Applied Informatics for Industry 4.0

Edited by
Nazmul Siddique
Mohammad Shamsul Arefin
Julie Wall
M Shamim Kaiser

CRC Press
Taylor & Francis Group
Boca Raton London New York

CRC Press is an imprint of the
Taylor & Francis Group, an **informa** business

A CHAPMAN & HALL BOOK

First edition published 2023
by CRC Press
6000 Broken Sound Parkway NW, Suite 300, Boca Raton, FL 33487-2742

and by CRC Press
4 Park Square, Milton Park, Abingdon, Oxon, OX14 4RN

CRC Press is an imprint of Taylor & Francis Group, LLC

Library of Congress Cataloging-in-Publication Data

Names: Siddique, N. H., editor.
Title: Applied informatics for industry 4.0 / edited by Nazmul Siddique,
    Mohammad Shamsul, Julie Wall, and M. Shamim Kaiser.
Description: First edition. | Boca Raton, FL : CRC Press, 2023. | Includes
    bibliographical references and index.
Identifiers: LCCN 2022028988 (print) | LCCN 2022028989 (ebook) | ISBN
    9781032164144 (hbk) | ISBN 9781032187501 (pbk) | ISBN 9781003256069
    (ebk)
Subjects: LCSH: Electronic data processing--Industrial applications. |
    Application software. | Information theory.
Classification: LCC QA76.76.A65 A687 2023 (print) | LCC QA76.76.A65
    (ebook) | DDC 005.3--dc23/eng/20221104
LC record available at https://lccn.loc.gov/2022028988
LC ebook record available at https://lccn.loc.gov/2022028989

ISBN: 978-1-032-16414-4 (hbk)
ISBN: 978-1-032-18750-1 (pbk)
ISBN: 978-1-003-25606-9 (ebk)

DOI: 10.1201/9781003256069

Typeset in Latin Roman font
by KnowledgeWorks Global Ltd.

Publisher's note: This book has been prepared from camera-ready copy provided by the authors.

This book is dedicated to all the researchers, professionals, and students who are continuously trying their best for the advancement of technologies for the betterment of humanity.

Contents

Preface   xi

Contributors   xiii

Editors   xvii

CHAPTER   1 ▪ Cloud-Based Smart Parking Systems Using IoT   1

ABHIJIT PATHAK, ABRAR HOSSAIN TASIN, MD. SHAHID UDDIN RAHAT, VICKY BARUA,
MUNNA DAS, AND SUDARSHAN DAS

CHAPTER   2 ▪ Empirical Study on Dimensionality Reduction Approach for
            F-Commoroc Dataoct by Principal Component Analysis   11

SHAHADAT HOSSAIN, MD. MANZURUL HASAN, AND TANVIR HOSSAIN

CHAPTER   3 ▪ Analysis of Online Purchase Intentions of Young Bangladeshi
            Social Network Users   20

ASLAM SIKDER, MD. WALIUR RAHMAN MIAH, BIMAL CHANDRA DAS, AND MD. MIJANUR
RAHMAN

CHAPTER   4 ▪ An Ethereum Blockchain-Based Healthcare System Using
            Smart Contract   34

TAMANNA TABASSUM, FATEMA AKTER, AND MOHAMMED NASIR UDDIN

CHAPTER   5 ▪ Bangla Fake News Detection Using Hybrid Deep Learning
            Models   46

MD. RAKIBUL HASAN SHEZAN, MOHAMMED NASIF ZAWAD,
YEASIR ARAFAT SHAHED, AND SHAMIM RIPON

CHAPTER   6 ▪ Adaptive Decay and Radius-Based Evolving Clustering
            Approach for Data Stream   61

SATHI RANI PAL, MD MANJUR AHMED, K. M. AZHARUL HASAN, AND RAHAT HOSSAIN FAISAL

CHAPTER   7 ▪ Solar-Powered Smart Street Light and Surveillance System
            Using IoT   74

SADIKA SULTANA MEEM AND NUSRATH TABASSUM

CHAPTER 8 ∎ Analysis of Aquaculture for Cultivating Different Types of Fish 83

NAYEEM ABDULLAH, AHNAF SHAHRIYAR CHOWDHURY,
MD. MEHEDI HOSSAIN, ORKO DUTTA, AND JIA UDDIN

CHAPTER 9 ∎ Crime-Finder: A System for Extraction and Visualization of Crime Data from Bengali Online Newspaper Articles 97

MD ABDULLA AL MAMUN, MD ABUL KALAM AZAD,
AND MD ILEAS PRAMANIK

CHAPTER 10 ∎ BERT-Based Emotion Classification Approach with Analysis of COVID-19 Pandemic Tweets 109

MD. SHAHAD MAHMUD CHOWDHURY AND BIPRODIP PAL

CHAPTER 11 ∎ Emotion Detection from Natural Text Using Embedding Techniques 122

SAMARIYA NAWRIN AND K. M. AZHARUL HASAN

CHAPTER 12 ∎ Performance Analysis of Energy-Aware DTN Routing Protocols in Opportunistic Networks 136

TASLIMA AKHTER AND MD. SHARIF HOSSEN

CHAPTER 13 ∎ Performance Investigation among Heterogeneous Routing Techniques in Wireless Sensor Networks 151

TASPIA SALAM AND MD. SHARIF HOSSEN

CHAPTER 14 ∎ Analysis of Physical and Psychological Impacts to Predict Satisfaction of Students toward E-Learning during COVID-19 Pandemic 163

SUDIPTA NATH

CHAPTER 15 ∎ SeniorsAid: Requirements, Elicitation, and Development of a Mobile App for Seniors 175

MALIHA SULTANA, AKASH PODDAR, MUHAMMAD NAZRUL ISLAM,
AND TASMIAH TAMZID ANANNYA

CHAPTER 16 ∎ Comparative Study of Big Data Visualization Tools and Techniques 188

KHADIJA BEGUM, MD MAMUNUR RASHID, AND MOHAMMAD ARAFATH UDDIN SHARIFF

CHAPTER 17 ■ Low-Cost IoT-Based Power Interruption Monitoring System   200

DEEPAK CHANDRA ROY, MD SHAZZAD HOSSAIN, AMIT KUMAR DAS, MD. ASHRAF ALI, AND MOHAMMAD AZAM KHAN

CHAPTER 18 ■ Multilevel Voting Models in Cyber Aggression Detection for Bangla Texts   212

SAMIN YASAR, MD. MAHFUZUL HAQUE GAZI, AND KAZI SAEED ALAM

CHAPTER 19 ■ A Cognitive Approach for Load Adaptive MAC Protocol in Wireless Body Area Networks   223

MD. MORTUZA HOSSAIN, MD. MONIRUL ISLAM, AND MD. OBAIDUR RAHMAN

CHAPTER 20 ■ Discrete Tone-Driven Directional Rate Controlled Communication System for Wireless Networks   236

SWEETY MONDAL, MD. TAREQ MAHMUD, AND MD. OBAIDUR RAHMAN

CHAPTER 21 ■ Blockchain-Based Secure Medical Data Management with Enabling IoT   251

NAYMUL EKRAM, MD. NAZMUL HASAN, MUHAMMAD SHEIKH SADI, AND MOHAMMAD SHAHRIAR RAHMAN

CHAPTER 22 ■ Bio-Inspired Meta-Heuristic Techniques for DC-DC Boost Converter with LQR Controller in a DC Microgrid   266

MD. HASSANUL KARIM RONI AND M. S. RANA

CHAPTER 23 ■ Mining Significant Pre-diabetes Features of Diabetes Mellitus: A Case Study of Noakhali, Bangladesh   280

MD. SHAHRIARE SATU, KOUSHIK CHANDRA HOWLADER, AVIJIT BARUA, AND MOHAMMAD ALI MONI

CHAPTER 24 ■ IoT-Based Smart Kitchen Security System   293

AL-AKHIR NAYAN, JOYETA SAHA, JANNATUL FERDAOUS, AND MUHAMMAD GOLAM KIBRIA

Index   305

Preface

We are in the era of the Fourth Industrial Revolution that is a new chapter in human development enabled by extraordinary technology advances and making a fundamental change in the way we live, work, and relate to one another. It is an opportunity to help everyone, including leaders, policy-makers and people from all income groups and nations, to harness converging technologies in order to create an inclusive, human-centred future.

Applied informatics combines the technologies of computer science and information sciences to assist in the management and processing of data to provide different types of services. Due to the adaptation of 4.0 IR related technologies, applied informatics is playing vital roles in different sectors.

The digital enterprise, which is already a reality, is growing increasingly prevalent in industry. Data is generated, processed, and evaluated on a continuous basis. The availability of large amounts of data nowadays serve as the foundation for the creation of digital representations of entire plants and systems. The use of digital twins has been around for quite some time to structure the planning and design of products and machinery – and even the actual manufacturing operations themselves – and to do so more flexibly and efficiently while producing high-quality, customized products faster and at a lower cost.

Industry 4.0 is already a reality for a significant number of businesses worldwide. Nonetheless, it is worth noting that the modifications necessary to fully participate in this industrial revolution and reap its rewards will not occur suddenly. In this book we consider 24 chapters of various topics such as such social network analysis, smart system design, security, healthcare and privacy related issues. The book can be used as a reference for advanced undergraduate or graduate students studying computer science or related subjects such as software engineering, information and communication engineering, security, industrial automation, etc. It will appeal more to those with a technical bent; sections are technically demanding and emphasize learning by experience: designing, constructing, and implementing systems.

Contributors

Nayeem Abdullah
BRAC University
Dhaka, Bangladesh

Md Manjur Ahmed
Department of CSE
University of Barishal
Barishal, Bangladesh

Taslima Akhter
Comilla University
Cumilla, Bangladesh

Fatema Akter
Jagannath University
Dhaka, Bangladesh

Md Abdulla Al Mamun
Begum Rokeya University
Rangpur, Bangladesh

Kazi Saeed Alam
KUET
Khulna, Bangladesh

Md. Ashraf Ali
Sigma Engineers Ltd.
Dhaka, Bangladesh

Tasmiah Tamzid Anannya
Department of CSE
MIST
Dhaka, Bangladesh

Md Abul Kalam Azad
Begum Rokeya University
Rangpur, Bangladesh

Avijit Barua
Department of CSTE
NSTU
Noakhali, Bangladesh

Vicky Barua
Department of CSE
BGC Trust University
Chattogram, Bangladesh

Khadija Begum
The People's University of Bangladesh
Dhaka, Bangladesh

Ahnaf Shahriyar Chowdhury
BRAC University
Dhaka, Bangladesh

Md. Shahad Mahmud Chowdhury
RUET
Rajshahi, Bangladesh

Amit Kumar Das
DPDC
Dhaka, Bangladesh

Bimal Chandra Das
Daffodil International University
Dhaka, Bangladesh

Munna Das
Department of CSE
BGC Trust University
Chattogram, Bangladesh

Sudarshan Das
Department of CSE
BGC Trust University
Chattogram, Bangladesh

Orko Dutta
BRAC University
Dhaka, Bangladesh

Naymul Ekram
KUET
Khulna, Bangladesh

Rahat Hossain Faisal
Department of CSE
University of Barishal
Barishal, Bangladesh

Jannatul Ferdaous
European University of Bangladesh (EUB)
Dhaka, Bangladesh

Md. Mahfuzul Haque Gazi
KUET
Khulna, Bangladesh

K. M. Azharul Hasan
Department of CSE
KUET
Khulna, Bangladesh

Md. Manzurul Hasan
AIUB
Dhaka, Bangladesh

Md. Nazmul Hasan
KUET
Khulna, Bangladesh

Md. Mehedi Hossain
BRAC University
Dhaka, Bangladesh

Md. Mortuza Hossain
Department of CSE
DUET
Gazipur, Bangladesh

Md Shazzad Hossain
DPDC
Dhaka, Bangladesh

Shahadat Hossain
City University
Dhaka, Bangladesh

Tanvir Hossain
Oklahoma State University
Stillwater, OK, US

Md. Sharif Hossen
Comilla University
Cumilla, Bangladesh

Koushik Chandra Howlader
Department of CSTE
NSTU
Noakhali, Bangladesh

Md. Monirul Islam
Department of CSE
DUET
Gazipur, Bangladesh

Muhammad Nazrul Islam
Department of CSE
MIST
Dhaka, Bangladesh

Mohammad Azam Khan
DPDC
Dhaka, Bangladesh

Muhammad Golam Kibria
IoT Lab
ULAB
Dhaka, Bangladesh

Md. Tareq Mahmud
Department of CSE
DUET
Gazipur, Bangladesh

Sadika Sultana Meem
International University of Business
Agriculture and Technology
Dhaka, Bangladesh

Md. Waliur Rahman Miah
DUET
Gazipur, Bangladesh

Sweety Mondal
Department of CSE
DUET
Gazipur, Bangladesh

Mohammad Ali Moni
School of Health and Rehabilitation
Sciences, Faculty of Health and
Behavioural Sciences
The University of Queensland
St Lucia, Australia

Sudipta Nath
Department of CSE
CUET
Chattogarm, Bangladesh

Samariya Nawrin
KUET
Khulna, Bangladesh

Al-Akhir Nayan
Chulalongkorn University
Bangkok, Thailand

Biprodip Pal
RUET
Rajshahi, Bangladesh

Sathi Rani Pal
Department of CSE
University of Barishal
Barishal, Bangladesh

Abhijit Pathak
Department of CSE
BGC Trust University
Chattogram, Bangladesh

Akash Poddar
Department of CSE
MIST
Dhaka, Bangladesh

Md Ileas Pramanik
Begum Rokeya University
Rangpur, Bangladesh

Md. Shahid Uddin Rahat
Department of CSE
BGC Trust University
Chattogram, Bangladesh

Md. Mijanur Rahman
Southeast University
Dhaka, Bangladesh

Md. Obaidur Rahman
Department of CSE
DUET
Gazipur, Bangladesh

Mohammad Shahriar Rahman
UIU
Dhaka, Bangladesh

M. S. Rana
RUET
Rajshahi, Bangladesh

Md Mamunur Rashid
Pukyong National University
Busan, South Korea

Shamim Ripon
East West University
Dhaka, Bangladesh

Md. Hassanul Karim Roni
RUET
Rajshahi, Bangladesh

Deepak Chandra Roy
DPDC
Dhaka, Bangladesh

Muhammad Sheikh Sadi
KUET
Khulna, Bangladesh

Joyeta Saha
University of Surrey
Guildford, UK

Taspia Salam
Comilla University
Cumilla, Bangladesh

Md. Shahriare Satu
Department of MIS
NSTU
Noakhali, Bangladesh

Yeasir Arafat Shahed
East West University
Dhaka, Bangladesh

Mohammad Arafath Uddin Shariff
Port City International University
Chattogram, Bangladesh

Md. Rakibul Hasan Shezan
East West University
Dhaka, Bangladesh

Aslam Sikder
DUET
Gazipur, Bangladesh

Maliha Sultana
Department of CSE
MIST
Dhaka, Bangladesh

Nusrath Tabassum
International University of Business
Agriculture and Technology
Dhaka, Bangladesh

Tamanna Tabassum
Jagannath University
Dhaka, Bangladesh
East West University
Dhaka, Bangladesh

Abrar Hossain Tasin
Department of CSE
BGC Trust University
Chattogram, Bangladesh

Jia Uddin
Woosong University
Daejeon, South Korea

Mohammed Nasir Uddin
Jagannath University
Dhaka, Bangladesh

Samin Yasar
KUET
Khulna, Bangladesh

Mohammed Nasif Zawad
East West University
Dhaka, Bangladesh

Editors

Dr. Nazmul Siddique is affiliated with the School of Computing, Engineering and Intelligent Systems, Ulster University. He obtained a Dipl.-Ing. degree in Cybernetics from the Dresden University of Technology, Germany, an MSc. in Computer Science from Bangladesh University of Engineering and Technology, and a Ph.D. in Intelligent Control from the Department of Automatic Control and Systems Engineering, University of Sheffield, England. His research interests include: cybernetics, computational intelligence, nature-inspired computing, stochastic systems and vehicular communication. He has published over 170 research papers including five books published by John Wiley, Springer and Taylor & Francis. He guest-edited eight special issues of reputed journals on Cybernetic Intelligence, Computational Intelligence, Neural Networks and Robotics. He is on the editorial board of seven international journals including *Nature Scientific Research*. He is a Fellow of the Higher Education Academy, a senior member of IEEE and member of different committees of IEEE SMC Society and UK-RI Chapter. He was involved in organising many national and international conferences and co-edited seven conference proceedings.

Dr. Mohammad Shamsul Arefin is on leave from Chittagong University of Engineering and Technology (CUET) and currently affiliated with the Department of Computer Science and Engineering (CSE), Daffodil International University, Bangladesh. Earlier he was the Head of the Department of CSE, CUET. Prof. Arefin received his Doctor of Engineering Degree in Information Engineering from Hiroshima University, Japan with support of the scholarship of MEXT, Japan. As a part of his doctoral research, Dr. Arefin worked with IBM Yamato Software Laboratory, Japan. His research includes privacy preserving data publishing and mining, distributed and cloud computing, big data management, multilingual data management, semantic web, object oriented system development and IT for agriculture and environment. Dr. Arefin has more than 120 referred publications in international journals, book series and conference proceedings. He is a senior member of IEEE, Member of ACM, Fellow of IEB and BCS. Dr. Arefin is the Organizing Chair of BIM 2021; TPC Chair, ECCE 2017; Organizing Co-Chair, ECCE 2019; and Organizing Chair, BDML 2020. Dr. Arefin visited Japan, Indonesia, Malaysia, Bhutan, Singapore, South Korea, Egypt, India, Saudi Arabia and China for different professional and social activities.

Dr. Julie Wall is a Reader in Computer Science, leads the Intelligent Systems Research Group and is the Director of Impact and Innovation for the School of Architecture, Computing and Engineering at the University of East London. Her research focuses on machine/deep learning and biologically inspired neural network architectures, algorithms and applications for audio, speech and natural language understanding; privacy-preserving intelligent systems for audio processing; developing industrial applications of automated decision-making machine and natural language understanding; and applications of intelligent systems to immersive virtual, augmented and mixed environments. Dr. Wall maintains close collaborative research and development links with industry.

Dr. M Shamim Kaiser is currently a Professor at the Institute of Information Technology of Jahangirnagar University, Savar, Dhaka-1342, Bangladesh. He received his bachelor's and master's degrees in Applied Physics Electronics and Communication Engineering from the University of Dhaka, Bangladesh, in 2002 and 2004, respectively, and a Ph.D. degree in Telecommunication Engineering from the Asian Institute of Technology, Thailand, in 2010. His current research interests include data analytics, machine learning, wireless network and signal processing, cognitive radio network, big data and cyber security, and renewable energy. He has authored more than 100 papers in different peer-reviewed journals and conferences. He is Associate Editor of the IEEE Access Journal, Guest Editor of Brain Informatics Journal and Cognitive Computation Journal. He is Life Member of Bangladesh Electronic Society, and Bangladesh Physical Society. He is also a senior member of IEEE, USA, and IEICE, Japan, and an active volunteer of the IEEE Bangladesh Section. He is the founding Chapter Chair of the IEEE Bangladesh Section Computer Society Chapter. He organized various international conferences such as ICEEICT 2015-2018, IEEE HTC 2017, IEEE ICREST 2018 and BI2020.

Cloud-Based Smart Parking Systems Using IoT

Abhijit Pathak, Abrar Hossain Tasin, Md. Shahid Uddin Rahat, Vicky Barua, Munna Das, and Sudarshan Das

Department of Computer Science and Engineering, BGC Trust University Bangladesh, Chattogram, Bangladesh

CONTENTS

1.1	Introduction	1
1.2	Literature Review	2
1.3	System Overview	3
1.4	System Framework	5
	1.4.1 Vehicle Panel	5
	1.4.2 Reservation Flowchart	5
1.5	System Implementation	7
	1.5.1 Data Flow of Merchandising App	7
	1.5.2 Data View	7
	1.5.3 Security	7
1.6	Use Case Scenarios of the Smart Parking System	7
1.7	Conclusion	9

C Loud-based smart parking systems that use IoT help a driver to find a parking space during peak hours in the city. Therefore, in this study, we present the development of such an application that can be embedded in smartphones. Finally, drivers will be able to check the availability of parking spaces in real-time. As a result, drivers can park their vehicles in less time. Therefore, this study presents an IoT-based architecture to transfer parking space information in real-time scenarios to the application. This Android-based system is developed in JAVA and MySQL environments and is used in the back-end.

1.1 INTRODUCTION

Bangladesh is a densely populated country. In addition to the population, the number of vehicles is also increasing day by day. However, the country's parking infrastructure is still not effectively developed. People usually park their cars in violation of traffic rules, resulting in poor management of the entire city traffic system. A smart parking system can handle such situations. Smart parking systems help drivers quickly find suitable parking spots and secure open spots. Also, with the establishment of a problem-free payment system, entry and exit points are provided.

Intelligent parking allocation systems are a hot topic in today's society. This is because the world's population is dense and people often buy cars and related equipment. Although every day such items are increasing, it can also help owners of the land that can be used as parking lots and benefit from revenue-sharing schemes for parking lots. A parking system is a tool for managing the flow of vehicles in a parking lot and ensuring that everyone has a place to park. In addition, the system monitors the number of vehicles passing through the gate and the duration of each vehicle's passage. It then determines how much the vehicle must pay at checkout.

The main objective is to connect vehicle and property owners. Users are provided with unique vehicle and parking information, so data can be retrieved from the vehicle or parking lot.

1.2 LITERATURE REVIEW

The Internet of Things (IoT) is a technology that uses everyday objects. IoT is classified as the next level of access to the Internet in use. IoT operations are controlled by system development. Currently, IoT is used in various fields. Smart parking proposes a system that uses the Google Maps application [1]. The ultrasonic sensor and the collected data are stored in the cloud. Android app map provides useful information about spaces. Each building has an LED display to find the right parking space. An IoT-based parking system using Google [1] is proposed to allow users to adjust parking lots. A mobile app finds your current parking space. This system uses IR sensors to identify spaces and is displayed at entry and exit gates. The RFID tag has been removed and you can enter the parking lot. If the person has an authorized signal, the gate will open [2]. The advanced parking system [3] uses Arduino and Raspberry PI to get free space. This app uses web server reservation with Google Maps using GPS. The results are displayed in a graph inside the label [4]. Verification is done using RFID tags. ZigBee is used for communication purposes. The Android app contains customer details like location, country, and other vehicles. It's an application that allows users to enter and exit on time and choose parking locations. User details are stored in the MYSQL database. LEDs indicate whether the parking space is empty or full. The camera is used to obtain the license plate and change the image to check whether the vehicle is authenticated by the user [5]. A smart parking system based on an embedded system [6] uses an integrated smart parking system and a network of sensors in Android applications and Windows applications. This program uses Raspberry PI. An IR sensor is used to detect empty parking spaces. V2I (Vehicle-to-Infrastructure) connectivity provides drivers submitting parking requests with useful information about matching reservations. Vehicle infrastructure (V2I) communication is used for parking requests and driving directions. The JSON format is used for data conversion. QR codes are used for security purposes. Scan the code using your webcam to allow viewing of park routes [6]. A private payment system over the phone has been proposed [7]. The proposed parallel parking system not only provides new directions for solving parking problems but also provides important guidance for the accurate implementation of parallel parking theory [8]. These features allow WSNs to work with VANETs to reduce limitations and make WSNs an effective complement to VANETs. On the other hand, WSN deployments can also use other communication technologies such as VANETs and cellular networks to disseminate collected information to remote locations. Therefore, WSN can also play a major role in ITS [9]. Both parkers and parking system managers can use an online platform that provides an open individual inquiry system and a fair and accurate reflection of the real-time situation, ensuring a fair process for issuing parking tickets [10]. They describe techniques for parking availability monitoring, parking reservation, and dynamic pricing and see how they are used in different settings [11]. In the cities considered here, parking policies are reoriented around alternative social goals. Several recent parking reforms have been implemented due to the need to meet EU air quality or national greenhouse gas targets [12]. Intelligent parking systems acquire and process information about available parking spaces to place cars in specific locations. A prototype of a park assist system was built based on the architecture proposed here. The hardware, software, and implementation solutions used to build this prototype are described in this white paper [13]. This IoT platform uses ThingSpeak [14] to display sensor data in the cloud environment. The average energy consumption of the sensor and the radio duty cycle are investigated. This facilitates the deployment of scalable and interoperable multi-hop WSNs, the placement of border routers, and the management of sensor energy consumption [15]. This paper proposes a new architecture for building decision support systems using heterogeneous wireless sensor networks. This architecture is built around standard hardware and existing wireless sensor network technology [16].

1.3 SYSTEM OVERVIEW

Using IoT geomagnetic tracker and NB-wireless vehicle owner authentication system, it is possible to identify vehicles and license plates in parking lots. If someone tries to move the vehicle without confirming its location, an alarm system sounds and connects to the nearest security room. A driver must confirm that he is the legal owner of the vehicle before allowing the vehicle to travel. Either he faces a security guard or he doesn't. Drivers must use their phone number to log in or sign up for the app. Phone numbers and license numbers are linked. And parking money is deducted from the criminal's phone account. Without payment, the app has no verification step. Therefore, no one can remove the car from the parking lot without paying. If the vehicle is moved without permission and payment, the alarm will sound and the police will be called.

To use the smart parking system, users must first register their cars with their identification number. They can do this in their account settings. Parking and payment application for Android. The user must specify the estimated time of arrival and the estimated first and last time of using the parking lot. Infrared sensors are used to detect empty parking spaces and full parking spaces.

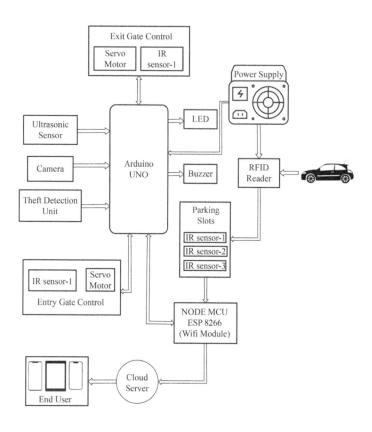

Figure 1.1: Block Diagram of Smart Parking System

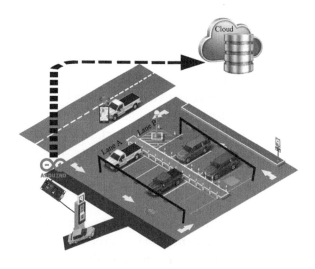

Figure 1.2: Overview of Smart Parking System

We use fog nodes because they can send data from local edge IoT or user devices much faster than sending it to the cloud for centralized processing. It is a micro-controller device that is considered an integral part of the device. It helps to collect sensor data using wireless communication, sensor data and data are processed locally through filters. This step is necessary to save energy by reducing the data sent over the network.

1.4 SYSTEM FRAMEWORK

The main goal is to work with car owners to park their cars. The car owner is the first and most important factor. Vehicle owners can easily create an account with their registration, username, phone number, and password. Valid information is necessary for this situation, so the original owner must accept the registration process to operate this platform. Therefore, the user needs an active phone number to register.

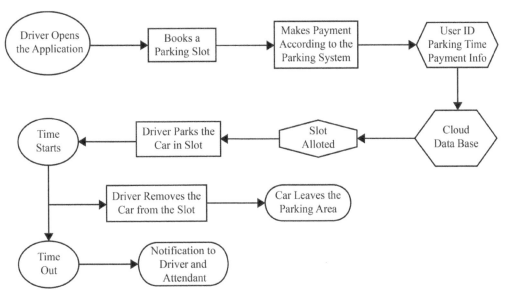

Figure 1.3: Functional Diagram of the Smart Parking System

1.4.1 Vehicle Panel

There is one panel for the owner of the vehicle where he or she may register and log in. Then he/she will be able to check the parking lots available, and he/she can book the parking lot for as much time as he/she needs. He/she can pay the owner of the lot through a payment gateway.

1.4.2 Reservation Flowchart

The following flowchart shows how this parking system can help users through an Android application. First, it guides the local user by executing appropriate commands and sending audio signals. The selected location will be saved for some time. If the user enters, he can access the parking lot and use the reserved space until the end of the day. Guests arriving after the reservation date must go to the parking lot through the front door.

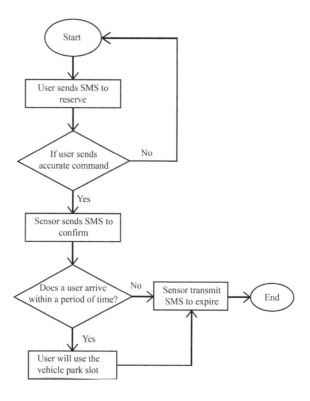

Figure 1.4: Flowchart of Slot Reservation

A car owner must enter the application first. Then he can search for nearby parking spaces. If he doesn't find a room in the parking lot, he will find a room and a place again to park his car.

We tried to demonstrate the effectiveness of the scheme at every stage, from monitoring the availability of parking spaces to parking a car in an empty parking lot. This is achieved by implementing a good parking plan inside the store parking lot. Below are the steps a driver must follow to park a car using the parking system.

- Step 1: Install the smart parking application.

- Step 2: Find the nearest parking spaces of the destination with the mobile app.

- Step 3: Choose a parking space.

- Step 4: Browse through the various parking spaces in that parking lot.

- Step 5: Select a parking area.

- Step 6: Choose the time (hours) you want to park.

- Step 7: Pay the parking fee.

- Step 8: Verify your stay using the mobile app once you have successfully parked your car in the designated parking area.

1.5 SYSTEM IMPLEMENTATION

Smart Parking Reservation System is an Android smartphone application that uses IoT. We have tried to focus on various processes such as small loads on the device that will help reduce problematic fraudulent use, avoid excessive battery usage and more. The approach used in the application is established so that the vehicle owner should first record the required details. The user can access all parking spaces, and the car owner will reserve the preferred parking space.

1.5.1 Data Flow of Merchandising App

Data migration refers to the entire process when data is sent to a server and received on an Android device. JSON (JavaScript Object Notation) has been used as a communication bridge between Android devices and web servers. The first Android device will generate an HTTP POST request to JSON during data transfer. JSON will then send the request to the fire support server, and JSON will receive the results from the server. The result will be translated into a Java object, and the Android device will be assigned a Java object. A user is required to provide a phone number, name, license number, and password. In this way, a user can book a parking space.

1.5.2 Data View

We tried to effectively reflect all user data in our smart parking system app. Finding the best parking space for a particular company is very easy. Owners can monitor the units in their vehicles. The owner adjusts the schedule according to his wishes. Vehicle owners can pay the company through their phone account.

1.5.3 Security

Smart parking system applications can create a powerful web server connection. HTTP session management is the essence of web security. When a web server receives a request from a user, the server must provide the information in the form of a JSON array. Any restriction to ensure that times are protected must be accepted.

1.6 USE CASE SCENARIOS OF THE SMART PARKING SYSTEM

Figure (1.5) provides a clear case for how different data sources can support potential services and access and manage much-needed parking data, from parking management and provider perspectives. Illustrated use of character smart parking device are shown. Process skills change the current status of the operator. Parking space availability in the parking data management system reserve the right of the user and the parking space intended for parking costs of the required parking space. The user must save the parking space.

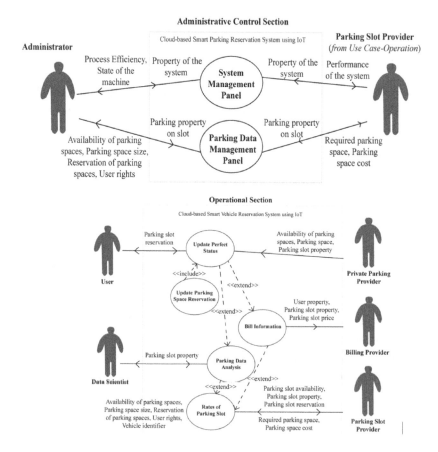

Figure 1.5: Use Case Scenarios of Smart Parking System

To find out if there is parking nearby, the users need to find a specific parking spot. By analyzing parking data to understand parking space availability, they can save parking space assets and parking spaces. They can find parking places using mobile applications. After successfully parking the car in the parking lot, the presence of the car must be confirmed using the mobile application. A fixed fee must be paid for parking.

Customer satisfaction with this project is important because the main goal of this project is to secure the parking lot. That's why we created a customer satisfaction chart [Figure (1.6)] based on customer reviews of this app. Customer satisfaction is high and the average satisfaction score is 95.25 percent.

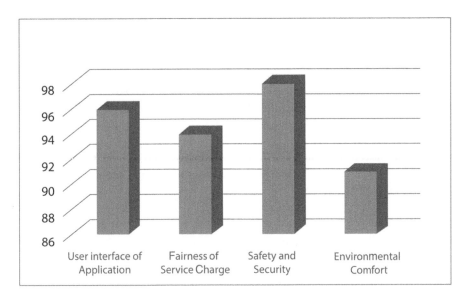

Figure 1.6: Average satisfaction rating of customers

1.7 CONCLUSION

Problems that may arise while working with an intelligent parking system, as well as solutions that provide a good platform for all users, have been explained. The system we are proposing provides information on the availability of parking spaces in the parking lot in real-time. By using our Android-based system, users can reserve a place to park. Therefore, users can save time looking for parking spaces.

Bibliography

[1] Abhirup Khanna, R. A. (2016). IoT based Smart Parking System. International Conference on Internet of Things and Applications (IOTA) (p. 5). Pune: IEEE

[2] Amir O. Kotb, Yao-chunShen, and Yi Huang "Smart parking Guidance, Monitoring and Reservation: A Review," IEEE-ITSM, pp.6-16, Apr 2017.

[3] Ching-FeiYang, You-HueiJu, Chung-Ying Hsieh "I parking a real-time parking space monitoring and guiding system", Elsevier, pp.301-305. Apr 2017.

[4] Chinrungrueng, S. Dumnin and Pongthornseri, "I Parking: A Parking Management Framework", 11th International Conference on ITS Telecommunications, pp.63-68, 2011.

[5] D.J. Bonde, "Automated car parking system Commanded by Android application", IEEE Conf., 05-03, Jan 2014.

[6] Deng, D. (2015). A Cloud-Based Smart-Parking System Based on Internet-of-Things Technologies. IEEE, 11. 3. O. Orrie, B. S. A Wireless Smart Parking System. IECON (p. 5). Yokohama: IEEE.

[7] Faiz Ibrahim Shaikh, Pratik Nirnay Jadhav, Saideep Pradeep Bandarakar "Smart Parking System based on embedded system and sensor Network" IJCA, vol. 140. pp. 45-51. Apr 2016.

[8] Fei-Yue Wang, Liu-Qing Yang, Fellow, Jian Yang, (2016), "Urban Intelligent Parking system based on Parallel Theory," IEEE-Computing, Networking and Communications, Mobile Computing and Vehicle Communications.

[9] Losilla, A.J Garcia-Sanchez, F. Garcia-Sanchez and J. Garcia-Haro, "On the Role of Wireless Sensor Networks in intelligent Transportation Systems", IC-TON, pp. 2161-2056, 2012.

[10] Huey-Der Chu, Yong-Quan Yeh, Yi-Cheng Lin, Meng-hung Lai, Yi-Jie Lin, (2017), "The Study Intelligent Roadside Park Charging Systems", IEEE- International Conference on Applied System Innovation, pp. 1064-67.

[11] Khaoula Hassoune, W. D. (2016). Smart parking Systems: A Survey. IEEE, 6.

[12] Kodransky, M. and Hermann, G. (2011). Europe's Parking U-Turn: From Accommodation to Regulation. New York: Institute for Transportation and Development Policy.

[13] M.A.R. Sarkar, A.A. Rokoni, M.O. Reza, M. F. Ismail, "Smart parking system with image Processing facility", I. J. Intelligent System and Application, 2012.

[14] Abhijit Pathak, A., AmazUddin, M., Abedin, M.J., Andersson, K., Mustafa, R., Hossain, M.S. IoT based smart system to support agricultural parameters: a case study. Procedia Comput. Sci. 155, pp. 648–653, 2019.

[15] Abedin, M., Chowdhury, A., Hossain, M., Anderson, K., Karaim, R. An interoperable IP based WSN for smart irrigation systems. In: IEEE Annual Consumer Communications and Networking Conference (CCNC), pp. 1–5, 2017.

[16] K. Andersson and M. S. Hossain, "Heterogeneous wireless sensor networks for flood prediction decision support systems," 2015 IEEE Conference on Computer Communications Workshops (INFOCOM WKSHPS), Hong Kong, 2015, pp. 133-137, doi: 10.1109/INFCOMW.2015.7179373.

CHAPTER 2

Empirical Study on Dimensionality Reduction Approach for F-Commerce Dataset by Principal Component Analysis

Shahadat Hossain

City University, Dhaka, Bangladesh

Md. Manzurul Hasan

American International University-Bangladesh, Dhaka, Bangladesh

Tanvir Hossain

Oklahoma State University, Stillwater, OK, US

CONTENTS

2.1	Introduction	12
2.2	Related Work	12
2.3	Methodology	13
	2.3.1 Sample Collection and Dataset	14
	2.3.2 Principal Component Analysis	14
	2.3.3 Random Forest Algorithm	15
	2.3.4 Artificial Neural Network	15
2.4	Experimental Analyses and Observations	15
2.5	Conclusion	17

DATA have been growing exponentially since the last decade. For further use and study, proper maintenance of these data is essential. Principal Component Analysis (PCA) is a dimensionality reduction technique that helps to reduce vast amounts of data without losing minor information. In this research, we applied PCA to existing survey data from consumers of different e-commerce groups from Facebook (F-Commerce) pages. We have shown that Artificial Neural Network (ANN) and

Random Forest (RF) perform nearly the same with the dimension reduced dataset compared to the previous experiment with the dataset that holds all the features. Our relevant contribution is to use PCA to reduce the components and determine the models' performances for different variances.

2.1 INTRODUCTION

PCA reduces the components and represents the dataset with limited loss of information. Due to the rapid increase of data every day, most of the generated data are unstructured. It is essential to manage these unstructured data to extract valuable data for human usage and development. Like other online platforms, a plethora of F-commerce data is being increased day by day. To use these data appropriately, scientists and data analysts are employing some innovative techniques. Among them, dimensionality reduction is used most widely in the field of data science.

These studies are based on real-world datasets from Facebook groups and pages. Using PCA, we evaluate the efficiencies of the models in different variances. The dataset includes several variables and multiple observations for each variable. We use ANN and RF models for the study, quantifying how the result matrices keep changing for different variances. These models are parts of the F-Commerce's consumers behavioral studies [1]. Our overall research aims to compare the models' performance matrices for different variances in PCA. The objectives of our overall research are as follows.

- To analyze changes in the result matrices applying PCA.

- To observe the number of principal components for different variances.

- To compare the systems concerning dimension reduced dataset and the real dataset.

The rest of this paper's sections are arranged as follows. First, Section 2.2 contains relevant works on consumer behavioral analyses and different machine learning algorithms and PCA. Then, in Section 2.3, we show the methodologies. Finally, in Section 2.4, we demonstrate the experimental analyses and observations, and in Section 2.5, we discuss future works before concluding.

2.2 RELATED WORK

Hossain et al. [1] demonstrated the effects of influencing factors on consumer behaviors and presented an analysis using ANN and RF. The models only identified the factors affecting F-Commerce consumer purchases. Heijden et al. [2] studied 228 online shoppers in their research. The responses of these shoppers are observed from a technological and trust-based perspective. They applied a model to the samples and analyzed the model's effectiveness. Kumar [4] found that consumer behaviors towards the online market depend on two contexts. One is physical, and another one is psychological. Khaniwale [5] identified a relationship between consumer activities and influencing factors behind those activities. Islam et al. [21] built an intelligent framework to analyze the product ratings and feedback. Business companies attempt with artificial intelligence to analyze consumer behaviors. There had been considerable research to examine consumer activities [14, 7, 13, 8], digital signage [15], and the shopping environment [16] that help companies to make the best decisions for their enterprises. Kumar et al. [13] also studied consumer sentiments using Natural Language Processing (NLP) and Machine Learning (ML) models from Amazon Web Resources Reviews. By implementing word embedding and LSTM RNN on consumers' tweets, Tirbefinder classified the consumers based on alternative certainties, lifestyles, and entertainment [7].

Dimensionality reduction plays a significant role in a system's performance. Numerous mathematical techniques are being applied to reduce the real-time [20] data dimensionality. The principal component analysis [19] is one of the most popular approaches among them. Its objective is to extract meaningful information from a large dataset to determine its principal components and to illustrate the observation patterns' similarities with point mappings. It has been applied to analyze fossil teeth data to elicit animals' dietary information [17] that existed 200 million years ago. It has also been widely used in atmospheric science to research sea-level pressure data [18]. Ng [22] used PCA to reduce the dimensionality of the digital images. In their study, internet image file transmission was improved significantly, especially mobile device transmission quality.

2.3 METHODOLOGY

This section depicts the study's most important steps. To begin, we use more data than that of the previous analytical survey conducted by Hossain et al. [1]. Then, we begin data pre-processing after collecting the dataset. PCA is being used to reduce the dataset's dimensions. Finally, we conclude our analysis with the result and observation derived from the dataset after ANN and RF have been applied. Figure 2.1 represents the workflow of our analysis.

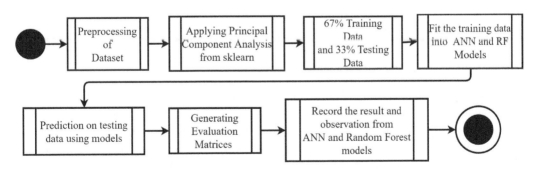

Figure 2.1: Workflow of the analysis.

2.3.1 Sample Collection and Dataset

Dataset is collected from the study of consumer behavior analysis in F-Commerce. Following that dataset, the total number of data is increased to 656 with 22 attributes [23]. Some attributes from the dataset are reduced during the pre-processing stage. Table 2.1 below contains descriptions of some selective attributes. The conceptual model developed by Fishbein et al. [6] is used for survey questioning.

Table 2.1: Participants' profile sample (N=656)

Question	Count	Percentage
Age		
11-30	634	96.6%
31-60	19	2.5%
61-90	02	0.3%
≥ 90	01	0.15%
Gender		
Male	534	81.5%
Female	119	18%
Other	03	0.5%
Profession		
Private Service	101	15.4%
Govt. Service	20	3%
Student	515	78.6%
Other	20	3%
Time spent in FB		
≤ 2 Hours	122	18.6%
≥ 2 Hours	534	81.4%
Buy anything from FB		
Buy from FB	356	54.3%
Not buy from FB	300	45.7%

When using machine learning, dataset imbalance can cause imbalanced learning. To balance the dataset, we utilize the synthetic minoring oversampling approach (*SMOTE*) from the python *imbalanced-learning* package.

2.3.2 Principal Component Analysis

Principal Component Analysis is a dimensionality reduction technique that can reduce the less important features and attributes of a dataset. It helps to make a process computationally efficient by keeping almost identical system performance. For transforming a dataset to the combination of principal components, the covariance has been calculated. For example, for a three-dimensional (X, Y, Z) features dataset, the covariance matrix is,

$$\begin{bmatrix} Cov(X,X) & Cov(X,Y) & Cov(X,Z) \\ Cov(Y,X) & Cov(Y,Y) & Cov(Y,Z) \\ Cov(Z,X) & Cov(Z,Y) & Cov(Z,Z) \end{bmatrix}$$

Here $Cov(X,X) = Var(X)$, variance of X and $Cov(X,Y) = Cov(Y,X)$. Then eigenvectors and eigenvalues [24] of that covariance matrix are calculated. These two essential parts belong to linear algebra and are for determining the principal components. Each column of the eigenvector represents a principal component. The first column represents the first principal component; likewise, the nth column represents the nth principal component. The first component carries the biggest amount of information. As much as the number of components increases, the amount of information decreases. The eigenvalue indicates the factor by which the data transformation to the principal component occurs. The component's eigenvalue is divided by the sum of eigenvalues and calculates the percentage of a component's variance. Finally, to achieve dimension-reduced data, the following mathematical operation is applied.

$$FinalData = (FeatureVector)^T * (DataAdjust)^T$$

2.3.3 Random Forest Algorithm

Random forest (RF) is a machine learning algorithm that is used to predict data from a dataset [9]. Ho [3] designed this algorithm. The fundamental justification for using RF is that it has a low bias and a low variance. However, in terms of correctness, RF outperforms other decision tree algorithms such as j48 [10]. The number of trees in RF improves efficiencies and makes predictions more accurate, but it also slows down the computation. In the RF algorithm, the maximum number of features it considers splitting a node and the minimum number of leaf nodes are needed. Since it can be used for both regression and classification, the RF algorithm is more robust than other decision tree algorithms. Furthermore, this algorithm is very convenient because it can provide a good prediction result when the default hyper-parameters are used.

2.3.4 Artificial Neural Network

A neural network is a sort of network that processes data like a human brain. The neurons are linked to each other among different units. The *Artificial Neural Network (ANN)* enables the machine using functions to make decisions on data for various purposes[11]. In our experiment three different layers are linked: *input layer, output layer* and *hidden layer*. A backpropagation algorithm in ANN is used to adjust weights to ensure that the network is perfectly learned [12].

2.4 EXPERIMENTAL ANALYSES AND OBSERVATIONS

Our experiment has applied PCA on the dataset using the sci-kit-learn Machine Learning (ML) Library, where first we have scaled the dataset with the *StandardScalar* class and then fit it with appropriate transformation. After that, we have obtained the eigenvectors and eigenvalues of the principal components for five different variances $(75, 80, 85, 90$ and $95\%)$. The number of components after reduction is shown in Table 2.2, along with the associated variances. On the dataset with different variances, we apply ANN and RF.

Table 2.2: Different variances and components

Variance	75%	80%	85%	90%	95%
Component	08	10	12	14	16

Table 2.3: Result table

Variance	Component	Matrices	ANN	RF
100% - Real Dataset [1]	18			
		Accuracy	0.98	0.98
		Precision	0.99	0.98
		Recall	0.98	0.99
		F1-Score	0.98	0.98

According to Figures 2.2 and 2.3, the Random Forest model has performed better than the ANN in all the result matrices, except for 75 and 80% variances in precision matrices. In all cases, the higher the variance, the higher performance of the models. However, when the variance exceeds 90%, the RF model's performance matrices have remained constant at 98% as shown in Figure 2.2a. On the other hand, in the ANN model, the performance matrices have slightly been increased except for the precision matrices, where a slight downturn has occurred.

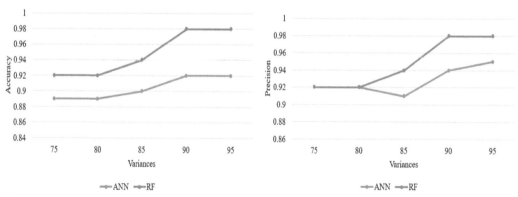

(a) ANN's and RF's accuracies with respect to different variances.

(b) ANN's and RF's precisions with respect to different variances.

Figure 2.2: Graph analyses of result matrices (Accuracy and Precision) for different variances after PCA.

However, the ANN model has achieved the highest precision $(94 - 95\%)$ when the variance percentage has risen over 90% as shown in Figure 2.2b. The graphs in Figures 2.3a and 2.3b also shows that the Random Forest result metrices are increasing, and at a certain point of variance 90%, the rate of change in results remains constant. In the case of the RF model, it reaches close to the result (in Table 2.3) of the actual dataset. Furthermore, after applying PCA, RF gets better results with the least number of components. When our data variation exceeds 90%, our ANN

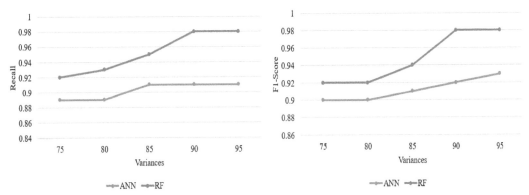

(a) ANN's and RF's recalls with respect to differ- (b) ANN's and RF's F1-scores with respect to dif-
ent variances.   ferent variances.

Figure 2.3: Graph analyses of result matrices (Recall and F1-Score) for different variances after PCA.

model achieves accuracy over 90%. Thus, we can conclude that the graphs of the RF and ANN models grow as the number of components and variances increases.

2.5 CONCLUSION

In this chapter, we have studied our ANN and RF models' performances by reducing the dataset's dimension using PCA. Though we have reduced the number of components, our models have performed as closely as models' performance on other lower dimensions of the dataset. We have reduced the component and have applied ANN and RF algorithms for performance analyses.

Although our research determines the effects of dimensionality reduction on our models' performances, numerous directions are yet to be explored. In the future, we would like to explain the reasons behind the encouragement of consumers to purchase products from F-Commerce. It is also welcomed that one can validate and verify our results considering a larger dataset. Furthermore, this work would allow us to extend our research into consumer behavioral analysis in F-Commerce in the near future.

Bibliography

[1] Hossain, S., Hasan, M. & Hossain, T. An Analytical Study of Influencing Factors on Consumers' Behaviors in Facebook Using ANN and RF. *International Conference on Intelligent Computing & Optimization*. pp. 744-753 (2020)

[2] Heijden, H., Verhagen, T. & Creemers, M. Understanding online purchase intentions: contributions from technology and trust perspectives. *Eur. J. Inf. Syst.* **12**, 41-48 (2003)

[3] Ho, T. The Random Subspace Method for Constructing Decision Forests. *IEEE Trans. Pattern Anal. Mach. Intell.* **20**, 832-844 (1998)

[4] Rakesh, K. Consumer Behaviour and Role of Consumer Research in Marketing. *In Journal of Commerce and Trade.* **12**, 65-76 (2017)

[5] Khaniwale, M. Consumer Buying Behavior. *In International Journal of Innovation and Scientific Research.* **14**, 278-286 (2015)

[6] Fishbein, M. & Ajzen, I. Predicting and changing behavior the reasoned action approach. (2015), http://www.vlebooks.com/vleweb/product/openreader?id=Exeter & isbn=9781136874734, OCLC: 1190691560

[7] Gloor, P., Colladon, A., Oliveira, J. & Rovelli, P. Put your money where your mouth is: Using deep learning to identify consumer tribes from word usage. *CoRR.* **abs/2105.13036** (2021), https://arxiv.org/abs/2105.13036

[8] Lang, T. & Rettenmeier, M. Understanding consumer behavior with recurrent neural networks. *Proceedings of the Workshop on Machine Learning Methods for Recommender Systems.* (2017)

[9] Rokach, L. & Maimon, O. Top-down induction of decision trees classifiers - a survey. *IEEE Trans. Syst. Man Cybern. Part C.* **35**, 476-487 (2005), https://doi.org/10.1109/TSMCC.2004.843247

[10] Ali, J., Khan, R., Ahmad, N. & Maqsood, I. Random forests and decision trees. *In International Journal of Computer Science Issues (IJCSI).* **9**, 272 (2012)

[11] Hassoun, M. Fundamentals of artificial neural networks. (MIT Press, 1995)

[12] Hecht-Nielsen, R. Theory of the backpropagation neural network. *Neural Networks.* **1**, 445-448 (1988)

[13] Kumar, P., Nandagopalan, S. & Swamy, L. Investigation of Emotions on Purchased Item Reviews Using Machine Learning Techniques. *Proceedings of the International Conference on Intelligent Computing & Optimization.* pp. 409-417 (2018)

[14] Alhendawi, K., Al-Janabi, A. & Badwan, J. Predicting the Quality of MIS Characteristics and End-Users' Perceptions Using Artificial Intelligence Tools: Expert Systems and Neural Network. *Proceedings of the International Conference on Intelligent Computing and Optimization.* pp. 18-30 (2019)

[15] Ravnik, R., Solina, F. & Zabkar, V. Modelling In-Store Consumer Behaviour Using Machine Learning and Digital Signage Audience Measurement Data. *Video Analytics for Audience Measurement - First International Workshop, VAAM 2014, Stockholm, Sweden, August 24, 2014. Revised Selected Papers.* **8811** pp. 123-133 (2014)

[16] Eroglu, S., Machleit, K. & Davis, L. Atmospheric Qualities of Online Retailing: A Conceptual Model and Implications. *In Journal of Business Research.* **34** pp. 177-184 (2001)

[17] Gill, P., Purnell, M., Crumpton, N., Brown, K., Gostling, N., Stampanoni, M. & Rayfield, E. Dietary specializations and diversity in feeding ecology of the earliest stem mammals. *Nature.* **512**, 303-305 (2014)

[18] Obukhov, A. Statistically homogeneous fields on a sphere. *Usp. Mat. Nauk.* **2**, 196-198 (1947)

[19] Jolliffe, I. & Cadima, J. Principal component analysis: a review and recent developments. *Philosophical Transactions of the Royal Society A: Mathematical, Physical and Engineering Sciences.* **374**, 20150202 (2016)

[20] Chowdhury, R., Adnan, M. & Gupta, R. Real-Time Principal Component Analysis. *Trans. Data Sci..* **1**, 10:1-10:36 (2020)

[21] Islam, M., Forhad, M., Uddin, M., Arefin, M., Galib, S. & Khan, M. Developing an Intelligent System for Recommending Products. *International Conference On Intelligent Computing & Optimization.* pp. 476-490 (2020)

[22] Ng, S. Principal component analysis to reduce dimension on digital image. *Procedia Computer Science.* **111** pp. 113-119 (2017)

[23] Hossain, S. Consumer Behavior in Facebook Dataset. (https://www.kaggle.com/shahadathossain1992/consumer-behavior-in-facebook-dataset), Accessed: 2021-02-24

[24] Jaadi, Z. A Step-by-Step Explanation of Principal Component Analysis. (https://builtin.com/data-science/step-step-explanation-principal-component-analysis), Accessed: 2021-03-24

Analysis of Online Purchase Intentions of Young Bangladeshi Social Network Users

Aslam Sikder

Dhaka University of Engineering & Technology, Gazipur

Md. Waliur Rahman Miah

Dhaka University of Engineering & Technology, Gazipur

Bimal Chandra Das

Daffodil International University

Md. Mijanur Rahman

Southeast University

CONTENTS

3.1	Introduction	21
3.2	Literature Review	22
3.3	Research Design and Data Collection	24
	3.3.1 Research Design	24
	3.3.2 Data Collection and Preprocessing	25
3.4	Result and Discussion	26
3.5	Conclusion and Future Direction	29

THE ubiquity of online shopping is rising due to availability and easy access to web-based vendors. Young people especially are very interested in such activities. As the customers cannot physically touch and feel the online product for making a purchase decision, they tend to depend on various factors, such as behavioural attitude, trust, reputation, satisfaction, and consumer engagement. This chapter aims to investigate the effects of those factors on the purchase intention from the perspective of Bangladeshi youths. In this research, we collected data through an online survey among undergraduate students of different universities in Bangladesh. The survey questionnaire focused on factors established by existing literature. We use both the single and multiple linear regression analysis for understanding the influence of different factors. The results of this investigation show that the mentioned factors have quantitatively different positive influences on the young consumers of Bangladesh when buying online.

3.1 INTRODUCTION

The emergence of the world wide web has changed the behaviour and lifestyles of many people. In the past, one had to go out to some distant marketplaces to buy necessary commodities; now, thanks to the Internet, one can get them through some clicks or taps of the fingers. About a half of the world population, that is 3.4 billion people are now using the web, and 67% of those users are dynamic social media users [1]. The huge user-base of the Internet has provided organizations an alternative mode of advertising. In order to increase sales, organizations can advertise in the web instead of physical mass gatherings [2]. Currently, in a world changed by the COVID-19 pandemic, importance of avoiding mass gatherings has increased enormously. Due to the ongoing COVID-19 restrictions, an ever-increasing number of retailers are moving towards web-based marketing. The social networks are a focal point in that drift. The prevalence of virtual networks are pulling in the clients to buy items or services, depending on their purchase interest.

The development of business through social media has changed the mode of buying. A number of elements, including factors identified in existing literature, influence a customer's purchase expectations via social networking sites. However, many of those elements might not have been analysed in the traditional literature on how they influence the purchase intention through social media [3]. Recently, researchers are showing a rapidly growing interest in such topics related with social media marketing. Our current research endeavours to identify and analyse the components affecting a customer's buying intention through social networks in Bangladesh. In this endeavour, we pose the following research questions:

1. Can a set of factors, established by existing literature, be used to understand the online purchase intention through the social networks of Bangladesh?

2. Can machine learning algorithms such as regression analysis be used to understand the influences of those factors for purchase intention of Bangladeshi young buyers?

In this research, we answer those questions through investigation, experiment, and analysis.

Our contributions in this work include tapping into the online habits of young Bangladeshi social media users, collecting data through survey, and using machine learning algorithm to analyse and find out which factors, documented in the literature, influence them in making buying intentions using online media.

The remaining part of this chapter is organized as follows: Section 3.2 reviews the existing literature related to the current research. A set of factors related to buying intention, established by existing literature, is discussed. Our research design and data collection are explained in Section 3.3. The hypotheses related to each of the factors are also mentioned in that section. Section 3.4 discusses the result and analysis. Finally, we conclude with our findings and future directions in Section 3.5.

3.2 LITERATURE REVIEW

In this section, we review contemporary literature related to buyers' purchase intention including the use of a social media platform. The social network sites have drastic influence on people's habits, manners, behavioural attitudes, and the way of life as a whole. Many people are using the web on a regular basis for searching information of necessary commodities and making a purchase. Today's business requires one to understand a consumer's need and behaviour in social networks which influence their buying intention [4]. This helps the business to increase the number of customers and keep a close relationship with them. In this context a term "s-commerce" has been coined recently. The s-commerce implies an online business that joins e-commerce with social media and informative communication with customers to achieve business objectives, capacities, and practices [5]. To influence buyers in the market, online vendors give positive data in their social sites. They also encourage buyers, sometimes with gifts, to post remarks in their social pages and advise them to partake in social gatherings. Social traders regularly work together with social networking services (SNS), for example Facebook, to spread their engagements with potential customers. Broadcasting the information about an item of an online vendor can simply be accomplished by buyers through SNSs. After buying an item, an online customer can share their feelings, knowledge, and satisfaction with their friends, relatives, and even apparently unknown individuals through social networks using messages or posts and giving online surveys in different sites. Social business firms can recruit such customers to uplift their marketing and sales goal, which is less expensive than conventional advertising platforms [6].

Different researchers defined "purchase intention" in different ways. According to behavioural science, the probability that a person performs a particular action is "intention" in a general sense [7]. Intention can also be defined as a plan to behave in a specific way, for example "I should do," and "I will do" [8]. When such behaviour is related with buying, it is considered as a purchase intention, that is, a purchase intention is an intention where a customer wants to buy an item. Purchase intention is also viewed as a component of a shopper's psychological conduct uncovering the manner in which an individual plans to buy a specific item [9]. Usually people would like to buy items from a known brand. Netizens tend to give reviews of the purchased items via web-based networking media. The purchase intention can be used as a tool to anticipate what items or brands customers would purchase next time when they go out shopping [10]. To increase sale, an online merchant should stock the items depending on the interest of buyers. In this regard, a seller should be able to anticipate which items would match potential buyers' purchase intention. Different researchers used different parameters for analysing purchase intention. After thorough investigation of existing literature, we selected a set of parameters including behavioural attitude, trust, reputation, satisfaction, and consumer engagement. We would like to analyse their influence on the purchase intention of Bangladeshi social network users. In the following paragraphs, we explain each of those parameters.

Behavioral Attitude: Behavioural attitude is a sort of propensity to do shopping on the web or buying items or services from the web. The theory of planned behaviour [11] is one of the prevailing speculations in the investigations of an online shopper's behaviour. The theory of planned behaviour clarifies human activities, and it gauges one's choice on whether to act on a particular behaviour or not [4, 12, 11]. The behavioural attitude clarifies an individual's positive or negative inclination towards an action depending on experience and earlier learning. George [11] investigated the effect of behavioural attitude on online purchase. He found that this factor positively affects online purchasing behaviour of American college students. Algeji et al. [13] also found that this factor has a positive impact on customer purchase intention in the bookstores in Kurdistan. We believe that the behavioural attitudes have similar effect on Bangladeshi consumers in social media and devised one of our hypothesis (H1) accordingly. All of our hypotheses are presented in Section 3.3.

Trust: Trust is a focal idea for an understanding of online purchasing and social behaviours, because its absence may hinder a purchase intention and cause mistaken assumptions among buyers and merchants [14, 15]. In the virtual world, a comment or review of a customer who completed a purchase is more trustworthy than a comment of a "window shopper." Getting information from the reviews of social-network companions turns into an effective method to develop trust among the online members. Thus, the customers settle on a choice and expect to purchase from a vendor. Kim et al. [6] suggested that trust depends on many things such as reputation, communication, and word-of-mouth. According to Pavlou and Fygenson [16] trust is an essential factor in clarifying buying expectation and market achievement. George [11], and Ventre and Kolbe [17] also found a positive relation of trust with purchase intention. According to Siddiqui et al. [18] trust in the social networking sites has a positive impact on online purchase intention in India. We adopted a hypothesis (H2) supporting these findings about trust.

Reputation: A good reputation is an important asset for a business. Reputation performs an imperative job among the customers to settle on a buying choice. People prefer to purchase an item that has a goodwill over an item that does not. Reputation is improved or harmed by the comparison between what an organization promises and what it really delivers [19, 20]. Morgan-Thomas and Veloutsou [21] point out that it is easy to lose a decent reputation than to gain it, because a negative activity has more severe effect on a buyer's perception than a positive one. A good reputation can only be obtained by a business after investing resources, time, and effort to provide the customers with sincere care [6, 22]. Consumers tend to favor companies with a good reputation in electronic commerce [22]. Individuals assume that reputed brands would not cheat due to their value of goodwill. The understanding of the reputation of an online store has a considerable influence on a customer to build a trust and hence making a purchase decision [23]. Our hypothesis in the next section mentions a positive relationship of reputation with purchase intention.

Satisfaction: Customer satisfaction is a measure of a buyer's feeling of happiness about a product or service from a seller. Low, Lee, and Cheng [24] defined customer satisfaction as the view of pleasurable fulfillment of a client in the exchange encounters of a product or service. A customer might be happy at the time of purchase, but becomes dissatisfied over the time due to low quality product or service. Kuo et al. [25] recommended that a complete satisfaction depends on each buy as well as on the utilization time of a product or service. Satisfaction is a kind of customized audit from the customer. Information about customer satisfaction, including surveys and ratings, can help a company determine how to update its products and services. When a buyer is satisfied, he or she tends to make purchases from the same brand or retailer again in the future. Also the customer would happily recommend this brand or retailer to friends, and will leave a positive review on social media. Ahmed et al. [26] observed the effect of customer satisfaction on an online purchase. The authors found that customer satisfaction is the most prominent positive influencer of online purchase intention of Pakistani university students. We believe that the satisfaction has similar effect on Bangladeshi consumers in social media. Saha et al. [27] found that satisfied customers desire to stay longer and are willing to pay more. After reviewing the literature, we hypothesize that satisfaction (SA) positively affects consumers' online purchase intention.

Consumer Engagement: Customer engagement is an association between buyers and the business organization or brand through different channels of correspondence. Consumer engagement suggests to the "dimension of a client's physical, subjective and passionate nearness in their association with a service or organization" [28]. This association can be a response, connection, effect or, in general, client interaction which happens on the web and offline. The term can likewise be utilized to define a customer-to-customer correspondence regarding an item, service, or brand. A higher consumer engagement tends to uplift the goodwill of a business. In this way, consumer engagement is a critical component, and it has significant impact on new customers in making a choice of purchase. Our hypothesis H5 is devised on this idea.

3.3 RESEARCH DESIGN AND DATA COLLECTION

In this section we discuss our research design, and data collection and preprocessing.

3.3.1 Research Design

After a thorough investigation of existing literature, we formalize a model shown in Figure 3.1 with the mentioned parameters and assume that they have influence on the purchase intention of Bangladeshi social network users. Our goal is to experimentally look at different components, such as behavioral attitude, trust, reputation, satisfaction, and consumer engagement, which affect the consumers' purchase intention in online shopping in Bangladesh.

According to Figure 3.1, we devised our hypotheses as follows:

H1: Behavioral attitude (BA) positively affects consumers' online purchase intention through social networks.

H2: Trust (T) positively affects consumers' online purchase intention through social networks.

H3: Reputation (R) positively affects consumers' online purchase intention through social networks.

H4: Satisfaction (S) positively affects consumers' online purchase intention through social networks.

H5: Customer engagement (CE) positively affects consumers' online purchase intention through social networks.

3.3.2   Data Collection and Preprocessing

To collect data, we conducted an online survey among undergraduate students of universities of Bangladesh. A five-point Likert scale is used to gauge the measurement with classifications of "1-Strongly Disagree, 2-Disagree, 3-Neutral, 4-Agree, and 5-Strongly Agree." Data was collected using web-based Google form. The link of the survey questionnaire was shared on different social network pages and groups to welcome users to take part. Also, it was sent through email and individual messages. At first, we looked for information about the respondents, for example age and gender. After that, we collected information related with the components of our hypothesis including the five independent factors of Behavioral Attitude (BA), Trust (T), Reputation (R), Satisfaction (S) and Consumer Engagement (CE), and one dependent factor of Purchase Intention (PI). The response of the last question related to PI reflects the buyers' buying intention through social networks. Any personal information that can trace and identify the respondents was avoided to prevent personal security threat and ethical issues.

We collected a good number of responses through our survey. In the preprocessing stage, a thorough inspection reveals that some questions were not answered by some

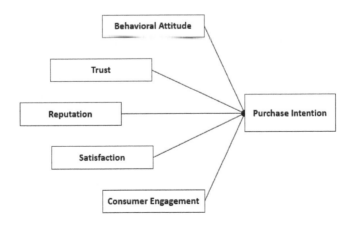

Figure 3.1: Proposed Research Model

Table 3.1: KMO and Bartlett's Test

Test Item	Value
Kaiser-Meyer-Olkin Measure of Sampling Adequacy	0.895
Bartlett's Test of Sphericity Approx. Chi-Square	5155.126
df	15
Sig.	0.000

of the responders. For some cases we had to discard the sample, and for some cases we replaced the missing value with the mean. Finally, we used 1530 samples in our experiment. Among those 1530 samples, 7.6% were under 19 years of age, 85.1% were 19 to 25 years of age, and 7.3% were over 25 years of age, while 60.4% were male and 39.6% were female.

After collecting the data, we used IBM SPSS tool for statistical and machine learning analyses. Our analyses include: reliability test, KMO and Bartlett's test, and simple and multiple linear regression.

3.4 RESULT AND DISCUSSION

First we try to understand whether our dataset has merits, such as consistency, reliability, and adequacy, to be acceptable for further factors analysis or not. For this purpose, we use popular statistical methods of Cronbach's alpha, and Kaiser-Meyer-Olkin (KMO) and Bartlett's test.

To measure the reliability and internal consistency of our data, we use Cronbach's alpha. It is computed by correlating the score for each scale item with the total score for each observation (usually individual survey respondents or test takers), and then comparing that to the variance for all individual item scores. The resulting Cronbach's α coefficient of reliability ranges from 0 to 1 in providing the overall assessment of internal consistency and reliability. Hair et al. [29] recommended that an α estimation of 0.7 and above is good and acceptable. The general rule of thumb also suggests that a Cronbach's alpha of 0.65 and above is good, 0.80 and above is better, and 0.90 and above is best; however less than 0.5 is usually unacceptable. Using SPSS tool, we computed Cronbach's alpha for our dataset and found its value as 0.891. The value indicates a good acceptable value for consistency and reliability.

We use the Kaiser-Meyer Olkin (KMO) and Bartlett's test for measuring adequacy of our data samples. High values (close to 1.0) of KMO generally indicate that the sample is adequate and a factor analysis may be useful. SPSS output for this test on our dataset is shown in Table 3.1, where we can see that the value of KMO is 0.895, which indicates that our data sample is adequate. The result of Bartlett's test shows the value Chi-square as 5155.126 with 15 degrees-of-freedom, and at 0.000 level of significance. Small values (less than 0.05) of the significance level indicate that we may proceed with further analysis with our data [30].

Now, we discuss the results of multiple linear regression first to understand the combined influence of the input variables. After that, we will find the effect of each individual factors on purchase intention through simple linear regression.

Table 3.2: Multiple Regression: values of β, t and p

Variables	β Coefficients	t Stat	p-value
Intercept	-0.245	-3.527	4.325E-04
Trust (T)	0.144	7.776	1.367E-14
Reputation (R)	0.261	12.747	1.937E-35
Consumer Engagement (CE)	0.235	11.494	2.212E-29
Satisfaction (S)	0.260	13.598	7.858E-40
Behavioral Attitude (BA)	0.179	11.278	2.168E-28

The multiple linear regression considers all input features (independent variables) to estimate the dependent variable at the output. The equation is of the form:

$$y = \beta_0 + \beta_1 X_1 + \beta_2 X_2 + \cdots + \beta_n X_n \tag{3.1}$$

where, y is the output dependent variable and β_i is the coefficient of input variable X_i. β_0 is the y-intercept (a constant).

In our experiment, X_is are the five input independent variables mentioned as Behavioral Attitude (BA), Trust (T), Reputation (R), Satisfaction (S), and Consumer Engagement (CE). The output y is the dependent variable of Purchase Intention (PI). We need to compute the β_i coefficients associated with each of the input variables. A popular method is to use least-squared-error. In this method, the best fit line is determined where the error is minimized. Table 3.2 shows the values of β coefficients, t statistics, and p values. Using the β coefficients we can rewrite Equation 3.1 as:

$$PI = -0.245 + 0.144T + 0.261R + 0.235CE + 0.260S + 0.179BA \tag{3.2}$$

Equation 3.2 gives a prediction of purchase intention (PI) of a customer according to the input factors of trust (T), reputation (R), consumer engagement (CE), satisfaction (S), and behavioural attitude (BA). The β coefficients are the slopes in each of the input dimensions indicating individual contribution in the group effort in predicting the value of the output. Observing the different values of the slopes, we can say that the factors have a different amount of influence. The highest influence, that is the highest contributing predictor, is reputation (R) with the β coefficient value of 0.261, and the second highest is satisfaction (S) ($\beta = 0.260$). The sequential ranking of the remaining predictors are consumer engagement (CE) ($\beta = 0.235$), behavioral attitude (BA) ($\beta = 0.179$) and then trust ($\beta = 0.14$). This proves all of the variables have positive difference influence in predicting the purchase intention, and the combination of the variables is useful.

Due to the least-squared-error method, our equation fits the data better than any other linear equation. However, it does not guarantee that the model fits the data well. To understand how well our equation fits the data, we look at the coefficient of multiple determination (R^2). The coefficient of multiple determination measures the proportion of variation in the dependent variable that can be predicted from the set of independent variables in the model [31, 32]. When the model fits the data well, R^2 will be large, that is close to 1. For our regression equation, we computed the value

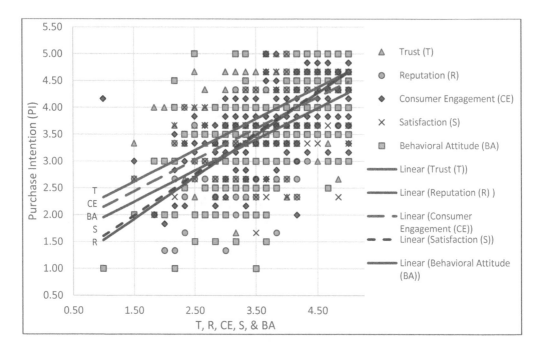

Figure 3.2: Simple linear regression lines of individual factors.

of R^2 as 0.728. This value suggests that the regression equation fits the data pretty well. For our sample problem, this means 72.8% of purchase intentions (PI) can be explained by the given input factors. We also find out the value of Durbin-Watson as d = 1.684. This value is between the two critical values of 1.5 <d <2.5. Therefore, we can assume that there is no first order linear auto-correlation in our multiple linear regression data.

With multiple regression, we are using more than one independent variable. Therefore, one may ask whether a particular independent variable contributes significantly to the regression after effects of other variables are taken into account. The answer to this question can be given with the t statistics and p values in Table 3.2. From the table we can see that the t-statistics are high for all of the five independent variables with the p values much less than 0.05 level. This means that each of the input factors contributes significantly to the regression after effects of other factors are taken into account. As an example, reputation (R) has the highest values of β, and t with a very low value of p. Therefore, the most significant among the five factors is the reputation (R), considering the effects of other factors as well. These outcomes also support this research's five hypotheses H1 to H5 mentioned in Section 3.3. Since, the coefficient beta is positive for all the variables and the significant value is 0.000 which is less than .005, we can say that all five of our hypotheses are asserted.

To understand the effect of each individual factor on the purchase intention, we conduct simple linear regression analysis. The linear regression lines for each individual factor are shown in Figure 3.2. The regression lines are produced considering each individual input factor independent of other factors.

A simple linear regression equation is given by $y = \beta x + \alpha$, here for our experiment y is the output purchase intention (PI), x is one of the input factors, β is the slope, and α is a constant (y-intercept) that works as a bias. The slope β explains how an input factor affects the output. The sign of β indicates whether the effect is positive or negative. The value of β expresses the amount of the effect. If the sign of the slope is positive and value is large, then it means that a small increase of the input would incur a large increase in the output. On the other hand, if the slope is negative, then increase in the input will result in a decrease in the output. We computed the values of α and β in the regression lines in Figure 3.2 and put them in individual equations associated with each input factor as below:

Reputation (R):   PI = 0.783R + 0.747;

Satisfaction (S):   PI = 0.766S + 0.84;

Behavioral Attitude (BA):   PI = 0.581BA + 1.372;

Consumer Engagement (CE):   PI = 0.585CE + 1.563;

Trust (T):   PI = 0.586T + 1.740;

From the above equations of linear regression lines, we can see that the slopes associated with each of the five input factors are all positive but have different quantitative values. This means that each of the factors has positive influence on the purchase intention. The values of α also show positive bias for all the factors. From the different values of the slopes, we can say that the quantitative amounts of influence differ for each of the associated factors. We can see that the highest contributor is the reputation (R) with a slope of 0.783, the second highest is the satisfaction (S) (slope 0.766). The other factors ranked sequentially with the slope values as trust (0.586), consumer engagement (0.585), and finally behavioural attitude (0.581). The ranking of the highest and second highest contributor in predicting the purchase intention remains the same as of multiple regression analysis.

In summary, we can say that all of our hypotheses are asserted through the results of this experiment. The chosen five factors of reputation, satisfaction, trust, consumer engagement, and behavioral attitude have positive influence in purchase intention for the online buyers of Bangladeshi youngsters.

3.5   CONCLUSION AND FUTURE DIRECTION

Trust, reputation, satisfaction, behavioural attitude, and consumer engagement are five important factors documented in the literature of purchase intention. In this research, we investigate how those factors influence online purchase intention of Bangladeshi young consumers. For this purpose, we collected data through an online survey among young university students of Bangladesh, who are also social media users. On those data, we conducted simple and multiple linear regression analysis to understand the individual and combined effects of the mentioned factors. Our result and analysis show that all five factors have, different in amount but, significant positive impact on the online purchase intention of the survey participants. Among all the factors, we found that reputation has the most significant effect on the online purchase intention. This corroborates natural intuition of a young buyer, usually one feels happy and tends to buy from a reputed brand or organization. The second most influencing factor is satisfaction. If a commodity fulfils the need of a buyer, s/he would normally favour the same organization in the next purchase. It is interesting to see that an important factor like 'trust' could not make it within the top most affecting factors. Perhaps this is because of the young age of the participants. In buying something, young people rely more on reputed brands and satisfaction than a trusted organization. This is also true that if a buyer is satisfied, then gradually trust will build up. Through the analysis of the coefficient of multiple determination (R^2), we found that the combined influence of the input factors on purchase intention is as high as 72.8%. In other words, one can say that 72.8% customers desire to shop online in Bangladesh when the mentioned five factors are satisfied.

Recently, the social commerce (s-commerce) is flourishing in Bangladesh, especially during the restrictions imposed due to the COVID-19 pandemic. Instead of only online dedicated websites, social networking sites such as Facebook, Instagram, or Twitter are also being used in s-commerce for advertising and selling products. Our above-mentioned conclusions also hold for s-commerce, as it is a subset of e-commerce. One interesting thing worth mentioning here is that s-commerce has more comprehensive customer engagement since customers can give feedback directly which helps other consumers making purchase decisions through SNS. We can also see this in the result section that consumer engagement is one of the important factors and ranked 3rd in Equation 3.2 for multiple regression analysis.

In this chapter, we limit our interest only to the mentioned five important factors. Other factors can be investigated in the future. Our analysis is made with only linear regression algorithm; other machine learning algorithms, including deep learning techniques, can be included in future endeavours. An observation on which algorithm performs better to predict purchase intention can also be made. Focus of our survey is limited to the target respondents. The respondents are undergraduate university students, who are comparatively young; older and general people could be future targets.

A prospective implementation of the findings of this research can be in online retail shops. If the mentioned five factors can be extracted from a social platform, then those can be used by the online retailers to target potential buyers. However, the extraction method requires further research.

Bibliography

[1] Kemp, S. (2016). *Digital Yearbook*. http://www.slideshare.net/wearesocialsg/2016digital-yearbook

[2] Wilson, S. G., & Abel, I. (2002). So you want to get involved in e-commerce. *Industrial Marketing Management*, 31 (2), 85–94.

[3] Kian, T. P., Boon, G. H., Fong, S. W. L., & Ai, Y. J. (2017). Factors that influence the consumer purchase intention in social media websites. *International Journal of Supply Chain Management (IJSCM)*, 6 (4), 208–214.

[4] Akar, E., & Dalgic, T. (2018). Understanding online consumers' purchase intentions A contribution from social network theory. *Behaviour & Information Technology*, 37 (5), 473–487.

[5] Noh, M., Lee, K., Kim, S., & Garrison, G. (2013). Effects of collectivism on actual s-commerce use and the moderating effect of price consciousness. *Journal of Electronic Commerce Research*, 14 (3), 244–260.

[6] Kim, S., & Park, H. (2013). Effects of various characteristics of social commerce (s-commerce) on consumers' trust and trust performance. *International Journal of Information Management*, 33 (2), 318–332.

[7] Fishbein, M., & Ajzen, I. (1977). Belief, attitude, intention, and behavior: An introduction to theory and research. *Philosophy and Rhetoric*, 10 (2).

[8] Triandis, H. C. (1979). Values, attitudes, and interpersonal behavior. In H. E. Howe Jr. & M. M. Page (Eds.), *Beliefs, attitudes, and values: Nebraska symposium on motivation, 1979* (Vol. 27, pp. 195–259). Lincoln, NE: University of Nebraska Press.

[9] Su, D., & Huang, X. (2011). Research on online shopping intention of undergraduate consumer in China – based on the theory of planned behavior. *International Business Research*, 4 (1), 86–92.

[10] Fandos, C., & Flavian, C. (2006). Intrinsic and extrinsic quality attributes, loyalty and buying intention: an analysis for a PDO product. *British Food Journal*, 108 (8), 646–662.

[11] George, J. F. (2004). The theory of planned behavior and internet purchasing. *Internet Research*, 14 (3), 198–212.

[12] Omran, E. E., & Van Etten, J. (2007). Spatial-data sharing: Applying social-network analysis to study individual and collective behaviour. *International Journal of Geographical Information Science*, 21 (6), 699–714.

[13] Algeji, A. F. M., Tahir, J. M., & Arije, U. M. (2021). Factors influencing consumer purchase intention: A study of bookstores in Kurdistan region of Iraq. *International Fellowship Journal of Interdisciplinary Research*, 1 (1), 19–35.

[14] Premazzi, K., Castaldo, S., Grosso, M., & Hofacker, C. (2010). Supporting retailers to exploit online settings for internationalization: The different role of trust and compensation. *Journal of Retailing and Consumer Services*, 17 (3), 229–240.

[15] Lee, C. K., Mjelde, J. W., Kim, T. K., & Lee, H. M. (2014). Estimating the intention–behavior gap associated with a mega event: The case of the expo 2012 Yeosu Korea. *Tourism Management*, 41, 168–177.

[16] Pavlou, P. A., & Fygenson, M. (2006). Understanding and predicting electronic commerce adoption: An extension of the theory of planned behavior. *MIS Quarterly* , 30 (1), 115–143.

[17] Ventre, I., & Kolbe, D. (2020). The impact of perceived usefulness of online reviews, trust and perceived risk on online purchase intention in emerging markets: A Mexican perspective. *Journal of International Consumer Marketing*, 32 (4), 287–299.

[18] Siddiqui, M. S., Siddiqui, U. A., Khan, M. A., Alkandi, I. G., Saxena, A. K., & Siddiqui, J. H. (2021). Creating electronic word of mouth credibility through social networking sites and determining its impact on brand image and online purchase intentions in India. *Journal of Theoretical and Applied Electronic Commerce Research*, 16 (4), 1008–1024.

[19] Hansen, H., Samuelsen, B. M., & Silseth, P. R. (2008). Customer perceived value in BtB service relationships: Investigating the importance of corporate reputation. *Industrial Marketing Management*, 37 (2), 206–217.

[20] Hongjiu, L., Rieg, R., & Yanrong, H. (2012). Performance comparison of artificial intelligence methods for predicting cash flow. *Neural Network World*, 22 (6), 549–564.

[21] Morgan-Thomas, A., & Veloutsou, C. (2013). Beyond technology acceptance: Brand relationships and online brand experience. *Journal of Business Research*, 66 (1), 21–27.

[22] Qalati, S. A., Vela, E. G., Li, W., Dakhan, S. A., Hong Thuy, T. T., & Merani, S. H. (2021). Effects of perceived service quality, website quality, and reputation on purchase intention: The mediating and moderating roles of trust and perceived risk in online shopping. *Cogent Business & Management*, 8 (1), 1869363.

[23] Jarvenpaa, S., Tractinsky, N., & Vitale, M. (2000). Consumer trust in an internet store information technology and management. *Journal of Information Systems*, 12 (1), 41–48.

[24] Low, W. S., Lee, J. D., & Cheng, S. M. (2013). The link between customer satisfaction and price sensitivity: An investigation of retailing industry in Taiwan. *Journal of Retailing and consumer services*, 20 (1), 1–10.

[25] Kuo, Y. F., Hu, T. L., & Yang, S. C. (2013). Effects of inertia and satisfaction in female online shoppers on repeat-purchase intention. *Managing Service Quality: An International Journal*, 23 (3), 168–187.

[26] Ahmed, M. E., Samad, N., & Khan, A. G. (2021). Factors influencing online purchase intention: A case of university students in Pakistan. *Eurasian Journal of Social Sciences*, 9 (1), 31–43.

[27] Saha, S. K., Duarte, P., Silva, S. C., & Zhuang, G. (2021). Supporting sustainability by promoting online purchase through enhancement of online convenience. *Environment, Development and Sustainability*, 23 (5), 7251–7272.

[28] Patterson, P., Yu, T., & De Ruyter, K. (2006, December 4–6). Understanding customer engagement in services. In *Advancing theory, maintaining relevance, proceedings of ANZMAC 2006 conference.* Brisbane, Queensland, Australia.

[29] Hair, J. F., Ringle, C. M., & Sarstedt, M. (2011). PLS-SEM: Indeed a silver bullet. *Journal of Marketing Theory and Practice*, 19 (2), 139–152.

[30] IBM. (2014). KMO and Bartlett's test. In *IBM SPSS Statistics*. IBM Corporation. https://www.ibm.com/docs/en/spss-statistics/23.0.0?topic= detection-kmo-bartletts-test.

[31] Witte, R. S., & Witte, J. S. (2017). *Statistics* (11th ed.). John Wiley & Sons, Inc.

[32] Berman, H. (2021). *Coefficient-of-multiple-determination. stattrek.com.* https:// stattrek.com/statistics/dictionary.aspx?definition=coefficient-of-multiple-determination.

CHAPTER 4

An Ethereum Blockchain-Based Healthcare System Using Smart Contract

Tamanna Tabassum, Fatema Akter, and Mohammed Nasir Uddin

Jagannath University, Dhaka, Bangladesh

CONTENTS

4.1	Introduction	35
4.2	Literature Review	36
4.3	Proposed System Design	38
	4.3.1 Prescription Mining	38
	4.3.2 Smart Contract Deployment	39
4.4	Experimental Setup and Analysis	40
	4.4.1 Simulation Environment	40
	4.4.2 Performance Analysis	40
4.5	Comparative Analysis	42
4.6	Conclusion	42

ONe of the prerequisites for the medical service industry is interoperability, handled by humans or machines to exchange medical records that contain confidential information of patients effectively and reliably. The fast take-up of digitization in the medical sector has increased the generation of massive records of healthcare information. Different organizations manage medical records in several ways and there is no standard procedure for maintaining medical records. Considering the confidentiality and integrity of patient information, this research work introduces a secure and transparent authentication approach for storing, sharing as well as having an authorized access of health records in the ethereum platform using decentralized technology blockchain. Each healthcare stakeholder (patient, doctor, and pharmacy) is authenticated with their cryptocurrency wallet address by Regulatory Authority (RA). Patients can migrate to other doctors without re-authentication of their distributed identity which minimizes the delay of information exchange throughout the same network. Pharmacies can generate a new ledger of the sold medicine list from recommendations. JavaScript VM and injected Web3 environment of Ethereum Virtual Machine (EVM) platforms are used for the implementation of smart contracts in solidity. The experimental outcome shows, with the use of the Markle tree and hash in the smart contract, integrity, verifiability, privacy, and security of the patient records have been achieved, and finally the comparison of the proposed and existing systems are shown.

4.1   INTRODUCTION

Trust is the basis of all economics and transactions, but with the exponential growth of the population, it is infeasible to verify everyone. In the case of sharing information, people trust a bank, government, etc. In this era of the internet, people are becoming more interested in exchanging sensitive information online, so the privacy and security of data is a major concern in all aspects of electronic healthcare in developing countries [1]. A trusted protocol called blockchain is a write-once-read-only (WORO), records digital events in a progressive series of distributed database systems within peer-to-peer (p2p) networks. Blockchain encompasses the mechanisms used to provide major security concern integrity and confidentiality [2]. Blockchain is gaining more popularity for solving issues related to exchange of information online using smart contracts; in smart contract, lines of code are automatically triggered defined actions when predetermined conditions are satisfied [3].

The traditional health record management system has a lack of integrity, confidentiality, and poor reliance on agents. Patients don't have control over their data being shared with unauthorized parties. When patients shift to other doctors, they go through the same treatment, and the overall process is delayed and the cost is increased. Furthermore, illegal medicine purchasing is causing an increase in the death rate; as per US Centers for Disease Control and Prevention, more than 42,000 have died from overdoses and illicit medication use was noted [4]. Another significant concern is the cost of smart contracts in the ethereum network when sharing confidential information.

The major contribution of this chapter is to bring all pharmacies together on a single platform, giving them access to view the patient medicine list and the ability to update the dispensed medicine list. Our designed proposed system can help in reducing the cost of implementing smart contracts in the healthcare sector. Proper management of patient prescriptions is important to ensure the best healthcare service so the proposed system solves the prescription problem and provides an easy way for sharing and getting prescriptions from a single platform by eliminating the centralized system. This system allows authorized specialists to create prescriptions, view patients' past medical records, and the pharmacy to view the recommended medicine to generate records of dispensed medicine for individuals. Thus prescriptions are stored in a distributed ledger, and the pharmacy is able to detect the abuse of medications.

4.2   LITERATURE REVIEW

Blockchain technology is being adapted into many verticals: healthcare, properties, automobiles, and even governments, simply as a chain of information creates blocks and shares the ledger on p2p networks [5], [6]. An unknown group proposed a currency system "Bitcoin" transactions on a platform where the online payments could be sent directly from one peer to another peer without going through a financial institution [7]. The main idea was to develop a trustful system that solves the double-spending problem through computational proof of the chronological order of transactions. In the blockchain, each transaction must be signed with the private key and validated by the public key to identify the validation of blocks [8]. After a block is accepted on the network, it will cryptographically be bounded in the distributed ledger that contains a full history of transaction records about the past, present, and future [9]. A list of transactions are linked together as a Merkle tree, a cryptographic hash of the previous block, nonce (used only once), and timestamp as information authentication [10]. This data stockpiling transmission allows the gateway to be straightforward, transparent, and secure, along with a spread over the number of nodes so that each node has a full copy of the same chain [11]. If an attacker attempts to make a change in a block, the local register will immediately stop being valid because the hash values inside the next block's headers will be completely different (see Figure 4.1).

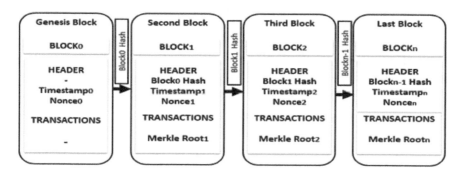

Figure 4.1: Blockchain Structure

Smart contract, a program that directly controls the share of digital currencies among users under certain conditions and works with "if/when...then...." rules. Nick Szabo, an American cryptographer first used the term "smart contract" in 1994 [12]. Rules are written as a code in solidity, the second-largest language of cryptocurrency in 2015 led by Christian Reitwiessner [13]. Smart contracts provide an exchange of currencies, reduce transaction costs by eliminating intermediaries, and data is encrypted on a shared ledger, making data impossible to share in an intelligible way as well as recognize any fraudulent activities [14]. Consensus algorithms achieve reliability and establish trust between unknown peers in a distributed system and ensure that each new block is added to the blockchain according to consensus [15]. Ethereum is a platform for sharing information across the world, described as a transaction-based state machine [16]. It allows a wide range of developers to assemble thousands of applications in the Ethereum Virtual Machine [17]. Metamask, a browser extension, and a cryptocurrency wallet act as a bridge between browsers and the ethereum network where users can build their decentralized applications and cryptocurrencies [18]. Before Smart contract dispatches on the ethereum networks, one version is sent to testnets, deploys, and allows to check resources [19].

A Secured Electronic Health Record Management System was proposed by M. Azhagiri et al. [20], for the improvement of health record management and services digitally. It is a centralized database system, and no specific mechanism is followed for the validation and authentication of the records as well as users before storing or accessing information. However, there are limitations in this system, such as single points of failure through centralization, unauthorized access to data, untrustworthiness, etc. It's also vulnerable to snooping and denial-of-service (DoS) attacks. Omotosho et al. [21] proposed a Secure Electronic Prescription System and showed the synergistic combination of steganography and cryptography technologies' capability of providing secure transmission of prescriptions. Manisree et al. [22], proposed an online medical advisory service which provides initial medical advice to patients by taking problems through voice input. These two are centralized systems, so patients are not able to access and share their health records with other doctors. Each time patients change doctors, patient identification and record retrieval are repeated, which is a time-consuming process. Our proposed system solves the unauthorized access problem of data and provides better security by using a decontralized platform

Seitz et al. [23] proposed a decentralized electronic prescriptions record system using smart contracts. This allowed medical records to be stored on a digital ledger for medical stakeholders. Authorized doctors can view patients' previous healthcare records and prescriptions but the pharmacy is not included in this research study. Proper management of medicine is important to ensure the best healthcare service, but illegal or additional medicine purchasing power may cause addiction and increase the overall death rate. So, our proposed healthcare system has included pharmacies to provide a better medication dispensing process.

Asma Khatoon [24] presented multiple medical workflows for different healthcare management organizations that integrate a private blockchain with the ethereum network's distributed file system. In this system, the doctor created prescriptions for the patient and the pharmacy can view this prescription through the smart contract. But it is not possible to generate the records of dispensed medicine by the pharmacy, which would be the cause of dispensing the same medicine many times or selling it illegally. This problem is solved in our proposed system by generating a new records of sold medicine list by the pharmacy.

Sultana et al. [25] proposed a blockchain-based information sharing and access control system for communication between the IoT devices. This system achieved trustfulness and authentication for data sharing in the networks by implementing multiple smart contracts to manage access control. The overall execution cost of the system is 6,900,000 gas units and the transaction cost is 5,200,000 gas units. In our proposed system, a single smart contract is used to manage the data sharing as well as access control among stakeholders. The transaction cost is 5,263,708 gas units and the execution cost is 3,954,740 gas units.

To overcome all the limitations discussed above, we proposed an ethereum blockchain-based healthcare system for sharing prescriptions. The main contribution in this research is to consolidate all pharmacies into a single platform to give them the access power to view the patient medicine list and update the sold medicine list. Smart contracts are implemented to solve all issues relating to prescription surveillance, illicit drug purchase control, and medication abuse by incorporating pharmacies into the system and allowing them to update the sold medicine list in a decentralized way. Our proposed system is also able to minimize the smart contract implementation cost in the healthcare system.

4.3 PROPOSED SYSTEM DESIGN

Medical blockchain will enable interaction with different healthcare stakeholders including doctors and pharmacies with patients' health records; besides each collaboration is auditable, straightforward, transparent, secure, and will be recorded as a transaction in a distributed ledger. The main determination of the proposed system is to secure medical prescriptions by eliminating the long waiting time process and reducing prescription mistakes due to doctor misinterpretations. Proposed system stakeholders involve a regulatory authority, doctor, patient, and pharmacy, who join using their ethereum wallet address and externally owned accounts (EOA) with ether balance in the ethereum network.

The regulatory authority performs as a system manager and controls the overall registration process to enroll stakeholders in the system. After the registration process, any registered doctor can create prescriptions for any registered patient as well as generate a code to corresponding prescriptions, and these records are stored in a block as hash value in the same ethereum network. Any patient can view prescriptions using code and can give access to the pharmacy when buying medicine. The pharmacy can access only the medicine lists of the shared prescriptions and generates new records with code of sold medicine lists. Doctors have to spend cryptocurrency (ether) for creating prescriptions with generation of code, and pharmacies have to spend cryptocurrency (ether) to create records of sold medicine quantity with code (see Figure 4.2).

4.3.1 Prescription Mining

One doctor has numerous patients with prescriptions. If Patient 1 has a health checkup with Doctor 1, and Doctor 1 provides Prescription 1 to Patient 1, then these three data are: Doctor 1 crypto wallet address, Patient 1 crypto wallet address, and Prescription 1 code are combined, and a transaction has to be performed to store these in a block as a hash value.

If the same patient (Patient 1) has another appointment with another doctor (Doctor 2) and the doctor generates Prescription 2, the crypto wallet addresses of Doctor 2 and Patient 1 with Prescription 2 are combined to create a hash, which is then stored through a transaction in another block of prescriptions (see Figure 4.3).

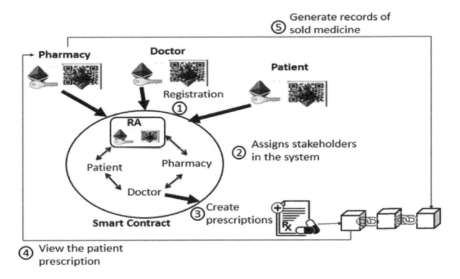

Figure 4.2: Proposed System Architecture

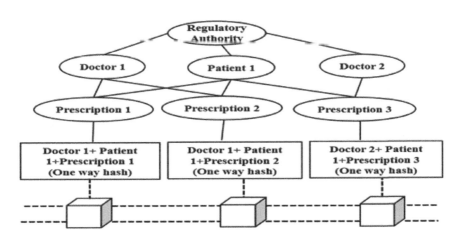

Figure 4.3: Prescription Mining

4.3.2   Smart Contract Deployment

The sharing and access-control policies are stored securely on the blockchain and smart contract is deployed just once for each node on ethereum (see Figure 4.4). The smart contract "MedicalPrescription" in Solidity follows some of the functions as:
contract MedicalPrescriptionContract{
function addDoctor () || addPatient() || addPharmacy () onlyRegulatoryAuthority
function createPresciption () constant onlyDoctor return (Code)
function generatePresciptionCode () private return index;
function getPrescriptionCode () onlyPatient
function getPresciption (Code) || getPharmacy () onlyDoctorOrPatientOrPharmacy
function getMedicinelist () onlyPatientOrPharmacy

function getSoldMedicineCode () onlyPatientOrPharmacy
function soldMedicinelist () payable onlyPharmacy}

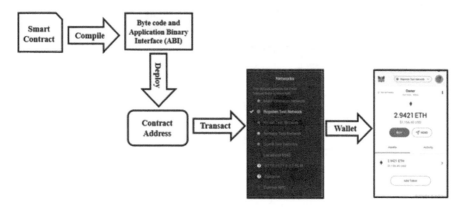

Figure 4.4: Injected Web3 Environment of Ethereum Virtual Machine

4.4 EXPERIMENTAL SETUP AND ANALYSIS

4.4.1 Simulation Environment

To execute all the computational tasks of the proposed system, Solidity programming language is used to implement smart contracts and the other configuration platforms are: Remix IDE, Metamask Wallet, Injected Web3, JavaScript VM, and Ganache.

4.4.2 Performance Analysis

Integrity

Merkle tree makes use of blockchain technology to ensure data integrity [26]. Throughout ethereum, the Merkle tree contains hashes of all the transactions in a block. If a node has to verify whether or not a transaction has been modified, it just needs to construct a Merkle tree in the transaction. In our proposed system, the Merkle tree is used to maintain consistency of the health records and prescription sharing process (see Figure 4.5).

Security Analysis

A Sybil attack is used against centralized networks, in which an individual creates a large number of nodes to disrupt network operation [27]. Only registered users will communicate in our system, and the hash value of each stakeholder is identical, so no individual can create one. Our proposed system mitigates this attack. Also the 51% chance of attack is a major weakness in bitcoin, which is solved in our proposed system using ethereum.

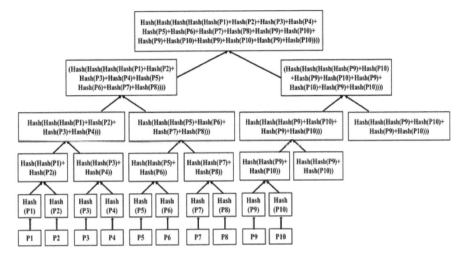

Figure 4.5: Markle Tree of Prescription Process

Verifiability

Each prescription is attached to the chain as a block. When a prescription block is generated, the smart contract returns a prescription code to the patients to verify that their health records are added to the chain and maintained without any modification.

Cost Analysis

Real time gas costs are ascertained by the EVM. Various functions are implemented to share and access control of records among system stakeholders. The smart contract deployment cost, function cost in JVM, and different test networks costs in injected Web3 environment of ethereum are calculated (see Figure 4.6, Figure 4.7, and Figure 4.8).

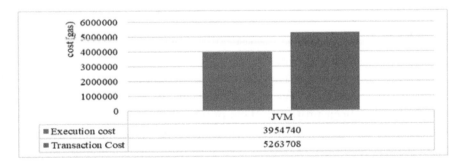

Figure 4.6: Smart Contract Cost

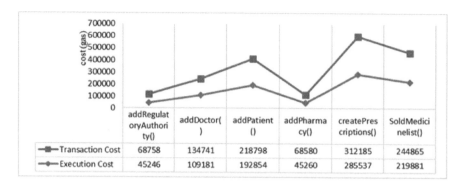

Figure 4.7: Function Cost in JVM

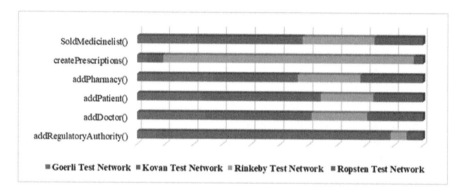

Figure 4.8: Function Cost in Different Test Networks

4.5 COMPARATIVE ANALYSIS

Another comparison is manifested to evaluate the performance of the proposed healthcare system in terms of cost (see Figure 4.9).

4.6 CONCLUSION

Many countries face significant difficulties to ensure security of information in the healthcare sector. To achieve the transparency and confidentiality of sensitive information, and sharing records without manipulation, an ethereum blockchain-based healthcare system has been proposed. This proposed decentralized system based on the smart contract has solved the prescription sharing problem, abuse of medicine, and unauthorized accessibility of patient health records which will improve any country's better healthcare informatics section. Additionally the proposed approach of medical healthcare system has implemented with the minimal cost of smart contract. In the ethereum network, consensus-based testnets are selected to reduce the computational cost. In the near future, this research intends to integrate with the supply chain in the blockchain network and real implementation in the hospital ecosystem to analyze the impact in the healthcare domain.

Table 4.1: Comparison with the Related Work

Properties	Azhagiri et al. [20]	Omotosho et al. [21]	Manisree et al. [22]	Seitz et al. [23]	Asma K. [24]	Sultana et al. [25]	Ours
Integrity	×	×	×	√	√	√	√
Privacy	√	×	×	√	√	√	√
Decentralization	×	×	×	√	√	√	√
Verifiability	×	×	×	×	×	×	√
Prescription creation	×	√	√	√	√	×	√
Sold medicine update	×	√	√	×	×	×	√

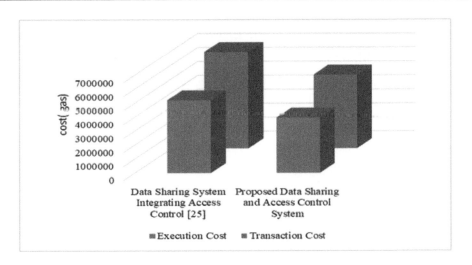

Figure 4.9: Cost Comparison

Bibliography

[1] Lin, I.C. and Liao, T.C., (2017). A survey of blockchain security issues and challenges.In *nt. J. Netw. Secur.*, 19(5), pp. 653-659.

[2] Leekha, S., (2018). Blockchain Revolution: How the Technology Behind Bitcoin Is Changing Money, Business, and the World. In *FIIB Business Review,* 7(4), pp. 275-276.

[3] Wang, S., Ouyang et al. (2019). Blockchain-enabled smart contracts: architecture, applications, and future trends. In *IEEE Transactions on Systems, Man, and Cybernetics: Systems*, 49(11), pp. 2266-2277.

[4] ABiswas, T., Islam et al. (2016). In Socio-economic inequality of chronic non-communicable diseases in Bangladesh, *PloS one,* 11(11), p. e0167140.

[5] Zile, K. and Strazdina, R., (2018). Blockchain use cases and their feasibility. In *Applied Computer Systems*, 23(1), pp. 12-20.

[6] Mohanta, B.K., Panda, S.S. and Jena, D., (2018), July. An overview of smart contract and use cases in blockchain technology. In *2018 9th International Conference on Computing, Communication and Networking Technologies (ICCCNT)* (pp. 1-4). IEEE.

[7] Nakamoto, S., (2008). Bitcoin: A peer-to-peer electronic cash system. In *Decentralized Business Review*, p. 21260.

[8] Sankar, L.S., Sindhu, M. and Sethumadhavan, M., (2017), January. Survey of consensus protocols on blockchain applications. In *2017 4th International Conference on Advanced Computing and Communication Systems (ICACCS)* (pp. 1-5). IEEE.

[9] Khatoon, A., Verma et al. (2019). Blockchain in energy efficiency: Potential applications and benefits. In *Energies*, 12(17), p. 3317.

[10] Giungato, P., Rana et al. (2017). Current trends in sustainability of bitcoins and related blockchain technology. In *Sustainability*, 9(12), p. 2214.

[11] Golosova, J. and Romanovs, A., (2018), November. The advantages and disadvantages of the blockchain technology. In *2018 IEEE 6th workshop on advances in information, electronic and electrical engineering (AIEEE)* (pp. 1-6). IEEE.

[12] Szabo, N., (1994). Smart Contracts, retrieved from: http://www. fon. hum. uva. nl/rob/Courses/InformationInSpeech/CDROM/Literature. LOTwinterschool2006/szabo. best. vwh. net/smart. contracts. html.

[13] Mukhopadhyay, M., (2018). Ethereum Smart Contract Development: Build blockchain-based decentralized applications using solidity. In *Packt Publishing Ltd*.

[14] Buterin, V., (2014). A next-generation smart contract and decentralized application platform. White paper, 3(37).

[15] Nguyen, G.T. and Kim, K., (2018). A survey about consensus algorithms used in blockchain. In *Journal of Information processing systems*, 14(1), pp. 101-128.

[16] Wood, G., (2014). Ethereum: A secure decentralised generalised transaction ledger. In *Ethereum project yellow paper*, 151(2014), pp. 1-32.

[17] Hirai, Y., (2017), April. Defining the ethereum virtual machine for interactive theorem provers. In *International Conference on Financial Cryptography and Data Security* (pp. 520-535). Springer, Cham.

[18] Choi, N. and Kim, H., (2019). A Blockchain-based user authentication model using MetaMask. In *Journal of Internet Computing and Services*, 20(6), pp. 119-127.

[19] Zhang, L., Lee et al. (2019), August. Ethereum transaction performance evaluation using test-nets. In *European Conference on Parallel Processing* (pp. 179-190). Springer, Cham.

[20] Azhagiri, M., Amrita et al. (2018), October. Secured electronic health record management system. In *2018 3rd International Conference on Communication and Electronics Systems (ICCES)* (pp. 915-919). IEEE.

[21] Omotosho, A., Adegbola et al. (2015). A secure electronic prescription system using steganography with encryption key implementation. In *arXiv preprint* arXiv:1502.01264.

[22] Manisree, A., Rushmitha, R. and Divya, M., (2020). Medical prescription generator using python (No. 4830). In *EasyChair.*

[23] Seitz, J. and Wickramasinghe, N., (2017), October. Blockchain technology in e-health: The case of electronic prescriptions in Germany. In *XVII international scientific conference on industrial systems* (pp. 156-159).

[24] Khatoon, A., (2020). A blockchain-based smart contract system for healthcare management. In *Electronics*, 9(1), p. 94.

[25] Sultana, T., Ghaffar et al. (2019), November. Data sharing system integrating access control based on smart contracts for IoT. In *International Conference on P2P, Parallel, Grid, Cloud and Internet Computing* (pp. 863-874). Springer, Cham.

[26] Rogers, B., Chhabra et al. (2007), December. Using address independent seed encryption and bonsai merkle trees to make secure processors os-and performance-friendly. In *40th Annual IEEE/ACM International Symposium on Microarchitecture (MICRO 2007)* (pp. 183-196). IEEE.

[27] Cramer, R., Gennaro, R. and Schoenmakers, B., (2000). A Secure and Optimally Efficient Multi-Authority Election Scheme. In *European Transactions on Telecommunications*, 8(5), pp. 481-490. Wiley Online Library, America.

CHAPTER 5

Bangla Fake News Detection Using Hybrid Deep Learning Models

Md. Rakibul Hasan Shezan, Mohammed Nasif Zawad,
Yeasir Arafat Shahed, and Shamim Ripon

East West University, Dhaka, Bangladesh

CONTENTS

5.1	Introduction	47
5.2	Related Work	48
5.3	Methodology	48
	5.3.1 The Dataset	49
	5.3.2 Dataset Preprocessing	49
	5.3.2.1 Removing Stopwords	50
	5.3.2.2 Removing Punctuations	50
	5.3.2.3 Tokenization	50
	5.3.2.4 Word Embedding	51
5.4	Proposed Models	51
	5.4.1 Hybrid Model Architecture	52
5.5	Results and Analysis	54
	5.5.1 Evaluation Metrics	55
	5.5.2 Result with Class Weights	55
	5.5.3 Result without Class Weights	57
5.6	Discussion and Future Works	58

FAKE NEWS has been one of the major concerns for the whole world because of the increasingly rapid pace of its spreading through social networks and websites. Fake news stories are frequently created for gaining financial and political advantages in order to deceive the general public. It has become easy to manipulate and mislead people with fabricated news because of the easy access to the online world through social media platforms. Determining the fakeness or reliability of an article automatically using linguistic analysis is currently an interesting area to investigate. However, most of the recent works are focused on the English language, whereas other low-resource languages like Bangla remain out of focus. In this study, we develop four hybrid deep learning models using Convolutional Neural Networks (CNN), Long Short Term Memory (LSTM), and Bi-LSTM trained on a publicly available Bangla fake news dataset and evaluate their performance. CNN model extracts the local features from the dataset, whereas LSTM detects the sequential patterns from those extracted features. Among the four hybrid models, the CNN + LSTM model gives the best result, as it achieves an accuracy of 97.69% and correctly predicted 77.7% of news as fake.

5.1 INTRODUCTION

Nowadays, we live in an era of the global village with advanced technology. Everyone is connected through the means of communication technology of different types. With the help of online news portals and social media platforms, it becomes easy for us to get attached to various news and views. The platform of social media (Facebook, Twitter, etc.) is increasing day by day as well as its users. We can see that there have been around 2.85 billion monthly active users of Facebook[1] and 187 million monthly active users of Twitter[2]. Undoubtedly, it is a great achievement for civilization that a huge number of people are interconnected under a certain network.

The main question is whether the information we get through different online platforms is real or fake. At first glance, it is hard to distinguish for ordinary people whether the news is fake or real.

Fake news refers to the spread of false information or disinformation, bluffs, false contexts, manipulated contents, clickbait, etc. There are some evil-minded people behind the unprecedented spread of fake news and even human programmed bots [1] are also spreading misleading information on platforms where a huge number of users are attached. The motive behind spreading fake news sometimes is to achieve a political advantage by playing dirty politics (spreading propaganda) against opposition and also to harm someone's life. During the 2016 US election, false news had a significant impact on the result [2].

It is a matter of great concern that we should come forward to mitigate the spread of fake news. Many researchers are also trying to develop some algorithms and applications to identify and mitigate the spread of fake news where most were conducted using English as a medium of communicating language. To our best knowledge, the amount of studies done on Bangla fake news detection is very little. As of now, there are around 230 million Bangla native speakers and 37 million who speak it as a second language[3], and it is also the 5th highest speaking language in the world. So, studies need to be done to develop some solutions and resources to tackle the spreading of Bangla fake news. So in this paper, we specifically focus on:

- Detecting Bangla fake news articles based on the headline and the news of an article.

---

[1] https://www.omnicoreagency.com/facebook-statistics/
[2] https://www.statista.com/statistics/242606/number-of-active-twitter-users-in-selected-countries
[3] https://en.wikipedia.org/wiki/Bengali_language

- Performance of the combination of deep learning models using GloVe embeddings of Bangla language on a publicly available Bangla dataset.

- Performance of the models on the dataset with and without the class weights and comparing their results when the dataset is imbalanced.

5.2 RELATED WORK

The spreading of fake news is not something new. It was also familiar in ancient times when news became a concept [3]. Detecting fake news from the news platforms in this modern era has become a great challenge for us. To identify fake news automatically, deep learning and machine learning approaches are mostly followed by researchers.

One research [4] developed models using CNN (Convolutional Neural Network), LSTM (Long Short-Term Memory network), and Bi-LSTM (Bidirectional LSTM), applied them on the dataset Fake News Challenge (FNC-1) published in 2016, and achieved 72.2% accuracy. Their model detects fake news in accordance with where article headline and article body relationship has followed.

A study [5] found that using a hybrid model consisting of CNN and RNN (Recurrent Neural Network) gives a better understanding of fake news classification than other non-hybrid baseline methods. Another study [6] used GloVe vectors for word embedding and develops a model on Bi-LSTM to detect fake news which gives above 90% accuracy.

On a Bangla dataset of their own [7], they used different types of traditional linguistic features (SVM) like lexical, semantic, syntactic, etc. and neural networks with pre-trained language models. They achieved a highest F1-score of 68% using the BERT model, and the CNN-based model achieved an F1-score of 59%.

Another study [8] utilized SVM and MNB classifier to detect Bangla fake news with the TF-IDF and CountVectorizer feature extraction techniques with an accuracy of 96.64% on SVM classifier with linear kernel.

A CNN-based architecture [9] trained on a hybrid feature extraction technique from texts by merging the Word2Vec and TF-IDF to detect whether a Bangla news is a satire or not with a precision of 96%.

As many studies are based on mainly the English language, the number of works on Bangla fake news detection is comparatively very low. A few studies have been done on Bangla fake news detection, but none of them discussed the implementation of deep learning models and their significance. In this study, we propose four deep learning models with the combination of CNN, LSTM, and Bi-LSTM with Bangla GloVe embeddings trained on a publicly available Bangla dataset [7] to detect Bangla fake news. Our experimental results show that our hybrid deep learning models can perform better than some of the existing studies.

5.3 METHODOLOGY

We discuss the methodology of the study in the sections below.

5.3.1 The Dataset

There are different fake news-related datasets available in many languages but not enough in the Bangla language. We have used a publicly available dataset named 'BanFakeNews' [7] which consists of around 50K instances of both fake and real news[4]. The whole dataset was created by collecting news from the 22 most popular and mainstream trusted news portals in Bangladesh. The dataset has overall 3 types of news which are: Misleading/False Context news, Clickbait news, and Satire/Parody news.

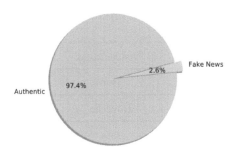

Figure 5.1: A pie chart showing the amount of authentic news and fake news in the dataset.

Among the total of 49977 pieces of news, 48678 instances are authentic or real news (label = 1) and only the remaining 1299 news are fake (label = 0). From these numbers, it is clear that the dataset is imbalanced, as the number of fake news compared to real news is pretty small. In machine learning classification problems, the class imbalance is a big concern. It simply indicates that the frequency of the target class is highly imbalanced, i.e., one of the classes is very common in comparison to the other classes present. We can look at Figure 5.1 to see the distribution of the target labels (fake and real) of the dataset that clearly shows imbalance as only 2.6% of total news is fake.

5.3.2 Dataset Preprocessing

We concatenated the fake and real datasets together and shuffled them randomly. Then we removed the first four columns of the dataset which are: articleID, domain, date, and category because we mainly focused on a piece of news only. Then we merged the headline of each piece of news with the content part to increase the overall context of the news and then dropped the headline column. So, the final dataset that we preprocessed and trained our models on consisted of only two columns: content and the label (0,1) of that news.

The dataset we have worked with is mixed with noisy and unnecessary data. So, we preprocessed our whole dataset before making it ready to use. Text preprocessing is a very crucial and necessary step in machine learning. Preprocessing your text means converting it into a format that is predictable and analyzable for your task.

---

[4]https://www.kaggle.com/cryptexcode/banfakenews

So, we have applied some steps to clean our dataset. The steps are described in the following section below.

5.3.2.1 Removing Stopwords

Stopwords[5] are words in English that add no extra special meaning to the context of a phrase. They can be ignored without affecting the meaning of the sentence. Some of the stopwords are like, the, he, this, have, etc. In Bangla language, the words are like the ones shown in Table 5.1.

Table 5.1: Bengali stopwords, their pronunciation and meaning in English.

In Bangla	Pronunciation	In English
হয়	Hoy	Is
হয়েছে	Hoyeche	Done
যারা	Jara	Those
তিনি	Tini	He
একটি	Ekti	A

To remove these Bangla stopwords from our dataset we have used the *BNLP* (Bengali Natural Language Processing) toolkit[6]. It is a toolkit that can be used to tokenize Bengali text, embed Bengali words, tag Bengali POS, and build a neural model for Bengali NLP.

5.3.2.2 Removing Punctuations

Each news in the dataset has different types of punctuations, like ?, !, :, -, etc. We created a function that takes each row of text data as input and removes all the punctuation symbols from it and replaces them with white spaces.

5.3.2.3 Tokenization

Machine learning algorithms cannot work with text datasets. The texts must have to be replaced with numbers. Tokenization[7] is a technique used in machine learning to represent texts or each word of a text with some numbers or vectors. We used the *nltk* library to use tokenizers for tokenizing each word of news in our dataset. These mappings of original words to the number are preserved in the *word_index* property of the tokenizer. Each of the texts is vectorized by tokenization.

The tokenizer is applied to a pre-processed training corpus mentioned above and transformed into integer sequences. The length of each of these sequences is set to

---

[5]https://en.wikipedia.org/wiki/Stop_word
[6]https://BNLP.readthedocs.io/en/latest/
[7]https://nlp.stanford.edu/IR-book/html/htmledition/tokenization-1.html

300, as the average number of words in the news in our dataset is 271.16 for authentic news and 275.36 for fake news. Then post-padding is added for news with less than 300 words. Because, to get each word of the same length, it is important to fill up each sequence with zeros that are shorter than the fixed length of 300.

5.3.2.4 Word Embedding

Word embedding[8] is a technique that refers to the vector representation of words with some numerical values. Machine learning techniques are not able to process string or text data as they expect vectors as input. There are techniques like Word2Vec, TF-IDF, CountVectorizer, etc. to convert words to vectors.

Neural networks can be used to train models for word vectors. Training these word vectors is time-consuming, as a huge text corpus and a good machine is necessary to train the model. There are also many pre-trained models available in different languages that contain these word vector matrices. But there is not much in the Bangla language.

Table 5.2: Embedded words showing the same team's other player names to a given player's name as input.

In Bangla		In English
তামিম(Tamim)	তামিম	Tamim
	মুশফিক	Mushfique
	সৌম্য	Soumya
	মাহমুদউল্লাহ	Mahmudullah
	ইকবালের	Iqbaler
	মুশফিকুর	Mushfiqur

We have used the *BNLP* toolkit to use the pre-trained GloVe model (BengaliGlove) with Bengali Wikipedia Dump Dataset. GloVe is an unsupervised neural network based learning algorithm for creating vector representations of words in order to derive semantic links. The Bengali pre-trained word vectors have 39 million tokens and the vectors are of 300 dimensions.

5.4 PROPOSED MODELS

We have used the following models to create hybrid models for our work:

- Bengali Global Vectors (GloVe) for representing the Bengali texts of our dataset and feeding them as inputs to the model.

- Long Short-Term Memory (LSTM): It is composed of layers with memory cells.

---

[8]https://www.tensorflow.org/text/guide/word_embeddings

To learn the long-term dependencies of words, LSTM has memory cell states. It incorporates a cell state and a carry in addition to the current word vector in the process as the sequence is processed at each time state. The carry ensures that no data is lost during the sequential process.

- Bidirectional Long Short-Term Memory (Bi-LSTM): Another RNN-based methodology for large text sequence prediction and text classification. In contrast to the LSTM model, the Bi-LSTM network processes the input sequence in both directions at the same time.

- Convolutional Neural Network (CNN): CNN is basically used for images to extract patterns and characteristics from the input. It is a normalized feed-forward neural network to represent multilayer perceptions. CNN actually works well with image data, but it has proven that it can perform well with text data. Max-pooling and dropout layers are often used to minimize the overfitting problem to CNN models.

5.4.1 Hybrid Model Architecture

All four hybrid models used in this study are created using the *keras*, a python library that includes the sequential models.

1. **Model 1: CNN + LSTM:** In this model, first, we implemented a single layer of Conv1D to handle the input vector and extract the local features. Then we added one single MaxPooling layer followed by one dropout layer to regularize the model.

   To learn the long-term dependencies, we have added two layers of LSTM that take the output of the dropout layer as the input. These LSTM layers use the local features that are extracted from the layers of CNN architecture and learn the long-term dependencies of the texts that finally classify whether the news is fake or real. As the important local features get selected from the CNN layer and then the LSTM layers use them to learn the dependencies, this hybrid model can perform better based on different scenarios. The overall structure of the model is as follows:

   - The first layer is the non-trainable embedding layer that takes the input train data, and the pre-trained Bangla GloVe embedding matrix is used to train the model.
   - The embedding layer is followed by a one-dimensional CNN layer (Conv1D) to extract the local features from the texts. The total number of filters used is 32 with only a single stride (strides = 1) and the ReLu (Rectified Linear Unit) activation function.
   - One Maxpooling1D layer is used with a *pool_size* = 5 to down-sample the vectors generated from the previous CNN layer. As there are a lot of parameters to train, adding a pooling layer helps to reduce the computational hazard without affecting the performance of the model.

- After that, a dropout layer with a dropout rate of 0.33 was added to reduce the overfitting problem.

- The long-term dependent features of the input feature maps are output by two LSTM layers of 128 and 64 units, respectively. A dropout of 0.25 is added with both of these layers.

- A dense layer is added to shrink the output of the LSTM layers with the ReLu activation function.

- Finally, the output dense layer with the sigmoid activation function outputs whether the news is fake or real (0 or 1).

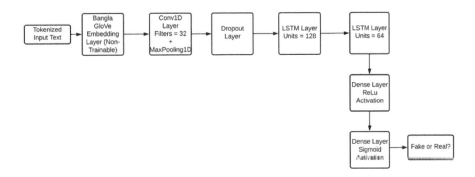

Figure 5.2: Structure of the hybrid CNN+LSTM model.

Pseudo Code for the CNN+LSTM hybrid model

<u>BEGIN</u>
Input: Tokenized train and test data of 300 dimensional.
Output: Prediction of whether a news is real or fake (1 or 0).
Method:

(a) **seq_input** ← **Input**(shape = (300), dtype = 'int32')

(b) **embedded_sequences** ← embeddings_layer (seq_input)

(c) **cov1** ← **Conv1DLayer**(filters=32,activation='relu')(embedded_sequences)

(d) **pool1** ← **MaxPooling1D Layer**(pool size = 5) (cov1)

(e) **Dropout** ← **Dropout Layer** (drop rate = 0.33) (pool1)

(f) **Lstm1** ← **LSTM** (units = 128, dropout = 0.25) (Dropout)

(g) **Lstm2** ← **LSTM** (units = 64, dropout = 0.25) (Dropout)

(h) **dense1** ← **Dense**(units = 32, activation = 'relu') (Lstm2)

(i) **Prediction** ← **Dense** (1, activation = 'Sigmoid') (dense1)

<u>END</u>

2. **Model 2: CNN (1 layer + 4 filters) + Bi-LSTM (2 Layer):** The structure of this hybrid model is the same as before but instead of using LSTM, we have used Bi-LSTM to see whether it can perform better than the previous model.

3. **Model 3: CNN (1 Layer + 32 filters) + Bi-LSTM (2 Layer):** In this model, we increased the number of filters in CNN's Conv1D layer to 32. All the other settings are the same as the previous Model 1.

4. **Model 4: CNN (2 Layer + 4 filters) + Bi-LSTM (2 Layer):** Finally, we implemented a hybrid model with 2 one-dimensional CNN architecture followed by 2 Bi-LSTMs.

We have used the Pandas framework library of Python to read the dataset and then we have split the dataset into train and test subsets (70-30% split). The adaptive moment estimation (Adam) optimizer was used to specify the learning rate in each iteration, the binary cross-entropy was used as the loss function, and the accuracy as the evaluation metric for evaluating the output results for all four hybrid models. The whole training was done with 20 epochs and a batch size of 256.

To get the best model while training, we used the *keras* callbacks functions which consisted of *Earlystopping* and *Modelcheckpoint*. *Earlystopping* is used to stop the training when no more improvement of the model is possible based on the validation set and *Modelcheckpoint* saves the best model to be used in the test phase of the experiment by monitoring validation loss.

We have incorporated class weights to balance the dataset, as it is highly imbalanced as Figure 5.1 shows. Class weights[9] are a technique used when the distribution of classes in a dataset is skewed or unbalanced. Different class weights are assigned to different classes to influence the classification of the classes during the training phase. The aim is to penalize the minority class for misclassification by giving them a higher class weight while giving the majority class a lower weight. In our case, as the number of fake news is pretty small, we give it a higher class weight and a lower class weight to the real news class as well.

5.5   RESULTS AND ANALYSIS

The experiments were made on the four hybrid models with different hyperparameters for optimization purposes and a better result. We have used the same class weights for all these four models. The results indicate that in terms of accuracy, precision, recall, and F1 score, the proposed hybrid CNN-LSTM model outperforms all other methods.

---

[9]`https://www.tensorflow.org/tutorials/structured\_data/imbalanced\_data#class\`
`_weights`

5.5.1 Evaluation Metrics

We used four metrics to evaluate the results of these models, all of which are based on the number of True Positives (TP), False Positives (FP), True Negatives (TN), and False Negatives (FN) in binary classifier predictions.

- The accuracy as an evaluation metric is used to verify if the news piece is correctly labeled as Real or Fake. The ratio of correctly predicted samples to total samples for a given data set is used to determine accuracy.

- The classifier's capacity to locate all of the positive samples is measured by the recall.

$$Recall = \frac{TP}{TP + FN}$$

- Precision refers to the classifier's ability to avoid labeling a negative sample as positive.

$$Precision = \frac{TP}{TP + FP}$$

- The F1 score is the harmonic mean of the individual precision and recall, which computes values between 0 and 1. It punishes extreme values of the dataset.

$$F1\ score = \frac{2 \times (Precision \times Recall)}{(Precision + Recall)}$$

5.5.2 Result with Class Weights

We tabulate the performance of the four models below in Table 5.3 to analyze their performance further.

Table 5.3: Precision, Recall, and F1-Scores of the four hybrid models for fake news prediction.

Model	Precision	Recall	F1-Score	Accuracy
CNN (4 filters) + Bi-LSTM	0.36	0.68	0.47	94.69
CNN (32 filters) + Bi-LSTM	0.41	0.73	0.53	96.75
CNN (2 layers + 4 filters)	0.34	0.62	0.44	96.06
CNN + LSTM	**0.52**	**0.78**	**0.63**	**97.69**

1. **CNN (1 layer + 4 filters) + Bi-LSTMs (2 layers)** In this model, we have used a one-dimensional CNN and 2 Bi-LSTM layers. The CNN layer has 4 filters of size 3 and strides of 1 with the ReLu activation function. After that, there is a Max Pooling layer of size 5 followed by a dropout layer. The two layers of Bi-LSTMs were 128 and 64 units followed by the ReLu and Sigmoid activation function.

The model achieves an accuracy of 94.68% on the test set with an F1-score of 0.47 and a low precision of 0.36. Among the total of 373 fake news instances from the test set, the model predicted 253 of them correctly as fake which is around 68% of the fake news from the test set. But it has misclassified 120 fake news instances also as shown in Table 5.4.

2. **CNN (1 layer + 32 filters) + Bi-LSTMs (2 layers)** The settings of this model are similar to the previous model (model 1). However, we have changed the number of filters to 32 to see whether it performs better, and the accuracy of this model increased to 96.75%. The precision also increased to 0.41 and recall to 0.73 with the overall F1-score of 0.53. The model predicted 273 news as fake, which is around 73% of the total fake news, and misclassified 100 fake news.

3. **CNN (2 layers + 4 filters) + Bi-LSTMs (2 layers)** This time, in the settings of the model we have added one extra one-dimensional CNN layer after the first CNN layer. The first layer consists of 4 filters, the second CNN layer has 8 filters, and both with the same strides of 1.

   The accuracy this model achieves is 93.37% on the test set with an F1-score of 0.44. The accuracy of this model is better than the previous two models but the Precision, Recall, and F1-score decreased. It is clearly reflected on the prediction rate, as it predicted 233 news as fake among 373 fake news from the test set. So, it means that the model predicted around 63% fake news correctly from the total fake news in the test set.

Table 5.4: The amount of fake news correctly classified by the hybrid models with class weights.

Model	Correctly Predicted	Prediction Rate (%)
CNN (4 filters) + Bi-LSTM	253	68
CNN (32 filters) + Bi-LSTM	273	73
CNN (2 layers + 4 filters)	233	63
CNN + LSTM	**290**	**77.7**

4. **CNN + LSTM**
   This model gives the best result among all the models created. The accuracy of this model hybrid model is around 97.64% on the test set with the highest F1-score of 0.63. But the actual improvement it has is on predicting the fake news instances.

   It achieves an accuracy of 77.7% on detecting fake news among the test set. The model successfully predicted 290 news among all the 373 news as fake which is pretty good compared to the other models we created. It also misclassified 83 fake news as the original. On the other hand, it misclassified 263 original news as fake.

The epochs vs. validation accuracy line graph is shown in Figure 5.3 to see the performance of the four models on unseen or validation data while training.

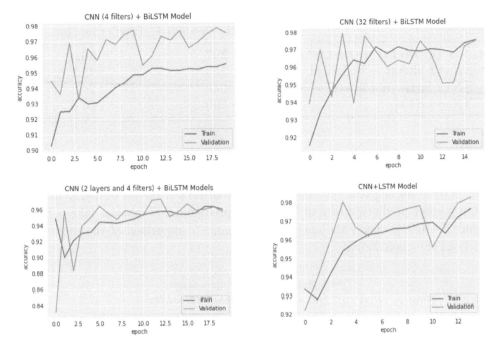

Figure 5.3: Line graphs showing train and validation accuracy in each epoch of four models.

As Figure 5.3 shows, the CNN(32 filters) + Bi-LSTM model and the CNN + LSTM model stopped before reaching the maximum epoch during training. It is because highest training loss was reached and no further improvement of the models was possible.

We note that one study [8] achieved an accuracy of 96.64% with the SVM classifier, while our CNN and LSTM based model achieved an accuracy of 97.64%. The performance difference can be an indication that using hybrid deep learning models can have more impact than the usual supervised models.

The CNN-based model [9] achieved an accuracy of around 96% combining the TFIDF and Word2Vec features. Compared to their result, our hybrid approaches performed satisfactorily and it may indicate that the use of GloVe embeddings can be a better choice than the use of Word2Vec as the features of the model.

5.5.3 Result without Class Weights

We have also trained all these four models without assigning any class weights to the class labels to see how they perform on differentiating fake news from the real.

As we can see from Table 5.5, all of the four models achieved less accuracy in predicting fake news among the test set compared to the accuracy of models trained with the class weights. The CNN + LSTM model performed well with the class

Table 5.5: The amount of fake news correctly classified by the hybrid models without the class weights.

Model	Correctly Predicted	Prediction Rate (%)
CNN (4 filters) + Bi-LSTM	**207**	**56.4**
CNN (32 filters) + Bi-LSTM	155	42.2
CNN (2 layers + 4 filters)	96	26.2
CNN + LSTM	200	54.6

weights as it has predicted 77.7% of the total fake news from the test set correctly as fake. However, without the class weights, it has predicted only 54.6% of the news as fake correctly from the test set. The CNN and Bi-LSTM model outperformed here as with a correct prediction rate of 56.4% and predicted 207 news as fake correctly.

Figure 5.4 below shows the overall performance comparison of the models with and without the class weights:

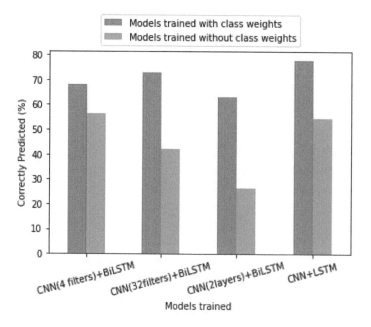

Figure 5.4: A compound bar chart showing the percentage of fake news classified correctly by the models trained with and without class weights.

5.6   DISCUSSION AND FUTURE WORKS

Fake news detection is not a new topic or research area, but it is completely a new thing whenever we are talking about Bangla fake news. There is a scarcity of Bangla fake news resources, as there are very few such initiatives taken to create Bangla datasets of fake news or misinformation. The Bangla dataset [7] created is the only publicly available dataset on Bangla fake news.

The four hybrid models we present here are all created by using state-of-the-art deep learning algorithms. The experimental results show that the hybrid CNN and LSTM model can perform better than the others on the dataset we used. As per our knowledge, no such work has been done in this sector for the Bangla language and with this dataset. The only available work is done by [8] on a Bangla satire news dataset to detect satire news automatically.

Due to the limited availability of the Bangla fake news dataset, we could not apply our proposed model on other datasets to analyze their performance in different contexts. We have tried to apply SMOTE (Synthetic Minority Over-sampling Technique) to balance the dataset [10], but as the dataset is pretty large and due to the limitations of our resources and time, we couldn't train the model with SMOTE. We needed to apply SMOTE on embedded sentences, which takes a very large memory. So, we have used class weights to balance the two classes by giving more importance to the minority class (fake = 0) compared to the majority class (real = 1).

In the future, we want to apply transformer-based models like BERT, DistilBERT, T5, etc. on Bangla datasets that work with the attention mechanism of the text [11]. Also, we are keen to work with several metadata of news, such as a source and the author who posted it, to extract different aspects of news to identify its reliability.

Bibliography

[1] Shao, C., Ciampaglia, G. L., Varol, O., Yang, K.-C., Flammini, A., & Menczer, F. (2018). The spread of low-credibility content by social bots. *Nature communications, 9(1)*, 1-9.

[2] Bovet, A., & Makse, H. A. (2019). Influence of fake news in twitter during the 2016 US presidential election. *Nature communications, 10(1)*, 1-14.

[3] Posetti, J., & Matthews, A. (2018). A short guide to the history of fake news and disinformation. *International Center for Journalists, 7*, 1-19.

[4] Abedalla, A., Al-Sadi, A., & Abdullah, M. (2019). A closer look at fake news detection: A deep learning perspective. *In Proceedings of the 2019 3rd international conference on advances in artificial intelligence* (p. 24-28).

[5] Nasir, J. A., Khan, O. S., & Varlamis, I. (2021). Fake news detection: A hybrid CNN-RNN based deep learning approach. *International Journal of Information Management Data Insights, 1*(1), 100007.

[6] Bahad, P., Saxena, P., & Kamal, R. (2019). Fake news detection using bi-directional LSTM-Recurrent neural network. *Procedia Computer Science*, 165, 74-82. (2nd International Conference on Recent Trends in Advanced Computing ICRTAC -DISRUP - TIV INNOVATION, 2019 November 11-12, 2019).

[7] Hossain, M. Z., Rahman, M. A., Islam, M. S., & Kar, S. (2020). Banfakenews: Adataset for detecting fake news in Bangla. *CoRR,abs/2004.08789.* Retrieved from https://arxiv.org/abs/2004.08789

[8] Hussain, M. G., Rashidul Hasan, M., Rahman, M., Protim, J., & Al Hasan, S. (2020). Detection of Bangla fake news using MNB and SVM classifier. In *2020 international conference on computing, electronics communications engineering (ICCECE)*(p. 81-85).

[9] Sharma, A. S., Mridul, M. A., & Islam, M. S. (2019). Automatic detection of satire in Bangla documents: A CNN approach based on hybrid feature extraction model. In *2019 international conference on Bangla speech and language processing (icbslp)* (p. 1-5).

[10] Chawla, N. V., Bowyer, K. W., Hall, L. O., & Kegelmeyer, W. P. (2002). Smote: synthetic minority over-sampling technique.*Journal of artificial intelligence research,16*, 321–357.

[11] Jwa, H., Oh, D., Park, K., Kang, J. M., & Lim, H. (2019). exbake: Automatic fake news detection model based on bidirectional encoder representations from transformers (bert). *Applied Sciences, 9* (19). Retrieved from https://www.mdpi.com/2076-3417/9/19/4062

Adaptive Decay and Radius-Based Evolving Clustering Approach for Data Stream

Sathi Rani Pal

Department of Computer Science and Engineering, University of Barishal, Barishal, Bangladesh

Md Manjur Ahmed

Department of Computer Science and Engineering, University of Barishal, Barishal, Bangladesh

K. M. Azharul Hasan

Department of Computer Science and Engineering (CSE), Khulna University of Engineering and Technology (KUET), Khulna, Bangladesh

Rahat Hossain Faisal

Department of Computer Science and Engineering, University of Barishal, Barishal, Bangladesh

CONTENTS

6.1	Introduction	62
6.2	Literature Review	63
6.3	Methodology	64
	6.3.1 Descriptions of Proposed Methodology	64
	6.3.2 Initialization of the System	65
	6.3.3 Update the Micro-cluster	65
	6.3.4 Kill the Micro-cluster	66
	6.3.5 Updating the Cluster Graph	66
6.4	Experimental Result and Analysis	67
	6.4.1 Cluster Formation on Mackey-Glass Data stream	67
	6.4.2 Space, Dimensionality and Cluster Quality	67
	6.4.2.1 Scalability	68
	6.4.2.2 Response to Variable Decay	69
	6.4.2.3 Cluster Purity and Accuracy	69

    6.4.2.4 Memory Efficiency 70

    6.4.2.5 Parameter Sensitivity Study 70

6.5 Conclusion 71

A S TIME PASSES, the application of data clustering in the data analysis field has increased dramatically. Forming micro-clusters is a typical approach of summarizing the online continuous data stream. These data clustering techniques are convenient for the field of data mining. For clustering data stream, an arbitrarily shaped density based clustering approach is proficient to produce clusters. Most of the existing data clustering approaches are hybrid, online, or offline. These approaches are able to find only hyper-elliptical clusters. Recently two fully online clustering algorithms called CEDAS and BOCEDS were proposed which are able to handle the property of data stream that evolves over time. In CEDAS, an optimal micro-cluster radius set globally needs to be initialized, which is a difficult task. It can be said that if the choice of radius is mistaken, then the performance of the algorithm will be reduced. In BOCEDS, a buffer is used for storing the temporarily irrelevant micro-clusters, and then a pruning method is used for extracting the micro-clusters. In these existing online clustering techniques, a permanent decay variable is specified and not updated over time (not evolving). This decay variable is predetermined when it is initialized. It can also be an erroneous choice like global optimal radius. In this chapter, we represent an online based evolving clustering approach based on adaptive decay and radius. In this approach, a graph structure is preserved where nodes are used to represent the micro-clusters, and edges are used to represent the pairs of intersecting micro-clusters. These cluster graphs are evolved over time. Furthermore, adaptive decay and adaptive radius are considered in order to avoid the arbitrary choice of these parameters. The experimental result of this algorithm is compared with the existing methods and it outperforms them.

6.1 INTRODUCTION

The uninterrupted flow of long succession of data is commonly known as data stream and the amount of continuous, time varying and rapid data stream generated is known as online data. As an example, Facebook has the highest registered users who produced more than 30 petabytes data per day according to statistics in September 2017 [1]. Analysis and clustering approaches have become significant for these unbounded data streams [2]. Clustering processes groups with similar and homogeneous data points in the same subsets or clusters, and dissimilar data objects are moved to others [3]. Most of the designed algorithms didn't work properly due to the infinite dimension, volume uncertainty, and gradual changes over time and data arriving speeds [4][5][6]. In general, clustering approaches are classified into five methods, namely, partitioning, hierarchical, grid based, model based and density-based methods [7]. All density connected data objects, and all the other objects which are density reachable from these objects, are formed as clusters [8]. Among these existing clustering calculations, a density-based clustering approach is known as a common and beneficial method for information streams because of its capability of discovering clusters with arbitrary shapes and its detection of noise [7]. The online phase generates micro-clusters by evaluating the arriving data streams, and the offline phase macro-cluster is achieved from the micro-clusters [4]. Furthermore, most of the algorithms are not fully online-based methods and can't handle the evolving characteristics of data points or low processing rates, or they suffer from high dimensionality or high requirements of memory [9].

In this chapter, we propose a clustering technique which is density based, namely adaptive decay and radius-based online clustering for stream data (ADROCS). It updates the radius between the range (R_{min}, R_{max}) and introduces a fading factor which is used to update the decay variable rather than a constant decay variable. It maintains the formation of clusters efficiently in dense and sparse areas. The proposed algorithm is discussed in Section 6.3. The performance of the proposed ADROCS algorithm is narrated with three datasets (Mackey-Glass [17], Helical Data streams, KDDCUP'99 [16]) in Section 6.4. Section 6.5 provides the conclusion of the study.

6.2 LITERATURE REVIEW

DBSCAN [11] is the fundamental algorithm which yields arbitrarily shaped clusters. The generated cluster size is different. Depending on Eps (radius) and MinPts (minimum points), it defines the data points as either core, border or noise points. It doesn't consider the limitation of memory. It is inappropriate to the high dimensional datasets. BIRCH [12] is one of the primitive calculations utilized for information stream clustering. It works by maintaining a CF tree where each node of the tree maintains some clustering features (CF). CluStream [13] is another clustering algorithm which is the extended version of BIRCH that clusters data over time horizons, for generating macro-clusters from micro-clusters based on k-means approach. However, it is effective but it only generates spherical-shaped clusters.

CODAS [14] is a newly online based clustering approach. It forms arbitrarily shaped clusters and is scalable to a high-dimensional data stream. The radius is set using expert knowledge. If the value of the radius is an erroneous choice, then it will give a worse performance than others. It does not have the feature to allow the clusters to evolve. CEDAS [9] was the improved version of CODAS by storing the adjacency information of micro-clusters in a graph structure that allows the evolving nature of clusters. It allows the rapid division and merging of macro-clusters. CEDAS is able to create high-dimensional clusters, and also handles noise and the evolving feature of clusters. It has a linear time penalty and complexity comparative to the number of dimensions of data. Similar to other density based clustering approaches, CEDAS has to choose the optimal value of radius and decay of a micro-cluster.

i-CODAS [15] is an improved version of CODAS which gives a better performance for a high-dimensional data stream. The number of micro-clusters in i-CODAS are reduced as the time increases than for CODAS. i-CODAS mean sample processing time is greater than CODAS for high-dimensional data. Like CODAS, the originated clusters do not evolve over time. Furthermore, BOCEDS [10], a buffer based method, is introduced where the irrelevant clusters are stored, and then a pruning operation is applied on the buffer for extracting the temporary irrelevant clusters. It also introduces the feature of adjusting micro-cluster radius sweep to its optimal. Moreover in BOCEDS [10], the decay parameter (number of specified data points) is used to diminish the irrelevant micro-clusters which are set by the user prior to execution. However, it is required to develop a fully online clustering approach which is able to adapt its radius and the decay parameter, and thus able to generate high-quality arbitrarily shaped clusters with minimal time and memory in the dynamic spatial environments.

6.3 METHODOLOGY

The proposed ADROCS algorithm produces high quality and highly scalable clusters which require less memory, and it also manages the evolving characteristics of the data stream. Generally, ADROCS algorithm is an information-driven approach which isolates the data field in shell and kernel regions. r is the radius of the micro-cluster, the inner region $(r/2)$ is the kernel region, and the outer region is the shell region $(r/2)$. Local density is the total number of data objects in any micro-cluster. The macro-clusters are formed by micro-clusters and they contain data objects more than a density threshold. A graph structure is used to define the connections of micro-clusters. The intersections of micro-clusters form the macro-clusters which are storing the connection in a cluster graph structure. Two connecting micro-clusters are the members of the same cluster. The methodology can be divided mainly into two fragments.

6.3.1 Descriptions of Proposed Methodology

The proposed algorithm has the following parameters: Maximum Radius (R_{max}) defines the maximum distance value in which the data point is in that cluster. Minimum Radius (R_{min}) is the lowest distance value in which out of that distance the data point belongs to another cluster. Density threshold $(Th_{density})$ is the requirement of minimum data samples to form a micro-cluster. It is a user-defined parameter. Energy is utilized to decide the length of time since a micro-cluster can get unused information. Micro-cluster energy is set to 1 when it is formed. Decay is a user-defined parameter that defines data rate. It is the number of data objects that come from the data stream, and this decay is used for updating the radius and energy values of the micro-clusters. Fading factor, λ, is a user-defined parameter. Micro-clusters are faded in each time step by this fading factor of $2^{(-\lambda)}$. The value of λ is greater than zero.

The proposed algorithm is composed of the following 4 distinct types of sub-algorithms: initialization of the algorithm, updating the micro-cluster, killing the micro-cluster and updating the cluster graph.

Definition 1: Kernel micro-cluster $(N_t, C_t, R_t, Energy_t, EL_t, M_t)$ is identified as the group of close points $X_1, X_2, \ldots \ldots X_{Nt}$ where the local density $N_t \geq Th_{density}$, radius $R_{min} \leq R_t \leq R_{max}, Energy > 0, center(C_{t+1}^k = \frac{X_k^t}{N_t^t})$, edge list $EL_t =$

$MC_1, MC_2, \ldots\ldots, MC_k$ and macro-cluster ID, M_t is a unique integer.

Definition 2: Non-kernel micro-cluster $(N_t, C_t, R_t, Energy_t, EL_t, M_t)$ is identified as the group of close points $X_1, X_2, \ldots\ldots\ldots X_{Nt}$ in a high-density area where the local density is not $\emptyset$, radius $R_{min} \leq R_t \leq R_{max}, Energy \leq 0, center(C_{t+1}^k = \frac{X_k^t}{N_t})$, edge list $EL_t = \emptyset$ and macro-cluster ID, M_t is empty.

6.3.2 Initialization of the System

Initially, create a new micro-cluster structure containing the data points which do not go under any micro-cluster. The data point X_i defines the center of the micro-cluster, MC_{new} in the data space. The MC_{new} local density is 1. The energy of MC_{new} is 1. $MC_{new}(Macro)$ refers to the macro in which the micro-cluster belongs is set to 1 and $MC_{new}(Edge)$ is 1. The radius of MC_{new} is R_{min}. Initially the value of t is set to 1. Only when another new micro-cluster is created then the value of t is increased by 1. Furthermore, another new micro-cluster creation is t=t+1.

6.3.3 Update the Micro-cluster

After a new data point arrives from the data stream, the proposed ADROCS algorithm attempts to give it to an existing micro-cluster $(N_t, C_t, R_t, Energy_t, EL_t, M_t)$ that works based on the Euclidean distance (d) between the data point, Xi and the micro-cluster center (C). If Euclidean distance (d) is less than the micro-cluster radius such that Distance, d $(X_i, C_t) < R$, Then the data point is mapped to the micro-cluster (Algorithm 1: Update the micro-cluster).

The number of data point in the kernel region is updated using Equation (6.1).

$$N_{t+1} = N_t + 1 \tag{6.1}$$

And the radius is updated by a fading factor (1/Decay) for every unit closeness

$$Radius, R_{t+1} = min([R_t + \{\frac{(2 \times d(X_{t+1}, C_t))}{R_t}\} \times 2^{(-\lambda \times Decay)}]), R_{max}) \tag{6.2}$$

The value of data objects in the shell region is updated using Equation (6.3).

$$N'_{t+1} = N'_t + 1 \tag{6.3}$$

The micro-cluster center is updated recursively using Equation (6.4).

$$C_{t+1}^k = \frac{(N'_{t+1} - 1) \times C_t^k + X_{t+1}^k}{N'_{t+1}} for\ k = 1, 2, 3 \ldots\ldots D, \tag{6.4}$$

where   D = dimension size of data objects.

For updating the energy (E_{t+1}) of a micro-cluster, an energy updating function is considered which is modified from BOCEDS [10].

$$Energy, E_{t+1} = E_t + \{\frac{(R_t - d(X_{t+1}, C_t))}{R_t}\} \times (t \times 2^{(-\lambda \times Decay)}) \tag{6.5}$$

Algorithm 1 Update micro-cluster

Sample X_i and Kernel Micro-cluster(N_t, C_t, R_t, $Energy_t$, $E\,L_t$, M_t) and distance defined as d(X_i, C_t)

    Step 1: Update the value of local density using equation (1) and the update the value t=t+1.

    Step 2: If(N_{t+1} = $Th_{density}$ And MC_{new} subset of MC_{kernel}) then

           Add MC_{new} to kernel micro-cluster

           Update radius(R_{t+1}) using equation (2)

           Update the Energy(E_{t+1}) of MC_{new} using equation (5)

        [End If]

    Step 3: If $\frac{R_{t+1}}{2}$ < d ≤ R_{t+1} , then

           Update the value of data point in the shell region(N'_{t+1}) following equation (3)

           Update the center(C^k_{t+1}) of the MC_{new} using equation (4)

        [End If]

    Step 4: Exit

6.3.4 Kill the Micro-cluster

To re-cluster the micro-cluster for evolving the clusters, energy parameter of the kernel micro-cluster is reduced by the fading factor. If the energy is less than zero, then the kernel micro-cluster is marked as a non-kernel micro-cluster. When any micro-cluster is deleted, then the value of t is updated by decreasing its previous value (Algorithm 2: Kill the micro-cluster).

Algorithm 2 Kill the micro-cluster

  Step 1: Decay value is updated by the following equation

        $Decay' = t * 2^{-\lambda(Decay+t)}$

  Step 2: Reduce the Energy by Decay' from all kernel micro-clusters

  Step 3: For every kernel micro-cluster, if micro cluster Energy ≤ 0 then it turns into a non-kernel micro cluster set.

  Step 4: For each non-kernel micro-cluster ,

        If Energy ≤ 0, then

           Remove $MC_{non-kernel}$ micro-cluster set

           t = t-1

           Remove all edges related with that micro cluster

           Reduce the number of micro clusters by 1

        [End If]

      [End For]

  Step 5: Exit

6.3.5 Updating the Cluster Graph

The cluster graph can be changed when the center of a kernel micro-cluster is changed. If two kernel micro-clusters (MC_{new} and MC'_{new} with centers C and C') exist, Euclidean distance between MC_{new} and MC'_{new} is s and then the intersecting center distance (s') between the two micro-clusters is calculated using the following Equations.

$$If\ c' > c, s' = c' + \frac{c}{2}\ Else\ s' = c + \frac{c'}{2} \qquad (6.6)$$

If $s \leq s'$ then add the edge (MC_{new} , MC'_{new}) to the edge list of (MC_{new} and MC'_{new}). If any of the edge list of the micro-cluster has changed, then it puts a new macro-cluster number within the graph. The edge list can be changed by moving the centers of the micro-clusters. Macro-cluster number will be changed only when the edge list values are changed. After changing, it will set a new value in the new graph. Therefore, the proposed ADROCS uses a fading factor which updates the decay and energy variable exponentially and adapts it with the data sample over time. The radius value is also updated over time using the fading factor. Moreover, the cluster graph is updated depending upon the changes of the micro-cluster.

6.4 EXPERIMENTAL RESULT AND ANALYSIS

The performance of the proposed ADROCS algorithm is discussed in this section based on three datasets: Mackey-Glass [17], Helical Data streams, KDDCUP'99 [16]. The sensitivity of parameters is discussed accordingly in this section, especially in Section 6.4.2.2 (Response to Variable Decay) and 6.4.2.5 (Parameter Sensitivity Study).

6.4.1 Cluster Formation on Mackey-Glass Data stream

The proposed ADROCS algorithm is a totally online clustering method where the micro-cluster is formed. After that, the micro-clusters are removed in order to reduce the number of micro-clusters. It changes the number of generated micro-clusters by a fading factor (see Section 6.3: Methodology).

$$\frac{dx(t)}{dt} = \frac{ax(t - \tau)}{1 + x(t - \tau)^{10}} \times bx(t) \tag{6.7}$$

The Mackey-Glass time series [17] dataset is originated from the following differential equation having a non-linear time delay. The equation is solved with various values for a and b using the fourth order Range-Kutta numerical method. The proposed approach is conducted on the clean Mackey-Glass data stream, and results of the clustering process are shown in Figure 6.1 for different time periods.

6.4.2 Space, Dimensionality and Cluster Quality

A circular helix consisting of three lists of helical data series forms the main helical data stream [10]. The clustering parameters for measuring scalability and response to variable decay are set as $Decay = 1000$ $data$ $points, \lambda = 0.010, Density$ $threshold, Th_{density} = 4$ $data$ $points, R_{max} = 0.06$ and $R_{min} = 0.04$. The quality of a cluster mainly depends on the three parameters of a cluster [10], namely, purity, accuracy and assignment percentage. KDDCUP'99 [16], a well-known data stream, has been used to measure the cluster quality in Section 6.4.2.3: Cluster Purity and Accuracy. For measuring cluster quality, clustering parameters are set as $Decay = 1000, \lambda = 0.010, Th_{density} = 3$, Maximum radius = 0.12, Minimum radius = 0.06 spaced at 10000 data points.

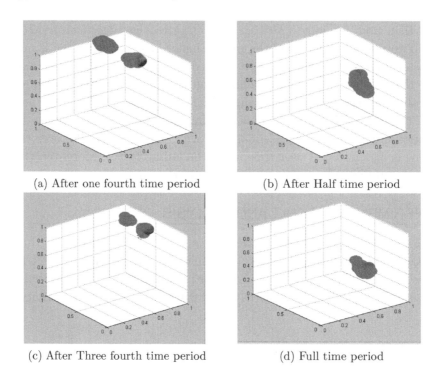

(a) After one fourth time period   (b) After Half time period

(c) After Three fourth time period   (d) Full time period

Figure 6.1: Micro-clusters formation using clean Mackey-Glass data stream.

6.4.2.1 Scalability

The term scalability defines the response of a clustering algorithm from low-dimensional to high-dimensional data stream in terms of processing time. As we know, a density-based clustering algorithm is efficient when processing time is low and also has low delay penalty [10]. As shown in Figure 6.2, the processing speed is

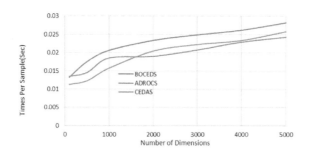

Figure 6.2: Scalability on helical data stream.

compared with the existing algorithms BOCEDS and CEDAS. It is noticed that the proposed ADROCS algorithm's processing speed is comparatively lower than the existing algorithms CEDAS and BOCEDS. Furthermore, the time penalty for ADROCS algorithm is less than the existing algorithms when dimension size increases.

6.4.2.2 Response to Variable Decay

The helical data streams are used for experimenting the response to variable decay. The mean processing time per sample is calculated for various decay periods in order to vary the dimensionality (the dimension of helical data streams is considered from low to high) for calculating the behavior of the proposed ADROCS algorithm. The relationship between time per sample, decay period and data dimensions is plotted in Figure 6.3. We have to choose decay value in order to get the highest performance of

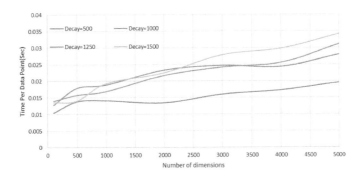

Figure 6.3: Processing time based on various decay.

the proposed ADROCS algorithm; otherwise, it does not work efficiently. Such as for decay value = 1000, it is efficient to choose $\lambda = 0.010$. And when the decay value = 500, it is efficient to choose $\lambda = 0.018$. From Figure 6.3, the relationship between the number of micro-clusters and decay variable indicates that the mean data processing time is increasing over the value of decay increases.

6.4.2.3 Cluster Purity and Accuracy

The purity and accuracy measurement of a cluster are for measuring the quality of a cluster. This is defined by the number of data objects which goes under a dominant cluster [10]. If n_i data samples are located in a cluster and among the data objects, and n_i^d data samples are located in the dominant cluster, then for N such cluster purity and accuracy is being calculated using the following Equations (6.8) and (6.9).

$$Purity = \frac{\sum_{i=1}^{N} n_i^d}{n_i} \times 100\% \tag{6.8}$$

$$Accuracy = \frac{\sum_{i=1}^{N} n_i^d}{\sum_{i=1}^{N} n_i} \times 100\% \tag{6.9}$$

For measuring the purity and accuracy of the proposed ADROCS, KDDCup'99 [16] data stream is used. The purity and accuracy are measured for the proposed ADROCS algorithm using Equations (6.8), (6.9) and compared with other four density based clustering algorithms, namely, DStream, MRStream, BOCEDS and CEDAS that are also applied on the same data stream. The mean purity, as well as

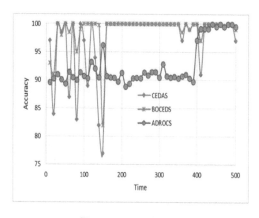 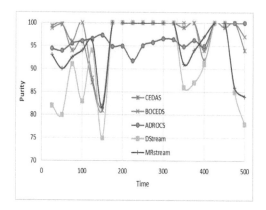

Figure 6.4: Accuracy and purity after clustering KDDCup'99.

accuracy, is applied at 10000 data points over 500 time intervals. Figure 6.4(b) is the experimental result of comparison of the purity of ADROCS with those of CEDAS, BOCEDS, MRStream and DStream. The ADROCS performs better most of the time compared with DStream and MRStream. The mean purities of the ADROCS for the initial and last time periods are quite better compared with the existing approaches. Moreover, the purity performance of the proposed ADROCS is more than 91% for all the time periods with respect to the previous methods.

As shown in Figure 6.4(a), the accuracy of the proposed ADROCS doesn't fluctuate much like other two existing algorithms. The accuracy is always more than 89% for all the time periods. Due to exponential changes in decay variable as well as energy, initially the accuracy is low but it increases over time.

6.4.2.4 *Memory Efficiency*

According to CEDAS [9], the number of generated micro-clusters in the density based approach directly defines the memory efficiency of that approach. As shown in Figure 6.5, the number of generated micro-clusters is less than the BOCEDS[10] algorithm and CEDAS algorithm. Therefore, it can be stated that the proposed algorithm's space complexity is less than the existing algorithms. The number of generated micro-clusters in BOCEDS algorithm is higher due to its pruning method to extract the temporary irrelevant clusters from the buffer. Unlike BOCEDS, the proposed ADROCS algorithm shows less memory requirement compared to the existing algorithms due to the changes in the decay variable which is updated exponentially.

6.4.2.5 *Parameter Sensitivity Study*

Like the density threshold, decay, fading factor, and Max and Min radii are user-defined. The sensitivity of decay and fading factor is already discussed in Section 6.4.2.2 (Response to Variable Decay). In order to get the best performance of the proposed ADROCS, it is necessary to check the sensitivity of the parameters ($Th_{density}$, Radii, etc.). For this, KDDCup'99 [16] dataset is used. By placing the value of $Th_{density} = 1$ to onward checking the value of purity and accuracy and when it

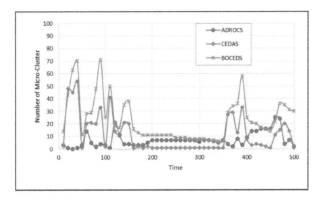

Figure 6.5: Memory after clustering KDDCup'99 data stream.

gets the highest, that's the final value for that dataset. For this KDDCup'99 dataset, $Th_{density} = 3$ provides the highest accuracy and purity. For example, in Figure 6.6(a) and Figure 6.6(b), accuracy and purity values are checked over 500 time intervals for various (R_{min}, R_{max}) values. However, for $R_{min} = 0.06, R_{max} = 0.12$, it provides the highest accuracy and purity.

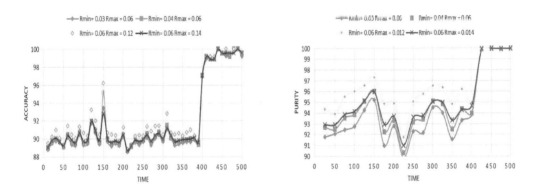

Figure 6.6: Accuracy and purity over various radius ranges.

6.5 CONCLUSION

This method is a fully online clustering algorithm named as ADROCS. The algorithm dynamically adopts the radius and decay parameters. As a result, it is not required to initialize the decay and global radius parameter by the expert of the application. The proposed ADROCS compares the performance of clustering with similar density based clustering approaches in terms of processing speed, scalability, cluster quality (accuracy and purity) and memory efficiency. ADROCS shows the linear relationship between the processing speed and dimension size and also the lowest increase in time complexity with respect to the existing methods. In terms of purity and accuracy, it shows comparatively better performance over time compared with other existing algorithms. In terms of memory efficiency, it provides better results, as in this algorithm the decay variable is adapting over time.

ACKNOWLEDGEMENTS

This research work was supported by Special Grant of ICT Division (Ministry of Posts, Telecommunications and Information Technology), Bangladesh, and Grant No. 56.00.0000.028.20.004.2 0-333. The authors would like to acknowledge University Grant Commission, Bangladesh, for their partial support through the Barishal University Research Grant Scheme under Grant No. BU/REG/Academic/Research/UGC/2020-2021/498/2403.

Bibliography

[1] Can, U., & Alatas, B. (2017). Big social network data and sustainable economic develop-ment. Sustainability, 9(11), 2027.

[2] Babcock, B., Babu, S., Datar, M., Motwani, R., & Widom, J. (2002, June). Models and is-sues in data stream systems. In Proceedings of the twenty-first ACM SIGMOD-SIGACT-SIGART symposium on principles of database systems (pp. 1-16).

[3] Nguyen, Hai-Long, Yew-Kwong Woon, and Wee-Keong Ng. "A survey on data stream clustering and classification." Knowledge and information systems 45.3 (2015): 535-569.

[4] Carnein, M., Assenmacher, D., & Trautmann, H. (2017, May). An empirical comparison of stream clustering algorithms. In Proceedings of the computing frontiers conference (pp. 361-366).

[5] Gama, J. (2010). Knowledge discovery from data streams. CRC Press.

[6] Jacques, J., & Preda, C. (2014). Functional data clustering: a survey. Advances in Data Analysis and Classification, 8(3), 231-255.

[7] Amini, A., Wah, T. Y., & Saboohi, H. (2014). On density-based data streams clustering algorithms: A survey. Journal of Computer Science and Technology, 29(1), 116-141.

[8] Merrell, Richard, and David Diaz. "Comparison of data mining methods on different appli-cations: clustering and classification methods." Information Sciences Letters 4.2 (2015): 61.

[9] Hyde, Richard, Plamen Angelov, and Angus Robert MacKenzie. "Fully online clustering of evolving data streams into arbitrarily shaped clusters." Information Sciences 382 (2017): 96-114.

[10] Islam, M. K., Ahmed, M. M., & Zamli, K. Z. (2019). A buffer-based online clustering for evolving data stream. Information Sciences, 489, 113-135.

[11] M. Ester, H.-P. Kriegel, J. Sander, and X. Xu, "A density-based algorithm for discovering clusters in large spatial databases with noise," in Kdd, 1996, pp. 226-231.

[12] Zhang, T., Ramakrishnan, R., & Livny, M. (1997). BIRCH: A new data clustering algorithm and its applications. Data Mining and Knowledge Discovery, 1(2), 141-182.

[13] Aggarwal, C. C., Philip, S. Y., Han, J., & Wang, J. (2003, January). A framework for clustering evolving data streams. In Proceedings 2003 VLDB conference (pp. 81-92). Morgan Kaufmann.

[14] Hyde, Richard, and Plamen Angelov. "A new online clustering approach for data in arbitrary shaped clusters." 2015 IEEE 2nd International Conference on Cybernetics (CYBCONF). IEEE, 2015.

[15] Islam, M. K., Ahmed, M. M., & Zamli, K. Z. (2019). i-CODAS: An Improved Online Data Stream Clustering in Arbitrary Shaped Clusters. Engineering Letters, 27(4).

[16] Bay, S. D., Kibler, D., Pazzani, M. J., & Smyth, P. (2000). The UCI KDD archive of large data sets for data mining research and experimentation. ACM SIGKDD explorations newsletter, 2(2), 81-85.

[17] Glass, L., and Mackey, M. (2010). Mackey-Glass equation. Scholarpedia, 5(3), 6908.

CHAPTER 7

Solar-Powered Smart Street Light and Surveillance System Using IoT

Sadika Sultana Meem and Nusrath Tabassum

International University of Business Agriculture and Technology, Dhaka, Bangladesh

CONTENTS

7.1   Introduction 75
7.2   Motivation 75
7.3   Methodology 76
    7.3.1   Components 78
    7.3.2   Working Procedure 79
    7.3.3   Software Development 79
7.4   Discussion and Result 79
    7.4.1   Advantages of Proposed Model 80
    7.4.2   Limitation of Proposed Model 80
7.5   Conclusion 80

ELECTRICITY is an essential part of all daily life activities. There is no complete system to prevent power wastage. Electricity is a national resource which is very important to avoid wastage. The main objective of the proposed experiment is to prevent wastage of energy and create an intelligent system that makes a choice for illumination control (dim/on/off) using a light-dependent resistor (LDR), which can detect the day and night mode by identifying the sunlight intensity value. In the night time, street lights will be controlled (full bright or dim) by a motion sensor by identifying any object. So, it will be able to save more energy. Another part of this project is the surveillance system. The mini wireless camera or IP camera inside the street light is used, which will ensure safety. This camera has wireless connectivity with a cloud server. Anyone can monitor surveillance areas from anywhere in the world. This system reduces the manpower cost. The most interesting part of our project is that the entire project runs through the solar system. If the solar system does not work at any time, the AC current of a secondary backup system handles this situation. All the components that we use in this experiment are cost-effective.

7.1 INTRODUCTION

Internet of things (IoT) has brought about a radical change in our daily lives. It makes a remarkable change in our traditional system and everyday home items that facilitate our lives [1-4]. IoT is a combination of operational and informational technology [1].

Its implementation depends on four different communication techniques: device-device, device-cloud, device-gateway, and back-end data-sharing. IoT-based projects are increasing day by day because they connect with objects that can collect and transfer data over a wireless network without human intervention. The advantages of IoT-based projects are the reduction in operational cost, enhanced security measures, gathering of huge data, and use of smart devices. For safe highways and increased home protection in all cities, street lighting is crucial for any nation [5]. According to a city survey, street lighting squanders 30% of electricity [1]. According to estimates, Bangladesh would be able to produce 20,000 megawatts of electricity annually by 2018. An average of 77.9% of the population had access to electricity in the country. The remaining 13% people are still without access to electricity. In this situation, energy-saving is most important. Our project is mainly based on a solar power system which is very helpful in conserving electricity. It primarily consists of two components: a camera or surveillance system and a street light. These two parts are created by using pieces of equipment such as ultrasonic sensors, wireless connectivity, rechargeable battery, solar panel, camera, and light-emitting diode (LED). This initiative will save a significant amount of energy while providing security.

7.2 MOTIVATION

In recent years, researchers have done a lot of research work based on street lights and surveillance systems. Tina et al. [6] designed an automatic lighting system using sensors controlled by a microcontroller for the house. The light will turn on and sound the alert if it detects any movement or heat. Parkash et al. [7] proposed IoT-based intelligent street light which is managed by the sensor. The light will be on when absolute darkness but when it is fuzzy dark, the chances of an accident are very high. Bhairi et al. [8] suggested an Arduino-based system for cheap, energy-efficient LED street lights that could be used to control traffic patterns both day and night. Their proposed method can automatically turn the light on/off and detect sunshine. Due to the lack of a dimming component in the plan, a significant amount of energy would be lost. B. Abinaya et al. [9] created a sensor-based smart weather adaptive lighting system for street lights using GSM technology. In the model, the system, CCTV, and panic buttons have all been manually turned on and off. This was not a power-saving project because using the lamp was a sodium vapor lamp which expended more energy and was expensive. Chitra et al. [10] proposed a smart street lighting system that totally depends on the sensor. The vehicle detection method, which costs a lot of money, primarily used video to control the entire process.

In this proposed project, LDR is used which detects the sunlight, and an ultrasonic sensor that can detect any kind of object. The street light will start to fade after sunset, and if anything is seen outside during the night or when it is completely dark, the light will be on brightly. If no object is detected at night time then the light will dim. We use the mini IP camera inside the lamp which gives surveillance to the area for 24 hours, captures all the footage, and delivers it to the database. At the same time, the camera can deliver live footage to a cloud server by wireless connectivity. For any need, anyone with access to the database can view any footage or live video footage from anywhere. This system is capable of giving full security to every person.

In our project, with a dimming system, we can prevent electricity wastage. Having lights with cameras at specific distances will allow for overall area monitoring. The usage of solar systems and a dimming system will both reduce energy waste by 30% and 20%, respectively. So the wastage of half of the country's electricity can be prevented. As a result, it will be possible to reach the places of the country where electricity has not been reached until now. The camera will have a limitation on how much area it will cover. We employ a very inexpensive, little camera. The lights will be accompanied by cameras that will monitor the roads at all times. The cameras will have separate codes through which we can connect to the camera via the internet and see the live situation on the road. There will also be a database for storing information. Videos that have already been saved and recorded by the surveillance system can be accessed at any time.

We will therefore be able to thoroughly review any incident that occurs in front of this camera subsequently. If we implement our concept, it might lower the cost of the gadget as well as the cost of maintenance because if we wanted to complete these duties manually, we would need to employ workers. However, since we are now controlling everything through automation, there is little need for upkeep, and since we are using light-emitting cameras, the expense of using separate CCTV cameras is also reduced.

7.3 METHODOLOGY

The solar system has been used for powering the systems and charging the batteries in the proposed project. The whole system is a complete module.

The Block diagram of the proposed model is represented in Figure 7.1. It implements the technology of IoT along with the conventional systems available. The main source of power for our current system's facilities is a solar system, which uses less energy when equipped with a dimming system. From the evening to morning, lights will be dim or full bright through detecting any object. Light will sometimes be bright when an object is detected and other times it will be dim. In our proposed project, we added another feature that is a surveillance system. The smart video surveillance system is an IoT-based digital system, as it uses the internet for various applications [11-14]. In this feature, the camera will monitor the street. The camera has an extra memory system and energy-saving system. Additionally, the camera uses solar energy. The camera will be used to monitor the entire street in this feature. The camera features an additional memory system, energy-saving technology, and it uses solar energy. Every time this system provides us with a surveillance or monitoring system. The microcontroller (Arduino UNO) is the brain system [15-16].

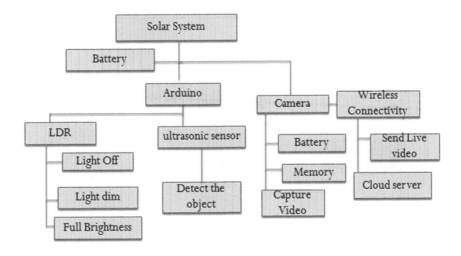

Figure 7.1: Block diagram of proposed model

Arduino decides when lights will be full bright or dim. An ultrasonic sensor detects the object and passes the detected report to Arduino. LDR controls the off, on, or dimming system of light. Although the project primarily uses solar energy, it also features a backup AC line. The battery will be recharged by an AC connection when solar energy is not present. For that reason, an extra relay has been used. It is an automatic switch system.

Figure 7.2 shows the street light system circuit diagram in the proposed model. This circuit diagram is directly connected with the solar system battery. This circuit is created on bread-broad, connecting cables, LDR, HC-SR04, ultrasonic sonar sensor, printed circuit board (PCB), LED, and Arduino nano.

Firstly, all the components are gathered and checked to ensure they are working. We make the circuit on the breadboard, and connect with the cathode of LED to GND (ground 5 v) & anode to 13 no pin of Arduino. Next, connect the Ultrasonic Sensor pins VCC (Voltage Common Collector), GND, Trig pin, and Echo pin to 5V, GND, 9, 10 no pin, respectively, to Arduino. Then we connect one end of LDR to 10K resister to A0 no pin of Arduino Uno and another end to 5V supply, and the other pin of resister to GND pin of Arduino Uno. Battery power cable is joined with Arduino nano.

Secondly, the surveillance system circuit is created by a mini camera or CMOS pinhole camera, extra battery, WIFI module, antenna, IP module, breadboard, cables, and inverter. An inverter is the connecting part to the battery or power supply system to the surveillance system. First, we link an Arduino board to the 2.4"/.64" board's GND (ground 5 volts), and then we attach a second 2.7"/1.16" board to the first. In the 2.7"/1.16" breadboard, connect the VIS WIFI module on the cathode side of

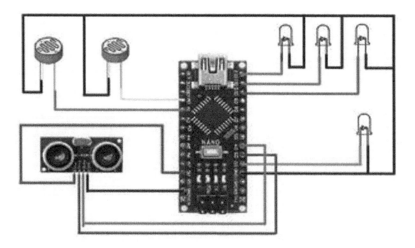

Figure 7.2: Circuit diagram.

the board. The antenna connects by a cable with a WIFI module. The IP module is attached with the anode part in the breadboard. The mini camera joins with the WIFI module by cables. The extra battery joins the Arduino and memory connects the WIFI module. This total circuit connects with the inverters which convert the current DC to AC. The inverter directly attaches to the main battery, solar system, or power supply system.

7.3.1 Components

The proposed system has a few key components that together make it incredibly effective.

Solar panel—Photo voltaic module that uses photons from direct sunlight to generate direct current electricity. It is mainly a PV module or PV panel types.

Battery—Store of electricity that has an electrochemical cell that generates the electricity by the chemical reaction called galvanic.

Motion sensor—A motion detector that automatically alerts users of motion in an area.

Wireless connectivity—wireless modules mainly help the system to send surveillance data to remote monitoring.

7.3.2 Working Procedure

The surveillance system will work 24 hours. The total system will be run on solar power. In the proposed system, we install a photovoltaic (PV) module. This panel collects energy from the sun during the day, converts it to DC current, and stores it in the batteries. From the battery, power will pass the total system through the cables. In the middle of the battery and camera, an extra inverter is used which converts DC to AC current for the camera and passes the current.

The surveillance system captures the footage stored in the database and sends it to the cloud server. Different IP modules have different IP addresses. By the cloud server, the user can see live footage when connecting the device with an IP address. The proposed system has backup power. It will be available when the solar system does not work properly. The backup system has a direct AC line. For that, we use an extra relay or automatic switch system.

The proposed model shows in Figure 7.3 that an ultrasonic sensor detects the object. This information sensor passes the Arduino and determines if an object is available or not. Arduino works like a brain and it takes the decision of when the light will be full, dim, or off. Arduino operates through the code. In this code, we give all instructions. We have a light sensor called an LDR that determines whether it is day, evening, or night. These choices are transmitted by LDR to the Arduino. LDR, ultrasonic sensor, and Arduino are combined as the project's core decision.

7.3.3 Software Development

In the proposed system, we used a microcontroller. A program is necessary for a microcontroller to function. The intended system is implemented and operated by the microcontroller in this software. Our software, which runs on the Arduino, is incredibly user-friendly. Those people who know only the C language can make the program [8]. Through this software development, different types of sensors like motion sensors, ultrasonic sensors, etc. will determine the operation of the system. For this proposed system, a program is required which can be generated by Arduino programming in C language.

7.4 DISCUSSION AND RESULT

The environment model is displayed in Figure 7.4. We are using solar to run the system for better efficiency and prevent a lot of power wastage. After analyzing various research works, we develop the proposed system. We actually developed the prototype of our proposed system. The entire city or country will have complete security thanks to this energy-saving scheme, which will also conserve all the power used by the street lights. The outside light will determine when this system starts. In the C program, we mention two-level light intensity. This system firstly detects darkness. The entire system will turn on when darkness is accessible. Light will be off during the day since sunlight is accessible, and it will be on at night because there will be no light during the night. In the night time, if any object is detected then the light will be on 100% and give full brightness. If an object is not detected then the

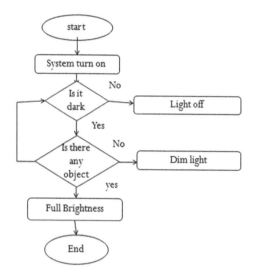

Figure 7.3: Flow chart of proposed system

light will be 30% bright or dim. The security system will always be active and provide surveillance.

7.4.1 Advantages of Proposed Model

- Prevent the wastage of energy

- Automated switching on/off/dim street lights

- Unlimited surveillance

7.4.2 Limitation of Proposed Model

- The proposed experiment has a somewhat higher initial cost, but after it is built, the solar system eliminates the requirement for manpower costs and electricity. Therefore, the project's overall cost is lower than that of the cited research.

7.5 CONCLUSION

Our assessment is at its very initial state. From the analysis of the results, it is clear that the training results and validation results of the assessment are overfitting with the model, which is the major weakness, but the accuracy of 88% is not bad at all. Maybe the dataset needs more preprocessing mechanisms to be processed and this

Figure 7.4: The environmental model

dataset may not be sufficient. Currently, we are working to perceive the basis of overfitting and trying to enhance the exactness. We are also working to implement this approach at the production level.

Bibliography

[1] Saifuzzaman, M., Moon, N. N., & Nur, F. N. (2017). IoT-based street lighting and traffic management system. In 2017 IEEE Region 10 Humanitarian Technology Conference (R10-HTC) (pp. 121-124). IEEE.

[2] Madakam, S. (2015). Internet of Things (IoT): A literature review. Journal of Computer and Communications, 3(05), 164.

[3] Zarpelão, B. B., Miani, R. S., Kawakani, C. T., & de Alvarenga, S. C. (2017). A survey of intrusion detection in Internet of Things. Journal of Network and Computer Applications, 84, 25-37.

[4] Maqbool, Z., Habib, R., Aziz, T., Maqbool, A., & Altaf, O. (2020). Internet Security Issues in Smart City Environment. Journal of Information Technology and Computing, 1(1), 14-30.

[5] Cho, S., & Dhingra, V. (2008). Street lighting control based on LonWorks power line communication. In 2008 IEEE International Symposium on Power Line Communications and Its Applications (pp. 396-398). IEEE.

[6] Singla, M. (2019). Smart Lightning and Security System. In 2019 4th International Conference on Internet of Things: Smart Innovation and Usages (IoT-SIU) (pp. 1-6). IEEE.

[7] Parkash, P. V., & Rajendra, D. (2016). Internet of things based intelligent street lighting system for smart city. International journal of innovative research in science, engineering and technology, 5(5).

[8] Bhairi, M. N., Kangle, S. S., Edake, M. S., Madgundi, B. S., & Bhosale, V. B. (2017). Design and implementation of smart solar LED street light. In 2017 International Conference on Trends in Electronics and Informatics (ICEI) (pp. 509-512). IEEE

[9] Abinaya, B., Gurupriya, S., & Pooja, M. (2017). Iot based smart and adaptive lighting in street lights. In 2017 2nd International Conference on Computing and Communications Technologies (ICCCT) (pp. 195-198). IEEE.

[10] Suseendran, S. C., Nanda, K. B., Andrew, J., & Praba, M. B. (2018). Smart street lighting system. In 2018 3rd International Conference on Communication and Electronics Systems (ICCES) (pp. 630-633). IEEE.

[11] Quadri, S. A. I., & Sathish, P. (2017). IoT based home automation and surveillance system. In 2017 International Conference on Intelligent Computing and Control Systems (ICICCS) (pp. 861-866). IEEE

[12] Memos, V. A., Psannis, K. E., Ishibashi, Y., Kim, B. G., & Gupta, B. B. (2018). An efficient algorithm for media-based surveillance system (EAMSuS) in IoT smart city framework. Future Generation Computer Systems, 83, 619-628.

[13] Gulve, S. P., Khoje, S. A., & Pardeshi, P. (2017). Implementation of IoT-based smart video surveillance system. In Computational intelligence in data mining (pp. 771-780). Springer, Singapore.

[14] Gupta, A. K., & Johari, R. (2019). IOT based electrical device surveillance and control system. In 2019 4th international conference on internet of things: Smart innovation and usages (IoT-SIU) (pp. 1-5). IEEE

[15] Hidayanti, F., Rahmah, F., & Wiryawan, A. (2020). Design of Motorcycle Security System with Fingerprint Sensor using Arduino Uno Microcontroller. International Journal of Advanced Science and Technology, 29(05), 4374-4391.

[16] Das, L., Kumar, A., Singh, S., Ashar, A. R., & Jangu, R. (2021). IoT Based Weather Monitoring System Using Arduino-UNO. In 2021 2nd International Conference on Computation, Automation and Knowledge Management (IC-CAKM) (pp. 260-264). IEEE.

CHAPTER 8

Analysis of Aquaculture for Cultivating Different Types of Fish

Nayeem Abdullah, Ahnaf Shahriyar Chowdhury,
Md. Mehedi Hossain, and Orko Dutta

BRAC University, Dhaka, Bangladesh

Jia Uddin

Woosong University, Daejeon, South Korea

CONTENTS

8.1   Introduction 84
8.2   Literature Review 85
8.3   Proposed Model 86
       8.3.1   Input 86
       8.3.2   Process 87
               8.3.2.1   Linear Regression Method 87
               8.3.2.2   K-Nearest Neighbor Method 87
       8.3.3   Linear Regression Method Output 87
       8.3.4   K-Nearest Neighbor Method Output 87
8.4   Experimental Setup and Result Analysis 89
       8.4.1   Hardware Specifications 89
       8.4.2   Linear Regression 90
       8.4.3   K-Nearest Neighbor 91
       8.4.4   Dataset and Environment 91
       8.4.5   Software Setup 91
       8.4.6   Selecting Fish for Cultivation 92
       8.4.7   Analysis between linear regression and K-Nearest Neighbor 93
8.5   Conclusion 95

Ensuring appropriate water quality is an indispensable part of aquaculture. The conventional methodology of monitoring water quality is being performed by biochemical research, which is expensive. Moreover, the conventional way requires collecting samples of water from various sources and sending them to a laboratory for analysis. Nonetheless, this takes a lot of time which can cause complications for aquaculture. Therefore, to decrease time consumption and reduce manual efforts, this chapter addresses a new approach to dealing with water quality testing utilizing Arduino and Machine Learning. We are linking an analog pH sensor with Arduino and sending input data to a computer in a CSV file and subsequently, we are using Linear Regression and K-Nearest Neighbor (KNN) algorithms to predict the amount of dissolved oxygen. We used two different machine learning algorithms to get their respective accuracy and also found which one is best suitable for the given data set. Besides, a temperature sensor is additionally used to monitor the water temperature. We are conducting our research based on the river water quality data-set to train our model. The fundamental motivation behind our proposed model is to verify water quality for aquaculture at a lower cost with a faster result. By analyzing and running our data-set, the model got an accuracy of 84.30% for the Linear Regression Model, and for KNN the model got an accuracy of 90%.

8.1 INTRODUCTION

Water is a crucial part of the ecosystem upon which human existence relies, yet additionally it keeps up with the equilibrium of eco-structure, ecological process, and regional environment ecosystem. Water is a sustainable resource since it is continually recyclable. The ascent in urbanization and throwing industrial waste in the water are dangerous for our lives, particularly for our aqua-firms. According to The State of World Fisheries and Aquaculture 2016, per capita fish supply reached a new record high of 20 kg in 2014, on account of enthusiastic development in aquaculture, which presently gives half of all fish for human consumption (FAO 2016) [1]. In the last two decades, there is a shift towards relatively greater consumption of farmed species compared with wild fish in recent times. It reached a milestone in 2014, at the point when the farmed sector's contribution to the supply of fish for human consumption outperformed that of wild-caught fish for the first time, the quality of water in which the fish will be produced will be a significant factor to meet the demand of fishes. Moreover, it tends to be perceived that the rate of total world fishery production (capture plus aquaculture) is projected to expand over the period, reaching 196 million tons in 2025 (Guadayol et al. 2014) [2]. As the demand for water-dwelling animals is increasing so does the need for these aquaculture farms. Therefore, the living quality in these farms for these aquatic animals is important for production. For this purpose, in this chapter, we are proposing a water monitoring system, which will observe the temperature and pH of water. A linear regression model is used to figure out the level of oxygen and predict the suitability for these aquatic animals to live in these aquaculture farms. Linear regression is a faster and efficient approach to process simultaneously. Similarly, the K-Nearest Neighbor (KNN) algorithm is used which determines the values of new data points depending on 'feature similarity'. This means that a value is assigned to the new point based on how similar it is to the points throughout the training set and as a result, it provides an accurate prediction. The pH value and oxygen level of water vary with time and season. There is a rise in the auto-monitoring system in the field of medical and agriculture fields. This monitoring system is one of the most efficient ways for monitoring aquacultures. Here pH value is used for measuring the acidity and alkalinity of the water. Every creature has a suitable temperature, which they will thrive on, and thus, by measuring the temperatures of water we can adjust that. Furthermore, by considering oxygen levels, we can see the safe level for these marine creatures, and we consequently hope to seek maximum productivity through this monitoring system.

8.2 LITERATURE REVIEW

Dissolved oxygen and aquatic life are strongly related and the researches based on these two terms were continuing for a long time to establish a healthier environment for both the aquatic animal and aquaculture. In a research paper written by Boyd and Terry, they did studies on some aquatic animals which include catfish, shrimp, and tilapia (Boyd et al. 2010) [3]. In their studies, they wanted to show how low dissolved oxygen concentration can have a negative impact on aquaculture. According to their analysis, the average minimum dissolved oxygen concentration is directly proportional to the rate of survival and the production rate. In the paper, the optimal dissolved oxygen concentration value found for catfish is not below 3.5mg/L; for shrimp, it is 3.89 mg/L; and for tilapia, 20% saturation in the dissolved oxygen increases the survival rate of tilapia fish. In another paper written by Zhang and Wei, they did studies based on the aquaponics system for anticipating the concentration of dissolved oxygen for aquaculture (Ren et al. 2018) [4]. They came up with a prediction model by implementing the Fuzzy Neural Network in combination with genetic algorithms, since it gives a better output when working with a large dataset. According to their result, they found out that the Fuzzy Neural Network along with genetic algorithms gave the lower prediction error among the other methods. Moreover, Yang and Zhang discussed the application of deep learning for fish farming along with its advantages and disadvantages (Yang et al. 2021) [5]. Initially, the research was done on how the other machine learning algorithms including Artificial Neural Network (ANN), Support Vector Machine (SVM), Convolutional Neural Network (CNN), Long Short Term Memory (LSTM), Random Forest algorithm, etc. works in the field of aquaculture (Islam et al. 2021; Islam et al. 2020) [6] [7]. From there they tabulated the behavioral analysis, species classification, size estimation, and water quality prediction. After the implementation of Deep Learning, they came up with the statement that deep learning can process different types of data-sets, but there are certain pros and cons that were being discussed after the implementation of deep learning. One of the advantages they found while using deep learning is that deep learning methods can automatically extract features from the data-set but in other traditional algorithms the need to be handled manually, which is time-consuming. On the other hand, a disadvantage of using deep learning is that it will take more time to train if the data-set is large. With the increase in the data-set, deep learning algorithms will start to take more time than before. Along with that, this process is found to be costly because different types of sensors are needed in order to implement deep learning algorithms.

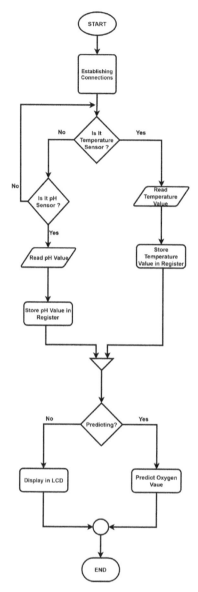

Figure 8.1: The component required for the proposed model and working flow.

8.3 PROPOSED MODEL

Figure 8.1 shows the working flow of the proposed model. To begin with, we utilized a temperature sensor and a pH sensor to collect the temperatures and pH values of the sample water at different times. From that point forward, numerical computations are performed which will provide the oxygen level in the sample water.

8.3.1 Input

In this project, the system is taking the temperature in degrees Celsius for the LCD display. After that, the system is taking the pH value as input for the prediction of oxygen. To train the model, a data-set of river water quality has been taken. Data-set features are pH and oxygen (mg/l).

8.3.2 Process

In Figure 8.1, the full working process of our project is demonstrated. Firstly, we are checking the temperature of the water and showing it on LCD. Then the pH values are taken if any keyboard interaction stops taking input. And after that, the input is taken in order to train our data for prediction.

8.3.2.1 Linear Regression Method

The extension of the training linear model is called the regularization method and it seeks both to minimize sum and squared error. The way to make a prediction using linear regression is by making a correlation between data and by creating a two-dimensional matrix and making a line to understand the relation. To prepare the data, it has to be linearly assumed, noise and collinearity removed, Gaussian distributed and re-scaled accordingly.

8.3.2.2 K-Nearest Neighbor Method

The KNN algorithm predicts the values of subsequent data points based on feature similarity. This means that a score is assigned to the new point based on how comparable it is to the points in the training set. Finding the distances between a query and all the instances in the data, selecting the defined number of examples (K) closest to the query, and voting for averaged labels are how KNN regression works. This distance is counted by the Minkowski distance.

8.3.3 Linear Regression Method Output

After training our model, when data is being fitted, we will have a straight line (Anderson 2013). The y-axis is our predicted oxygen value, and the x-axis is the independent pH value.

$$Y(\text{dissolved oxygen}) = m * X(\text{pH value}) + c \tag{8.1}$$

In Figure 8.2, plotted data is being shown. Here oxygen and pH are correlation coefficients. These are represented by the red dotted area. The blue line is for measuring accuracy. The closer the red dots are to the blue line, the more accurate the result will be. In linear regression, the accuracy is -1 to $+1$.

8.3.4 K-Nearest Neighbor Method Output

After training our model, by fitting the data, there will be patterns. The KNN algorithm uses feature similarity to predict the values of any new data points. This means that the new point is assigned a value based on how closely it resembles the points in the training set to calculate the distance between the nearest point by following

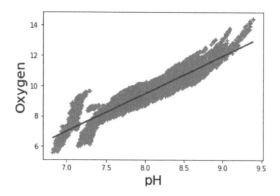

Figure 8.2: Y label oxygen (mg/l).

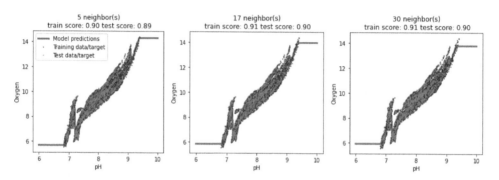

Figure 8.3: Train and Test Score Compare for different k values.

the Minkowski distance method (Walters-Williams et al. 2010) [8].

$$L_m = (\sum_{i=1}^{n} |p_i - q_i|)^{\frac{1}{r}} \tag{8.2}$$

Here, from (8.2) n = Number of dimensions; p_i,q_i=data points; p = order of norms / k-value; p = 1, Manhattan Distance;p = 2, Euclidean Distance; p = ∞, Chebyshev Distance

The model is being trained for leaf-size 30. Numbers of neighbors vary from 5, 17 and 30. while p is 2. Thus the sample value will follow these patterns.

In Figure 8.3, the data have been plotted. Here train and test scores are being compared based on different values of k. Training data are represented by the red dotted area. The blue line is for measuring testing data. While the green line is the prediction on how the relationship between pH and Oxygen will be. The closer the red dots and the blue dots are to the green line the more accurate the result will be. In KNN regression, the train and test scores are -1 to +1. If the value is closer to 1 the model is more accurate and the opposite is true for -1.

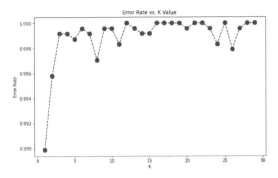

Figure 8.4: Error rate vs K value.

Figure 8.5: pH meter hardware setup.

8.4 EXPERIMENTAL SETUP AND RESULT ANALYSIS

In this section, we will describe the device and the environment which is needed for water quality detection for cultivation. The dataset and parameters used for this experiment will also be described in the following section.

8.4.1 Hardware Specifications

To explain this research, some sample data of pH and temperature were gathered, which is shown in Table 8.1. Along with that, the predictive value of oxygen is in that table. Moreover, in Table 8.2, the data represents the productivity and survival range of some aquatic animals based on pH, oxygen, and temperature. Some components that are used to build the model are listed below:

- Arduino Uno: The Arduino Uno R3 is a micro controller board based on a detachable, dual-inline-package (Plunge).

- DS18B20 Digital Temperature Sensor: DS18B20 gives 9-bit to 12-bit (configurable) temperature readings over a 1-wire interface (Figure 8.5).

- Analog pH Sensor: The pH sensor, or pH meter, is an instrument used to measure the acidity or alkalinity of the fish farm's water. pH is the unit of measurement that describes acidity or alkalinity. Figure 8.5 shows that the measuring

Figure 8.6: Temperature sensor.

Figure 8.7: Hardware setup for temperature sensor.

scale of pH ranges from 0 to 14. In Figure 8.7, we can see the hardware setup for the pH meter.

- 16x2 LCD: In Figure 8.7, we can see the 16x2 LCD.

8.4.2 Linear Regression

Step 1: Connect the pH sensor with Arduino and send data using serial communication

Step 2: Read dataset

Step 3: Plot dataset and calculate correlation

Step 4: Train the dataset for prediction using scikit-learn

Step 5: Fit our data in the trained model

Step 6: Get the predicted values

Step 7: Calculate accuracy

Table 8.1: Correlation and description

	temp	spcond(ms/cm)	pH	Ox	do_present
temp	1	-0.309181	0.377783	0.12158	0.446837
spcond(ms/cm)	-0.309181	1	0.293552	0.313457	0.156739
pH	0.377783	0.293552	1	0.920925	0.955451
Ox	0.121258	0.313457	0.920925	1	0.940846
do_present	0.446837	0.156739	0.955451	0.940846	1
turbidity	-0.013292	0.021905	0.256044	0.289516	0.266441
chlorophyll	-0.22022	0.420438	0.403227	0.520148	0.391506
phycocyanin	0.180565	0.107436	0.67669	0.668493	0.669557
sysbattery	0.553171	-0.065153	0.350102	0.258131	0.411199

8.4.3   K-Nearest Neighbor

Step 1: Load the data

Step 2: Initialize K to your chosen number of neighbors

Step 3.1. For each sample in the data, calculate the minkowski distance between the query example and the current example from the data

Step 3.2: Add the Minkowski distance and the index of the example to an ordered collection

Step 4: Sort the ordered collection of distances and indices from smallest to largest (in ascending order) by the distances

Step 5: Pick the first K entries from the sorted collection

Step 6: Get the labels of the selected K entries

Step 7: Return the mean of the K

8.4.4   Dataset and Environment

A river water data-set has been taken that contains temperature in degree celsius, pH value, and oxygen in mg/l (Live Water Quality Data For The Lower Charles River | US EPA 2020) [9]. For the purpose of demonstration, here pond water has been used as a sample. In Figure 8.2, the correlation between pH and oxygen can be understood and the linear regression model depends on this correlation. If the correlation is closer to 1, there is a linear relation. If closer to zero, then it means no relation.

8.4.5   Software Setup

Firstly, PyCharm, a Python IDE, is used for plotting the pH value on the y-axis. This process is called the serial communication process. Python package matplotlib allows the system to plot and show a relational graph. Then the pH value is saved in a CSV file manually, which will be used for oxygen prediction. In the prediction part, the jupyter notebook and anaconda environment help to visualize the data and prediction. By using linear regression, prediction of the oxygen in mg/l has been done.

8.4.6 Selecting Fish for Cultivation

In order to explain this research, some sample data of pH and temperature were gathered and shown in Table 8.2. Along with that, the predictive value of oxygen is shown in that table. Moreover, in Table 8.3, the data represents the productivity and survival range of some aquatic animals based on pH, oxygen, and temperature.

Table 8.2: Sample Value Taken by Sensors and Oxygen Prediction

Sample No.	pH	Temperature(°C)	Oxygen(mg/l)		Linear Regression
			K- Near Neighbour		
			K-value	Oxygen(mg/l)	
1	6.98	25.7	5	6.64	6.9461319
			17	6.76823529	
			30	6.78866667	
2	6.83	25.75	5	5.698	6.5749492
			17	5.80823529	
			30	5.885	
3	6.88	25.6	5	6.284	6.6986768
			17	5.99235294	
			30	6.11233333	

Table 8.3: Cultivation Parameter for fishes (*Productivity = Pd, *Survival = Sl, *Oxygen = Ox, Temperature = temp)

pH	Parameter for Aquatic Animals								Temp(°C)
	Ox(mg/l)								
	Carp		Hardy		Crustacean		Salmonid		
	Pd	Sl	Pd	Sl	Pd	Sl	Pd	Sl	
6.5-9.0	6.0-7.0	>1.5	>5	3.0-5.0	6.5-8.5	>1.4	6.17	0.09	14-41

In Table 8.2, the samples 1, 2, 3 pH are in range for productivity according to Table 8.3, which is based on JDEP Division of Fish & Wildlife - Fish Fact Sheets 2021 [10]; Tiwari et al. 2016 [11]; Zafar et al. 2015 [12]; Yovita 2007 [13]. Moreover, the temperatures are around 25-26°C. According to Table 8.2, the mentioned values are the best temperature for carp fishes (NJDEP Division of Fish & Wildlife - Fish Fact Sheets 2021). However, from Table 8.3, it is seen that the temperature is too low for shrimps and prawns (Tiwari et al. 2016; Yovita 2007). For hardy and salmonid fishes, it can be seen in Table 8.3 that the temperature is too low. Thus, if the focus is shifted to the oxygen level of these samples then they are in ranges from 6.5-6.95 when the prediction was done via linear regression. Again, while considering KNN, the oxygen sample is in the range of 5.69-6.79. So, it can be said it is in the range for most carp fishes. Now, the oxygen level is good for shrimp and prawn (Zafar et al. 2015) [12]. Furthermore, from the table, it can be seen that the oxygen level is good for hardy fishes (NJDEP Division of Fish & Wildlife - Fish Fact Sheets 2021). On the other hand, the oxygen level is very low for salmonid fishes (Yovita 2007) [13]. Thus, from the discussion of the parameter, it can be decided that the water environment is a suitable environment for the cultivation of carp fish. Finally, it can be concluded that the sample environment is not suitable for cultivating crustaceans, salmonids, and hardy fishes.

8.4.7 Analysis between linear regression and K-Nearest Neighbor

Table 8.4: Comparison between KNN and LR

Algorithms	R2 coefficient of determination	Accuracy(%)
Linear Regression	0.920925	84.3
k-Nearest Neighbor		
k=5	Train Score : 0.90 Test Score :0.89	87.81
k=17	Train Score : 0.91 Test Score :0.90	89.65
k=30	Train Score : 0.91 Test Score :0.90	90.22

In this research, it can be seen in linear regression from the result that the correlation between oxygen and pH value is 0.920925, which has been seen in Table 8.4. If the correlation is in -1 to 1, that means there is a strong linear relation. Therefore, it can be stated that there is a strong relation between pH and oxygen level in the water. Furthermore, a common method of measuring the accuracy of a regression model is to use the R square statistic (Anderson 2013) [14].

$$R^2 = 1 - \frac{RSS}{TSS} \qquad (8.3)$$

Here,

- The RSS (residual sum of squares) measures the variability left unexplained after performing the regression

- The TSS measures the total variance in Y

- Therefore, the R2 statistic measures the proportion of variability in Y that is explained by X using our model

After the experiment, the score of RSS is 0.8430215710800057. So, it can be said that the model has 84.30% accuracy. In this analysis, three random parameters have

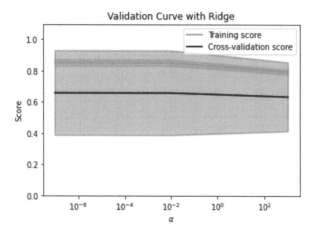

Figure 8.8: Cross Validation (Leave-One-Out).

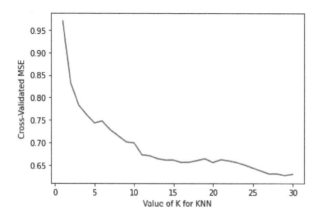

Figure 8.9: Cross Validation (k-Fold).

been chosen as the sample. In Figure 8.4, there are both samples and the parameter for fish cultivation shown in a tabular format. Again, it also can be seen during KNN regression via the result that the training score is 0.90 and the testing score is 0.89 when k- value is 5 when k-value is 17 or 30 is training score and testing score are increased to 0.91 and 0.90 respectively. As it is close to 1 the relation between oxygen and pH is strong in the water. Considering more neighbors will just make the relationship more accurate. Now, for finding the model accuracy R_squared statistic has been used. Thus, this KNN model gives 87.81% when considering only 5 nearest neighbors. again considering 17 neighbors gives the model accuracy of 89.65%. Finally, if the k-value is 30 this model gives 90.22% accuracy.

In Figure 8.9, during linear regression, it can be seen that the variance between training score and validation is almost constant. This model fits perfectly. Again, in Figure 8.8, re: KNN regression it can be seen that cross-validating that MSE (Mean Square Equation) gets closer to 0 when we use the k-value. So, the model is fitting better over time. Thus, the model fits perfectly. In conclusion, KNN regression is better than linear regression. As linear regression established the relation between pH and oxygen. This only gives the prediction based on that. However, KNN provides a pattern for the changes in relation. The more nearest neighbors are taken the better the model performs, thus, giving more accurate results.

8.5 CONCLUSION

Here, we have come up with a device that will be able to detect the dissolved oxygen concentration along with the temperature and pH value of the water, and from that output, we can easily deduce which fish will give better net profit when it comes to cultivation. A chart is being constructed where the values of oxygen, pH level, and temperature are listed along with the productivity and survival rate of the fish that we chose in our experiments. Linear regression is implemented on the dataset and the model is giving an accuracy of 84.30%. While using KNN we got better accuracy than linear regression, almost close to 90%. Using these methods, we can identify the suitable conditions for different types of fish and provide those conditions to have the maximum output. Moreover, from the overall result analysis, it is seen that carp fish will have a better productivity and survival rate in the water sample that we did our experiment with as both the temperature and the dissolved oxygen concentration indicate a better result in cultivating carp fish. In this project, we only used a laptop for data training and storage but we have a plan to store and train the data in a specific remote server for better safety access. The set-up for this project is significantly cheaper as this can run for an extended period of time. Therefore, the production of fish can be improved a lot over time to meet the rising demand. This project can contribute to the economic development of the nation since people will get attracted to fish cultivation.

Bibliography

[1] FAO. (2016). The State of World Fisheries and Aquaculture Contributing to Food Security and Nutrition for All. Rome.

[2] Guadayol, Oscar, Nyssa J. Silbiger, Megan J. Donahue, & Florence IM Thomas. (2014). Patterns in temporal variability of temperature, oxygen and pH along an environmental gradient in a coral reef. PloS one 9, no. 1 : e85213.

[3] Boyd, Claude E. & T. Hanson (2010). Dissolved-oxygen concentrations in pond aquaculture. Ratio 2.

[4] Ren, Qin, Long Zhang, Yaoguang Wei, & Daoliang Li. (2018). A method for predicting dissolved oxygen in aquaculture water in an aquaponics system. In *2018 International Conference on Bangla Speech and Language Processing Computers and electronics in agriculture.* Computers and electronics in agriculture 151 : 384-391.

[5] Yang, Xinting, Song Zhang, Jintao Liu, Qinfeng Gao, Shuanglin Dong, & Chao Zhou (2021). Question Classification on Question-Answer System using Bidirectional-LSTM.

[6] Islam, Md Monirul, Mohammod Abul Kashem, and Jia Uddin (2021). Fish survival prediction in an aquatic environment using random forest model. Int J Artif Intell ISSN 2252, no. 8938 : 8938.

[7] Islam, Md Monirul, Jia Uddin, Mohammod Abul Kashem, Fazly Rabbi, & Md Waliul Hasnat, (2020). Design and Implementation of an IoT System for Predicting Aqua Fisheries Using Arduino and KNN. In *2020 In International Conference on Intelligent Human Computer Interaction*. Cham, Switzerland: Springer.

[8] Walters-Williams, Janett, & Yan Li.(2010). Comparative study of distance functions for nearest neighbors. In Advanced techniques in computing sciences and software engineering. In *2010 IEEE 11th International Conference on Software Engineering and Service Science*. Dordrecht, Netherlands: Springer.

[9] https://www.epa.gov/charlesriver/live-water-quality-data-lower-charles-river (2020). Live Water Quality Data For The Lower Charles River. In *2020 EPA*. US: EPA.

[10] https://www.nj.gov/dep/fgw/fishfact.htm. (2021). *NJDEP Division of Fish & Wildlife - Fish Fact Sheets*

[11] Tiwari, A., A. C. Dwivedi, & Priyank Mayank.(2016). Time scale changes in the water quality of the Ganga River, India and estimation of suitability for exotic and hardy fishes. In *2016 Hydrology Current Research 7, no. 3 : 254*.

[12] Zafar, M. A., M. M. Haque, M. S. B. Aziz, & M. M. Alam (2015). *Study on water and soil quality parameters of shrimp and prawn farming in the southwest region of Bangladesh*. Journal of the Bangladesh Agricultural University 13, no. 1 : 153-160.

[13] Mallya, Yovita John. (2007). The effects of dissolved oxygen on fish growth in aquaculture. In *2007 The United Nations University Fisheries Training Programme, Final Project*.

[14] Anderson, Alan.(2013). *Business statistics for dummies* John Wiley & Sons.

CHAPTER 9

Crime-Finder: A System for Extraction and Visualization of Crime Data from Bengali Online Newspaper Articles

Md Abdulla Al Mamun, Md Abul Kalam Azad, and Md Ileas Pramanik

Begum Rokeya University, Rangpur, Bangladesh

CONTENTS

9.1	Introduction	98
9.2	Related Work	99
9.3	Methodology	100
	9.3.1 Driver	100
	9.3.2 News Crawler and Crime News Collector	101
	9.3.3 Sentence Classifier	102
	9.3.4 Named Entity Recognizer	102
	9.3.5 Geocoder	103
	9.3.6 Database	103
	9.3.7 Location Mapper	103
9.4	Experiments and Results	104
	9.4.1 Parameter Tuning for the Classifiers	104
	9.4.1.1 Random Forest Classifier	104
	9.4.1.2 Logistic Regression	105
	9.4.1.3 Linear Support Vector Classifier	105
	9.4.1.4 Stochastic Gradient Descent Classifier	105
	9.4.2 Performance Comparison of Sentence Classifiers	105
9.5	Discussions	106
9.6	Conclusion	107

INFORMATION EXTRACTION (IE) is the task of automatic extraction of relevant information from unstructured or semi-structured documents and other electronically represented sources. In this chapter, we present a system to extract and visualize crime information from Bengali online newspaper articles. Although law enforcement agencies can possess this kind of information, they do not usually make them publicly accessible. Apart from this, newspaper articles can also be a good source of such information in an unstructured form. Therefore, this paper focuses on the automatic extraction of publicly available yet unstructured crime information and visualization to make them readily available to the general public. To demonstrate the feasibility of our approach, we focus on crime location data in Bengali newspaper articles. A news article contains many location data as part of the sentences in it. We first employ four different machine learning algorithms to classify the crime location sentences, compare their accuracy, and deploy Named Entity Recognizer (NER) to extract the actual address from these location sentences. We then use geocoder to get geo-coordinates. Finally, we built a data visualization tool that utilizes the end result of our approach to further demonstrate that our results can be used for data visualization purposes (i.e., crime-prone area).

9.1 INTRODUCTION

With the ever-increasing adoption of the Internet to propagate a plethora of information every day, large volumes of data (a.k.a. big data) are being generated every day. In the past few decades, access to the Internet has become more available to the mass people thanks to the growing use of smart devices. Many are extending their business targeting this trend, and some are even migrating completely to online-based services. Bengali newspaper portals are also targeting this trend by having their electronic version online. Newspaper readers are getting the latest news every moment, as the reporters are reporting hundreds of news instantly to the newspaper outlets, and the newspaper publisher is publishing them on their website with no delay. Therefore, newspaper websites are being enriched with a large amount of information every moment. Although they contain various valuable information such as crimes, politics, accidents, and sports in human-friendly format on their online version, automatic extraction of relevant information and presentation in a specific format from such sources has been of significant importance to the research community in the Information Extraction (IE) field [3].

Although people can get reliable information by reading newspaper articles, collecting all the relevant and related information by organizing or storing them manually can become tiresome and unrealistic. Search engines can also provide information to user-specific queries. However, one has to go through all the search results to gain insights such as the increase in numbers of specific crimes in a city. In this work, we aim to develop a system to automatically extract information from Bengali newspaper articles and conveniently gain insights by visualizing them.

In Bangladesh, there are about 30 daily Bengali newspapers and most of them have an electronic version available online. Newspapers are a good source of timely and mostly authentic information. In this chapter, we focus particularly on crime information extraction from these news sources. Our proposed system can collect this information and present them in a user-friendly way to understand the trend of criminal activities across the country or in a locality and point out the crime-prone areas of the country. We chose this domain for our study because crime information is a key variable that helps us in decision-making in various situations such as whether to move to a new area (high crime rates) or avoid traveling to specific places. To the best of our knowledge, there is no IE system currently available for Bengali newspaper articles.

To accomplish our task, we first divide the whole task into several smaller tasks. Our approach uses a rule-based technique to crawl crime-related news articles from the web. As those articles are unstructured or semi-structured, we then extract the crime location sentences using machine learning algorithms such as supervised classification algorithms. In our work, we use four different machine learning algorithms and compare their accuracy. Afterward, we employ a voting system to classify a sentence as a crime location sentence or non-crime location sentence. Next, we use a Bengali Named Entity Recognizer (Bengali NER) to extract the necessary information, particularly crime location, from the selected news articles available on the newspaper websites. Finally, this information is visualized on top of a Map by marking the locations.

This chapter is structured as follows. In Section 9.2, we discuss the related tasks and how they are related to our work. The structure and workflow of our system are presented in Section 9.3 with a detailed explanation of the technical aspects. Section 9.4 consists of the experiments and their results to come up with a robust solution. Direction to further works and some final words are in Section 9.5 and 9.6.

9.2 RELATED WORK

In this section, we provide an overview of the related work in the area of crime information extraction and the Natural Language Processing (NLP) tools we use for information extraction from articles written in Bengali newspapers.

Peng & McCallum [4] have employed Conditional Random Fields (CRFs) to extract information from research papers. They have extracted various common fields from the headers and citations of research papers. Other than CRFs, we have used machine learning methods to extract crime data from online news articles. Kim & Gil [16] have classified the research articles using K-means clustering algorithm based on the TF-IDF values of the research papers. They have considered the whole research paper as a document and took the TF-IDF value of the papers. Most recently, Bhakta, Dash, Bari & Shatabda [2] have classified Bengali news articles to generate tags for news articles. In our work, we consider a sentence as a document and use its TF-IDF value. Pirana, Sertbas, & Ensar [5] have investigated three deep learning approaches: Convolutional Neural Network (CNN), Recurrent Convolutional Neural Network (RCNN), Long Short-Term Memory (LSTM) to classify Turkish texts to use the classifiers in virtual assistants. Alam, Rahoman & Azad [9] have classified Bengali comments from various sources with CNN. However, we are interested in classifying crime location-related sentences to apply NER on them to get crime location information.

Rahem & Omar [7] have studied the extraction of drug-trafficking-related crime information including ways to hide drugs, find nationality of drug dealers, types of drugs, quality, and prices of drugs, etc. They have tried a rule-based approach to extract this information based on a set of drug crime gazetteers and a set of grammatical and heuristic rules. Chowdhury, Tumpa, Khatun & Rabby [14] have performed a lexical-based analysis to study crime monitoring by analyzing sentiment of headlines posted on Twitter. In our work, we are mainly depending on machine learning techniques to help us in extracting data. Apart from these, Sulieman [6] has studied the coverage of crime news in an online Saudi newspaper by collecting data by structured content analysis. They have done that to see the coverage preference of newspapers to various types of crime news. Though their intention is different from ours, our work is somewhat related to them in the sense that both are working with crime news.

Arulanandam, Savarimuthu & Purvis [12] have shown how theft-related crime information can be extracted and analyzed from news articles of newspapers from three different countries. They have tested several English NER to evaluate their performance on different countries' news writing styles. They have shown the possibility of doing this kind of work. Hassan & Rahman [10] have analyzed two English newspaper articles published from Bangladesh to extract the location name and ranked the locations concerning crime frequency. By taking inspiration from these works, we focus on crime information extraction in the Bengali domain, as there is no previous research work for huge volumes of news articles resting in Bengali newspaper websites. Although there are many NER tool sets available for the English language, such a tool for the Bengali language is lacking. Therefore, we use NER by [13] in the process of building our system. The results of our system show that we can build a more robust tool in the future, given a state-of-the-art Bengali NER tool set. We aim to work in this direction in the future.

9.3 METHODOLOGY

The goal of this work is to classify crime sentences and extract crime information (i.e., crime locations) from Bengali online newspaper articles. In this section, we describe the methodology used in our system to accomplish these tasks. Our proposed system consists of several modules as shown in Figure 9.1 with their interactions.

In the following subsections, we discuss these modules used in our methodology in detail.

9.3.1 Driver

In our work, we utilize a *driver program* which controls the flow of execution inside the system. It maintains the sequence of execution of the subsystems by sharing and collecting intermediate data among them. It also sanitizes the input sentences to remove undesired contents like punctuation or number to gain higher accuracy as mentioned by Ayedh, Tan, Alwesabi & Rajeh [1]. The sequence of operation that the driver performs is listed below:

1. Start the news-article crawler and wait until it exits.

2. Take crawled articles, split them into sentences, and remove unwanted symbols.

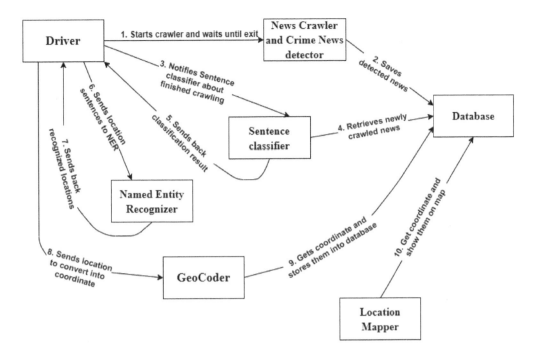

Figure 9.1: Overview of all the components in our system and their interactions

3. Send sanitized sentences to the Sentence Classifier and produce location sentences as a result of the classification.

4. Feed the location sentences to the NER and extract location address to visualize the results through *Geocoder* on a map.

9.3.2 News Crawler and Crime News Collector

The News Crawler retrieves news articles from the online version of the newspaper, *Kalerkantho*[1]. For this purpose we use a popular framework, Scrapy[2] to build a web-spider. The spider loads the news list[3] page by page. In a page, there are several news article summaries along with their headlines. We search the headlines to see if there is a match with a keyword from the Figure 9.2 list and label the news article with that keyword's crime type.

After a match is found, this subsystem checks the database if that news article is already crawled. If that is the case, it stops crawling as the subsequent news articles have already been crawled. If that is not the case, the crawler enters into that news article link and grabs the article id, the article text, the publication date, and the reporter's district and saves them to the database. In this way, a piece of news can have multiple labels, as the news headline can contain multiple such keywords.

---

[1] A popular Bengali newspaper of Bangladesh

[2] https://scrapy.org. Title: Scrapy | A Fast and Powerful Scraping and Web Crawling Framework

[3] https://www.kalerkantho.com/online/country-news/0. Title: Kalerkantho | online

Crime Type	Keywords to match
ABDUCTION_TYPE	অপহরণ, অপহরণকারী, অপহৃত, মুক্তিপণ, অপহরণে
DRUGS_TYPE	মাদক, মাদকে, হেরোইন, হেরোইনে, ইয়াবা, ফেনসিডিল, ফেন্সিডিল
MURDER_TYPE	হত্যা, খুন, ছুরিকাঘাত, কুপিয়ে
THEFT_TYPE	চুরি, চোর, ডাকাত, ছিনতাই, ডাকাতি
RAPE_TYPE	ধর্ষণ, ধর্ষক, ধর্ষিত, শ্লীলতাহানি, সম্ভ্রমহানি

Figure 9.2: Crime types and their corresponding keywords

9.3.3 Sentence Classifier

At the end of the crawling and before starting sentence classification, the driver program processes the articles in the following sequence: First, we separate the sentences using either of '|', '?' or '!' as sentence end markers. Second, for each sentence, we perform some preprocessing such as removing numbers and special characters from the sentence. Third, we send that sentence to the 'Sentence Classifier' to find if it is a location sentence. The Sentence Classifier classifies the sentences in the article as follows:

1. Transform the sentence to get a Bag of Words representation.

2. Transform the Bag of Words with TF-IDF to get another representation.

3. Feed the latest representation to the four pre-trained models.

4. Record the classification result of each of the models.

5. Count the 'positive' and 'negative' result frequencies from recorded results.

6. Label this sentence to be a 'location sentence' if 'positive' frequency is greater than or equals to 'negative' frequency.

For example, if a sentence is classified as 'location sentence' by Logistic Regression, Random Forest Classifier, and Linear Support Vector Machine Classifier but 'non-location sentence' by Stochastic Gradient Descent Classifier, then we will consider it as 'location sentence' because 3 classifiers have classified as 'location sentence' and 1 classifier has classified as 'non-location sentence' so 'location sentence' class wins the voting system. Similarly, if a sentence is classified as 'location sentence' by Logistic Regression but 'non-location sentence' by Random Forest Classifier, Linear Support Vector Machine Classifier, and Stochastic Gradient Descent Classifier, then we will consider it as 'non-location sentence'.

After that, it sends back the result of classification to the driver program.

9.3.4 Named Entity Recognizer

We pass the positively classified (Crime Location) sentences to a Named Entity Recognizer (NER) to extract the location from that sentence. Karim et al. [8] created a rich data-set for Bengali Named Entity Recognition task. Sarkar [13] used the data-set to create a NER using CRF, and we also utilize that tool for our work.

9.3.5 Geocoder

This subsystem receives the location address and finds the approximate geographic coordinates (latitude and longitude) and stores them in the database. Here we use OpenCage[4] geocoder API to convert the location address to the coordinates. The coordinate is approximate, because it is not guaranteed that we will get an exact coordinate for a given address according to Manoruang & Asavasuthirakul [11].

We send the extracted address to the API and wait for the response; if after consulting the response we get a geographic coordinate, we report that coordinate as the approximation. If we do not get any geographic coordinate for that address, we generalize the address by dropping the specific parts from that address and send the new address again to the API and this continues until we get a geographic coordinate or the address becomes empty. If the address becomes empty, we use the district name of the reporter as the crime location (as a reminder, we have extracted the district of the reporter beforehand when crawling the article using a rule-based approach).

As an example of generalizing address, we can consider the address: 'Balapara, Madhupur, Badarganj, Rangpur' becomes 'Madhupur, Badarganj, Rangpur' after dropping the village name from the address.

9.3.6 Database

A database is used to store information like crawled news, storing news types, saving location of the crime and also the location coordinate so that we don't repeat tasks like crawling, crime type detection, running NER, and getting coordinates. A database is also convenient for querying various data efficiently and we use various queries to get data from the database. We use SQLite3[5] as our database.

9.3.7 Location Mapper

This is an independent subsystem that only uses the database from the previously stated subsystems and is not controlled by the 'driver program'. It is a GUI application that can filter and show the results on top of a map and a bar chart. The map here used is the OpenStreetMap[6] with support from the LeafletMap[7] library to show the location markers.

At the start, the application will show a user interface that is not populated with any data. At the top, there are some filtering options like date range selection, district selection or crime type selection. After selecting some filtering criteria, the user presses the 'Apply' button, at the top-right corner, and the application connects to the database to retrieve the appropriate information and show them as shown in Figure 9.3.

---

[4]https://opencagedata.com. Title: OpenCage Geocoder - Easy, Open, Worldwide, Affordable Geocoding

[5]https://www.sqlite.org. Title: SQLite Home Page

[6]https://www.openstreetmap.org. Title: OpenStreetMap

[7]https://github.com/N1k145/LeafletMap. Title: N1k145/LeafletMap: LeafletMap is a JavaFX component for displaying an OpenStreetMap based map inside a JavaFX WebView by using the Leaflet JavaScript library.

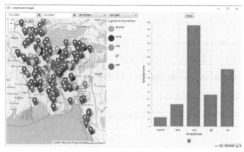
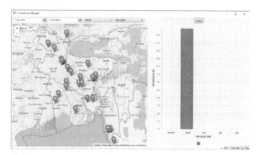
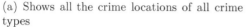

(a) Shows all the crime locations of all crime types

(b) Figure shows the filtered crime locations of crime type 'Drugs'

Figure 9.3: Graphical User Interface of the proposed application

9.4 EXPERIMENTS AND RESULTS

For experimental purposes, we have collected Bengali news articles from the online version of Kalerkantho. To collect these articles, we have created a separate crawler to label sentences manually (this crawler is different from the earlier stated crawler in a sense that it prompts to mark the 'crime location sentences' in the article).

We have taken about 650 Bengali news articles by applying the procedure stated in Section 9.3.2. For each of these articles, we have separated the sentences using either of '|', '?' or '!' as sentence end markers (as described in Section 9.3.3) then labeled them as 'crime location sentence' or 'non-crime location sentence' by hand. After doing this, we had 830 sentences labeled as 'crime location sentence' but 'crime location sentence' was smaller in number than 'non-crime location sentence'. So we have chosen the same number of sentences from these two categories by selecting all the 'crime location sentences' and selecting the same number of sentences randomly from 'non-crime location sentences'. So we have used $2 \times 830 = 1660$ sentences to train and test the models.

There are four machine learning algorithms we use to classify the sentences: Logistic Regression, Random Forest Classifier, Linear Support Vector Machine Classifier and Stochastic Gradient Descent Classifier. The implementation of the mentioned algorithms used here is from the Scikit-Learn[8] library.

9.4.1 Parameter Tuning for the Classifiers

Parameter tuning for a particular kind of task is very important as the default parameters of the algorithms are not applicable in general to all the problems. So we have done some parameter searches to tune them for this task.

9.4.1.1 Random Forest Classifier

The important parameter for Random Forest Classifier is the number of estimators (n_estimators) and maximum depth (max_depth). The number of estimators means

---

[8]https://scikit-learn.org. Title: scikit-learn: machine learning in Python - scikit-learn 0.24.2 documentation

Table 9.1: Performance Comparison of Different Classification Algorithms

Algorithm	Accuracy	Sentence Class	Precision	Recall	F1-Score	Support
Random Forest	0.87	Non-Location	0.86	0.89	0.88	215
		Location	0.88	0.84	0.86	200
Logistic Regression	0.90	Non-Location	0.88	0.93	0.91	215
		Location	0.92	0.87	0.89	200
Linear SVM Classifier	0.90	Non-Location	0.88	0.94	0.91	215
		Location	0.93	0.86	0.90	200
SGD Classifier	0.88	Non-Location	0.85	0.94	0.89	215
		Location	0.93	0.82	0.87	200

the number of trees in the forest to be built, and maximum depth means the maximum allowed depth of any tree. We have used $n\_estimators = 25$ and $max\_depth = 20$.

9.4.1.2 Logistic Regression

We had to set the inverse-regularization parameter (C) for this algorithm parameter to deal with overfitting. A smaller value means a stronger regularization. We have used $C = 0.9$.

9.4.1.3 Linear Support Vector Classifier

We had to set the inverse-regularization parameter (C) for this algorithm parameter to deal with overfitting. A smaller value means a stronger regularization. We have used $C = 0.06$ where the default value of this parameter is 1.0.

9.4.1.4 Stochastic Gradient Descent Classifier

We have changed the constant that multiplies the regularization term. The higher the value, the stronger the regularization. This is named 'alpha' in Scikit-Learn implementation. We have set it to 0.003 where the default value is 0.0001.

9.4.2 Performance Comparison of Sentence Classifiers

We have used a training data-set of 75% of all the 1660 sentences considered, and the rest were used for testing purposes. Below are the performances by different algorithms used.

Table 9.1 shows the different performance measures for the classification algorithms used in our system. The accuracy varies between 87% to 90% for all the four classifiers. The precision is also satisfactory as all of them score above 85%. F1-Score also indicates their efficiency as a candidate classifier.

Additionally, Table 9.2 shows the performance of our proposed voting system, and Table 9.3 shows the accuracy gain by the proposed voting system.

Table 9.2: Performance of the Proposed Voting System

Accuracy	Sentence Class	Precision	Recall	F1-Score	Support
0.91	Non-Location	0.89	0.93	0.81	215
	Location	0.93	0.88	0.90	200

Table 9.3: Accuracy Gain after Incorporating our Voting Scheme

Compared Algorithm	Accuracy Gain
Random Forest Classifier	4%
SGD Classifier	3%
Logistic Regressing	1%
Linear SVM Classifier	1%

Due to the absence of similar work for Bengali language, we could not report a comparison with other work in terms of accuracy. Although there are numerous works available in this direction for the English language, such as [12, 14], we believe these are not a fair comparison for our method as, unlike English, an effective NER is still unavailable in the Bengali language. We left the improvement of the current NER for future exploration.

9.5 DISCUSSIONS

From the above experimentation result, we can see that every algorithm is working almost in the same way, indicated by its accuracy. This argument is true for other performance metrics. So instead of choosing a single algorithm, we have employed a voting system to get feedback from all the classifiers. The Class getting more votes is decided as the class of the sentence. By investigating some sentences on the voting system, we have found that the votes become 4:0 or 3:1 for classifying a sentence as Crime Location or Non-Crime Location and a ratio of 2:2 is very rare. So this approach is more fruitful.

To utilize the gathered data effectively, we have developed a minimal Graphical User Interface that can connect to the database and show the collected data on a map. In the Graphical User Interface (Figure 9.3), we have brought the ability to filter the news we have collected and their related location data correspondingly. We can select a date range to see the crimes only in that time frame. We can also select a particular district to see the crimes in that district. For a particular crime, we can see that crime's affected areas by filtering the news articles for that crime category. When multiple crime types are selected we display the different crimes in different colors. A bar chart is also drawn from the relevant data to compare the crime numbers.

The presented system has some limitations, and those limitations are directions to future works. Firstly, we have considered only a single newspaper as the source. The challenge in using multiple newspapers as sources is the possibility of overcounting the same crime because the same news can be covered by different newspapers. Secondly, we have used the traditional machine learning approaches only but we could use the latest deep learning approaches as mentioned by Tabashum, Hossain, Islam, Zahara & Fami [15]. Thirdly, we have considered the follow-up news as new news, this can contribute to the count of a particular crime in a wrong way. A possible solution to this can be news chain detection. Fourthly, we have approximated the location of the crime using the geocoding service. Finally, for the Bengali language, we don't have a full-featured stammer, so we are not using any stammer. Developing a stammer for the Bengali language can increase the efficiency and accuracy of the models used here.

9.6 CONCLUSION

In this chapter, we discuss and implement a way to extract crime location sentences from Bengali online news articles from newspapers in Bangladesh. We employed machine learning algorithms to distinguish between crime location and non-crime location sentences inside a news article. We then use Named Entity Recognition (NER) to extract crime location from crime location sentences. We also show the accuracy of different models used in our work and the results have shown promising performance. To demonstrate the applicability of our work, we built a GUI application to visualize the results of our system.

Bibliography

[1] Ayedh A, Tan G, Alwesabi K, Rajeh H. (2016). The Effect of Pre-processing on Arabic Document Categorization *Algorithms*. 2016; 9(2):27. https://doi.org/10.3390/a9020027.

[2] Bhakta D., Dash A. A., Bari M. F., Shatabda S. (2020). Supervised Machine Learning for Multi-label Classification of Bangla Articles *Bhuiyan T., Rahman M. M., Ali M. A. (eds) Cyber Security and Computer Science. ICONCS 2020. Lecture Notes of the Institute for Computer Sciences, Social Informatics and Telecommunications Engineering, vol 325. Springer, Cham.* https://doi.org/10.1007/978-3-030-52856-0_38

[3] Cowie, Jim, and Wendy Lehnert (1996). Information extraction *Communications of the ACM 39.1* pp. 80-91.

[4] F. Peng and A. McCallum (2006). Information extraction from research papers using conditional random fields *Information Processing and Management* pp. 963-979 vol. 42. doi: 10.1016/j.ipm.2005.09.002

[5] G. Pirana, A. Sertbas and T. Ensar (2019). Sentence Classification with Deep Learning Method For Virtual Assistant Applications *2019 3rd International Symposium on Multidisciplinary Studies and Innovative Technologies (ISMSIT)*, Ankara, Turkey.

[6] H. Sulieman (2020). Coverage of crime news: content analysis of Al-Yaum Saudi online newspaper *Utopia y Praxis Latinoamericana* vol. 25.

[7] K. R. Rahem and N. Omar (2014). Drug-related crime information extraction and analysis *Proceedings of the 6th International Conference on Information Technology and Multimedia* pp. 250-254, doi: 10.1109/ICIMU.2014.7066639.

[8] Karim, Redwanul & Islam, M. A. & Simanto, Sazid & Chowdhury, Saif & Roy, Kalyan & Neon, Adnan & Hasan, Md & Firoze, Adnan & Rahman, Mohammad. (2019). A step towards information extraction: Named entity recognition in Bangla using deep learning *Journal of Intelligent & Fuzzy Systems* 37. 1-13. doi: 10.3233/JIFS-179349.

[9] M. H. Alam, M. Rahoman and M. A. K. Azad (2017). Sentiment analysis for Bangla sentences using convolutional neural network *2017 20th International Conference of Computer and Information Technology (ICCIT)* pp. 1-6, doi: 10.1109/ICCITECHN.2017.8281840.

[10] M. Hassan & M. Z. Rahman (2017). Crime news analysis: Location and story detection *2017 20th International Conference of Computer and Information Technology (ICCIT)* pp. 1-6, doi: 10.1109/ICCITECHN.2017.8281798.

[11] Manoruang, D. & Asavasuthirakul, D. (2019). Quality analysis of online geocoding services for Thai text addresses. *Engineering and Applied Science Research*, 46(2), 86-97.

[12] Arulanandam, B. T. R. Savarimuthu and M. A. Purvis (2014). Extracting crime information from online newspaper articles *The second Australasian web conference, Auckland*.

[13] Sarker, Sagor. (2021). BNLP: Natural language processing toolkit for Bengali language.

[14] S. M. M. H. Chowdhury, Z. N. Tumpa, F. Khatun and S. K. F. Rabby (2019). Crime Monitoring from Newspaper Data based on Sentiment analysis *2019 8th International Conference System Modeling and Advancement in Research Trends (SMART)* pp. 299-304 doi: 10.1109/SMART46866.2019.9117513.

[15] S. Tabashum, M. M. Hossain, A. Islam, M. Y. Mahafi Taz Zahara and F. N. Fami (2020). Performance Analysis of Most Prominent Machine Learning and Deep Learning Algorithms In Classifying Bangla Crime News Articles *2020 IEEE Region 10 Symposium (TENSYMP)* pp. 1273-1277 doi: 10.1109/TENSYMP50017.2020.9230785.

[16] S. W. Kim and J.M. Gil (2019). Research paper classification systems based on TF-IDF and LDA schemes *Hum. Cent. Comput. Inf. Sci.* 9, 30 https://doi.org/10.1186/s13673-019-0192-7.

BERT-Based Emotion Classification Approach with Analysis of COVID-19 Pandemic Tweets

Md. Shahad Mahmud Chowdhury and Biprodip Pal

Rajshahi University of Engineering & Technology, Rajshahi, Bangladesh

CONTENTS

10.1	Introduction	110
10.2	Datasets	111
	10.2.1 ISEAR dataset	111
	10.2.2 Tweets dataset	111
10.3	Proposed approach	112
	10.3.1 Data preprocessing	112
	10.3.2 Emotion detection model structures	113
	10.3.2.1 LSTM	113
	10.3.2.2 BERT	113
	10.3.2.3 Model-1: Embedding and LSTM with Dense Layers	114
	10.3.2.4 Model-2: Using BERT	114
	10.3.2.5 Model-3: BERT with LSTM and Dense Layers	114
10.4	Experiments	114
	10.4.1 Emotion Recognition from ISEAR Dataset and Effect of Stop Words	115
	10.4.2 Explaining the Model Predictions Using LIME	115
	10.4.3 Emotion Dynamics and Contributing Factors during Pandemic	117
10.5	Conclusion	119

THE continuous spread of coronavirus disease requires active research on interactions, activities, and emotional state dynamics of people, as it is significant to policymakers. While social media are broadly used to express opinions and emotions, emotion detection and classification from text is a challenging problem due to the lack of facial or voice expressions. This chapter proposes a machine-learning model that, unlike manual feature extraction techniques, leverages the neural attention approach to detect emotions through meaningful feature extraction. Firstly, this research contributes to taking a deep learning approach for the classification of six types of emotions from the text using the benchmark ISEAR dataset. Secondly, the model predictions have been explained using the model agnostic approach. Thirdly, emotions in tweets related to COVID-19 have been classified and quantified along with an illustration of the emotion dynamics during the pandemic before and after the start of vaccination. Finally, N-gram analysis has been used in the summarization of the contributing factors. In terms of emotion classification from ISEAR data, our approach comes out with a better F1 score of .72 compared to some other state-of-the-art works.

10.1 INTRODUCTION

Emotion is a strong feeling generated based on one's different situations or moods that can affect decision-making, behavior, and thinking. But it is a challenging task to find out the emotional state of textual content, as it lacks voice or facial reactions. Emotion detection has drawn the attention of several researchers due to its increasing applications. Detecting emotion has several applications like Human-Computer Interaction (HIC), artificial intelligence based assistants, marketing, and attitude or personality detection. Due to a long lockdown during the COVID-19 pandemic, the emotional state of people during this time has become an area of active research. According to a survey in the United States, it has been predicted that the usage of online social media Facebook, Twitter, and Linkedin would increase by 62.3%, 34.4%, and 15.4% accordingly during the time of lockdown [7]. To analyze the emotion flow during the pandemic, English tweets from Twitter have been considered in this research, as most of the tweets are public. Research attempts are common to design efficient methods for emotion classification. A study in [2] showed a method of emotion classification using supervised machine learning with SNoW learning architecture. Wang and Zheng proposed an improved latent semantic analysis algorithm to detect emotion on ISEAR dataset [20]. Mohammad and Kiritchenko used emotion-word hashtags and captured categories of fine emotions from tweets [13]. Balahur et al. have represented a method to detect emotion based on commonsense knowledge. They also built an EmotiNet representing situations that trigger emotions. They have modeled the situations as a chain of actions and their corresponding emotional effect using an ontological representation [4]. In a study [17], Sear et al. have used keyword extraction and analysis techniques along with phrasal verb identification, intensity check, and negation check to find the emotion affinity of a sentence. They have associated an emotion score along with each text. Bandhakavi et al. have generated a domain-specific emotion lexicon for feature extraction and they used a machine learning approach to classify emotion from the text [5]. Ho et al. have transformed the text into a sequence of events that cause mental states, then used the high-order Hidden Markov Model to model the process that state sequence causes the emotion [10]. Udochukwu and He have presented a rule-based approach to sentence-level implicit emotion detection based on the OCC model. They used a set of pre-defined rules to identify an emotion for a given text [18]. Most of these studies used manual feature extraction for specific emotion classification tasks and the model decisions are not explained. However, Choudrie et al. have taken transfer learning and RoBERTa based approaches to identify, explore and understand emotions during the pandemic. They used over two million tweets collected between February to June 2020 [6]. Zhu et al. analyzed the spatiotemporal characteristics of big data on social media sentiment during the COVID-19 pandemic. They used LDA modeling and obtained 8 topics with 28 interactive topics. They have shown the topic and the rate of topic discussion dynamic, correlation with economic zone division, and the existence of rumor topics [21].

In this chapter, a transfer learning approach has been proposed that adopts LSTM and BERT-based deep learning for emotion classification. The proposed technique outperforms some state-of-the-art emotion detection approaches in terms of the ISEAR emotion classification dataset. Unlike previous Black-Box approaches, the effect of stop words and relevant features has been illustrated through the model agnostic explanation approach LIME. COVID-19 related tweets have been collected from April 2020 to July 2020, January 2021 to April 2021, and comprehensively analyzed the trajectories of emotion through our proposed model to help policymakers decide on optimal policy. The tweets were summarized using word cloud for proper visualization that can help the design of recommendation systems.

10.2   DATASETS

For this study, two datasets are used. In this section, the datasets, distribution, and collection processes will be discussed.

10.2.1   ISEAR dataset

ISEAR data contains texts categorized into seven significant emotions: anger, fear, guilt, disgust, sadness, joy, and shame [16]. This data was collected by psychologists for the ISEAR project and is one of the frequently used datasets for this task. The dataset contains a total of 7666 labeled texts and 7503 unique texts. The dataset is distributed as shown in Table 10.1.

Table 10.1: Data distribution of ISEAR dataset

Emotion	Anger	Disgust	Fear	Guilt	Joy	Sadness	Shame
Count	1096	1096	1095	1093	1094	1096	1096

10.2.2   Tweets dataset

The COVID-19 tweets dataset includes CSV (comma-separated values) files [12]. These files contain COVID-19 related tweet ids. An ongoing project is monitoring the real-time Twitter feed for coronavirus-related tweets using 60+ different keywords and hashtags that are commonly used while referencing the pandemic. These tweet IDs have been collected by this project. Some of the keywords are: "#corona", "corona", "#coronavirus", "coronavirus", "#covid", "covid", "covid19", "#covid19" [12]. The dataset contains only tweet ids. Later data was pulled out using tweet ids. For this study, the tweets were collected using tweet ids for 90 consecutive days. From each day, randomly 50,000 tweets were chosen based on the ids for the experiments. The tweets were collected twice, each for 90 consecutive days of duration. Firstly, the tweets were collected from 05 April 2020 to 03 July 2020, at the early stage of the pandemic. Later the tweets were collected from 04 January 2021 to 04 April 2021, during the time of vaccination.

10.3 PROPOSED APPROACH

The primary objective of this work is to develop a system that can identify the emotion of text and analyze the impact of a pandemic on society. Figure 10.1 shows a schematic process of our approach that is comprised of four major parts: data preprocessing, structuring the models, extraction of COVID-19 related tweets followed by analyzing the emotion flow during the pandemic.

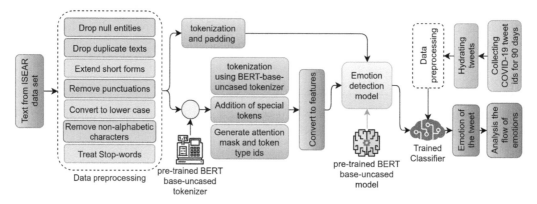

Figure 10.1: Work flow of proposed approach for emotion classification

10.3.1 Data preprocessing

To preprocess data, at first, the null and duplicate entries were removed. After this step, the anger, disgust, fear, guilt, joy, sadness, and shame types of sample count were 1086, 1078, 1083, 1063, 1079, 1057, and 1057, respectively. Next, the whole text was converted to lowercase, and the short forms like "I'm" were replaced with corresponding longer forms like "I am". Later all the punctuation and non-alphabetic symbols were removed.

Stop words play a vital role in the case of emotional state in text. So at first, some negative contextual words like 'not', 'nor', etc. were removed from the stop words list. Later to evaluate the impact of stop words, experiments have been carried out by training the classifier models with samples containing stop words and samples without stop words.

For tokenization, the stop words processed text was tokenized using the Tokenizer class functionalities from the deep learning library - Keras. It is the text preprocessing module to use with model-1. For model-2 and model-3, BERT base-uncased pre-trained tokenizer was used. BERT requires adding special tokens to separate sentences. So a token [CLS] was added at the beginning of a sentence and another token [SEP] at the end of the sentence. The token type ids and attention masks were also generated while tokenizing. Later with these tokens and targets, the examples were converted into features and fed into corresponding models.

10.3.2 Emotion detection model structures

In this study, the experimentation was done with three models leveraging BERT and LSTM models.

10.3.2.1 LSTM

Long Short-Term Memory (LSTM) is broadly used in cases where the current state reflects the effects of previous states [11]. Information can be added or removed by a mechanism called *gate*. The *input gate unit* protects the cell state or memory contents from perturbation by irrelevant information. An *output gate unit* protects other units from perturbation by current irrelevant memory contents. A forget gate is responsible for removing information from the memory. The formula of each LSTM component can be formalized as:

$$f_t = \sigma(W_f x_t + U_f h_{t-1} + b_f)$$
$$i_t = \sigma(W_i x_t + U_i h_{t-1} + b_i)$$
$$o_t = \sigma(W_o x_t + U_o h_{t-1} + b_o)$$
$$\hat{c}_t = \tanh(W_c x_t + U_c h_{t-1} + b_c)$$
$$c_t = f_t \circ c_{t-1} + i_t \circ \hat{c}_t$$
$$h_t = o_t \circ \tanh(c_t)$$

Here f_t, i_t, o_t, and c_t are the forget gate, input gate, output gate, and cell activation function, respectively, at time t. σ represents the logistic sigmoid function, which produces outputs in the range $[0, 1]$, $\circ$ represents multiplication operation, and b represents bias. Finally, h_t is the output of the hidden state [14].

10.3.2.2 BERT

The Bidirectional Encoder Representations from Transformers (BERT) consists of two steps processing: *pre-training* and *fine-tuning*. During pre-training, the model is trained on a large unlabeled corpus. For fine-tuning, the pre-trained parameters are fine-tuned using labeled data for a specific task [9].

BERT is a multi-layer bidirectional Transformer model. The Transformer model is structured with stacked self-attention and pointwise fully connected layers for both encoder and decoder. A stack of 6 identical layers of multi-head attention and feedforward sublayers constitute both decoder and encoder sections of the transformer. A residual connection from its previous inputs is taken by each sublayer. These sublayers add it to the sublayer output and normalize it to produce the final output of the sublayer. To allow for residual addition, all sublayers produce an output of dimension 512. The decoder has an additional sublayer that performs attention over the output of encoding shifted by one position to ensure the predictions from positions can depend only on the known outputs at positions less than i [8]. Concerning multi-head self-attention, *scaled dot product attention* is defined as:

$$Attention(Q,\ K,\ V) = softmax(\frac{QK^T}{\sqrt{d_k}})V$$

Here, Q, K, and V are the matrixes of queries, keys, and values where d_k is the dimension of the Q and K matrix. Now, the multi-head attention can be defined as: $MultiHead(Q,\ K,\ V) = Concat(head_1,\ head_2,\ ...,\ head_h)W^O$.

Here, $head_i = Attention(QW_i^Q,\ KW_i^K,\ VW_i^V)$. Multi-head attention consists of projecting the queries, keys, and values h times with different, learned linear projections. Then, on each of these projected versions of the queries, keys, and values, the attention function is performed in parallel, yielding in dv-dimensional output values. Finally, these are concatenated and projected, resulting in the final values [9, 19].

10.3.2.3 Model-1: Embedding and LSTM with Dense Layers

This is the model with the most simple structure. It contains an Embedding layer followed by an LSTM layer and two Dense layers. For the embedding layer, a vocabulary of 20000 words was used. The dimension of the dense embedding is 64. In the dropout layer, a dropout probability of 0.1 is used.

10.3.2.4 Model-2: Using BERT

In this model, BERT is used that is structured with a sequence classification/regression head on top [1]. For the study, 'BERT-base-uncased' pre-trained weights were used. While configuring BERT, a hidden dropout probability of value 0.3 was used along with Adam optimizer with a learning rate of 0.0003.

10.3.2.5 Model-3: BERT with LSTM and Dense Layers

In this model, both our model-1 and model-2 structures were combined. On the top, there is a BERT layer followed by a dropout layer. The output of this layer is fed into an LSTM layer followed by several dropout and Dense layers. The structure is shown in Figure 10.2.

10.4 EXPERIMENTS

While training the model, 5-fold cross-validation was used. So each time, 4 groups of data (about 6000 texts) were used during training, and the remaining group was used for validation (about 1503 texts).

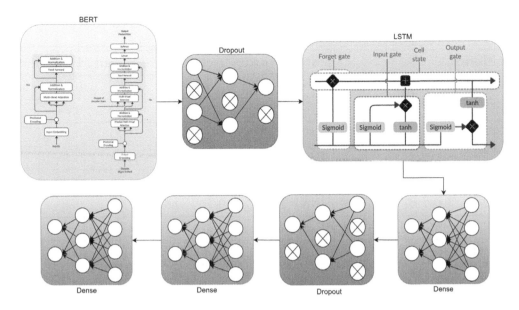

Figure 10.2: Structure of model-3

10.4.1 Emotion Recognition from ISEAR Dataset and Effect of Stop Words

To evaluate the model performances, the average validation scores of all the folds have been considered. Table 10.2 represents the outcomes of the models using the ISEAR dataset. In the table, the *stop words* column indicates the experimentation with stop words. The row with a *Yes* value in the *stop words* column indicates that the stop words were not removed during this experiment. The proposed model-3 also outperforms some research works done on the ISEAR emotion detection dataset as depicted in Table 10.2.

Table 10.2 indicates the accuracy, F1, recall and precision score of model-3 have increased by around 8%, 5%, 8%, and 1%, respectively, when the stop words were not removed. Clearly, stop words play a significant role in the case of emotion or sentiment analysis, and on average all three models have performed better when the stop words were not removed. Overall, it was noticed that model-3 has the best accuracy, F1, and precision score. On the other hand, the loss curve indicates if a model converges or not. Figure 10.3 shows the validation loss of the proposed model. It can be seen that the model converges quickly.

10.4.2 Explaining the Model Predictions Using LIME

Deep neural networks can understand complex structures but are difficult to interpret. LIME has been used to explain the prediction of the proposed model (model-3) [15]. LIME considers a query point and generates many neighbor hypothetical points. An interpretable model like a decision tree is trained on the neighborhood to generate the explanation. For these experiments, the neighborhood to learn the approximate linear model has been set to 5000, and *cosine similarity* has been used to measure distance.

Table 10.2: Performance of proposed models on ISEAR data

Model	Stop Words	Acc.	F1	Recall	Precision
LSTM + Dropout + Dense + Dense	Yes	0.50	0.42	0.33	0.71
	No	0.54	0.48	0.37	0.75
BERT + Dropout + Dense	Yes	0.79	0.59	**0.96**	0.41
	No	0.72	0.55	0.92	0.38
Proposed Model	Yes	**0.83**	**0.72**	0.70	**0.80**
	No	0.75	0.67	0.62	0.79
Balahur et al. [4]	-	0.42	-	0.30	-
Seal et al. [17]	-	0.65	0.66	0.63	0.70
Udochukwu and He [18]	-	-	51.3	-	-
Anusha and Sandhya [3]	-	-	63.1	-	-
Bandhakavi et al. [5]	-	-	39.48	-	-
Ho and Cao [10]	-	-	35.3	-	-

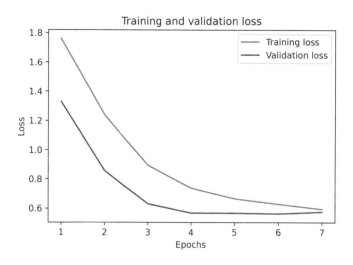

Figure 10.3: Loss curves of model-3

Figure 10.4(a) shows a sample output result generated for correctly classified *Anger* emotion. For the sample "When I was driving home after several days of hard work, there was a motorist ahead of me who was driving at 50 km/hour and refused, despite his low speed, to let me overtake", it can be observed that the word 'refused' has the most impact (around 75% having the stop words) to determine that the text is expressing anger with around 0.98 probability.

Figure 10.4(b) shows a sample "When a car is overtaking another and I am forced to drive off the road" misclassified as Fear emotion instead of correct prediction

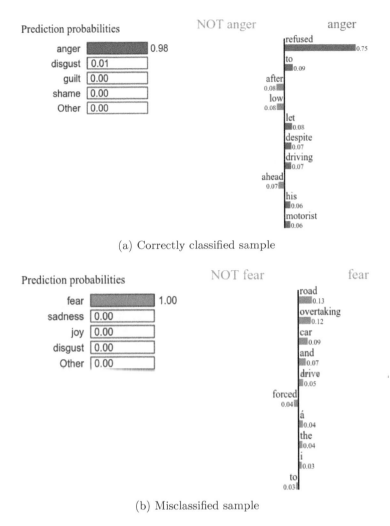

(a) Correctly classified sample

(b) Misclassified sample

Figure 10.4: Model prediction interpretation with LIME analysis

Anger. From the LIME analysis, it can be observed that although the word 'forced' contributed to correct prediction, other words like 'road' or 'overtaking' mislead the sentence towards class 'Fear' as they appeared in many examples to represent Fear.

10.4.3 Emotion Dynamics and Contributing Factors during Pandemic

The COVID-19 tweets dataset was preprocessed in the same manner as preprocessing the text from the ISEAR dataset. The stop words were not removed, as not removing stop words gives better results in model-3. The proposed model-3 classifier was then used for the classification of the emotions in the tweets. The flow of all emotions is shown in Figure 10.5. From Figure 10.5(a), it can be seen that at the very beginning of the pandemic, there were more posts with the emotions of joy and disgust. Reviewing the tweets, it was noticed that this is because of the opportunity people got to stay at home with their family, while some people did not enjoy it. Around the start of

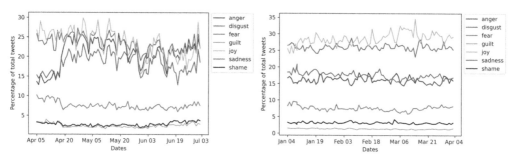

(a) Flow of all emotions during COVID-19 pan- demic before vaccination

(b) Flow of all emotions during COVID-19 pandemic after vaccination

Figure 10.5: Emotion dynamics during pandemic

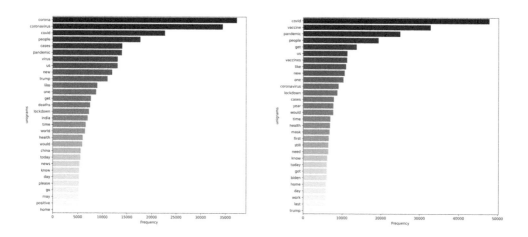

(a) Unigrams of most contributing factor in tweets before vaccination

(b) Unigrams of most contributing factor in tweets after vaccination

Figure 10.6: Unigrams of most contributing factor during pandemic

May, sadness and anger bumped up. Continuing the same situation started to build up sadness, anger, and disgust from May and increased. Figure 10.5(b) indicates that in recent times, during the vaccination period, tweets mostly contained the 'joy' emotion and kept continuing. The second highest emotional tweets are from the disgust category as the COVID-19 pandemic continues, and everyone asks for an improvement of the situation.

Some text-based analyses were performed to understand deeply the contributing factors towards the COVID-19 related emotions. Unigram analysis is used to draw valuable insight from a lot of words related together as shown in Figure 10.6. Figure 10.6(a) shows that most contributing factors towards the emotion before vaccination are: 'corona', 'coronavirus', 'covid', 'people', 'cases', 'pandemic' etc. On the other hand, Figure 10.6(b) reflects that 'covid', 'vaccine', 'pandemic', 'people', 'get', etc. are the most contributing factors after vaccination started. 'Vaccine' is one of the most contributing factors during 2021. Inventing and getting the vaccine is an important factor in joy. However, some side effects, lack of production, etc. reasons have also encouraged the 'disgust' feeling.

10.5   CONCLUSION

This study focuses on the development of an efficient emotion classification model and interpretation of the model prediction. After intuitive analysis, a deep learning-based novel approach has been proposed for detecting emotions from the text. The model performance was tuned based on explanation from LIME analysis and validated on the benchmark dataset. It has been illustrated based on tweets that, at the very beginning of the pandemic, the feeling of joy was at its peak. After that, sadness and anger spread out among people covering up the joyous feelings due to the pandemic that represents the degradation of mental health. Because of the lockdown, isolation, and no suitable measures, it turned into feelings of disgust that continued over time. After the start of vaccination, the feelings of joy dominated the tweets as observed over several months. Thus it is clear that taking necessary steps based on the emotion of people at a particular time can play a vital role to improve mental health. Individual anonymous analysis or locality-based analysis on sufficient data availability could be an interesting extension of this task. As the pandemic situation continues, frequent analysis of activities and emotions is significant for proper decision-making and the betterment of the people.

Bibliography

[1] BERT — transformers 3.0.2 documentation. `https://huggingface.co/transformers/model\_doc/bert.html`

[2] Cecilia Ovesdotter Alm, Dan Roth, and Richard Sproat. Emotions from text: machine learning for text-based emotion prediction. In *Proceedings of human language technology conference and conference on empirical methods in natural language processing*, pages 579-586, 2005.

[3] Vajrapu Anusha and Banda Sandhya. A learning based emotion classifier with semantic text processing. In *Advances in intelligent informatics*, pages 371-382. Springer, 2015.

[4] Alexandra Balahur, Jesús M Hermida, and Andrés Montoyo. Detecting implicit expressions of sentiment in text based on commonsense knowledge. In *Proceedings of the 2nd Workshop on Computational Approaches to Subjectivity and Sentiment Analysis(WASSA 2.011)*, pages 53–60, 2011.

[5] Anil Bandhakavi, Nirmalie Wiratunga, Deepak Padmanabhan, and Stewart Massie. Lexicon based feature extraction for emotion text classification. *Pattern recognition letters*, 93:133–142, 2017.

[6] Jyoti Choudrie, Shruti Patil, Ketan Kotecha, Nikhil Matta, and Ilias Pappas. Applying and understanding an advanced, novel deep learning approach: A Covid 19, text based, emotions analysis study. *Information Systems Frontiers*, pages 1–35, 2021.

[7] J. Clement. Estimated U.S. social media usage increase due to coronavirus home isolation 2020 - emphStatista. `https://www.statista.com/statistics/1106343/social-usage-increase-due-to-coronavirus-home-usa/`, June 2020.

[8] Jacob Devlin, Ming-Wei Chang, Kenton Lee, and Kristina Toutanova. Bert: Pre-training of deep bidirectional transformers for language understanding. In *Proceedings of the 2019 Conference of the North American Chapter of the Association for Computational Linguistics: Human Language Technologies, Volume 1 (Long and Short Papers)*, pages 4171–4186, 2019.

[9] Santiago González-Carvajal and Eduardo C. Garrido-Merchán. Comparing BERT against traditional machine learning text classification. *arXiv preprint arXiv:2005.13012*, 2020.

[10] Dung T. Ho and Tru H. Cao. A high-order hidden Markov model for emotion detection from textual data. In *Pacific rim knowledge acquisition workshop*, pages 94–105. Springer, 2012.

[11] Sepp Hochreiter and Jürgen Schmidhuber. Long short-term memory. *Neural computation*, 9(8):1735–1780, 1997.

[12] Rabindra Lamsal. Coronavirus (Covid-19) tweets dataset. `http://dx.doi.org/10.21227/781w-ef42`, 2020.

[13] Saif M. Mohammad and Svetlana Kiritchenko. Using hashtags to capture fine emotion categories from tweets. *Computational Intelligence*, 31(2):301–326, 2015.

[14] Guozheng Rao, Weihang Huang, Zhiyong Feng, and Qiong Cong. LSTM with sentence representations for document-level sentiment classification. *Neurocomputing*, 308:49–57,2018.

[15] Marco Tulio Ribeiro, Sameer Singh, and Carlos Guestrin. "Why should I trust you?" Explaining the predictions of any classifier. In *Proceedings of the 22nd ACM SIGKDD international conference on knowledge discovery and data mining*, pages 1135–1144, 2016.

[16] K.R. Scherer and H. Wallbott. International survey on emotion antecedents and reactions (ISEAR), 1990.

[17] Dibyendu Seal, Uttam K. Roy, and Rohini Basak. Sentence-level emotion detection from text based on semantic rules. In *Information and Communication Technology for Sustainable Development*, pages 423–430. Springer, 2020.

[18] Orizu Udochukwu and Yulan He. A rule-based approach to implicit emotion detection in text. In *International Conference on Applications of Natural Language to Information Systems*, pages 197–203. Springer, 2015.

[19] Ashish Vaswani, Noam Shazeer, Niki Parmar, Jakob Uszkoreit, Llion Jones, Aidan NGomez, Łukasz Kaiser, and Illia Polosukhin. Attention is all you need. In *Advances in neural information processing systems*, pages 5998–6008, 2017.

[20] Xuren Wang and Qiuhui Zheng. Text emotion classification research is based on improved latent semantic analysis algorithm. In *Proceedings of the 2nd International Conference on Computer Science and Electronics Engineering*. Atlantis Press, 2013.

[21] Bangren Zhu, Xinqi Zheng, Haiyan Liu, Jiayang Li, and Peipei Wang. Analysis of spatiotemporal characteristics of big data on social media sentiment with Covid-19 epidemic topics. *Chaos, Solitons & Fractals*, 140:110123, 2020.

Emotion Detection from Natural Text Using Embedding Techniques

Samariya Nawrin and K. M. Azharul Hasan

Khulna University of Engineering and Technology, Khulna, Bangladesh

CONTENTS

11.1	Introduction	123
11.2	Related Work	124
11.3	Embedding Techniques for Emotion Detection	124
	11.3.1 fastText Embedding	124
	11.3.2 Sentence-BERT Method	126
	11.3.3 Doc2Vec	126
	11.3.4 Examples of Emotion Detection Methods	126
11.4	DocDict: A Hybrid Embedding Technique	128
	11.4.1 Hybrid Model	128
	11.4.2 Classification Method	130
11.5	Experiments	130
	11.5.1 Datasets	130
	11.5.2 Results Analysis	130
11.6	Conclusion	133

AUTOMATIC emotion detection from natural text, reviews, or blog posts is a part of affective computing and a challenging area of research that has attracted growing attention due to its potentially useful applications, especially for computational social systems. Though there has been ample research on the topic of determining sentiment based on 'positivity' or 'negativity' from texts, detecting emotions such as 'anger', 'happiness', 'sadness', or 'fear' has yet to meet a lot of advances. Emotion detection from texts such as posts and feedback can provide a better view of the public sentiment and a richer feature space for neural networks. Recent text embedding techniques have achieved promising results in different natural language processing tasks. Thus, this chapter has mulled over the current state-of-the-art embedding techniques and suggested emotion detection models that identify emotions such as 'anger', 'happiness', 'sadness', or 'fear' from texts using them. We have also introduced a new hybrid text embedding approach for emotion detection named Doc-Dict. The proposed approach effectively detects emotions from the texts using the combined effects of the popular Doc2Vec embedding technique and the Keyword-based technique. From experimental results, we have observed that the proposed DocDict method can significantly outperform other approaches for the same benchmark datasets.

11.1 INTRODUCTION

An emotion is an affective aspect of consciousness that states the feelings, such as happiness, anger, love, fear, and so on. From the recent survey of Paul Ekman, he considered discrete emotions to be within the emotions such as 'anger', 'awe', 'compassion', 'contempt', 'disgust', 'embarrassment', 'envy', 'fear', 'gratitude', 'guilt', 'happiness', 'hatred', 'love', 'shame' and 'surprise' [1]. Among them, the emotion types 'surprise' and 'disgust' can be considered subsets of other different emotions in the Emotion Space depending on the domain of use. For example, "What just happened..!" can be considered as an expression of surprise, however, depending on the context, it can also be considered as 'anger' or 'fear'. Thus in the scheme of things the context space of emotion type 'surprise' is quite ambiguous. Also, the emotion 'disgust' can be considered as a part of the emotion 'anger' and so on. So, quite surprisingly the basic emotions a human generally expresses can be broadly divided into four categories: 'happiness'/'awe'/'gratitude'/'love', 'sadness'/'guilt'/'embarrassment', 'fear'/'surprise', and 'anger'/'disgust'/'contempt'/'envy'/'hatred'. Affective computing often refers to recognizing, interpreting, processing, and simulating the emotion expressed by speech, body language, facial expressions, texts, and others [2]. Though there have been numerous works on emotion detection such as [3], very few of them are based on natural texts. From 2010 to 2020 the quantity of work on emotion detection has increased significantly based on facial expression, speech, etc. along with text-based emotion detection but only around 11.16% of the total work is based on texts [4]. This work has solely focused on text-based emotion detection. It is considered difficult to determine the expressions from texts since there is no label or speech to pinpoint the accuracy due to the high context-dependence of texts. Therefore, the first challenge is to find a way for extracting the context of a sentence and thus the emotions that can be conveyed via texts. By representing sentences with feature vectors, we can capture hidden information about a language such as text analogies or context [5]. Using this information, it is possible to detect emotions from texts. However, finding out the most probable feature vector for the machine learning model is another factor to consider. In this chapter, we show the emotion detection approach from texts using the latest embedding techniques, such as Doc2Vec [6], which is an extension of word2vec [7], Sentence-BERT or the Bidirectional Encoder Representations from Transformers (BERT) based algorithm [8] and fastText by Facebook [9]. We classify the emotions into four classes, such as 'anger', 'happiness', 'sadness', and 'fear', and have applied multiclass classification using the "one-vs-all" scheme. We extract the numerical features from the text using keywords and then give those features as input to a machine learning model for multiclass classification. We introduce a hybrid embedding method called Document Dictionary (DocDict) which combines the facilities of the keyword-based method with Doc2Vec. Therefore, the scheme is not only applicable to emotion detection but also sentence embedding and text clustering.

The rest of the chapter is organized as follows: In Section 11.2, we provide a literature review of the emotion detection methods. In Section 11.3, we briefly describe the embedding techniques. In Section 11.4, we describe our proposed hybrid method for emotion detection. In Section 11.5, we show experimental results to compare the proposed method with different embedding techniques. Finally, we briefly conclude in Section 11.6.

11.2 RELATED WORK

Emotion Detection from texts, a part of the broader area of Affective Computing, is essentially a context-based classification problem involving concepts from the domains of Natural Language Processing as well as Machine Learning. The basic difference between sentiment analysis and emotion detection is that sentiment analysis is focused on the 'positivity' and 'negativity' of sentences [10]. But emotion detection focuses on determining different human affects. The concept of affective computing started with computer recognition of human emotion in 1997 by Picard [11]. Since then various methods for emotion detection have been proposed. According to Saxena [2] (2020), emotion detection is carried out based on four major methods, such as facial expression recognition, physiological signals recognition, speech signals variation, and text semantics. Among them, the text semantics or text-based detection approach is usually divided into three main categories: keyword-based, learning-based, and hybrid recommendation approaches [12]. In this chapter, emotion recognition based on textual data using embedding techniques has been attempted and this work mainly focuses on the latest embedding techniques for emotion detection and also introduces a new approach, DocDict intending to produce better results.

11.3 EMBEDDING TECHNIQUES FOR EMOTION DETECTION

In this section, we discuss models for emotion detection using some of the latest embedding techniques that can extract features from the text. All these methods learn a d-dimensional embedding from a given text sample which represents the intrinsic properties of the text. Afterward, we introduce our extension for capturing the emotions of sentences using a hybrid approach derived from one of these methods. The process for emotion detection can be shown with a generalized workflow where the underlying method is an embedding technique (see Fig. 11.1). Here the input is a text sample and the output is a machine learning model.

11.3.1 fastText Embedding

The fastText method is a very popular idea in modern machine learning and is optimized for text representations and text classification [9]. This method instead of learning vectors for words directly represents each word using character n-grams [13]

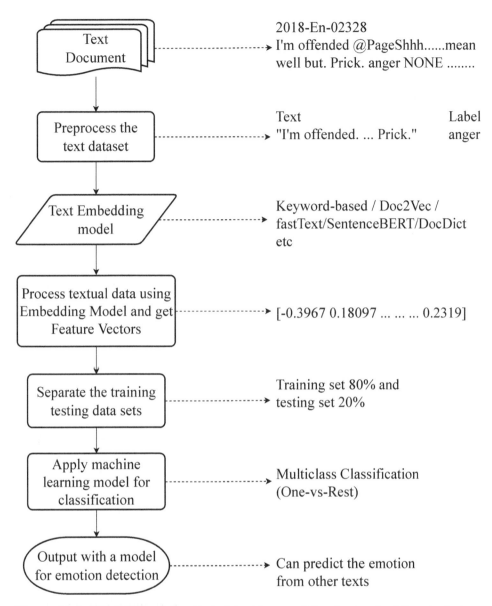

Figure 11.1: Workflow of emotion detection model using embedding techniques

and trains a skip-gram model to learn the embeddings and uses negative sub-sampling to distinguish dissimilar contexts which perform well on both large and small datasets [14]. As a result, the fastText-based emotion detection model is able to understand suffix-prefixes and the context of the text quite efficiently. We applied fastText with the pretrained unsupervised model, 'cc.en.300.bin' which produces a representation of dimension 300. The original fastText is a word embedding technique that does not return sentence embeddings. So, we used the function *get_sentence_vector* of the tool in our model that divides each word vector by its norm and then finds the average of them to create feature vectors for sentences of the text data written in

English. With these feature vectors, we produce an emotion detection model which provides fast performance compared to other approaches following the workflow of Fig. 11.1.

11.3.2 Sentence-BERT Method

The pre-trained BERT (Bidirectional Encoder Representations from Transformers) model is designed by jointly conditioning on both left and right context [15]. Sentence-BERT (SBERT) is a modification of the pre-trained BERT network to derive semantically meaningful sentence embeddings using siamese and triplet network structures and can find the foremost similar pair by comparing two sentences using cosine-similarity while maintaining the accuracy [8]. So we used SBERT with the pretrained 'bert-base-nli-mean-tokens' model from the sentence-transformers-repository that allows generating a 768-dimensional embeddings vector. We used the vector to produce an emotion detection model from texts following the steps of Fig. 11.1, though the time it takes for embedding the complete dataset is considerable because of the large vector size.

11.3.3 Doc2Vec

Doc2Vec is used to create a numeric representation of a document and the document can be of many sentences [6]. This method is based on the operational logic that the meaning of a word also depends on the document that it occurs in. The feature vector represented by Doc2Vec for classification is a concatenation of two vectors, one from the Distributed Bag of Words version of Paragraph Vector (PV-DBOW), and the other from Distributed Memory version of Paragraph Vector (PV-DM), both vector representations have 400 dimensions, though, in PV-DM, the learned vector representations for both words and paragraphs have 400 dimensions. We have used Doc2Vec model training and testing using gensim-3.8.3, iterating over the training corpus 100 times with window size 3, and used the trained model to generate embeddings for the text by passing the dataset as a list of words to the model.infer_vector function. The process of training the Doc2Vec model with word embeddings from the dataset is optional, but this method significantly affects the outcome of determining the context [16]. We trained the model with both PV-DM and PV-DBOW methods with different vector sizes up to 300, but the latter one performs significantly better.

11.3.4 Examples of Emotion Detection Methods

In Table 11.1, a few examples of each model along with the underlying methods, maximum vector size used for each emotion detection model, and the Euclidean distances of their embeddings have been shown to see the performance of different methods. As we can see from Table 11.1, the sample sentences are, "The happy days go by fast", "How unpleasant I feel right now!!", "It makes me angry" and "It is scary", where the sentences express 'happiness', 'fear'/'anger', 'anger', and 'fear' according to different models. Now even if we consider all the emotions a person might have felt while writing the text, the results remain ambiguous. There are quite a few words that showcase different meanings in different sentences and those express different emotions. Likewise, there are quite a few sentences that show different emotions in different contexts. But these methods cannot separate the words or sentences with dual meanings based on contexts. Also, this method fails to separate the emotions hidden in sarcastic reviews or sentences. All the methods in Table 11.1, other than the keyword-based method, provide very different Euclidean distances among different emotions due to having varied contexts, though even having a similar context does not guarantee to carry the same emotion.

Table 11.1: Summary of Emotion Detection Methods with Examples

Methods	Base model	Max vector size used	Examples						
			Sentences	Euclidean Distance				Predicted Class
				(i)	(ii)	(iii)	(iv)	
Keyword-based	Dictionary	300	(i) "The happy days go by fast"	0	1.4	1.4	1.4	joy
			(ii) "How unpleasant I feel right now!!"	1.4	0	1.4	1.4	fear
			(iii) "It makes me angry"	1.4	1.4	0	1.4	anger
			(iv) "It is scary"	1.4	1.4	1.4	0	fear
fastText	Skip-gram	300	(i) "The happy days go by fast"	0	0.5	0.5	0.7	joy
			(ii) "How unpleasant I feel right now!!"	0.5	0	0.5	0.6	fear
			(iii) "It makes me angry"	0.5	0.5	0	0.5	anger
			(iv) "It is scary"	0.7	0.6	0.5	0	fear
Sentence-BERT	BERT	768	(i) "The happy days go by fast"	0	19.3	19.5	18.4	joy
			(ii) "How unpleasant I feel right now!!"	19.3	0	8.7	10.3	fear
			(iii) "It makes me angry"	19.5	8.7	0	9.6	anger
			(iv) "It is scary"	18.4	10.3	9.6	0	fear
Doc2Vec	PV-DBOW, PV-DM	300	(i) "The happy days go by fast"	0	3.3	2.9	3.1	joy
			(ii) "How unpleasant I feel right now!!"	3.3	0	2.6	2.6	anger
			(iii) "It makes me angry"	2.9	2.6	0	2.1	anger
			(iv) "It is scary"	3.1	2.6	2.1	0	fear

11.4 DOCDICT: A HYBRID EMBEDDING TECHNIQUE

In this section, we propose a new hybrid model inspired by the word embedding techniques. In an attempt to find a better emotion detection model capable of removing the issues with existing methods, we intend to make more specifications on the models for emotion detection. The approach, DocDict is introduced by merging the keyword-based method with the Doc2Vec method. Surprisingly, this approach surpassed the performance of both Doc2Vec and keyword-based methods in terms of accuracy for detecting emotions from texts which have been discussed in the experimental section. In the following, we provide a detailed description of our hybrid model.

Keyword-based emotion detection is the simplest of all the methods where we can detect the associated emotions just by considering the presence or absence of a few specific words. As a baseline, we have used the keyword-based method and applied it to the dataset. To apply embedding techniques, the dataset needs to be normalized. A dictionary that includes the words or phrases expressing decisive characteristics regarding public emotion such as 'nice', 'pitiful', 'waste', 'scary', etc. These words express a few emotions like 'happiness', 'sadness', 'anger', or 'fear'. This approach is easy to implement and straightforward since it involves identifying words to search for in the text. However, it is domain-specific that relies on the presence of keywords for accurate results and often causes ambiguity. For example, we may assume two sentences, "He is happy" and "He is not happy", where the dictionary contains the word 'happy'. The feature vector will provide the same vector for both of these if no additional condition is provided. So there comes the need to preprocess the dataset. However, even after the preprocessing step, the problem with this method depends on the variety of usages and different contexts where the meanings of the keywords could be ambiguous. So, this problem is in need of finding better techniques for emotion detection.

11.4.1 Hybrid Model

From each of the above-mentioned models, we get an embedding or feature vector per text. To create a hybrid model, we take the element-wise mean of the Doc2Vec embedding vector and Keyword-based embedding vector. As a result, the process ends up adding weight to the feature vector of the Doc2Vec model which stores the contextual information based on the presence of the words collected in the dictionary. The dictionary contains words that are directly related to the emotions presented via different texts. Adding weight to such words produces a vector that specifies the emotions. The vector size for the DocDict approach has been kept up to 300. In Table 11.2, the same examples of Table 11.1 have been shown using our DocDict method. We can see that DocDict determines the emotion of the sentence, "How unpleasant I feel right now", as 'anger' even when the Keyword-based method (see Table 11.1) detects the emotion as 'fear'. In other words, this method performs well even if the context is ambiguous and is advantageous when the words present in the dictionary are also present in the text. Otherwise, this method performs the same as Doc2Vec. The Euclidean distances between the texts have also been different from that of the Keyword-based method (see Table 11.1). In addition, we provide the pseudocode of the proposed DocDict method in Algorithm 1.

Table 11.2: Examples of DocDict Method-based Emotion Detection

Sentences	Euclidean Distance				Predicted Class
	(i)	(ii)	(iii)	(iv)	
(i) "The happy days go by fast"	0	1.759	1.656	1.738	joy
(ii) "How unpleasant I feel right now!!"	1.759	0	1.494	1.501	anger
(iii) "It makes me angry"	1.656	1.494	0	1.318	anger
(iv) "It is scary"	1.738	1.501	1.318	0	fear

Algorithm 1 Create a Learning Model for DocDict Emotion Detection

---

Input: A list of sentences representing training data with known labels, T, where T_i represents i-th sentence and an ordered dictionary D, where D_j represents j-th word in the dictionary. $|T| = n$, and $|D| = m$
Output: A machine learning model $\mathcal{M}$

1: Initialize a feature matrix $F \in \mathbf{R}^{n \times m}$ with all entries being 0's.
2: **for each** $i \in n$ **do**
3:      **for each** $j \in m$ **do**
4:          $F_{ij} \leftarrow \text{Preprocess}(T_i, D_j)$
5:      **end for**
6: **end for**
7: Initialize a Doc2Vec model $Doc \in \mathbf{R}^{n \times m}$ with fixed text embedding vector size for i-th sentence $|Doc_i| = m$ and train it with the dataset words.
8: **for each** $i \in n$ **do**
9:      $Doc_i \leftarrow \text{Doc2Vec}(T_i)$
10: **end for**
11: Initialize a DocDict model $DocDict \in \mathbf{R}^{n \times m}$.
12: **for each** $i \in n$ **do**
13:      **for each** $j \in m$ **do**
14:          $DocDict_{ij} \leftarrow \text{Mean}(Doc_{ij}, F_{ij})$
15:      **end for**
16: **end for**
17: $\mathcal{M} \leftarrow$ Train a one vs. rest logistic regression model using matrix $DocDict$
18: **return** $\mathcal{M}$

11.4.2 Classification Method

Once we get the embeddings from the above technique, we treat them as features and create a classification model for the input texts. Since our dataset has more than two classes, this is a multi-class classification problem. We have used the Support Vector Classification (SVC) [17] and One-vs-Rest strategy (also called One-vs-all) of *scikit-learn* in our model which uses binary classification algorithms for multi-class classification per class with a train-test ratio of 80:20. We have four classes: 'happiness', 'sadness', 'anger', and 'fear'. So when we work on the class 'happiness', we consider 'happiness' as 1 and the rest of the classes as 0s. Again, when we work on the class 'sadness', we consider the element of the 'sadness' class to be 1, and the rest of the classes to be 0s, and so on. We use the logistic regression method of *scikit-learn* to build a model using the training dataset and predict the output for the testing dataset.

11.5 EXPERIMENTS

The experimental details are explained in the Datasets and Results Analysis subsections.

11.5.1 Datasets

The datasets we used are from WASSA-2017 shared task [18] (only the data kept as training set), SemEval [19] (only the new addition part of 2018) and ISEAR[1]. For preprocessing, we only took the data labeled as 'joy', 'sadness', 'anger', and 'fear' and discarded the texts with other labels such as 'disgust', 'guilt', etc. The different formats of datasets from varied sources have been ignored by only taking the texts and label separately. The preprocessing has been done by removing all unnecessary columns (every other column except text and emotion label) and normalizing the text (with tokenization, punctuation removal, stemming, etc.). After preprocessing the repeated texts, the number of sentences labeled 'joy', 'sadness', 'anger', and 'fear' has been 4638, 4390, 4656, and 5480, respectively. For our experiment, we merged all the raw data, shuffled them to remove any kinds of bias, and each experiment took almost up to 20,000 of the data or text sentences.

11.5.2 Results Analysis

The performance of the keyword-based method is equivalent to the number of relevant words or phrases in the word dictionary which causes an increase in the size of the feature vector (see Fig. 11.2(a)).

By varying the size of the dictionary with the size of the text document being unchanged, it has been observed that the keyword-based method is highly dependent on embedding size as shown in Fig. 11.2(a). Due to the embedding size dependency and the action of ignoring the context, the performance of the keyword-based method is poor.

---

[1]https://github.com/sinmaniphel/py_isear_dataset

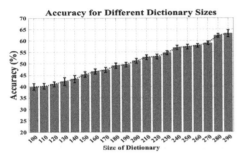

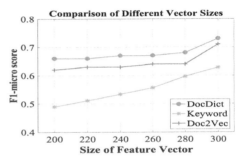

(a) Emotion Detection (keyword-based method) accuracy percentages for different dictionary sizes

(b) F1-micro score for different embedding sizes (Doc2Vec, keyword and DocDict based method)

Figure 11.2: Comparative results of different methods

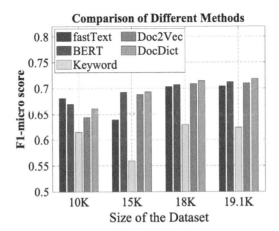

Figure 11.3: The F1-micro score comparison of different embedding methods

The DocDict method also relies on the size of the feature vector. However, the main difference from the keyword-based method is that it considers the context, and compared to Doc2Vec, it determines emotion better. After acquiring the embedding vector averaging Doc2Vec and Keyword-based vectors, we apply machine learning to train the dataset with a training testing ratio of 80:20 and then apply One-vs-Rest Classifier to them. We plot the F1-micro score for embedding sizes 200 to 300 with an interval of 20 of Doc2Vec, keyword-based method, and DocDict (see Fig. 11.2(b)), we can see that all these three methods rely on the embedding vector size but even for each vector size, the DocDict outperforms both keyword-based and Doc2Vec methods.

We have calculated the F1-micro score by measuring the F1-score of the aggregated contributions of all classes and plotted for different sizes of the dataset for each method in Fig. 11.3. In each case, we take the average result of ten runs. From Fig. 11.3 we see that among all the methods fastText and Sentence-BERT perform comparatively well, in most of the cases and Doc2Vec also performs well with a higher number of data. The keyword-based method does not perform satisfactorily in most cases. However, the proposed DocDict performs the best when adequate data is

Table 11.3: Confusion Matrix of FastText-based Model

FastText Confusion Matrix				
All Classes	anger	fear	joy	sadness
anger	0.553	0.136	0.112	0.199
fear	0.042	0.817	0.063	0.078
joy	0.059	0.092	0.693	0.156
sadness	0.077	0.088	0.092	0.743

taken. To measure the probability of misclassification, we have shown the normalized confusion matrix [20] of each emotion detection method (see Table 11.3, Table 11.4, Table 11.5, Table 11.6, and Table 11.7) that is often used to describe the performance of a classification model on the test data for which the labels are known. Since we worked on multiclass classification and the labels are binarized under a One-vs-Rest way, the confusion matrix calculates one confusion matrix between every two classes for misclassification [21]. Here the higher probability values are highlighted using green shades and the lower probability values are highlighted using red shades. As we can see, DocDict predicts most classes accurately but confuses mostly in the case of 'anger' class with 'sadness', 'fear' and 'joy' and between 'joy' and 'sadness'.

Table 11.4: Confusion Matrix of Sentence-BERT-based Model

Sentence-BERT Confusion Matrix				
All Classes	anger	fear	joy	sadness
anger	0.577	0.099	0.154	0.170
fear	0.048	0.843	0.047	0.062
joy	0.086	0.079	0.682	0.153
sadness	0.113	0.082	0.114	0.691

Table 11.5: Confusion Matrix of Keyword-based Model

Keyword-based Confusion Matrix				
All Classes	anger	fear	joy	sadness
anger	0.686	0.087	0.162	0.065
fear	0.385	0.395	0.194	0.026
joy	0.293	0.055	0.605	0.047
sadness	0.322	0.065	0.167	0.446

We also performed the Friedman test on the models' F1 scores of 15 consecutive runs to determine the statistical significance of our model [22]. The experiment was run with a different number of data in a similar environment for all the models and we found that the $\tilde{\chi}^2$ statistic is 30.7067 (degree of freedom = 4, N = 15). The p-value for our model is less than 0.00001 which indicates statistically very strong evidence

Table 11.6: Confusion Matrix of Doc2Vec-based Model

Doc2Vec Confusion Matrix				
All Classes	anger	fear	joy	sadness
anger	0.557	0.131	0.143	0.169
fear	0.051	0.811	0.066	0.072
joy	0.074	0.080	0.720	0.126
sadness	0.073	0.079	0.080	0.768

Table 11.7: Confusion Matrix of DocDict Model

DocDict Confusion Matrix				
All Classes	anger	fear	joy	sadness
anger	0.596	0.129	0.117	0.158
fear	0.049	0.814	0.070	0.067
joy	0.078	0.071	0.740	0.111
sadness	0.066	0.067	0.068	0.799

against the null hypothesis as the result is significant at $p < 0.01$. Therefore, we may reject the null hypothesis for the entire population and accept the alternative hypothesis and conclude that the proposed hybrid model works well for sentence embedding and emotion detection from natural text.

11.6 CONCLUSION

In this chapter, we have evaluated the current state-of-the-art embedding techniques for emotion detection along with a Keyword-based method. Then, we have proposed and evaluated a hybrid sentence embedding technique. With varying dictionary elements, the proposed method can be specified for any type of problem related to text embedding. We compared different types of emotion detection models using a benchmark dataset and found that our proposed hybrid model outperforms all other methods. More specifically the proposed method achieved an F1-micro score of 0.74 for a widely used benchmark dataset. With a well-performing model, we empirically showed that there is ample scope for specification in the latest text embedding techniques.

ACKNOWLEDGMENTS

We would like to thank all the anonymous reviewers for their feedback. We would also like to thank Md. Khaledur Rahman for helpful discussion on embedding techniques.

Bibliography

[1] Ekman, P. What scientists who study emotion agree about. *Perspectives On Psychological Science.* **11**, 31-34 (2016)

[2] Saxena, A., Khanna, A. & Gupta, D. Emotion recognition and detection methods: A comprehensive survey. *J. Of Artificial Intelligence And Systems.* **2**, 53-79 (2020)

[3] Torres P, E., Torres, E., Hernández-Álvarez, M., Yoo, S. EEG-based BCI emotion recognition: A survey. *Sensors.* **20**, 5083 (2020)

[4] Acheampong, F., Wenyu, C. & Nunoo-Mensah, H. Text-based emotion detection: Advances, challenges, and opportunities. *Engineering Reports.* **2**, e12189 (2020)

[5] Kusner, M., Sun, Y., Kolkin, N. & Weinberger, K. From word embeddings to document distances. *Proceedings Of ICML.* pp. 957-966 (2015)

[6] Le, Q. & Mikolov, T. Distributed representations of sentences and documents. *Proceedings Of ICML.* pp. 1188-1196 (2014)

[7] Mikolov, T., Chen, K., Corrado, G. & Dean, J. Efficient estimation of word representations in vector space. *ArXiv:1301.3781.* (2013)

[8] Reimers, N. & Gurevych, I. Sentence-bert: Sentence embeddings using siamese bert-networks. *ArXiv:1908.10084.* (2019)

[9] Joulin, A., Grave, E., Bojanowski, P. & Mikolov, T. Bag of tricks for efficient text classification. *ArXiv:1607.01759.* (2016)

[10] Mukherjee, S. Sentiment analysis. *ML. NET Revealed.* pp. 113-127 (2021)

[11] Picard, R. Affective computing. MIT Press (2000)

[12] Kao, E., Liu, C., Yang, T., Hsieh, C. & Soo, V. Towards text-based emotion detection a survey and possible improvements. *Proceedings Of ICIME.* pp. 70-74 (2009)

[13] Wang, S. & Manning, C. Baselines and bigrams: Simple, good sentiment and topic classification. *Proceedings Of ACL.* pp. 90-94 (2012)

[14] Mikolov, T., Sutskever, I., Chen, K., Corrado, G. & Dean, J. Distributed representations of words and phrases and their compositionality. *ArXiv:1310.4546.* (2013)

[15] Devlin, J., Chang, M., Lee, K. & Toutanova, K. Bert: Pre-training of deep bidirectional transformers for language understanding. *ArXiv:1810.04805.* (2018)

[16] Lau, J. & Baldwin, T. An empirical evaluation of doc2vec with practical insights into document embedding generation. *ArXiv:1607.05368.* (2016)

[17] Cortes, C. & Vapnik, V. Support-vector networks. *Machine Learning.* **20**, 273-297 (1995)

[18] Mohammad, S. & Bravo-Marquez, F. WASSA-2017 shared task on emotion intensity. *ArXiv:1708.03700.* (2017)

[19] Mohammad, S., Bravo-Marquez, F., Salameh, M. & Kiritchenko, S. Semeval-2018 task 1: Affect in tweets. *Proceedings Of International Workshop On Semantic Evaluation.* pp. 1-17 (2018)

[20] Stehman, S. Selecting and interpreting measures of thematic classification accuracy. *Remote Sensing Of Environment.* **62**, 77-89 (1997)

[21] Piryonesi, S. & El-Diraby, T. Data analytics in asset management: Cost-effective prediction of the pavement condition index. *Journal Of Infrastructure Systems.* **26**, 04019036 (2020)

[22] Eisinga, R., Heskes, T., Pelzer, B. & Te Grotenhuis, M. Exact p-values for pairwise comparison of Friedman rank sums, with application to comparing classifiers. *BMC Bioinformatics.* **18**, 1-18 (2017)

CHAPTER 12

Performance Analysis of Energy-Aware DTN Routing Protocols in Opportunistic Networks

Taslima Akhter and Md. Sharif Hossen

Comilla University, Cumilla, Bangladesh

CONTENTS

12.1 Introduction 137
12.2 Related Work 138
12.3 Considered DTN Routing Protocols 138
    12.3.1 Epidemic 138
    12.3.2 Spray-and-Wait (SAW) 138
    12.3.3 PRoPHET 138
    12.3.4 MaxProp 139
    12.3.5 Spray-and-Focus (SNF) 139
12.4 Opportunistic Network Environment Simulator 139
12.5 Simulation and Results 139
    12.5.1 Delivery Probability 139
        12.5.1.1 Delivery Probability with Varying Number of Nodes and Buffer Sizes 140
        12.5.1.2 Delivery Probability with Varying Simulation Time and TTL (Time-to-live) 141
    12.5.2 Average Remaining Energy 142
        12.5.2.1 Average Remaining Energy with Varying Number of Nodes and Buffer Sizes 142
    12.5.3 Average Remaining Energy with Varying Simulation Time and TTL 143
    12.5.4 Average Latency 144
        12.5.4.1 Average Latency with Varying Number of Nodes and Buffer Sizes 144
        12.5.4.2 Average Latency with Varying Simulation Time and TTL (Time-to-live) 145
    12.5.5 Overhead Ratio 146

12.5.5.1   Overhead Ratio with Varying Number of Nodes and
Buffer Sizes 146
12.5.5.2   Overhead Ratio with Varying Simulation Time and
TTL (time-to-live) 147
12.6   Conclusion and Future Work 147

I N CHALLENGING ENVIRONMENTS where a fully connected path does not exist between source and destination, data can be transferred using Delay Tolerance Networking. Generally, neighboring nodes receive transmitted message copies from source nodes. Receiving transmitted copies of the message from one neighbor to another neighbor node is continued until it reaches its exact destination. Several DTN routing protocols are proposed to improve the performance and reduce resource consumption. Hence, most of the protocols are not aware of energy consumption. Modern technology proposed various significant features in smartphones, tablets, PCs, etc., which consume most of the power of batteries but the available power in the devices is limited. Reducing the consumption of energy resources is important in the protocol implementation. In this chapter, we design and investigate the performance of energy-aware routing protocols based on five well-known DTN routing protocols: Epidemic, spray-and-wait, spray-and-focus, PRoPHET, and MaxProp. The simulation results indicate that energy aware spray-and-focus deserves higher delivery probability, lower average latency, and lower overhead ratio compared to other considered routings. While energy aware MaxProp ensures maximum average remaining energy.

12.1 INTRODUCTION

The path between sending and receiving nodes in the delay tolerance network is highly unstable. Paths from source to destination for a specific connection are often discovered changed or broken frequently while the network is quite sparse [1]. There are lots of applications of a delay tolerance network. It is mostly used in deep-sea communication, internet access to vehicles by connecting to roadside wireless base stations, monitoring and tracking wildlife, environmental monitoring like water quality monitoring and roadside noise monitoring, interplanetary internet, etc. [2]. Energy consumption is a major concept in the performance and deployment of modern computational and communication systems [3]. Energy is the main factor in delivering the message from node to node. Hardware devices have limited energy. It is essential to consider the remaining energy of the node [4]. If a device does not contain sufficient energy, a message will not be delivered. To investigate the energy, various factors are considered like threshold value, the remaining energy of the node, and the number of dead nodes, scan energy, transmit energy, base energy, and response energy. Based on these factors comparison is made. The goal of this research is to implement DTN routing protocols Epidemic, PRoPHET, MaxProp, spray-and-wait, spray-and-focus with energy-efficient constraints. Here, we consider four performance parameters message delivery probability, average latency and overhead ratio, average remaining energy with the changing values of the number of nodes, simulation time, TTL (time-to-live), and buffer size, respectively. When energy is the main factor, it is essential to choose a router with less energy consumption. This comparison gives a better idea in the cases where choosing routers depends on different area requirements. The chapter is organized as follows. In Section 12.2, we discuss the protocols considered in this research. In Section 12.3, we present the simulation environment. In Section 12.4, we compare and discuss simulation results with parameters. Finally, in Section 12.5, we discuss the overall outcome and future works.

12.2   RELATED WORK

Cabacas et al. investigated the comparison between the average remaining energy and the number of dead nodes. The average remaining energy is decreased with the increasing value of nodes. Here, message generation time is an important factor in reducing message flow in the network. Less message flow results in dead nodes that reduce the energy consumption of nodes [10]. The amount of energy needed for sending and receiving a message is investigated in Rodrigues et al. (2012). This chapter also discusses how much energy is needed for finding a neighboring node [11]. Bista et al. (2014) use three mobility models to analyze their energy expense rate. Also, they compare their message delivery probability and message overhead ratio [12].

12.3   CONSIDERED DTN ROUTING PROTOCOLS

In this chapter, five popular routing protocols are used, which are described below.

12.3.1   Epidemic

Epidemic routing protocol is a flooding-based routing protocol [13]. It ensures high message delivery and latency because it sends message copies to all neighboring nodes. As messages are stored in the buffer it consumes resources.

12.3.2   Spray-and-Wait (SAW)

Spray-and-wait is a forwarding-based routing proposed by Spyropoulos et al., which attempt to gain benefits of delivery probability in replication based routing with low resource utilization. It consists of two phases [1]. **Spray:** L copies forwarded by the source to L relays, then go to the second phase after being received by intermediate nodes. **Wait:** Messages received in the node buffer and wait for direct transmission to the destination.

12.3.3   PRoPHET

PRoPHET maintains a probability set for the successful delivery of messages and also exploits the non-randomness of the real world. It only replicates the message when there is a better chance of delivering it. This strategy was first documented in a paper from 2003 [5].

12.3.4 MaxProp

MaxProp is naturally flooding-based. The destination of each message is stored in an ordered queue. Based on this queue, it determines which messages should be transmitted first and which messages should be dropped first [15]. All encounters do not attempt to be replicated and transferred [6].

12.3.5 Spray-and-Focus (SNF)

Spray-and-focus is similar to spray-and-wait protocol. The first step of both protocols is similar. The only difference is the focus step. It does not wait for direct delivery to the destination node. It uses a utility driven model, keeps the relay message transmission copy for the individual message, and it is an instant alternative to the focusing stage [8].

12.4 OPPORTUNISTIC NETWORK ENVIRONMENT SIMULATOR

For making complex simulations more realistic, the Opportunistic Networking Environment (ONE) simulator is used [9]. The simulation environment can be set up by Java programming language. Inter-node contacts, routing and message handling are the main functions of the ONE simulator. The result can be visualized by one simulator using graphical user interface. Energy module set up is an important factor in this case. Based on the available energy resources, DTN protocols make forwarding decisions. Energy module is set up using the routing module (as shown in Figure 12.1). Energy resources are replenished from sources such as solar cells.

12.5 SIMULATION AND RESULTS

Parameters of simulation and node energy setting are specified in Table 12.1 and Table 12.2, respectively. Shortest path map-based movement model controls mobile node movement in simulation environments. We assume that nodes do not charge their batteries during simulation; if all the energy consumed nodes become dead. The varied parameters are No. of nodes, buffer size, TTL, and simulation time, which are changed with time. Initial energy, scan energy, and transmit energy are node energy parameters.

12.5.1 Delivery Probability

Delivery probability is the ratio of number of delivered messages and total created messages [14].

$$Delivery\ Probability = \frac{Number\ of\ Messages\ Delivered}{Number\ of\ Messages\ Created} \qquad (12.1)$$

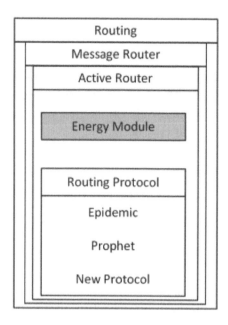

Figure 12.1: Energy module implementation in ONE simulator [9].

Table 12.1: Simulation Settings

Parameters	Value
Simulation area	4500m x 3400m
No. of node	50-260
Movement model	Shortest path map based movement
Message size	1M
Buffer size	5M-50M
Message generation interval	20s-40s
Simulation time	12-96 hours
Update interval	100
Message TTL	60-300

Table 12.2: Node Energy Parameters

Parameters	Value
Initial energy	3000k, 3240k
Scan energy	38.61
Transmit energy	51.47

12.5.1.1 Delivery Probability with Varying Number of Nodes and Buffer Sizes

Figures 12.2 and 12.3 show delivery probability with changing nodes and buffer size. In both cases, delivery probability is higher with increasing value of buffer size and node. Energy aware spray and focus shows the highest delivery probability. On the other side, energy aware PRoPHET and energy aware epidemic show the lowest performance. Energy aware MaxProp and energy aware spray-and-wait show medium performance.

12.5.1.2 Delivery Probability with Varying Simulation Time and TTL (Time-to-live)

Figures 12.4 and 12.5 depict delivery probability with changing the value of simulation time and TTL. The energy aware spray-and-focus router shows a higher delivery probability in both cases and is constant with the increasing simulation time. Energy aware PRoPHET shows minimum performance in this case. Energy MaxProp and spray-and-wait show slightly better performance than energy aware epidemic and PRoPHET with TTL.

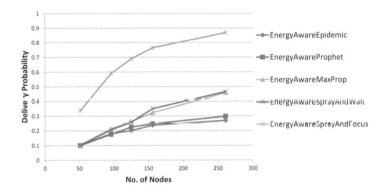

Figure 12.2: Delivery probability vs number of nodes.

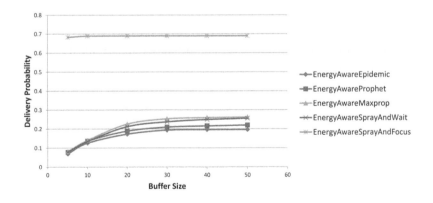

Figure 12.3: Delivery probability vs buffer size.

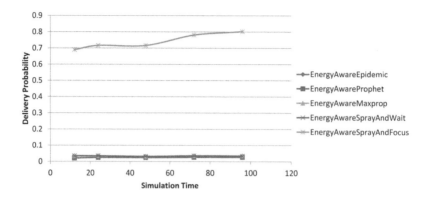

Figure 12.4: Delivery probability vs simulation time.

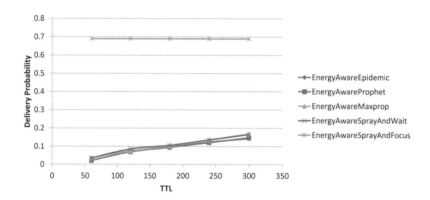

Figure 12.5: Delivery probability vs TTL.

12.5.2   Average Remaining Energy

The average remaining energy is the average amount of the node's energy remaining after the complete simulation.

$$Average\,Remaining\,Energy = \frac{Total\,Remaining\,Energy}{Total\,Number\,of\,Nodes} \qquad (12.2)$$

12.5.2.1   Average Remaining Energy with Varying Number of Nodes and Buffer Sizes

When node density is increased it needs more energy for scanning and transmitting messages. Here we use energy aware routers which take into account the energy constraints for improving performance. From Figures 12.6 and 12.7, we can see the remaining energy in energy aware spray-and-wait, MaxProp, and Epidemic router is higher. Following the figures we cannot say energy aware PRoPHET is energy efficient; energy aware spray-and-focus is better than energy aware PRoPHET.

12.5.3 Average Remaining Energy with Varying Simulation Time and TTL

In Figures 12.8 and 12.9, if simulation time and TTL increase the average remaining energy will decrease. If a message remains in network for more time it consumes more energy. In both figures, we can see energy aware MaxProp shows the best performance, while energy aware PRoPHET shows the worst performance. Energy aware spray-and-wait, epidemic, and spray-and-focus exhibit intermediary performance in this case.

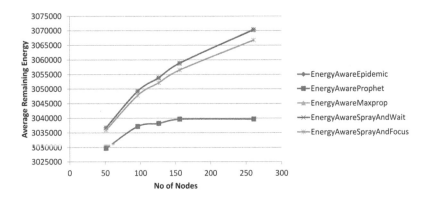

Figure 12.6: Average remaining energy vs number of nodes.

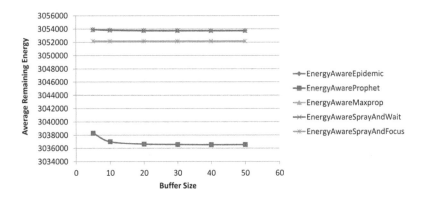

Figure 12.7: Average remaining energy vs buffer size.

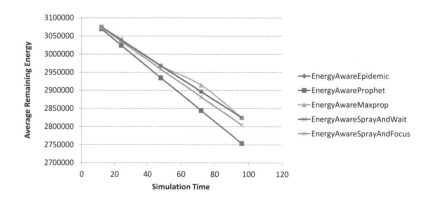

Figure 12.8: Average remaining energy vs simulation time.

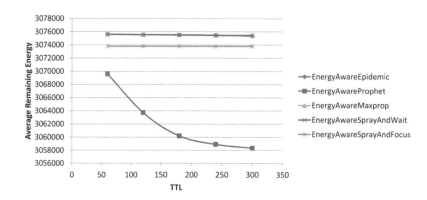

Figure 12.9: Average remaining energy vs TTL.

12.5.4 Average Latency

Average latency is the average time taken by the message to reach the destination node from source node [14].

$$Average\,Latency = \sum_{i-1}^{n} \frac{Time\,Message\,Received - Time\,Message\,Produced}{Number\,of\,Messages\,Received}$$

$$(12.3)$$

12.5.4.1 Average Latency with Varying Number of Nodes and Buffer Sizes

Figures 12.10 and 12.11 show average latency with increasing number of node and buffer size. Energy aware spray-and-focus has the lowest value for both cases. In Figure 12.10 energy aware PRoPHET has height average latency. In Figure 12.11

energy aware MaxProp shows high latency within buffer size 20M, and PRoPHET shows high latency for buffer size exceeding 30M. Energy aware spray-and-focus show lower average latency.

12.5.4.2   Average Latency with Varying Simulation Time and TTL (Time-to-live)

Figure 12.12 shows average latency with changing simulation time. In Figure 12.13 we can see energy aware spray-and-focus gives higher latency for simulation time for more than two days. We can see energy aware PRoPHET also gives lower latency while other routers give slightly higher latency. In Figure 12.13 we can see the average latency of energy aware spray-and-focus is constant with TTL (time-to-live). The average latency of other routers gives almost the same latency as TTL (Time-to-live).

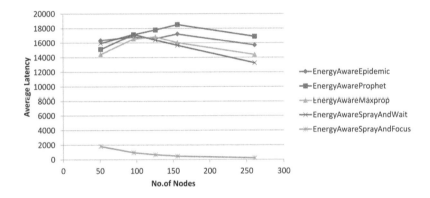

Figure 12.10: Average latency vs number of nodes.

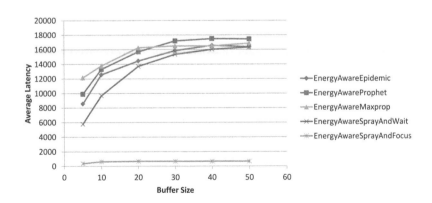

Figure 12.11: Average latency vs buffer size.

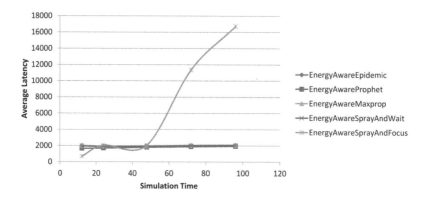

Figure 12.12: Average latency vs simulation time.

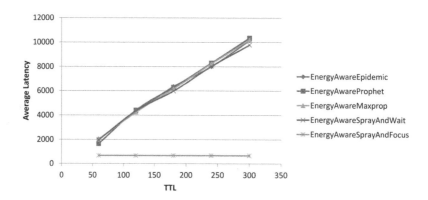

Figure 12.13: Average latency vs TTL.

12.5.5 Overhead Ratio

The number of message transmissions performed for each created message is called overhead ratio [14].

$$Overhead\,Ratio = \frac{R\;\;D}{D} \qquad (12.4)$$

where R is the number of messages forwarded by relay nodes, and D is the number of messages delivered to their destination.

12.5.5.1 Overhead Ratio with Varying Number of Nodes and Buffer Sizes

Figures 12.14 and 12.15 show overhead ratio with changing node density and buffer size. Graphs show that energy aware epidemic has a maximum overhead ratio. The overhead ratio of energy aware spray-and-focus router is almost zero because spray-and-focus follows the most technical way to limit the replication of copies.

12.5.5.2 Overhead Ratio with Varying Simulation Time and TTL (time-to-live)

Figure 12.16 shows the overhead ratio with increasing simulation time. Energy aware MaxProp shows higher overhead ratio within a simulation of two days (48 hours). Energy aware epidemic shows a higher overhead ratio for simulation time 2-4 days. Figure 12.17 shows overhead ratio with TTL. As TTL is increased, overhead ratio is decreased. Energy aware Epidemic has a high overhead ratio and energy aware spray-and-focus has the lowest overhead ratio for both cases.

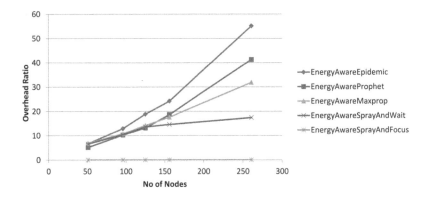

Figure 12.14: Overhead ratio vs number of nodes.

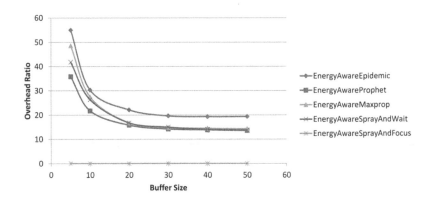

Figure 12.15: Overhead ratio vs buffer size.

12.6 CONCLUSION AND FUTURE WORK

Energy is an important factor in data transmission processes; it consumes more energy results in dead nodes. In this chapter, we implement five DTN routing protocols with energy-efficient strategies and name them as energy aware Epidemic, energy

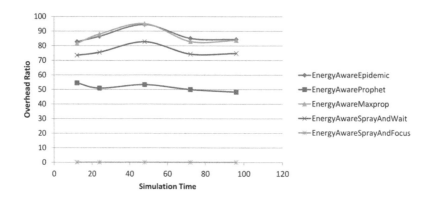

Figure 12.16: Overhead ratio vs simulation time.

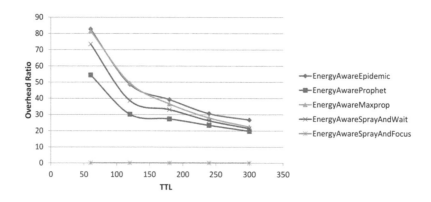

Figure 12.17: Overhead ratio vs TTL.

aware spray-and-wait, energy aware spray-and-focus, energy aware MaxProp, and energy aware PRoPHET. We do the simulation using ONE simulator and investigate the performance of these routing techniques for number of nodes, simulation time, TTL, and buffer size. Here, we consider four performance metrics, namely, average remaining energy, delivery probability, average latency, and overhead ratio. From all the analysis, we can say that energy aware spray-and-focus has a high delivery probability among others routing protocols. Energy aware MaxProp shows high average remaining energy. Next, energy aware Epidemic and energy aware spray-and-wait have higher average remaining energy. For long distance message transfer and long life, these three routing protocols will be useful. Energy aware spray-and-focus shows lower average latency and overhead ratio, which is essential for improving network performance. Although our energy resources are limited, we have to get the best performance within these resources. All routing protocols have some limitations and benefits; it is essential to integrate the benefits of the routing protocols. In the near future, we would like to introduce a new routing protocol that will consume less energy with high delivery probability and reduce network overhead and latency.

Bibliography

[1] T. Spyropoulos, K. Psounis, and C. S. Raghavendra, "Spray and wait: An efficient routing scheme for intermittently connected mobile networks," in Proc. ACM SIGCOMM Workshop on Delay-tolerant Networking, New York, NY, USA, 2005, pp. 252-259.

[2] Vandana Kushwaha and Ratneshwer Gupta, "Delay Tolerant Networks: Architecture, Routing, Congestion, and Security Issues," in proc. IGI global, 2019.

[3] Huang, C. M., Lan, K. C., and Tsai, C. Z., "A survey of opportunistic networks," In Advanced Information Networking and Applications-Workshops, 2008, AINAW 2008, 22nd International Conference on (pp. 1672-1677), IEEE.

[4] Friedman, R., Kogan, A., and Krivolapov, Y., "On power and throughput trade-offs of wifi and bluetooth in smartphones. Mobile Computing," IEEE Transactions on, 12(7), 1363-1376, 2018.

[5] Doria, and O. Scheln, "Probabilistic routing in intermittently connected networks". In Proceedings of the Fourth ACM International Symposium on Mobile Ad Hoc Networking and Computing (MobiHoc), 2003.

[6] J. Burgess, B. Gallagher, D. Jensen, and B. N. Levine, "MaxProp: Routing for Vehicle-Based Disruption-Tolerant Networks," in Infocom, pp. 1-11, 2006.

[7] Agussalim and Masato Tsuru, "Spray Router with Node Location Dependent Remaining-TTL Message Scheduling in DTNs".

[8] A. Keranen, "Opportunistic network environment simulator," Special Assignment report, Helsinki University of Technology, Department of Communications and Networking, 2008.

[9] Kaviani, M., Kusy, B., Jurdak, R., Bergmann, N., Liu, V., "Energy-Aware Forwarding Strategies for Delay Tolerant Network Routing Protocols," Journal of Sensor and Actuator Networks, 5(4), 18,2016, doi:10.3390/jsan5040018.

[10] Cabacas, R. A., Nakamura, H., and Ra, I. H. "Energy Consumption Analysis of Delay Tolerant Network Routing Protocols", International Journal of Software Engineering and Its Applications, 8(2), 1-10, 2014.

[11] Silva, D. R., Costa, A., and Macedo, J. "Energy impact analysis on DTN routing protocols", 2012.

[12] Bista, B. B. and Rawat, D. B. "Energy Consumption and Performance of Delay Tolerant Network Routing Protocols under Different Mobility Models", 2016.

[13] E.P. Jones and P.A. Ward, "Routing strategies for delay-tolerant networks," http://citeseerx.ist.psu.edu/viewdoc/download?, 2006.

[14] Md. Sharif Hossen and Muhammad Sajjadur Rahim, "Performance Analysis of Delay-Tolerant Routing Protocols in Intermittently Connected Mobile Networks", 2015.

[15] M. Boudguig and A. Abdali, "New DTN Routing Algorithm," International Journal of Computer Science Issues (IJCSI), vol. 10, 2013.

CHAPTER 13

Performance Investigation among Heterogeneous Routing Techniques in Wireless Sensor Networks

Taspia Salam and Md. Sharif Hossen

Comilla University, Cumilla, Bangladesh

CONTENTS

13.1   Introduction 152
    13.1.1 Motivation 152
    13.1.2 Shortcomings of this Research 153
13.2   Literature Survey 153
13.3   Representation of Hierarchical Routing Techniques 153
    13.3.1 Low Energy Adaptive Clustering Hierarchy Routing Protocol .. 154
    13.3.2 Energy-Aware Multihop Multipath Routing Protocol 154
    13.3.3 Threshold Sensitive Energy Efficient Sensor Network Routing
            Protocol 154
13.4   Simulation Tools and Environmental Settings 154
13.5   Performance Evaluation 155
    13.5.1 Network Lifetime 155
    13.5.2 Energy Consumption 156
    13.5.3 Time and Space Complexities 157
    13.5.4 Throughput 158
13.6   Discussion 159
13.7   Conclusion and Future Works 160

IN recent years, the necessity of Wireless Sensor Networks (WSNs) is growing in the field of communication that consists of randomly organized sensors in the network. Moreover, these sensors can sense temperature, humidity, and many more environmental parameters that are provided to the relevant users. However, this genus of the network is resource constraint, whilst to have the best outcomes from this network, researchers design various routing strategies to reduce energy consumption. One of the most essential techniques is hierarchical routing protocols that use the clustering method. Furthermore, through this technique, the network life can be extended and data can be conveyed efficiently. This chapter explores the investigation of the performance among heterogeneous LEACH, EAMMH, and TEEN routings in terms of network lifetime, stability period, consumed energy, time and space complexity, and throughput using MATLAB. For the heterogeneous networks, TEEN outperforms other routings, e.g., EAMMH and LEACH, because it ensures extended network lifetime with longer stability period, lower energy consumption, lower time and space complexity, and lower throughput as it reduces data redundancy.

13.1 INTRODUCTION

Wireless communication technology has advanced rapidly with its low power consumption, low cost, and self-organization. Particularly, energy savings is the major concern of this network. There are numerous techniques through which it is possible to save the energy of these sensor nodes. The clustering technique is such a method of picking up energy efficiency; moreover, this method can be incorporated with homogeneous and heterogeneous setups [Dahiya et al., 2017]. Homogeneous nodes have the same energy, memory space, processing speed, and the nodes of different energy and processing speed are known as heterogeneous nodes [Ngangbam et al., 2019]. WSNs require dissimilar routing protocols to enhance the performance of numerous applications that are crucial to convey data. The first hierarchical and cluster-oriented routing technique that is intended to overcome energy consumption is known as Low Energy Adaptive Clustering Hierarchy (LEACH) routing. However, it is just suitable for single-hop communication [Huang et al., 2018]. On the other hand, a routing technique that is generally heuristic and balances the communication load according to the residual node energy is known as Energy-Aware Multihop Multipath (EAMMH) routing procedure [Chaudhary et al., 2021]. Another hierarchical and reactive routing technique that utilizes energy efficiently and provides less throughput is called Threshold Sensitive Energy Efficient sensor Network (TEEN) strategy [Dener, 2018].

We will analyze the outcome of the heterogeneous LEACH, EAMMH, and TEEN routing procedures in this chapter by utilizing MATLAB in terms of considered metrics. From the outset, in Section 13.2, we shortly describe the literature survey. LEACH, EAMMH, and TEEN routings are described in Section 13.3. At that point, Section 13.4 contains the simulation tools and environmental settings. From that point onward, in Sections 13.5 and 13.6, we address the performance metrics of considered routing techniques and discussion consecutively. Finally, Section 13.7 covers the conclusion of this research and future works.

13.1.1 Motivation

Our investigation is based on a heterogeneous environment and we compare three heterogeneous routing strategies, namely, LEACH, EAMMH, and TEEN, to show which works better for the real world. For example, if we think of a smart city, there will be some light sensors that can light up when someone passes. If any accident occurs, the temperature of the atmosphere will be increased and will inform the specific traffic to handle it. In that case, we need to have a protocol that is event-driven and can properly send data to the user without any delay and error. These practical events stimulate us to compare these three methods in the heterogeneous environment.

13.1.2   Shortcomings of this Research

In this research, simulation results outline that TEEN works better than others. However, the selection of Cluster head (CH) in TEEN is only based on a threshold value which is not sufficient. CH plays a significant role in data transfer to the BS, and in the heterogeneous environment, both the normal and advanced nodes have the chance to be a CH. If any normal node can select as CH, then it will die soon and the energy of the network will run out rapidly. As a consequence, the efficiency of TEEN will be diminished.

13.2   LITERATURE SURVEY

There are numerous routing strategies in WSNs that are intended to extend the lifetime of a network and make interactive communication. Some of them are direct communication and others are low-energy multihop communication, but they are inefficient in terms of network lifetime. The concept of hierarchical structures, along with the clustering method, provides a thought for improving energy savings in WSNs. Some of the works on hierarchical routings are shown in Table 13.1 which is given below.

Table 13.1: Related works on hierarchical routings.

Strategies	Consumption of Energy	Stability Period	Lifetime of Network
LEACH [Heinzelman et al., 2000]	High	Limited	Medium
B-LEACH [Depedri et al., 2011]	Medium	Good	Medium
K-LEACH [Bakaraniya et al., 2013]	Medium	Good	Moderate
ME-LEACH [Kumar et al., 2008]	Medium	Limited	Medium
TEEN [Manjeshwar and Agrawal, 2001]	Maximum	Good	Good

13.3   REPRESENTATION OF HIERARCHICAL ROUTING TECHNIQUES

WSNs are comprised of stationary or mobile sensor nodes that are exceedingly adaptable and may be used to facilitate a wide range of applications in several settings.

In this network, the consumption of energy is one of the most important issues. The traditional routing protocols for WSN may not be optimal in terms of energy consumption. Hierarchical routing protocols are more energy-efficient than other protocols. These strategies can be efficient in terms of energy and scalability.

13.3.1 Low Energy Adaptive Clustering Hierarchy Routing Protocol

Low Energy Adaptive Clustering Hierarchy (LEACH) is the first hierarchical routing technique that is self-organized, cluster-based, and propagates energy evenly through randomized rotation of CH to all sensors. This technique follows two methods, namely, set-up and steady-state phase, which are responsible for creating clusters and data transmission respectively (Ahmed et al., 2019). Cluster head (CH) is a high energy sensor node which creates and manipulates a Time Division Multiple Access (TDMA) schedule after all nodes have been integrated into the cluster and conveys the message by using the Code Division Multiple Access (CDMA) procedure (Liang et al., 2019).

13.3.2 Energy-Aware Multihop Multipath Routing Protocol

This is a hierarchical protocol for multihop and energy-aware intra-cluster techniques. It uses a similar clustering process as LEACH. However, there is a difference between LEACH and EAMMH. EAMMH utilizes neighbor search algorithms to find out adjacent nodes and a routing table is maintained by all nodes for updated data communication. As it supports the multihop features, this methodology is applicable for long-distance data transmission [Salam and Hossen, 2020].

13.3.3 Threshold Sensitive Energy Efficient Sensor Network Routing Protocol

Threshold Sensitive Energy Efficient Sensor Network (TEEN) is a kind of reactive hierarchical procedure in which all of the sensors uninterruptedly sense the environment and convey the data when any event occurs which assists the users to have time-critical data (Lee et al., 2013). It utilizes the procedure of LEACH to form a cluster. A CH drives two categories of data to its neighbors:
(i) Hard threshold (HT) is for the identification of the characteristics.
(ii) Soft threshold (ST) is a simple difference in the assessment of the characteristic identified that stimulates the switching node. The nodes persistently recognize their environment and identify the transmission value. The nodes can communicate the identified value if they can fulfill the following criteria:
(a) The current estimation of the identified attribute is greater than HT.
(b) The current estimation of the identified attribute from the sensed value is greater than or equal to ST. Both of these threshold values restrict the superfluous transmissions [Ge et al., 2018].

13.4 SIMULATION TOOLS AND ENVIRONMENTAL SETTINGS

We concentrate on the investigation of routing performance among heterogeneous LEACH, EAMMH, and TEEN in terms of network lifetime, stability period, consumed energy, time and space complexity, and throughput using MATLAB simulator. The simulation environment is presented in Table 13.2 and the following metrics are used to compare among routing strategies which are given below:

(a) Network Lifetime signifies the number of alive nodes per round.

(b) Stability Period defines the interval between the start of the network and the death of the first sensor node.

(c) Energy Consumption defines how much energy is depleted for data transmission.

(d) Throughput signifies the overall rate of data sent across the network.

(e) Time Complexity defines how much time and space a procedure requires for completion.

(f) Space Complexity defines how much space a procedure requires for completion.

Table 13.2: Parameters for simulation.

Strategies	Values
Region of Simulation	(100×100) m^2
Position for Base Station	(50 m, 50 m)
Number of Nodes (n)	100,200,600,1000
Initial Energy (Eo)	0.5 J
Number of Rounds (r)	2500
Initial Optimal Probability (P)	0.1, 0.2
Proportion of Advanced Nodes (m)	0.2
Energy for Free Space (Efs)	10 pJ
Energy for Multipath Propagation (Emp)	0.0013 pJ
Energy for Data Aggregation (EDA)	5 nJ/bit
Energy for Transmission (ETX)	50 nJ/bit
Energy for Reception (ERX)	50 nJ/bit
Size of Packet	4000 bits
The portion of Additional Energy for Advanced Nodes (a)	1 J

13.5 PERFORMANCE EVALUATION

In our investigation, the routing performance is analyzed among heterogeneous LEACH, EAMMH, and TEEN in terms of network lifetime, stability period, consumed energy, time and space complexity, and throughput.

13.5.1 Network Lifetime

The lifetime of a network is an essential parameter that identifies the number of alive nodes per round. Figures 13.1 and 13.2 demonstrate that the number of alive nodes of the heterogeneous TEEN is higher than heterogeneous LEACH and EAMMH. This is because the TEEN routing technique is only activated for a specific event, and for this, it saves some energy, and the nodes remain alive for a longer time. Likewise, it is more stable than the other considered routing procedures. On the other hand, heterogeneous LEACH and EAMMH networks sense the environment all the time and transmit all the data that they receive, which requires more energy to convey data.

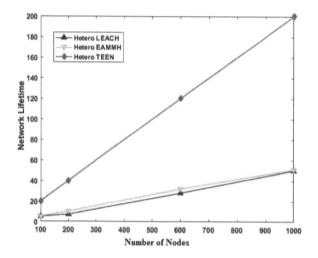

Figure 13.1: Network lifetime for 100, 200, 600, and 1000 nodes at $P=0.1$, $m=0.2$, and $a=1$.

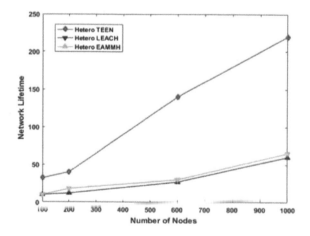

Figure 13.2: Network lifetime for 100, 200, 600, and 1000 nodes at $P=0.2$, $m=0.2$, and $a=1$.

13.5.2 Energy Consumption

A protocol that consumes less energy for data transmission is considered a good one. Figures 13.3 and 13.4 illustrate that the consumed energy of TEEN is lower than considered LEACH and EAMMH routings. It also signifies that the amount of energy consumption is reduced for the increasing number of nodes in heterogeneous TEEN. On the contrary, LEACH and EAMMH are proactive routings and convey redundant data which consumes more energy than TEEN.

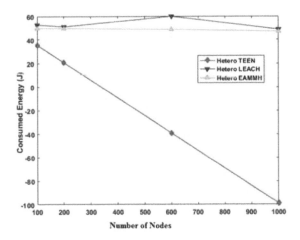

Figure 13.3: Energy consumption for 100, 200, 600, and 1000 nodes at $P=0.1$, $m=0.2$, and $a=1$.

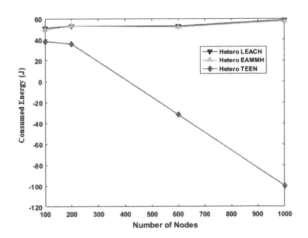

Figure 13.4: Energy consumption for 100, 200, 600, and 1000 nodes at $P=0.2$, $m=0.2$, and $a=1$.

13.5.3 Time and Space Complexities

A procedure that requires less time to execute and less memory space is recognized as a good strategy.

Figures 13.5, 13.6, 13.7, and 13.8 illustrate that the time and space complexities for heterogeneous TEEN are less than other considered routing techniques. This is because TEEN utilizes thresholds to reduce redundant data and, as a result, it

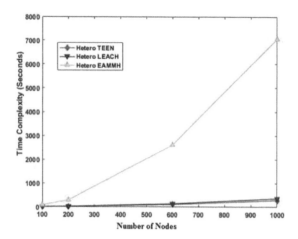

Figure 13.5: Time complexity for 100, 200, 600, and 1000 nodes at $P=0.1$, $m=0.2$, and $a=1$.

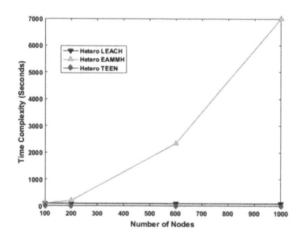

Figure 13.6: Time complexity for 100, 200, 600, and 1000 nodes at $P=0.2$, $m=0.2$, and $a=1$.

requires less memory space. Moreover, it is an event-driven strategy, so time is not wasted which saves more time than LEACH and EAMMH.

13.5.4 Throughput

A routing strategy that transfers higher data at the BS implies that the technique performs splendidly.

Figures 13.9 and 13.10 illustrate that TEEN has lower throughput than other considered routing techniques. Although TEEN has higher alive nodes along with a longer stability period, it omits the transmission of redundant data. For this reason, the throughput of TEEN is lower than LEACH and EAMMH routing procedures.

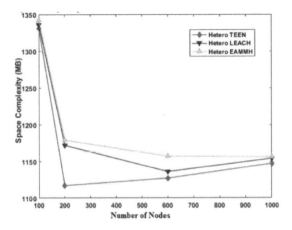

Figure 13.7: Space complexity for 100, 200, 600, and 1000 nodes at P=0.1, m=0.2, and a =1.

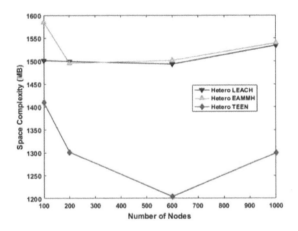

Figure 13.8: Space complexity for 100, 200, 600, and 1000 nodes at P=0.2, m=0.2, and a =1.

13.6 DISCUSSION

The heterogeneous TEEN routing is an event-driven strategy that continuously senses the environment but activates for a specific event. As a consequence, the energy of this network is saved, and that network can have more alive nodes that can convey data to the relevant users. Hence, TEEN has a longer network lifetime that makes it more stable. Moreover, it uses hard and soft threshold values that can be witnessed to reduce redundant data, and this can save more time and space for TEEN strategy, whereas it has a lower amount of throughput. On the other hand, heterogeneous LEACH and EAMMH continuously sense parameters, and transfer all data to the BS. As a result, they consume more energy, have fewer alive nodes with lower network lifetime, require more time to execute, and require more space for sensing data. It

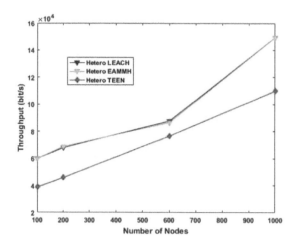

Figure 13.9: Throughput for 100, 200, 600, and 1000 nodes at $P=0.1$, $m=0.2$, and $a=1$.

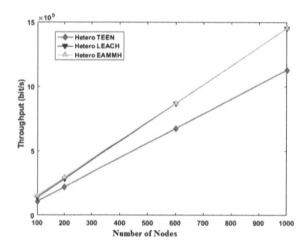

Figure 13.10: Throughput for 100, 200, 600, and 1000 nodes at $P=0.2$, $m=0.2$, and $a=1$.

is undeniable that heterogeneous TEEN can be more applicable than other routings considered for real-world applications.

13.7 CONCLUSION AND FUTURE WORKS

A vital standard for WSNs is to significantly transfer error-free data with less energy consumption. Subsequently, numerous techniques are expected to deal with the network appropriately. The biggest challenge is to improve energy efficiency, spanning the network life, and mitigate the delay with low-powered sensors. Throughout this chapter, in terms of various metrics, we examined the performance of heterogeneous LEACH, EAMMH, and TEEN routings. TEEN is a reactive protocol that can save more time. Moreover, it uses thresholds to reduce redundant data transmission. As a result, it saves more memory space, and energy, has a lower throughput, extended stability period, and a longer network lifetime compared to the heterogeneous, proactive LEACH and EAMMH. However, in TEEN, the CH is only selected based on the threshold value which is not sufficient for a routing strategy.

In the near future, we would like to update the CH selection criteria of the TEEN routing technique, implement the updated procedure on NS3, and compare the results with MATLAB to have a better outcome.

Bibliography

[1] Dahiya, M. S. and Singh, P. K. (2017). Clustering of Nodes in Wireless Sensor Network (WSN): A Survey. International Journal of Engineering Research and Technology, [online] 5.

[2] Ngangbam, R., Hossain, A. and Shukla, A. (2019). Lifetime Improvement for Hierarchical Routing with Distance and Energy-Based Threshold. International Conference on Intelligent Data Communication Technologies and Internet of Things (ICICI), Springer, Cham, [online] 38, pp. 77-83.

[3] Huang, W., Ling, Y. and Zhou, W. (2018). An Improved LEACH Routing Algorithm for Wireless Sensor Network. International Journal of Wireless Information Networks, [online] 25, pp. 323–331.

[4] Chaudhary, C. and Kumar, V. (2021). Performance Analysis of LEACH-C and EAMMH protocols in WSN in MATLAB. In Proc. of 2021 3rd International Conference on Advances in Computing, Communication Control and Networking, [online], pp. 1367-1370.

[5] Dener, M. (2018). A New Energy Efficient Hierarchical Routing Protocol for Wireless Sensor Networks, Wireless Personal Communications, Springer, [online].

[6] Heinzelman, W., R, Chandrakasan, A. and Balakrishnan, H. (2000). Energy-Efficient Communication Protocol for Wireless Microsensor Networks, In Proc. of Hawaii International Conference on System Sciences, [online] 8, pp. 1-10. Available at: 10.1109/HICSS.2000.926982.

[7] Depedri, A., Zanella, A. and Verdone, R. (2011). An Energy-Efficient Protocol for Wireless Sensor Networks, In Proc. of AINS, [online] 134, pp. 1-6.

[8] Bakaraniya, P., Mehta, S. and Sheetal (2013). K-LEACH: An improved LEACH Protocol for Lifetime Improvement in WSN, International Journal of Engineering Trends and Technology (IJETT), [online] 4 (5), pp. 1521-1526.

[9] Kumar, G., S, Paul, S. and Jacob, K. (2008). Mobility Metric Based Leach-Mobile Protocol, In Proc. of 16th International Conference on Advanced Computing and Communications, Available at: 10.1109/ADCOM.2008.4760456.

[10] Manjeshwar, A. and Agrawal, D., P. (2001). TEEN: A Routing Protocol for Enhanced Efficiency in Wireless Sensor Networks, In Proc. of the 15th International Parallel and Distributed Processing Symposium (IPDPS), [online] pp. 2009–2015.

[11] Ahmed, S. R., Kadhim, M. A., and Karim, T. A. (2019). Wireless Sensor Networks Improvement using LEACH Algorithm. In Proc. of 2nd International Conference on Sustainable Engineering Techniques, [online].

[12] Liang, H., Yang, S., Li, L., and Gao, J. (2019). Research on routing optimization of WSNs based on improved LEACH protocol. EURASIP Journal on Wireless Communications and Networking, [online] 194.

[13] Salam, T. and Hossen, M., S. (2020). Performance Analysis on Homogeneous LEACH and EAMMH Protocols in Wireless Sensor Network, Wireless Personal Communications, Springer, [online].

[14] Lee, S., Noh, Y. and Kim, K. (2013). Key Schemes for Security Enhanced TEEN Routing Protocol in Wireless Sensor Networks. International Journal of Distributed Sensor Networks, [online] 9.

[15] Ge, Y, Wang, S. and Ma, J. (2018). Optimization on TEEN Routing Protocol in Cognitive Wireless Sensor Network, EURASIP Journal on Wireless Communications and Networking, Springer, [online] 27. Available at: https://doi.org/10.1186/s13638-018-1039-z.

CHAPTER 14

Analysis of Physical and Psychological Impacts to Predict Satisfaction of Students toward E-Learning during COVID-19 Pandemic

Sudipta Nath

Department of Computer Science and Engineering, Chittagong University of Engineering and Technology, Chattogram, Bangladesh.

CONTENTS

14.1	Introduction	164
14.2	Related Work	165
14.3	Methodology	165
	14.3.1 Data Requirements Specification	166
	14.3.1.1 Demographic Data	166
	14.3.1.2 Physical Impacts	166
	14.3.1.3 Psychological Impacts	166
	14.3.1.4 Satisfaction	167
	14.3.2 Collection of Data	167
	14.3.3 Pre-processing of Data	167
	14.3.4 Data Cleaning	167
	14.3.5 Analysis of Data	167
	14.3.6 Applying Classification Algorithms	167
	14.3.6.1 Logistic Regression	168
	14.3.6.2 Naive Bayes	168
	14.3.6.3 K-Nearest Neighbours	168
	14.3.6.4 Decision Tree	168
	14.3.6.5 Random Forest	168
	14.3.6.6 Support Vector Machine	168
14.4	Result and Discussion	168
	14.4.1 Relativity and Demographic Analysis	169
	14.4.1.1 Relativity Analysis	169

14.4.1.2   Demographic Data Analysis 169

14.4.2 Physical Impacts of E-learning System (online classes) 170

14.4.3 Psychological Impacts of E-learning System 170

14.4.4 Satisfaction towards E-learning System 170

14.4.5 Correlation and Regression Analysis 171

14.4.6 Accuracy of Classification Algorithms 172

14.5 Conclusion 172

T He world is fighting a pandemic named COVID-19. The world's health system, economical condition, and education system are all in crisis as a result of the pandemic. The leaders are trying their best to deal with these crises while the doctors and the scientists are fighting the deadly virus. Education is considered the backbone of a nation. It has also been interrupted due to COVID-19. To mitigate this interruption, the E-learning system (online classes) is playing an important role. However, many students are coping with this system, which should be a major concern because the base of education depends on the learning rate and the satisfaction of a student. Therefore, the satisfaction towards the E-learning system with regard to physical and psychological impacts is very important. This chapter represents the analysis of physical and psychological impacts and the satisfaction of students towards the E-learning system. The application of linear regression and classification algorithms is also included here to check and predict the satisfaction or dissatisfaction of a student, which can be useful to build satisfaction model for instructors.

14.1 INTRODUCTION

COVID-19 is a highly infectious virus that is a consequence of SARS-CoV-2 (Severe Acute Respiratory Syndrome Coronavirus 2). In December 2019, the first instance of COVID-19 was confirmed in Wuhan, China [1]. The disease now has become an ongoing pandemic worldwide. COVID-19 causes a variety of symptoms like fever [2], breathing difficulties, cough, fatigue, headache [3], and loss of smell and taste [4], which can start anywhere from one to fourteen days following viral exposure. COVID-19 is primarily transferred when an infected person comes into close contact with another person [6, 7]. To reduce the chances of infection, some precautionary measures have been established including avoiding large gatherings, using facial masks in public, staying home, keeping a respectful distance from others, cleaning hands with soap frequently and for at least twenty seconds, maintaining proper respiratory hygiene, and refraining from rubbing the eyes, nose, or mouth with unclean hands [8, 9]. Social distancing is regarded as an important prevention method. Therefore, to combat the spread of COVID-19, most governments decided to close educational institutions temporarily [10, 11, 12, 13]. For educational and academic purposes, the E-learning system (online classes) has become a critical lifeline [14, 15]. However, how concerned are individuals with the physical, psychological, and overall satisfaction of students with this system? A healthy physical and psychological condition is a necessary prerequisite for gaining knowledge. The goal of this study is to determine the overall satisfaction of students from various study levels with regard to physical and psychological effects. The main objectives of this research are:

- To analyze the physical and psychological impacts of the E-learning system.

- To check the overall satisfaction towards the E-learning system using correlation and linear regression analysis.

- To apply and check the accuracies of different classification algorithms (Logistic Regression, Naive Bayes, K-Nearest Neighbours (KNN), Decision Tree, Random Forest, and Support Vector Machine) to predict whether a student is satisfied or dissatisfied.

The following is an overview of the remainder of this work. Section 14.2 discusses relevant literature and studies. Section 14.3 describes the survey and the study's methodology. Section 14.4 presents the findings and discussions. Section 14.5 brings the chapter to a conclusion.

14.2 RELATED WORK

COVID-19 is a present hot topic. The whole world is regularly researching on it to find out the impacts and remedies. Some intriguing studies have been uncovered while reviewing related work.

Authors et al.'s [16] major goal was to see if students were pleased or disappointed with their online lessons, as well as the psychological effects of online classes. In this study, the authors concluded that students are displeased with their online classes due to limitations such as a weak network connection and an inconsistent electricity supply. However, the survey of this study was done only on university students. The impacts of online classes on college students were examined by [17]. The problems that arise when taking online classes were also highlighted in this study. The goal was to discover the elements that influenced students' contentment and performance in virtual classes during the COVID-19 epidemic [18]. The conclusions of this study suggest various important facts, such as teacher quality and student satisfaction during online classes, which investigated the direct relationship between academic performance and satisfaction. A research was done [19] which included 67 students, 41.8 percent of whom reported having difficulty with online education, whereas 29.9 percent strongly disagreed with that statement.

In the current study, a survey with 510 datasets collected from students of different study levels has been done effectively on their overall satisfaction towards the E-learning system during the COVID-19 pandemic. Correlation and linear regression analysis has been used to check the overall satisfaction. To predict whether a student is satisfied or dissatisfied, classification algorithms are also applied here.

14.3 METHODOLOGY

This study is mainly based on a survey of students of different study levels. The survey was conducted over a period of three weeks using questionnaires that students answered regularly after their classes to record their physical and psychological status and their overall satisfaction level. Some important steps are followed to perform the research effectively. These steps are:

- Data Requirements Specification

- Collection of Data

- Pre-processing of Data

- Data Cleaning

- Analysis of Data

- Applying Classification Algorithms

These steps are discussed.

14.3.1 Data Requirements Specification

This study mainly focuses on the physical and psychological impacts along with the overall satisfaction of students towards the E-learning system. Therefore, questionnaires based on these impacts and the overall satisfaction towards the E-learning system were made to gather datasets. Questionnaires were mainly grouped into four parts:

14.3.1.1 Demographic Data

This section provides the demographic datasets of participants, such as gender, study level, and so on.

14.3.1.2 Physical Impacts

The questions related to physical impacts were included in this part. Example: Did you feel a headache during or after your E-learning classes (online classes)? (a) Yes. (b) No.

14.3.1.3 Psychological Impacts

The questions related to psychological impacts were included in this part. Example: Did you feel mental stress/depression during or after your E-learning classes (online classes)? (a) Yes. (b) No.

14.3.1.4 Satisfaction

The questions related to psychological satisfaction were included in this part. Example: Do you have overall satisfaction with your E-learning classes (online classes)? (a) Not satisfied. (b) Rarely satisfied. (c) Satisfied. (d) Strongly satisfied.

14.3.2 Collection of Data

A form was used to collect datasets from several web platforms. Simple binary type and some simple four points Likert-scale type questionnaires were designed for the survey using a form. The form was then sent to the target audience via email and various social media sites. This survey received 622 replies; however, 112 of them were discarded due to various inaccuracies.

14.3.3 Pre-processing of Data

RStudio and a built-in library in Python named Pandas have been used to process data sets. For basic binary type questions, students' opinions were divided into two sections and assessed: "Yes = 1 and No = 0," which investigated the physical and the psychological impacts. For Likert-scale type questions, opinions were divided into four categories and assessed as "Not satisfied = 0, Rarely satisfied = 1, Satisfied = 2, Strongly satisfied = 3," determining satisfaction with the E-learning system (online classes).

14.3.4 Data Cleaning

Due to certain inaccuracies and incomplete responses, 112 responses were eliminated from the survey, and all blank data were replaced with some high garbage value. Finally, 510 responses were obtained to conduct this study.

14.3.5 Analysis of Data

RStudio and some built-in libraries like NumPy and Matplotlib were used to analyze data and to apply the linear regression. The mean value of responses was used to evaluate the conclusion of this study. For binary type questions, a mean value of more than 0.5 denotes positive responses, whereas a mean value less than 0.5 denotes negative responses. A mean value of more than 2 indicates the satisfaction for questions of the type Likert scale and a mean value less than 2 indicates the dissatisfaction. In this research, the correlation between the overall satisfaction and the physical and psychological impacts is also studied. The linear regression analysis is also discussed in this study to measure the overall satisfaction.

14.3.6 Applying Classification Algorithms

Classification algorithms (Logistic Regression, Naive Bayes, K-Nearest Neighbours (KNN), Decision Tree, Random Forest, and Support Vector Machine) are also applied here to predict whether a student is satisfied or dissatisfied with the E-learning system with the training of physical and psychological impacts.

For applying classification algorithms (Logistic Regression, Naive Bayes, K-Nearest Neighbours (KNN), Decision Tree, Random Forest, and Support Vector Machine), a built-in library in Python named 'sklearn' has been used. The responses of "overall satisfaction" have been selected as the dependent variable and classified into two classes. The responses of "Not Satisfied (0)" and "Rarely Satisfied (1)" have been classified as "Dissatisfied" and the responses of "Satisfied (2)" and "Strongly Satisfied (3)" as "Satisfied".

14.3.6.1 *Logistic Regression*

Logistic regression is a suitable analysis to carry out with the binary variables. The link between a binary type dependent variable and one or more ordinal, nominal, interval independent variables is mostly explained by the application.

14.3.6.2 *Naive Bayes*

Naive Bayes is a Bayes theorem classification technique. Simply put, this classification analysis presumes that a certain aspect is totally unrelated to other features in various classes.

14.3.6.3 *K-Nearest Neighbours*

One of the simple learning machine techniques that assumes that related items stay close to each other is the K-Nearest Neighbours (KNN).

14.3.6.4 *Decision Tree*

The Decision Tree algorithm provides a problem-solving model using the representation of the tree in which a class label is referred to in the node, and the internal tree nodes are the characteristics.

14.3.6.5 *Random Forest*

The Random Forest method is mostly assembled of decision trees. This classifier is typically learned using the bagging method, which is a collection of learning models that improves overall performance.

14.3.6.6 *Support Vector Machine*

The support vector machine algorithm sets a hyper-plane in a dataset of N-features that distinctly classifies the data points.

14.4 RESULT AND DISCUSSION

In this section, the results and the discussions of this research will be analyzed.

Table 14.1: Relativity analysis.

Construct	Cronbach's Alpha	Result	Items
Physical impacts	0.776	Acceptable	4
Psychological impacts	0.754	Acceptable	3
Satisfaction	0.702	Acceptable	3

Table 14.2: Demographic data analysis.

Demographics	Categories	Frequency	Percentage
Gender			
	Male	267	52.35
	Female	243	47.65
	Total	510	100
Age			
	4-10 years	67	13.13
	11-15 years	84	16.47
	16-20 years	161	31.57
	21-25 years	198	38.83
	Total	510	100
Study level			
	Class 1-5	67	13.13
	Class 6-8	84	16.47
	Class 9-10	87	17.05
	Class 11-12	54	10.61
	University (under-graduate)	218	42.74
	Total	510	100

14.4.1 Relativity and Demographic Analysis

Relativity and demographic analysis are critical components of any research project.

14.4.1.1 Relativity Analysis

Cronbach's alpha is a measure of scale dependability, which is a measure of a group's internal consistency. Table 14.1 displays the Cronbach's Alpha result, which indicates that the following sections are acceptable and dependable because the Cronbach's Alpha value is greater than 0.7.

14.4.1.2 Demographic Data Analysis

According to Table 14.2, male and female respondents are almost equally represented in the survey. A total of 38.83 percent of respondents are between the ages of 21 and 25, 31.57 percent are between the ages of 16 and 20, 16.47 percent are between the ages of 11 and 15, and 13.13 percent are between the ages of 4 and 10. The replies of students aged 4 to 10 years were gathered with the assistance of their guardians. The

Table 14.3: Physical impacts of the E-learning system (One-sample Statistics).

Items	Opinion (Viewed as percentage)		Mean
	Yes (1)	No (0)	
Eyesight problems during or after class	70.9	29,1	0.709091
Headache during or after class	71.36	28.64	0.713636
Neck pain during or after class	62.27	37.73	0.622727
Back pain during or after class	60	40	0.600000

Table 14.4: Psychological impacts of the E-learning system (One-sample Statistics).

Items	Opinion (Viewed as percentage)		Mean
	Yes (1)	No (0)	
Depression during or after class	68.18	31.82	0.681818
Mental irritation/stress during or after class	67.73	32.27	0.677273
Worried about future	65.91	34.09	0.659091

majority of study level is university (undergraduate), accounting for around 42.74 percent of total respondents.

14.4.2 Physical Impacts of E-learning System (online classes)

Table 14.3 demonstrates that over 71 percent of the total students experience eyesight issues and headaches during or after their online classes, with approximately 60 percent experiencing neck pain and back pain concerns. Thus, it is obvious from Table 14.3 that the E-learning system is having a negative physical impact on the students, since the mean values of each item are larger than 0.5, indicating that the majority of respondents have positive responses to dealing with physical problems.

14.4.3 Psychological Impacts of E-learning System

According to Table 14.4, over 68 percent of students have mental irritations and depressions during or after their online classes, and approximately 66 percent of students are severely anxious about their future. As a result, the majority of students are experiencing psychological problems, because the mean values of each item are around 0.65, implying the majority of positive reactions of the participants to the questions and the negative psychological impacts of the E-learning system.

14.4.4 Satisfaction towards E-learning System

According to Table 14.5, the majority of participants are rarely satisfied with what they have learned, their teachers' behavior, and teaching approaches. The total

Table 14.5: Satisfaction towards E-learning System.

Items	Opinion (Viewed as percentage)				Mean
	Not Satisfied (0)	Rarely Satisfied (1)	Satisfied (2)	Strongly Satisfied (3)	
Satisfaction with what students have learned	25.6	38.8	28.3	7.3	1.763636
Satisfaction with the instructors' behaviors and the teaching methods	18.2	36.8	40	5	1.668182
Overall satisfaction	17.1	51.1	28.5	3.3	1.222727

Table 14.6: Correlation matrix.

Variables	Physical impacts	Psychological impacts	Overall satisfaction
Physical impacts	1	0.307	-0.172
Psychological impacts	0.307	1	-0.617
Satisfaction	-0.172	-0.617	1

Table 14.7: Regression analysis.

Variables	R	R square	Adjusted R square	df	P value
Overall satisfaction	0.842	0.709	0.698	8	.000

satisfaction scale also indicates participants' dissatisfaction. Table 14.5 demonstrates that 17.1 percent of respondents are dissatisfied with the E-learning system, whereas 51.1 percent are rarely satisfied with online classes.

14.4.5 Correlation and Regression Analysis

Table 14.6 reveals that overall satisfaction with the E-learning system (online classes) has negative relationships with physical and psychological impacts, indicating that the E-learning (online classes) system is causing physical and psychological problems among students. These issues should be addressed to enhance general satisfaction and assure the greatest possible outcome for students.

In Table 14.7, the R square value for the dependent variable overall satisfaction is .709, indicating that the independent variables can demonstrate around 70.9 percent of the instances of this dependent variable. The P-value for all dependent variables is .000, which is less than 5 percent, indicating that the null hypothesis cannot be accepted with 95 percent confidence.

among the accuracies of different classification algorithms.pdf

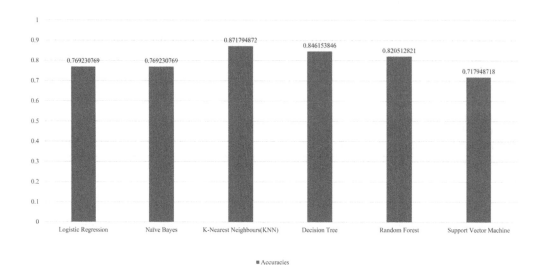

Figure 14.1: Differences among the accuracies of different classification algorithms.

14.4.6 Accuracy of Classification Algorithms

Here in Fig. 14.1, the accuracies of classification algorithms are given with respect to other independent variables (physical impacts and psychological impacts).

In Fig. 14.1, it is shown that the K-Nearest Neighbours (KNN) model acquires the best accuracy which is 87.18 percent following, respectively, Decision Tree, Random Forest, Logistic Regression, Naive Bayes, and Support Vector Machine models. As the accuracy of these algorithms is in the range of 70-90 percent, it can be said that a good model to predict the satisfaction of students towards the E-learning system can be established using these classification algorithms.

14.5 CONCLUSION

The physical and psychological impacts of the E-learning system (online classes) during the COVID-19 pandemic were efficiently explored in this article. According to the findings of this study, students are suffering from a variety of physical and psychological issues such as poor vision, headaches, mental irritability, depression, and so on. We must be worried about these impacts to get the best output from the E-learning system (online classes). Using classification algorithms, a model can be built for instructors which can predict the satisfaction and dissatisfaction of students regarding physical and psychological problems with maximum accuracy of around 87.18 percent. Finally, it is a must to care about the impacts of this system on students as well as their overall satisfaction levels.

Bibliography

[1] Page J., Hinshaw D., McKay B. (26 February 2021). *"In Hunt for Covid-19 Origin, Patient Zero Points to Second Wuhan Market – The man with the first confirmed infection of the new coronavirus told the WHO team that his parents had shopped there"*. The Wall Street Journal.

[2] Islam, M. A., Kundu, S., Alam, S. S., Hossan, T., Kamal, M. A., & Hassan, R. (2021).*Prevalence and characteristics of fever in adult and paediatric patients with coronavirus disease 2019 (COVID-19): A systematic review and meta-analysis of 17515 patients.* PloS one, 16(4), e0249788.

[3] Islam, M. A., Alam, S. S., Kundu, S., Hossan, T., Kamal, M. A., & Cavestro, C. (2020).*Prevalence of headache in patients with coronavirus disease 2019 (COVID-19): a systematic review and meta-analysis of 14,275 patients.* Frontiers in neurology, 11.

[4] Saniasiaya, J., Islam, M. A., & Abdullah, B. (2021). *Prevalence of Olfactory Dysfunction in Coronavirus Disease 2019 (COVID-19): A Meta-analysis of 27,492 Patients.* The Laryngoscope, 131(4), 865-878.

[5] World Health Organization (2020) *Coronavirus disease (COVID-19): How is it transmitted.* Geneva, Switzerland: WHO.

[6] Saniasiaya, J., Islam, M. A., & Abdullah, B. (2020). *Prevalence and characteristics of taste disorders in cases of COVID-19: a meta-analysis of 29,349 patients.* Otolaryngology–Head and Neck Surgery, 0194599820981018.

[7] Barile, J. P., Guerin, R. J., Fisher, K. A., Tian, L. H., Okun, A. H., Vanden Esschert, K. L., ... & Prue, C. E. (2021). *Theory-based behavioral predictors of self-reported use of face coverings in public settings during the COVID-19 Pandemic in the United States.* Annals of Behavioral Medicine, 55(1), 82-88.

[8] Wan, K. S., Tok, P. S. K., Yoga Ratnam, K. K., Aziz, N., Isahak, M., Ahmad Zaki, R., ... & Said, M. A. (2021). *Implementation of a COVID-19 surveillance programme for healthcare workers in a teaching hospital in an upper-middle-income country.* PloS one, 16(4), e0249394.

[9] Mustafa, N. (2020). *Impact of the 2019–20 coronavirus pandemic on education.* International Journal of Health Preferences Research, 1-12.

[10] Skulmowski, A., & Rey, G. D. (2020).*COVID-19 as an accelerator for digitalization at a German university: Establishing hybrid campuses in times of crisis.* Human behavior and emerging technologies, 2(3), 212-216.

[11] Cortese, K., & Frascio, M. (2021). *New Settings in Anatomy and Surgery Teaching During the Covid-19 Pandemic.* Anatomical Sciences Education.

[12] Cortese, K., & Frascio, M. (2021).*Bridging the gap between basic science and clinical curricula: lessons from SARS-COV-2 pandemic.* Surgical and Radiologic Anatomy, 1.

[13] Skulmowski, A., & Rey, G. D. (2020).*COVID-19 as an accelerator for digitalization at a German university: Establishing hybrid campuses in times of crisis.* Human behavior and emerging technologies, 2(3), 212-216.

[14] Murphy, M. P. (2020).*COVID-19 and emergency eLearning: Consequences of the securitization of higher education for post-pandemic pedagogy.* Contemporary Security Policy, 41(3), 492-505.

[15] Bishwas, P. C., Hakim, M. U., & Alam, D. M. S. (2020, August). Online Class and Its Psychological Impact on Satisfaction of University Students In Bangladesh During Covid-19 Pandemic. In Proceeding of the International Virtual Conference on Multidisciplinary Research (IVCMR) (Vol. 27, p. 28).

[16] T.K., Avvai Kothai & Sekar, S. Ramya. (2020). *Impact of Online Classes on College Students in Chennai During Covid-19 Pandemic.* 54. 68-74.

[17] Gopal, R., Singh, V., & Aggarwal, A. (2021). *Impact of online classes on the satisfaction and performance of students during the pandemic period of COVID 19.* Education and Information Technologies, 1-25.

[18] Batool, F., Saeed, B., Rehman, A. U., & Waseem, H. (2021). *Impact Of Online Classes During COVID-19 Pandemic Situation on Undergraduate University Students Pakistan.* Asian Journal of Allied Health Sciences (AJAHS).

CHAPTER 15

SeniorsAid: Requirements, Elicitation, and Development of a Mobile App for Seniors

Maliha Sultana, Akash Poddar, Muhammad Nazrul Islam, and Tasmiah Tamzid Anannya

Department of Computer Science & Engineering, Military Institute of Science and Technology, Mirpur Cantonment, Dhaka, Bangladesh

CONTENTS

15.1	Introduction	176
15.2	Related Work	176
15.3	Design and Development	178
	15.3.1 Need Findings	178
	15.3.2 Conceptual Framework	178
	15.3.3 Developing the Application	180
15.4	Evaluation	181
	15.4.1 Study Procedure	181
	15.4.2 Evaluation and Results	181
15.5	Conclusion	184

A SIGNIFICANT portion of the world population consists of senior citizens. They mostly require assistance from their loved ones and doctors for meeting their social and health needs. The world today is technology-driven and mobile applications (apps) have become an indispensable part of everyday life. Since these apps are usually not developed focusing on the usability and user experience from the perspective of senior citizens, they are largely being deprived of such benefits. As a result, they have to go through the trouble of adjusting themselves with the interface of several apps for performing various activities. Again, most of these apps rarely cater to their social needs. Thus, the objective of this research is to develop a usable and useful standalone (one-stop) app for the senior citizens of Bangladesh. With this aim in mind, 13 Bangladeshi senior citizens aged 60 and above were interviewed for eliciting their requirements; and then a mobile application called *SeniorsAid* was developed to address these requisites. The *SeniorsAid* app allows elders, both literates and illiterates, to maintain connectivity with their loved ones and local community as well as address their health concerns by contacting hospitals and getting reminders for medicines and doctor appointments. The application was later evaluated by those 13 participants. The evaluation results show that the developed application is effective, efficient, useful, and acceptable to senior users.

15.1   INTRODUCTION

Nowadays, people are highly mobile dependent. But not all age groups are equally advanced in the world of technology. Smartphones and mobile apps are still intimidating to the older generation who contribute to a significant portion of our population. In Bangladesh, around 5% of the total population is above the age of 60 and it will reach 7% by 2025. Telenor's local subsidiary, Grameenphone has observed that only 2% of their user base is above the age of 60. In other words, only 1 million out of their 52 million users are seniors [11]. And even though the number of smartphone users is on the rise, overall, only 1% of Bangladeshis over the age of 65 use a smartphone [11]. In the US, about 46 million seniors live today [12]. Among them, about 42% seniors (of ages 65 and above) now own a smartphone which was just 18% back in 2013 while 67% of seniors use the internet which is a 55% increase in just under two decades. Also, half of them now have broadband at home [13].

Thus, to make the lives of senior citizens a lot easier and more comfortable, the need to make inclusive apps cannot be over-emphasized. To provide such support, various types of IT/ICT-based solutions exist [20]. For example, the app, 'Trip 4 All', developed in Brazil acts as a gamified virtual assistant to the elderly during a walking tourist visit [6] while the 'Interaktor' app developed in Sweden supports older people to receive home care [5]. However, in the context of Bangladesh, only few such apps were developed to provide a limited number of services while not explicitly focusing on usability and not exploring the (real) needs of the senior citizens beforehand.

Therefore, the objectives of this research are to elucidate the primary requirements for addressing the daily needs of aging people through mobile apps in the context of Bangladesh and to develop a usable mobile app addressing those needs. For this, 13 senior citizens were interviewed, their primary requirements were identified and then an app named *SeniorsAid* was developed. The developed app has a senior-friendly interface that allows the users to meet their social as well as health-related needs in a single platform. Both literate and illiterate users can operate it due to its pictorial format. It provides the user with a wide range of features like communicating with loved ones, getting updates on social events, accessing a list of nearby hospitals, setting up reminders, etc.

The rest of the article is organized as follows: Section 15.2 presents the related works in this field along with their limitations. Section 15.3 discusses the system requirements, conceptual design and development of the proposed application, Section 15.4 discusses the evaluation process, and, finally, Section 15.5 concludes the chapter.

15.2   RELATED WORK

This section briefly discusses the works related to ICT-based mobile apps catered to the various needs of senior citizens.

Table 15.1: Comparing the features of senior-friendly Android Apps on Google Play Store

Serial No.	Features	Jestho	Elderly Care	Seniors Phone	Pocket Physio	Senior Safety
1	Call and Text	✓	✓	✓	✗	✓
2	Distress Signal and Location	✓	✓	✓	✗	✓
3	Health/Physio Information	✗	✓	✗	✓	✗
4	Get Advice and Share Story	✗	✓	✗	✗	✗
5	Find Pharmacy	✗	✓	✗	✗	✗
6	Links to other Apps	✗	✗	✓	✗	✗
7	Access other Pre-installed Apps	✗	✗	✗	✗	✓
8	Vision Enhancer	✗	✗	✗	✗	✓
9	Fall Detection	✗	✗	✗	✗	✓
10	Medicine Reminder	✗	✗	✗	✗	✓

Lorenz and Oppermann [10] provided a special focus on many desirable features of mobile app interface for senior citizens. Again, Gao and Koronios [9] suggested considering suitable font size, navigation, button arrangement and color-neutral display while developing a mobile app catered to them. Another study [17] found out that designing familiar icons reduced system complexity and increased usability in apps for older adults. However, mobile apps must be able to meet the specific needs (physical and non-physical) of senior citizens in their daily lives like health monitoring, personal information, social interaction, leisure, safety and privacy [9]. One study [16] reported the differences in the types of apps used by older and younger smartphone users and found out that senior smartphone users are more likely to use personal information manager applications. Another study [15] found that seniors prioritize calling functions the most, followed by phone books, clocks, emergency buttons, alarms, cameras and calculators. The researchers concluded that seniors prefer phone functions that require the lowest mental effort. Interestingly, Gao and Koronios [9] found that although several health apps are available, there is no integrated app with all the health features in one platform. So, a user has to use multiple apps to complete multiple tasks which can be daunting given the fact that senior adults are slower to adopt new forms and tend to be more selective in their use of technology [14]. For a better understanding of the types of apps catered towards senior citizens that were available for download at the time of this research, Table 15.1 shows feature comparisons.

In sum, throughout the world, many senior-friendly apps have been developed. A few apps have also been developed in the context of Bangladesh ('Jestho') which mainly focuses on calling, sending distress signals or setting up alarms. However, to the best of our knowledge, no research work has been conducted thoroughly to provide both social and health-related support to Bangladeshi senior citizens. This research work will focus on finding out the user requirements of this demographic and later develop a mobile app in the context of Bangladesh which can handle social and health-related needs.

15.3 DESIGN AND DEVELOPMENT

This section discusses the steps that were followed for developing the mobile application.

15.3.1 Need Findings

It is a crucial activity to identify and understand the user needs properly for developing an efficient and usable system [21, 22]. For this, a semi-structured interview was conducted with 13 senior citizens whose average age was 66.42 ± 5.30 years. Firstly, basic information of the interviewees (name, age, gender, etc.) was collected. Secondly, they were asked if they own any smartphones and use the internet. Ten participants were smartphone users and on an average spent $1 \pm .25$ hours using the internet daily. Thirdly, they were asked if they use any mobile apps. If so, they were requested to elaborate on the app and the features they liked the most. Next, they were asked whether they would like an integrated mobile app that can provide both social and medical support in their daily lives. Once they replied in the affirmative, the final step involved asking them about certain features they think should be included in the app. Each interview lasted about 20 minutes. A summary of their frequency of agreement on various requirements is presented in Table 15.2. Once all the user requirements were gathered, they were analyzed and divided into four categories: usability, health, social, and self-assistive.

15.3.2 Conceptual Framework

A conceptual framework (see Figure 15.1) was proposed to develop a mobile app considering the user requirements revealed through the need-finding study. Features of the application are categorically discussed below:

Usability: This a key quality attribute of any application to ensure ease-of-use and user friendliness. Almost all the participants mentioned 'font size' and 'recognizable icon' to design and develop the user interfaces (UIs) while nine out of 13 participants mentioned 'interface language'. Accordingly, all the contents and information have been presented using a large font in the app to help the senior citizens notice them easily. Similarly, pictures and icon-based buttons (or navigation links) were used instead of text-based buttons so that both the literate and the illiterate senior citizens can easily understand their referential meanings. As per their suggestions, Bengali language was also used to represent the contents of the UIs in order to make them more readable and understandable.

Health: This includes two features: 'Find Hospitals' and 'Set Reminders'. 'Find Hospitals' provides a list of nearby hospitals, their address and contact number. It also allows the user to search for a specific hospital. Users can view a history of the hospitals they had contacted before to facilitate their future correspondence. 'Set Reminders' allows users to set two types of reminders. One helps to remind

Table 15.2: Summary of the revealed requirements.

Category	User Requirement	Example of Translated Quote	Frequency
Usability	Use large font and recognizable icons	'I want an app with big writings and pictures.'	12
	UI in Bengali language	'If the app is in Bengali, I can easily understand everything.'	9
Social	Contact with people	'I talk to a few people and want to easily find their phone numbers.'	10
	Find local events	'I like to attend musical programs. It would be convenient to know when the next one is going to happen.'	5
Health	Find hospitals	'It would be nice to easily get phone numbers of hospitals.'	10
	Set reminders	'I often forget about taking my medicines. A reminder for that would be helpful.'	11
Self-Assistive	Send distress signal	'In case of emergency, I want to quickly contact my family.'	11
	Vision enhancer	'I have an app that helps me read medicine labels clearly just by holding the phone camera in front of it.'	3
	Access other pre-installed applications	'I use an app that lets me visit other apps I have on my phone.'	2

them when to take their medications and another one reminds them of their doctor appointments.

Social: This includes features like 'Contact People' and 'Find Local Events'. 'Contact People' provides a large, easy-to-use interface to place phone calls and send SMS. Users can add, search, delete, and import contacts easily. Users can also mark some of the saved contacts as 'Emergency Contact'. Users can view 'Call History' to access recently contacted numbers. Moreover, the home page displays the names of three of the most contacted people at the top, clicking on which the user can quickly and directly place a call. 'Find Local Events' focuses on the recreational aspect of senior citizens' lives. Users can view information about all the nearby senior-friendly social events taking place (yoga, morning jogs, classical music programs, etc.) and can participate in the ones they like.

Self-Assistive: This includes three features: 'Send Distress Signal', 'Vision Enhancer' and 'Access Other Apps'. 'Send Distress Signal' allows the user to simply press the power button twice and an SMS for help is sent to his/her emergency contacts along with the GPS location. 'Vision Enhancer' is like a camera that can be zoomed in and out by pressing two buttons. It helps the user read medicine labels or daily newspapers written in small fonts just by holding the phone in front of it. 'Access Other Apps' allows senior citizens to access other pre-installed apps on their phones from this app. A list of all the other apps is presented in large font with easy navigation.

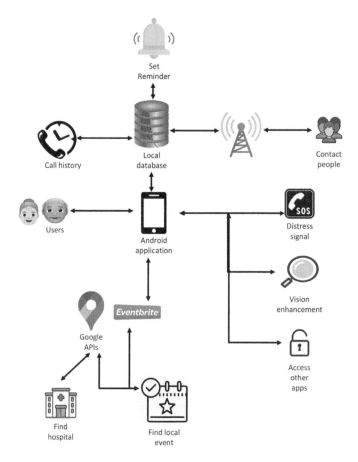

Figure 15.1: Proposed conceptual framework

15.3.3   Developing the Application

An application was developed by including all the key features shown in the conceptual framework. To ensure usability, the interface was designed using large fonts, recognizable icons and in Bengali language [23, 24, 25]. The development was carried out in stages in an organized manner. Given the large number of Android users worldwide and in Bangladesh [7], Android OS was used as the mobile platform. The app was built using Android Studio. The local database of the phone was used to store contacts, reminders, call history, etc. using SQLite. The user interface was developed using JAVA language. Google Maps and Google Places API were used to find nearby hospitals. Eventbrite and Google Maps API were used to find nearby local events. The home page and find local events page of the developed mobile application are illustrated in Figure 15.2.

 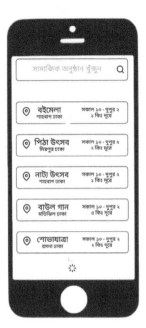

Figure 15.2: The Home Page and Find Local Events Page of the *SeniorsAid* app

15.4 EVALUATION

The *SeniorsAid* app was assessed through a user study to evaluate its usability which indicates the quality of an app in terms of effectiveness, efficiency, and user satisfaction [18]. The evaluation study was replicated with the 13 participants who had previously participated in the need-finding study.

15.4.1 Study Procedure

Participants who were previously involved in the need-finding stage were invited back and informed about the purpose of this study and how they would contribute. Next, they were asked to perform several tasks mentioned in Table 15.3. Corresponding data related to task completion time, frequency of wrong navigation, frequency of asking for help, input error and system error were collected while the users were performing these tasks. Finally, all the participants were asked to complete a set of questionnaires that had both open- and close-ended questions. Close-ended questions asked them to rate their overall satisfaction level, willingness to recommend the app to others, and willingness to use it in the future on a scale of 1 (strongly disagree) to 5 (strongly agree). Open-ended questions asked them for feedback, recommendations, and evaluation.

15.4.2 Evaluation and Results

Usability parameters (effectiveness, efficiency, satisfaction) defined by ISO [4] were measured to evaluate the app. The resultant outcomes are shown in Table 15.3 and Table 15.4.

Table 15.3: Summary result of app efficiency and effectiveness

Task	Task Completion Time (mins)	Asked for Help (frequency)	Wrong Navigation (frequency)	Input Error (frequency)	System Error	Task Completion Status
Set Reminder	2.5±0.5	1.1 ± 0.5 (3 part. asked 1 time, 1 part. asked 2 times)	1.8±0.3	3 (tried to set reminder without setting all parameters)	0	Successfully completed (3 part. needed 2 trials, others needed single trial)
Access list of nearby hospitals	0.8±0.3	2.2±.4 (3 part. asked 3 times, 2 part. asked 2 times, 3 part. asked 1 times)	3.1±0.6	4 (tried to access list without giving permission to access location)	2 (internet failure)	Successfully completed (4 part. needed 2 trials, others needed single trial)
Access list of social events	0.7±0.3	3.3±0.2 (4 part. asked 2 times, 3 part. asked 2 times)	2.7±0.4	3 (tried to access list without giving permission to access location)	3 (internet failure)	Successfully completed (2 part. needed 2 trials, others needed single trial)
Save New Contact	1.3±0.5	1±0.2 (2 part. asked 1 time)	1.6±0.2	2 (tried to save without entering name)	0	Successfully completed (3 part. needed 2 trials, others needed single trial)

Table 15.3: Continued on next page

Table 15.3: continued from previous page

Task	Task Completion Time (mins)	Asked for Help (frequency)	Wrong Navigation (frequency)	Input Error (frequency)	System Error	Task Completion Status
Send Distress Signal	1.2±0.1	2.2±0.3 (4 part. asked for 1 time, 2 part. asked 2 times)	3.1±0.2	3 (pressed button once)	0	Successfully completed (3 part. needed 3 trials)
Use Vision Enhancer	0.8±0.5	1±0.2 (2 part. asked 1 time)	0.3±0.1	0	0	Successfully completed (everyone needed single trial)
Access Other Apps	0.7±0.1	1.5±0.3 (3 part. asked 1 times)	0.6±0.1	0	0	Successfully completed (everyone needed single trial)
Total	1.1±0.3	1.8±0.2	1.7±0.3	12	8	

1. Effectiveness: It is the accuracy and completeness to achieve goals [2]. Indicators of effectiveness may include the successful completion of tasks with minimum possible attempts [3]. In this study, four variables were considered to measure the effectiveness of the app: Wrong Navigation (frequency), Input Error (frequency), System Error and Task Completion Status. From Table 15.3, it is seen that all the participants were able to complete all the given tasks. For two of the tasks, all the participants were successful on their first trial. For the remaining tasks, only around 23% of the participants required more than one trial. The frequency of wrong navigation was also very low (1.7±0.3 on average). The only two tasks that the participants had difficulty with were 'Access List of Nearby Hospitals' and 'Send Distress Signal'. This is because both of these features require users to do tasks (providing permission to access location, pressing the power button twice) that most of them were not previously acquainted with. The Input Error (frequency) was also low. All the participants completed two of the tasks without any input error. Moreover, for the rest of the tasks, it is seen that the participants quickly learned from their mistake (not providing permission to access location reduced from 4 to 3, not filling up all the parameters reduced from 3 to 2). Except for internet failure, no other system error was observed. The results from all four variables indicate that the participants completed their tasks effectively using the app.

2. Efficiency: It is defined as the resources expended to complete a task [2]. In this study, two variables were used to measure the efficiency of the app: Task

Table 15.4: Summary results of user satisfaction

Participants (Age in Years)	Overall Satisfaction	Recommending Others	Future Use
60 - 69 (n=8)	4.6±0.15	4.5±0.2	4.7±0.2
70 - 75 (n=3)	4.5±0.1	4.3±0.2	4.5±0.1
76 - 80 (n=2)	4.2±0.12	4.15±0.13	4.13±0.12
Total (n=13)	4.45±0.12	4.31±0.17	4.44±0.14

Completion Time (mins) and Asked for Help (frequency). From Table 15.3, it is seen that all the participants completed the given tasks successfully in a short period of time (1.1±0.3 mins on an average). The frequency of asking for help was also low. For three of the given tasks, none of the participants asked for any assistance. So, it can be presumed that they were able to perform the tasks efficiently.

3. Satisfaction: It is defined as the users' comfort with and positive attitudes towards the app [2]. In this study, three close-ended questions were asked to measure satisfaction based on the study of Laugwitz et al. [1] and the results are shown in Table 15.4. The overall satisfaction level of the participants was comparatively high (4.45±0.12). Their willingness to use the system in the future (4.44±0.14) and recommend it to others (4.31±0.17) was also overwhelming; thus indicating that the participants were very satisfied with the app. From the open-ended questions, the study found that a vast majority of the participants thought that the app will provide an easy-to-use and convenient way to support their daily needs. A few of them also provided helpful suggestions; for example adding features like an alarm clock, a radio station and making the app a bit more colorful.

In sum, the outcome of the evaluation study shows that the app is indeed effective, efficient, and satisfactory to the targeted end-users.

15.5 CONCLUSION

This chapter provides a brief overview of the design and development of a mobile app that will be very effective for assisting the daily needs of senior citizens. Through an extensive interview, their needs and requirements were identified in the context of Bangladesh and the light weighted evaluation study highlighted the app as a useful and innovative means to provide support to the aging population.

Undoubtedly, this app will overcome the existing problems senior citizens face while using mobile apps for their social and health-related needs. The app does so by providing vital features for fulfilling the user requirements identified through literature review, existing applications study and need-finding study. Among the context-based requirements that were extracted, the need for a simple interface and recognizable icons [17, 24], phone books, calling functions and emergency buttons [16, 15] were in common with those identified in prior studies. However, customized requirements like user interface in Bengali language, phone numbers of hospitals, vision enhancer, access to other apps, medicine/appointment reminders and updates on social events were discovered in the context of Bangladesh. Combining both these common and distinct yet helpful features into the app allows it to provide holistic support to the senior citizens by meeting their health and social needs all in one place.

The mobile app is based on the idea to simplify the lives of the elderly by compiling the key features in a single app. Although it manages to solve and tackle a lot of the issues previously discussed, it does have a few limitations. Because the app is Android-based, although it covers a significant portion of smartphone users, those using other platforms cannot access it. Moreover, a language selection option would have made the application more global. The research work was also conducted on a small scale involving a small group of people for requirement collection and app validation. For the future, the plan is to work with a larger group of people consisting of at least 50 potential users. For user benefit, future work will also look into the usefulness of features like: adding pictures with contact numbers, linking news sites, providing contact information for emergency services (firefighters, police, pharmacy), etc. All in all, further development of this app will emphasize addressing the limitations identified, discovering more requirements, as well as experimenting with different design layouts to enhance user experience.

Bibliography

[1] Laugwitz, B., Held, T. & Schrepp, M. Construction and evaluation of a user experience questionnaire. *Symposium Of The Austrian HCI And Usability Engineering Group.* pp. 63-76 (2008)

[2] Frøkjær, E., Hertzum, M. & Hornbæk, K. Measuring usability: are effectiveness, efficiency, and satisfaction really correlated? *Proceedings of the ACMCHI Conference on Human Factors in Computing Systems.* pp. 345-352 (2000)

[3] Raisamo, R., Patomáki, S., Hasu, M. & Pasto, V. Design and evaluation of a tactile memory game for visually impaired children. *Interacting With Computers.* **19**, 196-205 (2007)

[4] ISO, M. Ergonomics of human-system interaction–part 11: Usability: Definitions and concepts. (2018)

[5] Góransson, C., Wengstróm, Y., Hálleberg-Nyman, M., Langius-Eklóf, A., Ziegert, K. & Blomberg, K. An app for supporting older people receiving home care–usage, aspects of health and health literacy: a quasi-experimental study. *BMC Medical Informatics And Decision Making.* **20**, 1-10 (2020)

[6] Signoretti, A., Martins, A., Almeida, N., Vieira, D., Rosa, A., Costa, C. & Texeira, A. Trip 4 all: A gamified app to provide a new way to elderly people to travel. *Procedia Computer Science.* **67** pp. 301-311 (2015)

[7] StatCounter Operating System Market Share Bangladesh | StatCounter Global Stats. (https://gs.statcounter.com/os-market-share/all/bangladesh,2021)

[8] Hossain, M. Aging in Bangladesh and its population projections. *Pakistan Journal Of Social Science.* **3**, 62-67 (2005)

[9] Gao, J. & Koronios, A. Mobile application development for senior citizens. *PACIS.* pp. 65 (2010)

[10] Lorenz, A. & Oppermann, R. Mobile health monitoring for the elderly: Designing for diversity. *Pervasive And Mobile Computing.* **5**, 478-495 (2009)

[11] Group, T. The unconnected senior citizens of Asia - Telenor Group. (https://www.telenor.com/the-unconnected-senior-citizens-of-asia/,2015,5)

[12] Anderson, M. & Perrin, A. Think older people are technophobes? Think again | World Economic Forum. (https://www.weforum.org/agenda/2017/05/think-older-people-are-technophobes-think-again,2017,5)

[13] Anderson, M. & Perrin, A. Technology use among seniors. *Washington, DC: Pew Research Center For Internet & Technology.* (2017)

[14] Olson, K., O'Brien, M., Rogers, W. & Charness, N. Diffusion of technology: frequency of use for younger and older adults. *Ageing International.* **36**, 123-145 (2011)

[15] Chen, K., Chan, A. & Ma, Q. Cell phone feature preferences among older adults: A paired comparison study. *Gerontechnology.* **13** (2014)

[16] Rosales, A. & Fernández-Ardèvol, M. Beyond WhatsApp: Older people and smartphones. *Romanian Journal Of Communication And Public Relations.* **18**, 27-47 (2016)

[17] Salman, Y., Kim, Y. & Cheng, H. Senior-friendly icon design for the mobile phone. *6th International Conference On Digital Content, Multimedia Technology And Its Applications.* pp. 103-108 (2010)

[18] Islam, M. & Tétard, F. Exploring the impact of interface signs' interpretation accuracy, design, and evaluation on web usability: a semiotics perspective. *Journal Of Systems And Information Technology.* **16**, 250-276 (2014)

[19] Islam, M. & Inan, T. Exploring the Fundamental Factors of Digital Inequality in Bangladesh. *SAGE Open.* **11**, 21582440211021407 (2021)

[20] Jahan, M., Aziz, F., Ema, M., Islam, A. & Islam, M. A wearable system for path finding to assist elderly people in an indoor environment. *Proceedings Of The XX International Conference On Human Computer Interaction.* pp. 1-7 (2019)

[21] Islam, M., Ahmed, M. & Islam, A. Chakuri-bazaar: A mobile application for illiterate and semi-literate people for searching employment. *International Journal Of Mobile Human Computer Interaction (IJMHCI).* **12**, 22-39 (2020)

[22] Hoque, S., Sharmee, S., Islam, M., Shahrin, D. & Kabir, F. Ponno Aalap: An Interactive Web Portal for Improving Consumer Experience. *2020 IEEE Region 10 Symposium (TENSYMP)*. pp. 1770-1774 (2020)

[23] Islam, M. & Bouwman, H. Towards user–intuitive web interface sign design and evaluation: A semiotic framework. *International Journal Of Human-Computer Studies*. **86** pp. 121-137 (2016)

[24] Islam, M. Exploring the intuitiveness of iconic, textual and icon with texts signs for designing user-intuitive web interfaces. *2015 18th International Conference On Computer And Information Technology (ICCIT)*. pp. 450-455 (2015)

[25] Islam, M., Bouwman, H. & Islam, A. Evaluating web and mobile user interfaces with semiotics: An empirical study. *IEEE Access*. **8** pp. 84396-84414 (2020)

Comparative Study of Big Data Visualization Tools and Techniques

Khadija Begum

The People's University of Bangladesh, Dhaka, Bangladesh

Md Mamunur Rashid

Pukyong National University, Busan, South Korea

Mohammad Arafath Uddin Shariff

Port City International University, Chattogram, Bangladesh

CONTENTS

16.1	Introduction	189
16.2	Big Data and Data Visualization	190
16.3	Challenges and Problems of Data Visualization	191
	16.3.1 Challenges of Big Data Analysis	192
	16.3.2 Problems with Big Data Visualization	192
16.4	Big Data Visualization Tools	193
16.5	Big Data Visualization Techniques	195
16.6	Conclusion	197

W E are living in an age where everything is getting recorded digitally, thanks to the rise of the Internet and Social Media. Exabytes of data are getting generated frequently which needs to be explored, cleansed and analysed to make them usable. Big Data is a term that represents a huge volume of structured, semi-structured, or unstructured data. Translating information into meaningful visual context such as graphs, maps or charts to make data easier as well as pulling insights are called Data Visualization. It also introduces numerous possibilities for solving the Big Data problem by creative ideation through visual means. Lots of challenges as well as problems are associated with Big Data analysis due to its complex characteristics. In this chapter, we'll discuss the reasons for Big Data visualization being necessary, as well as some Big Data Visualization tools. We will also summarize different types of challenges in visualization methods as well as suggest a possible way forward for complications pertaining to the visualization of Big Data. In addition, the working procedure, characteristics, and drawbacks of several tools and techniques for Big Data visualization are examined in our research.

16.1 INTRODUCTION

Big Data has become one of the most sought-after topics in almost every industry, including academia, IT companies, and government agencies. Owing to many factors such as the Internet, Social Media, Telecommunication, IoT sensors, and the digitization of all offline information such as our medical history, the volume of data has risen exponentially in the last few years. The massive data that got produced from these sources is called the Big Data. Big Data represents larger, more complex datasets from various data sources that can be displayed in a variety of data formats, with the majority of them not being structural data flows [1]. The main concerns of Big Data are capturing, storing, analysing, and visualizing data. Interesting patterns can be found from Big Data analysis and when visualized, it helps our brain making better decisions.

The representation of raw, unprocessed data using various visual elements such as graphs, maps, and diagrams is known as data visualization. It's been around for millennia and is a simple and fast way to communicate messages and reflect complex objects. Due to its dynamic nature, visualizing Big Data is a difficult task and traditional visualization tools often are incapable of representing the significance of Big Data. Current researches in Big Data visualization are focused on inventing and improving visualization tools and techniques that enable them to get effective results.

This research is based on recent scholarly research and publicly available Big Data related articles. Most of the research articles were focused on challenges of Big Data and also on various data visualization tools and techniques. The contributions of this research are:

- A brief study of the current scenarios of Big Data, highlighting the main challenges and errors which need to be avoided for Big Data visualization.

- Exploration of some popular visualization tools and their features.

- Discussion over the most common and latest tools for Big Data visualization along with their advantages and disadvantages.

- Review of the complex techniques and methods to represent the data visualization output.

- Suggestion of future research scope based on the limitations of current tools and techniques.

The succeeding sections of our study are as follows: Section 16.2 describes the definition of Big Data and provides a brief introduction to data visualization; Section 16.3 discusses the challenges and problems of data visualization in details depending on the different variations of the data; Section 16.4 accommodates the most popular visualization tools currently in the practice; Section 16.5 provides some insight into the visualization methods which can be used to effectively represent the Big Data. This study's major propositions, a number of possible future research directions and study's concluding statements are detailed in the last section.

16.2   BIG DATA AND DATA VISUALIZATION

Nowadays a huge amount of data from numerous data sources are available all over the world. Social network, IoT sensors, meteorological data, streams from mobile subscribers, text messages, recordings (audio and video) are continuously contributing as the data sources. As a consequence of this, Big Data is getting used more frequently all over the world and is an emerging research field.

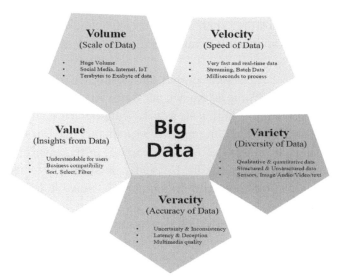

Figure 16.1: Characteristics (5 Vs) of Big Data.

Big Data is usually represented by the 5Vs, namely, Volume, Velocity, Variety, Veracity, and Value [2]. Figure 16.1 above represents the meaning of 5Vs and attributes of these characteristics. As per [3] the short description of the 5Vs are as follows:

- Volume: It refers to the vast amount of data being produced and stored.

- Variety: It reflects the variety of data in terms of types, contents, and formats.

- Velocity: It denotes the rate at which data is produced and gathered.

- Veracity: It means the quality (uncertainty and consistency) of data.

- Value: It refers to usefulness of the data to derive insights from it.

Visualization of Big Data comes with massive research challenges and opportunities. Processing the huge amount of data is not only the main concern but also processing of data with huge diversity is of prime importance. The application's response time is usually hampered by high data diversity and uncertainty, so visualization tools must devise new ways to process, analyze, and visualize this massive volume of complex data. Many businesses and open-source initiatives are focusing on developing new digital technologies and promoting Big Data analysis to aid analytics through visualization. Designing visualization tools with proper indexing is a very complex and tiresome process in Big Data. Tools need to handle a variety of semistructured and unstructured data types, including speech, audio, tables, graphs, text, video and other metadata formats. Because of bandwidth and power constraints, visualization should get as close to the data as possible to obtain useful information [4].

Users can currently combine disparate data sources to generate custom analytical views using a variety of visualization-based data exploration methods. The creation of interactive graphics with meaningful insights can be derived if advanced analytics can be integrated with these methods. Over the years, Big Data visualization has helped organizations from various perspectives such as decision making and data analytics. The use of advanced visualization software/technique allows for rapid exploration of all customer/user data in order to enhance customer-company relationships, product sales correlations, and customer profiles. So, organizations can get a great amount of assistance through visualized data to find a variety of successful marketing solutions as cited by [5]. Figure 16.2 depicts the few benefits of data analytics and visualization.

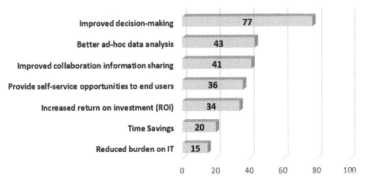

Figure 16.2: Benefits of using data visualization according to a survey [*Source: IDG Research Services, August 2012*].

16.3 CHALLENGES AND PROBLEMS OF DATA VISUALIZATION

One of the most complex aspects of dealing with Big Data is displaying the results of data analysis in a coherent and non-overwhelming manner. It's high time to develop a modern approach to data visualization that is both intuitive and useful to users while displaying graphs and charts. Traditional architecture and software can struggle to process the vast collection of data in a cost-effective manner, necessitating visualization compromises. Due to storage limitations and inadequate support for various data types, even the most basic statistical calculations can become complicated when dealing with Big Data [6].

16.3.1 Challenges of Big Data Analysis

Uncovering interesting patterns and connections among large sets of data is the prime concern for data visualization. We must be cautious while selecting the data dimensions, minimizing the dimensions to keep visualization small risks missing important patterns; on the other hand, if we use all dimensions, we risk making a visualization that is too heavy to be beneficial to users [7]. Due to the following attributes of Big Data, we face many obstacles when we are dealing with Big Data analysis [8].

Heterogeneity: Machine analysis algorithms are typically designed for homogeneous data and struggle to comprehend heterogeneous data. As a result, data should be meticulously organized before being analyzed.

Scale: Data growth outpaces CPU speeds and other compute resources.

Inconsistency and incompleteness: The resources are more diverse than ever and lack reliability. There is uncertainty, error, and missing value issues which must be managed.

Timeliness: It is necessary to filter and analyze data in real-time since it is not economically viable to store all of the raw data.

Privacy and data ownership: Privacy and ownership of the data such as inappropriate use of personal data is a massive concern.

The human perspective: For Big Data to achieve its full potential, it must be viewed from a human viewpoint. We, as humans, must be able to absorb the result of Big Data analysis.

16.3.2 Problems with Big Data Visualization

Since Big Data has such a large volume and magnitude, visualizing it becomes extremely difficult. The majority of current visualization tools perform poorly in terms of scalability, functionality, and response time [9]. The following are several other significant visualization issues for Big Data as mentioned by [10].

Visual Noise: Since a large share of the elements in a dataset are too relevant to one another, users often can't split them into separate objects. As a result, users often struggle to extract even a small amount of useful information from whole data visualizations that do not include any pre-processing tasks.

Large Image Perception: Humans lose their ability to extract any useful information from a data-overloaded view after reaching the highest level of awareness, and they have trouble understanding data visualization [10].

Information Loss: Due to aggregation and filtration in visualization approaches it's possible to sometime miss interesting hidden objects and visualization can be misleading.

High Performance Requirements: As there is a requirement for dynamic visualization, the above problems often get bigger due to the requirement of high performance.

High Rate of Image Change: When the audience viewing the data fails to react or respond to the data change, simply slowing down the changing rate will not achieve the desired result.

16.4 BIG DATA VISUALIZATION TOOLS

Currently, there are lots of data visualization platforms available for data analysis, each with its own set of features and limitations. Some could be better suited for a specific format of information, whereas some are good for a specific segment of information. The tools gather data from various sources and graphically represent the results/output. Some visualization tools automatically demonstrate the characteristics of the data and determine the relationship between the variables, after which they determine the form of chart to use to show the results [11]. We've gone through some of the most common visualization tools in this section. In Figures 16.3 and 16.4, we have presented few samples of the data visualization tools already existing in the industry.

Tableau: Tableau is a dashboard-based visual analytics platform that allows users to construct immersive visual analytics. These dashboards enable transforming data into understandable, interactive graphics simpler for non-technical analysts as well as end users [12]. The main features are: numerous data import options, capability of mapping, free public version and lots of video tutorials available to help one become an expert. The few limitations are: licensed versions are expensive and there is no privacy of source data for the public version.

Microsoft Power BI: Power BI is a feature-rich cloud-based advanced analytics service. It consists of software services and apps that work together to process data from unrelated sources and present visually interactive insights [13]. The main features are: visualizations are interactive and rich, publishes reports securely, no memory or speed constraints, and integrates seamlessly with many applications. Mentionable limitations are: crowded user interface and rigid formulas and difficult to understand and master.

Infogram: This web-based data visualization and infographics tool enables users to create and share graphs, illustrations, diagrams, and maps. In Infogram, there is a WordPress plugin that makes embedding visualizations much simpler for WordPress users [14]. The main features are: offers interactive visualization, no coding skill required, free version available, API for data sources. The limitations are: basic product does not allow users to adjust the font size or style. As a result of the lack of such basic features, details can be misleading at times.

Google Charts: Google Charts is a data visualization tool available for browsers and mobile devices that is efficient, easy to use, and interactive. Google charts can be integrated with Google Spreadsheets, Google Fusion Tables, Salesforce, and some other SQL databases [15]. The features are: completely free, offers huge collection of chart types, dynamic, and compatible with browsers. The limitations are: very limited support, Google chat is not added yet, coding knowledge required.

Jupyter: Jupyter is another open-source unique tool which enables us to interactively analyze and visualize Big Data. It supports real-time software development

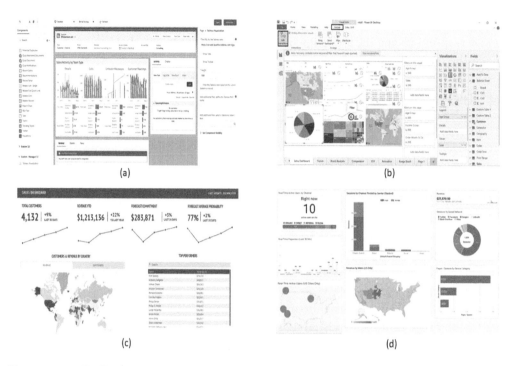

Figure 16.3: Different popular and trendy Big Data visualization tools currently getting used extensively. (a) Tableau interactive visual analytics [12]; (b) Sales and Return analysis in Power BI [13]; (c) Basic visualization in Infogram [14]; (d) Different types of Google Charts [15].

collaboration through a variety of programming languages [16]. The advantages are: can interact with multiple frameworks, both the code and the results are visible, very easy to host server side, better security. The limitations are: doesn't play very well with other tools, bad for running long asynchronous tasks.

D3.js: D3.js is a JavaScript based library that allows us to manipulate documents with data. Data can be encapsulated in HTML, SVG, and CSS files using D3. It is capable of producing dynamic, interactive data visualizations in web browsers [4]. The main features are: easy to customize the visualization, extremely fast and works well with large datasets, open-source. The limitations are: not enough official tutorials, coding knowledge is required.

SocNetV: Social Network Visualizer (SocNetV) is a cross-platform software application for social network analysis and visualization. This software enables users to construct networks on a virtual environment in a variety of formats. The main features of this software include network cohesion metrics such as density, diameter, geodesics and distances, clustering, etc. Different algorithms, matrix routines, and layout models are also available in this tool [17]. The main limitation is it is only available for social network analysis.

Tulip: Tulip is a data analysis and visualization platform for relational data. Its primary goal is to provide a comprehensive library for developers to use in creating interactive visualization applications for relational data that can be customized to

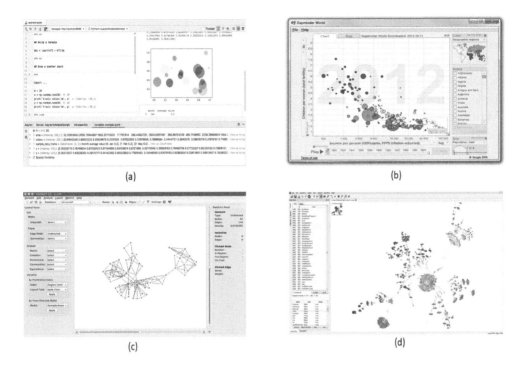

Figure 16.4: Few more commonly used popular Big Data visualization tools. (a) Interfaces of Jupyter with input and output [16]; (b) Visualization D3.js (Data-Driven Documents) [4]; (c) SocNetV Visualization [17]; (d) Visualization in Tulip [18].

address specific issues. The system is written in C++, allowing the development of latest algorithms, data types, visual mappings, and strategies for visualization [18]. The main limitation is that there are limited resource/tutorials to master.

16.5 BIG DATA VISUALIZATION TECHNIQUES

The different characteristics of Big Data requires users to leave their comfort zone and ask for more exploration and innovation in visualization techniques to derive insights and decisions. Every now and then, new and more advanced visualization techniques are developed based on the fundamentals of data analysis, which include not only cardinality but also data structure and origin. We have provided some popular data visualization methods in Figures 16.5 and 16.6, which are going to be vital for the Big Data visualization sector.

Kernel Density Estimation: Kernel Density Estimation started by plotting the data and aiming to generate a distribution curve. The curve is calculated by weighing the distance between each point in the distribution. It is a non-parametric method for evaluating and visualizing a random variable's probability density function. It can be used in determining the class-conditional marginal densities of data that can improve its prediction accuracy [19].

Box and Whisker Plot: Binned box plots with whiskers are used to graphically represent classes of numerical data by their quartile distribution of large data, allowing outliers to be easily identified. In a Box and Whisker plot, there are lower, upper edges and the middle line to represent percentile. Whiskers that stretch out from the box's edges reflect extreme values that are beyond the lower and upper percentiles. They save space, which is beneficial for comparing distributions across multiple groups or datasets [20].

Word Clouds and Network Diagrams: A word cloud is useful to visualize uncoded text responses that are not possible to show in a conventional bar chart or a table. Cluster of words of different sizes are used for its depiction and a word with more frequency and more importance in the given text appears bigger and bolder [21]. Semi-structured or unstructured data can be visualized in Network Diagrams. They use nodes, actors, and elements to portray relationships and their connections (relationships between individuals).

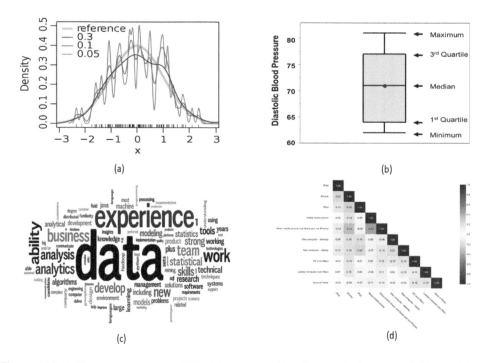

Figure 16.5: Some examples of Big Data visualization techniques. (a) Kernel density estimation [19]; (b) Box and Whisker Plot [20]; (c) A word cloud [21]; (d) Correlation matrices [6].

Correlation Matrices: By combining large amounts of data, a correlation matrix allows for fast visualization of relationships between variables [6]. In essence, it is a table that displays correlation coefficients between various variables, with each cell representing a relationship between two variables. It could come in handy when analyzing numerous linear regression models.

Decision Trees: A decision tree is a tool for making decisions that uses a tree-like model of selections and their likely responses, such as chance event outcomes, overhead charges, and utility. In a dataset, decision trees reflect the relationship between input and target values. When a close relationship between the target and input values is discovered, all of these values are grouped into a bin that becomes a decision tree branch [6].

Histograms: Histograms are one of the simplest visualizations to create for huge datasets because they simply require the inclusion of frequency weights in the bar size computation and display the bins as segmented columns [22]. The set of values must first be binned, and then each interval's number of values should be counted. The next move is to draw a rectangle with a height comparable to the tally and a width equal to the bin dimension.

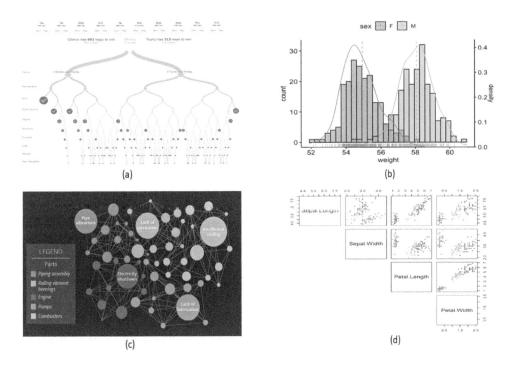

Figure 16.6: Some more examples of common Big Data visualization techniques. (a) Data segmented in a Decision Tree; (b) Visualization in Histogram [22]; (c) Connectivity charts [23]; (d) Scatterplot Matrices [24].

Connectivity Charts: The links between marvels or events are depicted in connectivity charts. The diagram above, for instance, shows the relationships between hardware failures and their causes, as well as the quality of these relationships [23].

Scatterplot Matrices: A scatter plot matrix is a powerful visualization technique that visualizes multivariate relationships between combinations of variables using a grid (or matrix) of scatter plots as stated by [24]. One can customize the scatterplots with density ellipses for all data or just groups of data for further study.

16.6 CONCLUSION

We have discussed several main characteristics of Big Data, as well as the complexities and problems of Big Data visualization throughout this paper. We have also reviewed some popular open-source multi-platform visualization tools and methods with their respective advantages and limitations from different perspectives. It is critical to first determine goals and then choose an appropriate tool from a variety of data visualization platforms. Visualization techniques/methods are equally important to understand the data, getting insights and making decisions. From our study, some startling revelations were made, all of which are valid in today's world. There is still scope for improvement, and subsequent works should be directed in optimizing the constrains of the tools and techniques. Future research in addressing and overcoming Big Data challenges such as data heterogeneity, inconsistency, and security offers enormous potential.

Bibliography

[1] Gorodov, E.Y.E. and Gubarev, V.V.E. (2013). *Analytical review of data visualization methods in application to Big Data.* Journal of Electrical and Computer Engineering, 2013.

[2] Andrienko, G., Andrienko, N., Drucker, S., Fekete, J. D., Fisher, D., Idreos, S., ... & Sharaf, M. (2020, March). *Big Data visualization and analytics: Future research challenges and emerging applications.* In BigVis 2020-3rd International Workshop on Big Data Visual Exploration and Analytics.

[3] Zion, G. D., & Tripathy, B. K. (2020). *Comparative analysis of tools for Big Data visualization and challenges.* Springer, Data Visualization, 33-52.

[4] Caldarola, E. G., & Rinaldi, A. M. (2017). *Big Data visualization tools: a survey* Research Gate.

[5] Olshannikova, E., Ometov, A., Koucheryavy, Y., & Olsson, T. (2015). *Visualizing Big Data with augmented and virtual reality: challenges and research agenda.* Journal of Big Data, 2(1), 1-27.

[6] Choy, J., Chawla, V. and Whitman, L. (2013). *Data visualization techniques: from basics to Big Data with SAS visual analytics.* SAS: White Paper.

[7] Manyika, J., Chui, M., Brown, B., Bughin, J., Dobbs, R., Roxburgh, C., & Byers, A. H. (2011). *Big Data: The next frontier for innovation, competition (Vol. 5, No. 6). and productivity.* Technical report, McKinsey Global Institute.

[8] Jagadish, H. V., Gehrke, J., Labrinidis, A., Papakonstantinou, Y., Patel, J. M., Ramakrishnan, R., & Shahabi, C. (2014). *Big Data and its technical challenges.* Communications of the ACM, 57(7), 86-94.

[9] Wang, L., Wang, G., & Alexander, C. A. (2015). *Big Data and visualization: methods, challenges and technology progress.* Digital Technologies, 1(1), 33-38.

[10] Hajirahimova, M., & Ismayilova, M. (2018). *Big Data visualization: Existing approaches and problems.* Problems of Information Technology, 9, 72-83.

[11] Gavin Mcleod. 30 Simple Tools For Data Visualization. *https://www.fastcompany.com/3029239/30-simple-tools-for-data-visualization.*

[12] Tableau Homepage. *https://www.tableau.com/.*

[13] Power BI Homepage. *https://powerbi.microsoft.com/.*

[14] Infogram Homepage. *https://infogram.com/.*

[15] Room, C. (2020). *Exploratory Data Analysis.* Machine learning, 8(39), 23.

[16] Top 4 Popular Big Data Visualization Tools. *https://towardsdatascience.com/top-4-popular-big-data-visualization-tools-4ee945fe207d.*

[17] Socnetv Homepage. *https://socnetv.org//.*

[18] Tulip Library. *https://tulip.labri.fr/site/.*

[19] Kernel Density Estimation. *https://deepai.org/machine-learning-glossary-and-terms/kernel-density-estimation.*

[20] Box and Whisker Plot. *https://www.simplypsychology.org/boxplots.html.*

[21] WordCloud Home. *https://www.wordclouds.com/.*

[22] Wilkinson, L. (2017). *Visualizing Big Data outliers through distributed aggregation.* IEEE transactions on visualization and computer graphics, 24(1), 256-266.

[23] Connectivity Charts. *https://datascience.foundation/sciencewhitepaper/a-quick-intro-into-big-data-visualization-techniques-and-tools.*

[24] Gandhi, P., & Pruthi, J. (2020). *Data Visualization Techniques: Traditional Data to Big Data.* Data Visualization: Trends and Challenges Toward Multidisciplinary Perception, 53.

CHAPTER 17

Low-Cost IoT-Based Power Interruption Monitoring System

Deepak Chandra Roy

Dhaka Power Distribution Company Limited (DPDC), 1 Abdul Gani Road, Dhaka-1000, Bangladesh.

Md Shazzad Hossain

Dhaka Power Distribution Company Limited (DPDC), 1 Abdul Gani Road, Dhaka-1000, Bangladesh and Federation University, Australia.

Amit Kumar Das

Dhaka Power Distribution Company Limited (DPDC), 1 Abdul Gani Road, Dhaka-1000, Bangladesh.

Md. Ashraf Ali

Sigma Engineers Ltd., Dhaka-1230, Bangladesh.

Mohammad Azam Khan

Dhaka Power Distribution Company Limited (DPDC), 1 Abdul Gani Road, Dhaka-1000, Bangladesh.

CONTENTS

17.1 Introduction 201
17.2 KPIs for Quality Control of Power Supply 202
17.3 IoT-based Device Design and Implementation 203
    17.3.1 Determination of Breaker Status 203
        17.3.1.1   CB Auxiliary Contacts 204
        17.3.1.2   Relay Output Contact 204
    17.3.2 IoT-based Device 205
17.4 Development of Web-based System 206
17.5 Results for Pilot Study 207
17.6 Discussion 207
17.7 Conclusion and Future Work 210

Today's world is more reliant on electricity in every sphere of its development than ever before. This has prompted energy regulators, utility companies and other associated entities to look at the quality aspect of electricity more closely. The quality of electricity is largely dependant on ensuring reliability at every stage of its distribution. Thus an economical and effective mechanism to measure the reliability of electricity is vital for any electrical distribution network. In this study, we propose a low-cost IoT-based solution to automatically evaluate two standard key performance indicators (KPIs) for the continuation of power supply in a distribution network: (i) system average interruption frequency index (SAIFI) and (ii) system average interruption duration index (SAIDI). Moreover, we develop a web-based real-time power interruption monitoring system (PIMS) for further power outage analysis, strategic decision-making, and improved customer service.

17.1 INTRODUCTION

The primary goal of the power distribution network is to provide sufficient electricity to customers with fair assurance of reliability. Hence, the utility companies must ensure the optimum strategic planning and lowest potential costs for the requirements of reliable power supply to its customers [1]. In this regard, monitoring of failures and outages in the distribution network is critical in order to determine the reliability of power supply. Gono et al. (2007) [2] analyzed data about failures and outages of the electrical power supply from multiple distribution areas to obtain reliability indices of a distribution network. A study conducted by Sekhar et al. (2016) [4] makes an attempt to measure different reliability indices including SAIFI, SAIDI and other indicators of power distribution network. Another study [5] attempts to determine the reliability index values for the electricity distribution network system, specifically the failure rate, the average output time, the average annual unavailability, SAIFI, SAIDI, among others. These values are accomplished by performing a simple data recapitulation on each unit in the network and then calculating the index of reliability using reliability index formulas. A further study [6] discussed many aspects of reliability research in distribution systems, focusing on three major areas: reliability principles in distribution systems, reliability indexes, and reliability assessment of distribution systems.

The review [7] provides a concise illustration of detailed comparisons and literature surveys for distribution substation reliability using various improvement mechanisms, measurement methods, and reliability indices. Olusuyi et al. (2014) [8] investigated the electrical power infrastructure, including the state of all related equipment and energy availability, to conduct a fault analysis of the 11 kV distribution power system. Diamenu et al. (2019) [9] evaluated the mean-time-to-failure (MTTF), mean-time-to-repair (MTTR), and other reliability indices to quantify the performance of a selected 33 kV electric power distribution network. Another research [10] examined the performance of a 22 kV overhead feeder line by identifying the causes of failure, analyzing outages, and developing a process for improving the feeder's performance.

Indeed, utility companies are concerned about supplying uninterrupted power to customers. Hence, these companies are concentrating on improving customer service by ensuring that their customers have constant access to quality supply of electricity. To achieve this goal, first of all, companies need to monitor power outages and restorations in real-time. As a result, they have to incorporate an integrated digitalized system within their distribution network [11, 12]. In particular, we can develop such system by determining the operating status of a circuit breaker (CB) located in two different types of substations: substation automation system (SAS) based and non-SAS-based substations. We require at least two separate statuses (manual shutdown and CB tripping due to faults) from CB to calculate reliability indices.

When CBs are integrated into SAS, i.e., when these instruments are mounted in SAS-based substations, it is relatively easy to obtain various statuses and other details. Tagging appropriate trip logics from an already established and running software system for SAS-based substations could be used to collect necessary statuses. Unlike SAS-based substation, however, non-SAS-based substations lack automation software and other requisite facilities to retrieve information to calculate reliability indices from CBs. The key topics covered in this study would be collecting, processing, and preparing reports using these statuses.

To sum up, this study has taken steps to develop a cost-effective solution and to evaluate quality of power supply in a distribution network considering non-SAS-based substations. The contributions of our work include:

- We develop an IoT-based device that captures the interruption signals from CB and then logs the processed signal into the server automatically.

- A web-based system called power interruption monitoring system (PIMS) has been developed and deployed for real-time power interruption monitoring, outage analysis, and strategic decision-making.

- Overall, the novelty of the chapter is that this study proposes a low-cost IoT-based solution to evaluate several key performance indicators (KPIs) for the continuation of the power supply.

17.2   KPIS FOR QUALITY CONTROL OF POWER SUPPLY

The Institute of Electrical and Electronics Engineers (IEEE) formulated several standards [13] of measurement as KPIs for electric power distribution reliability indices. System average interruption frequency index (SAIFI) and system average interruption duration index (SAIDI) are two critical indicators to assess continuation of power supply to customers.

SAIFI is the average number of interruptions for each customer served over the course of a year, and is computed as:

$$SAIFI = \frac{\sum \lambda_i N_i}{N_T} \tag{17.1}$$

where λ_i is the failure rate and N_i is the number of customers for location i. N_T is the total number of customers served.

On the other hand, SAIDI is the average outage duration that a customer would experience throughout the year, and is calculated as:

$$SAIDI = \frac{\sum U_i N_i}{N_T} \qquad (17.2)$$

where N_i is the number of customers and U_i is the annual outage duration for location i. N_T is the total number of customers served.

17.3 IOT-BASED DEVICE DESIGN AND IMPLEMENTATION

An indispensable process of SAIFI and SAIDI calculation is to determine the exact operating status of the CB of the respective feeder. The method of determining the operating status of CB and feeding the captured signal to an IoT-based device is described in the following subsections.

17.3.1 Determination of Breaker Status

An electrical CB normally operates in two binary states: OPEN/OFF State and CLOSE/ON State. At any given time, the breaker is either OFF or ON. A CB can be operated manually using push buttons or automatically using protection relays. Manual operations are subject to scheduled maintenance, outage operations, etc. On the contrary, automatic operations are performed primarily due to power system faults inhibiting tripping signals from the relay protecting the circuit. Manual operation and tripping status are then fed to the external IoT device for further process and pass the information to the web-based power interruption management system (PIMS) through secure VPN connectivity to calculate SAIFI and SAIDI later on. The breaker status data feed mechanism is shown in Figure 17.1(a).

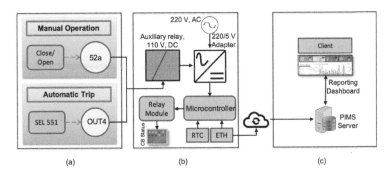

Figure 17.1: Overall architecture: (a) Breaker status data collection, (b) IoT-based device, and (c) Web-based system

17.3.1.1 CB Auxiliary Contacts

One way to determine the CB status is to check the status of auxiliary contacts. Conventionally a CB has two such contacts: one that mimics its exact status and the other does the opposite. As per ANSI, these contacts are named 52a and 52b, respectively. 52a is a normally open (NO) contact and 52b is a normally closed (NC) contact. Change of status of these two auxiliary contacts with CB status is shown in Table 17.1.

CB	52a (NO)	52b (NC)
Closed	Closed	Open
Open	Open	Closed

Table 17.1: Auxiliary contact status with respect to CB

17.3.1.2 Relay Output Contact

Any SAIFI and SAIDI application should be able to differentiate between planned outages and tripping due to faults. This can be realized by obtaining status of tripping signal from the protection relay. Modern microprocessor based relays are equipped with several output contacts which can be configured to send the tripping signal to external IoT devices [14]. The process covered in this manuscript utilizes an output contact of SEL 551 Overcurrent and Reclosing relay manufactured by Schweitzer Engineering Laboratories as a pilot study. This is a feeder protection relay [15]. The protection functions incorporated in this relay are shown in Figure 17.2. Although SEL 551 relay has built-in reclosing functions, it is omitted to keep the design in the simplistic form for this project.

This relay has a special feature called SELogic control equations which can be configured to achieve desirable operations of the relay. The trip logic of SEL 551 relay is shown in Figure 17.3, where TR is trip conditions, ULTR is unlatch trip conditions, TRGTR is target reset, TRIP is the relay word bit initiating trip signal and TDURD is the minimum trip duration time.

As depicted in Figure 17.3 TRIP asserts to logical 1 whenever TR equals logical 1 irrespective of other trip logic conditions. TR asserts to logical 1 whenever any of the protection functions described in Figure 17.2 asserts to logical 1 defined by SELogic control equation of TR. Incorporating all protection functions into TR, it can be defined for instance as shown in Eq. 17.3.

$$TR = 51P1T + 51N1T + 50P1 + 50N1 \qquad (17.3)$$

SEL 551 relay has four user configurable output contacts of which Output 04 (designated as 'OUT4') is spared by default. This spare contact is used to send tripping data to external IoT device. SEL 551 has ten SELogic variables having timer outputs. The relay word bit TRIP is piped through any of those timers to account for breaker failure timing. OUT4 is set as $OUT4 = SV5T$ where $SV5 = TRIP$. $SV5T$ is the timed output of SELogic variable $SV5$ as shown in Figure 17.4. The timer's

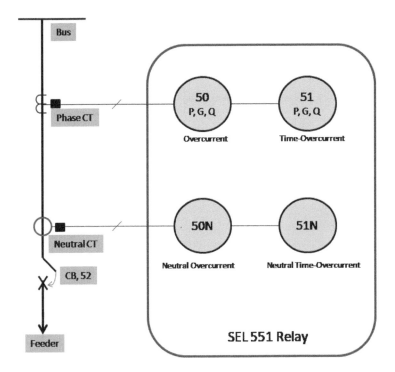

Figure 17.2: Protection functions of SEL 551 relay

output can be controlled by modifying its pickup ($SV5PU$) and dropout ($SV5DO$) cycles. For this project, these values are set to 12 and 2 cycles, respectively.

17.3.2 IoT-based Device

We prepare an IoT-based device to automatically capture the interruption signals from CB located in substation in which substation automation system (SAS) is not available. The device is composed of several components. One of the main components is the microcontroller and we have used the Arduino mega 2560 as the microcontroller. The other components are: a real-time clock (RTC), Ethernet shield (ETH) and an SD card. When a feeder is tripped, the microcontroller senses the different voltage signals and makes the decision whether it is a controlled tripped or uncontrolled trip. These decisions are simultaneously sent to a central web server through the Ethernet shield and written into the internal SD card. The IoT device makes a bridge by establishing a network between the non-SAS substation and the central server and provides different types of interruption data by analyzing the electrical signals.

The changes of CB statuses due to planned outages and protection tripping are collected via two separate NO contacts from breaker auxiliary contact 52a and SEL 551 relay OUT4 contact. These two contacts are then fed to two separate auxiliary DC-110 volts relays. When a tripping/manual opening event of CB occurs, a relay particular to that event energizes and activates an 220/5 volt, AC adapter connected to its circuit. The adapter's output is connected to the microcontroller input. When the microcontroller receives an input at one of its ports, it recognizes the event.

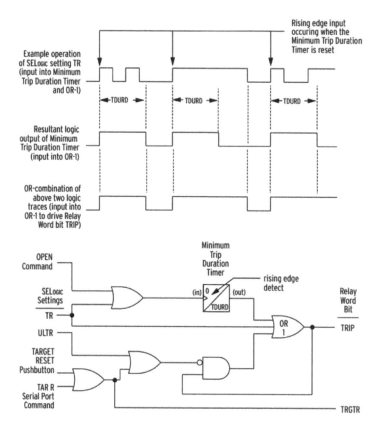

Figure 17.3: Trip logic of SEL 551 [15]

This particular event is then sent to a PIMS server via a secured VPN channel. The mechanism is shown in Figure 17.1(b).

17.4 DEVELOPMENT OF WEB-BASED SYSTEM

As soon as any power interruption occurs, the IoT device immediately records the data and sends it to the server in which web-based PIMS has been deployed as shown in Figure 17.1(c). The device sends the affected feeder information along with the trip time. A web-based dashboard and reporting tool has been developed to organize and to analyze these interruptions in real-time. LogRegister, Interruption, Feeder, Substation, and Location are the major entities of the web-based system. Figure 17.5 shows an entity-relationship diagram (ERD) for various entities.

The *LogRegister* is the actual logbook that records the time of each power off and power on of feeders as shown in Figure 17.1. The property *Event_Status* captures the power off or on flag. Feeders can be shut down for two reasons: one is for routine maintenance (controlled), and the other is for an earth fault or a system fault (uncontrolled). The property *Interruption_Type* is also a flag that determines these controlled and uncontrolled trips. The *Interruption* entity is a processed table that deals with the raw data of the *LogRegister* entity and finds out the actual duration

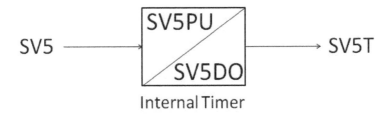

Figure 17.4: SELogic variable SV5

between powers off and on time. Both the *Feeder* and *Interruption* entities hold the *No_of_customer* attribute. The number of customers assigned to a feeder usually change over time. We must store the historical demographic value of affected customer numbers against any power interruptions in order to accurately calculate SAIFI and SAIDI.

The web-based system allows users to create a variety of reports. The system can provide a breakdown of interruption data by customer service unit/office, substation, and feeder. A few screenshots of the system are shown in Figures 17.6 and 17.7 (information is partly withheld not to disclose the authors' identities). While the first screenshot indicates an overall interruption for all feeders, the second provides a more fine-grained interruption report for a specific feeder. Interruption reports can be generated by the hour, day, week, month, and year.

17.5 RESULTS FOR PILOT STUDY

As a test result of pilot implementation at Mogbazar Substation of DPDC, we have collected data for several CBs for February 2021 and March 2021. The data pushed from the developed device at the substation in this interim period are shown in Table 17.2. During those two months, a total of 8,764 customers were served through four CBs, with 52 interruptions and 21.3 hours (1278 minutes) of power outages. On the basis of the data, we can compute the SAIFI and SAIDI indices for the aforementioned two months, which are 14.8 times and 390.77 minutes, respectively. Due to human interventional error, the data from the manual log register of the substation sometimes differs from the machine-generated data. In practice, the data generated by the proposed device is more accurate and validated.

17.6 DISCUSSION

When a substation is equipped with a substation automation system (SAS), it is easy to capture power interruption signals (e.g., CB ON, CB OFF) and operating mode (e.g., test mode, service mode and so on) from the system. However, such a system comes at a substantial cost of investment for utility companies. As a result, many organizations have been unable to implement SAS-based systems in many substations. Given this, our developed system may be a viable alternative for assessing reliability indices in a distribution network. It would, in the end, ensure a more focused customer service and more efficient use of limited resources available to utility

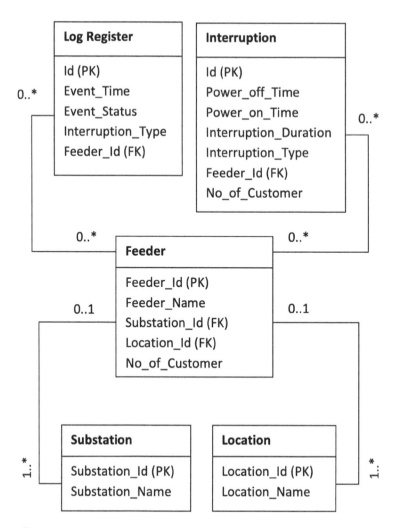

Figure 17.5: ERD for different entities of web-based system

companies. Second, several non-SAS systems have already been installed in the utility network. To calculate KPIs, we need to capture CB status in these substations. A mechanism should be implemented to properly and safely handle interruption information. Indeed, a few systems are available on the market, but they are all proprietary and expensive. Hence, we attempt to develop a cost-effective IoT-based solution where SAS-based implementation is not available. In addition, our newly developed web-based monitoring system will assist utilities in real-time monitoring of power interruption.

There are certain limitations to this research. For handling a single CB in a substation, we consider a single IoT-based unit for collecting different statuses of a CB. This will require a moderate number of IoT devices for each substation. In the future study, the architecture will be improved to accommodate multiple CBs in a single IoT-based device. It would lower the cost of instruments while also taking up less space in the substation.

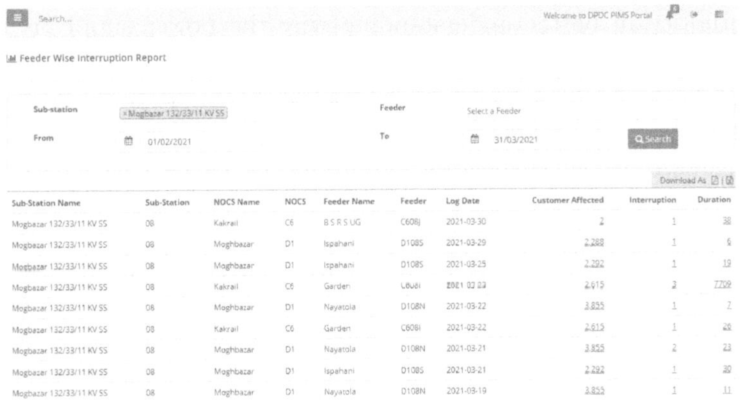

Figure 17.6: Overall interruptions for all feeders

Figure 17.7: Interruption report for an individual feeder

Our web-based system is currently handling data for non-SAS-based substations. In the future, we may enhance this system to accommodate data collected from SAS-based substations as well. This can be accomplished by correctly tagging the trip logic from an already installed and running software system for SAS-based substations. We then utilize a data-pulling mechanism in the terminal unit (e.g., the computer in which the SAS software is installed) located in substations to retrieve and send data at the PIMS server on a regular interval basis.

Importantly, the web-based reporting tool can be utilized for predictive maintenance of a feeder. Using this reporting tool, we can extract information about frequently tripped feeders, their causes, and other relevant information. This will

Table 17.2: Number of interruption and duration

Feeder Name	Customers Served	No. of Interruption	Duration (Minutes)
BSRSUG	2	1	38
Garden	2615	16	428
Ispahani	2292	19	437
Nayatola	3855	16	375
Total	8764	52	1278

assist the authority in better understanding why the power supply is usually disrupted. The authority would finally have enough room to make an informed decision on how to enhance customer service in a timely manner. Past performance evaluation is necessary, because it aids in identifying the areas of the network that performs poorly and the need for improvements [16].

17.7   CONCLUSION AND FUTURE WORK

In this study, we present a low-cost IoT-based solution along with a web-based reporting tool for automatic power interruption monitoring in a power distribution network. This system will aid the distribution utilities to monitor the reliability of the power supply to its customers. Our developed web-based tool can be utilized for predictive maintenance of a feeder as well by leveraging the information about frequently tripped feeders, their causes, and other relevant information.

Instead of adopting a single feeder into a single IoT device, in the future study, we will improve our solution by incorporating multiple CBs into a single IoT unit to decrease expenses even further. Moreover, our developed web-based system can be utilized to capture, process, and visualize information using data collected from SAS-based substations as well. All of these interventions will accelerate the research activities for reliable power supply to customers and eventually will enhance customer service in the long run.

ACKNOWLEDGMENT

We are very thankful to Mr. Joni Barua (Sub-Divisional Engineer, DPDC), Mr. Arif Shahriar (Sub-Divisional Engineer, DPDC), Mr. Md. Shafiqul Islam (Executive Engineer, DPDC), Mr. Md. Abdul Wahed Halim (Executive Engineer, DPDC), and a few other personnel for their enormous help and engagement during the implementation of the pilot project at Mogbazar grid substation of DPDC.

Bibliography

[1] Anthony, R. (2014). Reliability Analysis of Distribution Network. *Technical Report*. Universiti Tun Hussein Onn Malaysia.

[2] Gono, R., Rusek, S. & Kratky M. (2007). Reliability analysis of distribution networks. In *2007 9th International Conference on Electrical Power Quality and Utilisation*. EPQU 2007 - Conference Proceedings. 1-5. doi: 10.1109/EPQU.2007.4424180.

[3] Gono, R., Rusek, S., Kratky, M. & Leonowicz, Z. (2011). Reliability Analysis of Electric Distribution System. In *2011 10th International Conference on Environment and Electrical Engineering*. EEEIC.EU 2011 - Conference Proceedings. 1-4. doi: 10.1109/EEEIC.2011.5874842.

[4] Sekhar, P.C., Deshpande, R.A. & Sankar, V. (2016). Evaluation and Improvement of Reliability Indices of Electrical Power Distribution System. In *2016 National Power Systems Conference (NPSC)*. p. 1–6.

[5] Sucita, T., Mulyadi, Y. & Timotius, C. (2018). Reliability Evaluation of Power Distribution System with Reliability Index Assessment (RIA). In *IOP Conference Series: Materials Science and Engineering*. 384, 012072.

[6] Lantharthong, T. & Phanthuna, N. (2012). Techniques for Reliability Evaluation in Distribution System Planning. *International Journal of Electrical and Computer Engineering*. 6(4), 405–408.

[7] Hussen, S., Ayalew, F. & Ibrahim, K. (2020). Assessment of Distribution System Reliability and its Possible Mitigations: A review. In *International Conference on Advanced in Management and Technology (ICAMT)*.

[8] Olusuyi, K., Oluwole, A., Adefarati, T., Babarinde, A., Babarinde, A., Oluwole, S. & Kayode, A. (2014). A Fault Analysis of 11 kV Distribution System (A Case Study of ADO Ekiti Electrical Power Distribution District. *American Journal of Electrical Power and Energy Systems*. 3, 27–36.

[9] Diamenu, G. & Kwarteng, J. (2019). Electric Power Distribution Network Performance Assessment Based on Reliability Indices. In *International Research Journal of Engineering and Technology (IRJET)*.

[10] Moloi, K. & Yusuff, A.A. (2018). Moehoek 22 kV Power Distribution Feeder Reliability Assessment. In *2018 IEEE PES/IAS Power Africa*. p. 53–57.

[11] Kulkarni, N., Lalitha, S. & Deokar, S. (2019). Real Time Control and Monitoring of Grid Power Systems using Cloud Computing. *International Journal of Electrical and Computer Engineering (IJECE)*, 9, 941.

[12] Salehi, V., Mazloomzadeh, A., Fernandez, J. & Mohammed, O. (2012). Real-time Power System Analysis and Security Monitoring by Wampac Systems. In *2012 IEEE PES Innovative Smart Grid Technologies (ISGT)*.

[13] IEEE (1999). IEEE Guide for Electric Power Distribution Reliability Indices. *IEEE Std 1366-1998*, pp. 1–21.

[14] Machidon, O., Stanca, A., Ogrutan, P., Gerigan, C. & Aciu, L. (2018). Power System Protection Device with IoT-based Support for Integration in Smart Environments. *PLOSONE*. 13, e0208168.

[15] Schweitzer Engineering Laboratories. *SEL-551 Overcurrent and Reclosing Relay Instruction Manual*.

[16] Billinton, R., Allan & R.N. (1996): *Reliability Evaluation of Power Systems*. (Second Edition). Plenum Press, New York, USA.

CHAPTER 18

Multilevel Voting Models in Cyber Aggression Detection for Bangla Texts

Samin Yasar, Md. Mahfuzul Haque Gazi, and Kazi Saeed Alam

Khulna University of Engineering & Technology, Khulna, Bangladesh

CONTENTS

18.1	Introduction	213
18.2	Related Work	213
18.3	Proposed Detection Model	215
	18.3.1 Dataset Description	215
	18.3.2 Data Preprocessing	215
	18.3.3 Dataset Splitting	216
	18.3.4 Feature Extraction	216
	18.3.5 Classification Process	216
18.4	Experimental Results	218
18.5	Conclusion and Future Works	220

CYBER AGGRESSION over social interactive platforms (Twitter, Facebook, Instagram, etc.) has increased extensively in the past few years.[1] People, especially teenagers, all over the world, are continuously becoming the victim of bullying, harassment, racism, sexism and toxicity irrespective of the language they speak. Motivated by the need for cyber aggression detection, we have analyzed a number of individual machine learning classifiers and ensemble-based techniques for detecting cyberbullying in the Bangla language. Ambiguity in the dialects and miscellaneous vocabularies and sentence structures in Bangla texts have been the main obstacles to achieve satisfactory classification performance so far. However, this research work aims to build multilevel-based voting models to automatically classify Bangla texts into two groups: toxic and non-toxic. Combining with various feature generation techniques and cross-validation techniques, we've achieved high accuracy individually for logistic regression and random forest ensemble technique which is surpassed by our proposed double-level ensemble (DLE) and triple-level ensemble (TLE) voting models. TLE also outperforms DLE yielding the maximum accuracy of 89%.

18.1 INTRODUCTION

The widespread popularity of social platforms has exerted a strong influence on people, allowing them to share their opinions and ideas more openly than ever before. Twitter and Facebook are examples of social networking platforms that have become indispensable. Because of their enormous popularity among people, especially among teenagers [2], it has become an integral part of our daily lives. The significant growth in the use of these media has some detrimental effects, as these adolescents are often subjected to a variety of psychological and behavioral attacks known as cyberbullying [3]. Furthermore, social media platforms provide users with the choice of anonymity, which may lead to persons misusing technological features to carry out criminal activities. When bullying happens more often over time, things get much worse.

On social media sites, offensive language involving aggressive acts with the intent to hurt others has become the most harmful activity. Aggressive comments, sexism, racism, harassment, toxic message, hate speech, etc. are all examples of cyber aggression [4]. In the majority of cases, these harmful texts result in horrific psychological consequences such as self-harm, depression, stress, emotional frustration, and even suicidal thoughts or attempts [5]. According to a Pew Research Center report over 60% of people in the USA who use social media sites have been subjected to cyberbullying, with teenagers, especially girls, experiencing the worst types of it.

Hence, a variety of prevention strategies have been implemented with the objective of improving online protection for consumers in order to reduce such egregious acts of cyberbullying. However, it's a difficult task to detect the offensive language in Bangla text. It faces a number of difficulties as the informal language used in social media messages, which is typically written in short forms and slangs that are difficult for the classifier to semantically process and understand. Moreover, the dialects and types of the Bangla language are varied and diverse, which makes it more complex for achieving high performance for the classifiers.

The need for automated detection of offensive content for Bangla texts prompted the development of this research. We worked on identifying offensive contents in Bangla that have been withdrawn from various social media sites. We implemented a Double Level Ensemble Model (DLE) and a Triple Level Ensemble Model (TLE) using several supervised learning models and Feature Extraction techniques to automatically classify the posts as: "toxic" and "non-toxic". Our proposed models outperform individual classifier techniques (Support Vector Machine, Logistic Regression, Decision Tree Model, Multinomial Naive Bayes, K-Nearest Neighbors) and Ensemble strategies (Gradient Boosting Classifier, AdaBoost and Random Forest). We conducted experimental evaluation using a dataset that included both toxic and non-toxic messages, and the findings were very promising. In addition, we used cross-validation techniques to ensure the accuracy of the data obtained and we reported the results in multiple performance measures.

18.2 RELATED WORK

Several methods for investigating social media abuse have recently been developed. This segment briefly describes recent scientific research on identifying cyberbullying

[6] on social media networks. For English data, Alam et al. [7] suggested a machine learning algorithm to detect and avoid cyberbullying on Twitter. Several generic ML models (SVM, NB, LR, etc.), ensemble models (Adaboost, Gboost, Bagging), and single-level and double-level voting classifiers were used to train and test social platform bullying items. In terms of accuracy, SLE outperformed most of the classifiers. Yadav et al. [8] used BERT, a language learning model that can create contextual embeddings as well as task-specific embeddings for classification. They used a single layer of linear neural network on top of the novel pre-trained BERT model as a classifier in this process.

Various researchers analyzed and projected cyberbullying terms in Facebook posts and comments using a text mining strategy focused on Naive Bayes. The method examines each instance of a Facebook post and estimates the incidence and the type of bully-related terms. Seven machine learning classifications have been used by Muneer et al. [9]. In order to calculate the identification rates used for the global dataset for the classifier, the individual algorithms are assessed by means of various performance metrics. The experimental findings indicate that LR had a superior accuracy of 90.57%. Baruah et al. [10] applied RoBERTa, English BERT (En-BERT), DistilRoBERTa and Support Vector Machine (SVM) for the English language.

In the case of Bangla, it becomes more difficult to detect abusive text. Hussain et al. [11] suggested a root level algorithm to identify abusive text. He also proposed unigram string features where they used a collection of 300 comment datasets. The authors in [12] have used a variety of machine learning (ML) and deep learning (DL) based algorithms to detect various classes of abusive Bangla text. RNN has outperformed other algorithms with an accuracy of 82.20%. Some authors [13] have used the SVM and NB algorithm on a dataset containing 1339 data. They obtained data from Facebook using a web scraper and reached the highest accuracy of 72%. Romim et al. [14] presented a new dataset tagged by crowdsourcing and verified by experts. They conducted baseline experiments and several deep learning algorithms with pre-trained Bangla word embedding on this dataset. The experiment illustrated that although all the deep learning models performed well, SVM achieved the best result with 87.5% accuracy.

Ghosh et al. [15] proposed a machine learning technique, to automatically remove emotion (positive or negative) from Facebook messages. The polarity of the emotion was determined using a multilayer Perceptron model. Regarding using deep learning and machine learning algorithms, in another paper [16], the authors created a model to detect cyberbullying in Bangla and Romanized Bangla texts. A comparison between the algorithms was proposed in various metrics. Datasets were trained using algorithms of machine training and deep learning. CNN algorithm worked best with 84% accuracy. Here, Multinomial Naive Bayes worked well with the other two datasets by achieving 84% and 80% accuracy.

In our proposed model, we implemented hard voting for double level and triple level voting classifiers. We trained our model on two classes and evaluated them on a few metrics: Accuracy, F1-score and AUC. Our proposed model obtained better results on the evaluation metrics.

18.3 PROPOSED DETECTION MODEL

To implement our proposed detection model, the methodology can be divided into the following segments:

- Dataset Description

- Data Preprocessing

- Dataset Splitting

- Feature Extraction

- Classification Process

18.3.1 Dataset Description

We have worked with a benchmark dataset [17] of 10220 comments gathered from various social media platforms. The data have been saved as a xlsx file with two columns: text and toxic. All offensive and non-offensive posts and comments have been grouped together as 'text' as examples given in Figure 18.1. These texts are labeled as 'toxic', 0 means non-offensive and 1 represents offensive. 41.64% (4256) of our data are marked as offensive and the remaining 58.36% (5964) are non-offensive.

Text	Toxic
হাহা ভাইকি গাঞ্জা একটু বেশি খাইছেন	1
গানটা খুব ভালো লাগছে	0
দুইডারে হিজরার মত লাগতাছে	1
চমৎকার লিখেখেছেন। ইসলাম জ্ঞান অর্জনের কথা বলে।	0

Figure 18.1: Sample Bangla texts for detecting cyberbullying.

18.3.2 Data Preprocessing

As our data were in raw format, they needed to be processed before we could use them in our models. At first, we have tokenized the data. Our tokenizer automatically removes white space, punctuation, number, special characters (e.g., #, @, (,),+). Our next step of preprocessing was stemming. This is a technique where derivatives of the same word are reduced to its root format. Detokenization has been performed as the last phase of preprocessing, resulting in clean data for heading to the next step. The workflow can be seen in Figure 18.2

Figure 18.2: Preprocessing steps.

18.3.3 Dataset Splitting

The cleaned data has been divided into two parts: train set and test set. Train data set was made up of 80%, while the test set contained 20% of the total dataset. After splitting the dataset, models have been fitted over the train set. Different cross-validation techniques have been used to improve the performance, such as Shuffle Split, K-Fold. We have used 10-fold cross-validation techniques in this case.

18.3.4 Feature Extraction

Feature extraction is a dimensionality reduction method that reduces an extensive amount of raw data into smaller groups that can be processed more easily. The raw data set includes a vast number of variables, which necessitates a significant amount of computational power to process. Moreover, the classification model's accuracy struggles when irrelevant and redundant elements are present. Feature extraction reduces the volume of redundant data without losing relevant data. In this study, we have applied two methods for extracting features: TF-IDF vectorization and Bag of Words (BoW). Both strategies transform words into numerical values that increase performance and efficiency. BoW analyzes the histogram of the text's words and produces a numerical mapping called vector features of a specific length. The method of representing documents in vector space is known as vectorization. The procedure entails creating a mapping from one word to the next. It counts the number of terms occurring in a text and displays them as a matrix. TF-IDF weights a term's frequency and inverse document frequency. In this process, rare terms get priority over commonly used terms. We have also used different types of string properties, such as unigram and bigram. The unigram features do not consider the word relevancy in a single sentence. However, this function can be used to determine which terms are more offensive. Bigram architectures consider the relationship between two consecutive terms in a sentence. Word and character analyzer has also been applied in our research.

10.3.5 Classification Process

Various machine learning algorithms have been implemented for detecting abusive texts from different social media. Among those, Support Vector Machine and Logistic Regression have performed better for detecting harassing texts. In this research work, we have applied algorithms such as LR, LSVC, DT, MNB, GBoost, AdaBoost, Random Forest along with all the previously mentioned features on the respective dataset. Furthermore, we have used an ensemble of these machine learning algorithms to improve the accuracy and other efficiency metrics of our models. Our ML algorithms have been proposed as a double layer ensemble and a triple layer ensemble. The architectures can be seen in Figure 18.3.

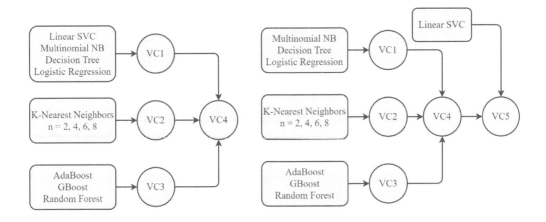

Figure 18.3: Architecture of the proposed voting models.

While implementing DLE, we have categorized the classifiers into three groups. After that, three voting classifiers have been made.
$VC1$: Linear SVC, LR, Multinomial NB, DT;
$VC2$: KNN (n = 2, 4, 6, 8) and $VC3$: AdaBoost, GBoost, Random Forest,
The DLE was built as follows:
$Level1$: $VC1$, $VC2$ and $VC3$ was constructed
$Level2$: $VC4$ was generated from $VC1$, $VC2$ and $VC3$

While implementing TLE, we classified models into three classes. And three voting classifiers have been made.
$VC1$: MNB, LR, DT;
$VC2$: KNN (n = 2, 4 , 6, 8), and,
$VC3$: AdaBoost, GBoost, Random Forest;
The TLE was built as follows:
$Level1$: $VC1$, $VC2$ and $VC3$ was constructed
$Level2$: $VC4$ was gained from $VC1$, $VC2$ and $VC3$
$Level3$: $VC5$ was achieved from $VC4$ and LSVC

Voting classifiers are divided into two levels in the DLE architecture. Three classes ($VC1$, $VC2$ and $VC3$) have been developed at the first stage so that generic machine learning models as well as ensemble based models are able to determine voting outcomes. Finally, the outcomes of $VC1$, $VC2$ and $VC3$ are then compared at the next level to determine the final result.

Three-level voting classifiers have been established in the TLE architecture. Three classes ($VC1$, $VC2$ and $VC3$) have been developed at the first stage. The results of $VC1$, $VC2$ and $VC3$ are then compared in "$Level2$" to get $VC4$ and then $VC4$ and LSVC are compared to determine the final outcome.

Furthermore, to develop the ensemble structures, we have used hard voting. To detect cyberbullying, we have constructed level-based voting classifiers. An overall workflow can be seen in Figure 18.4.

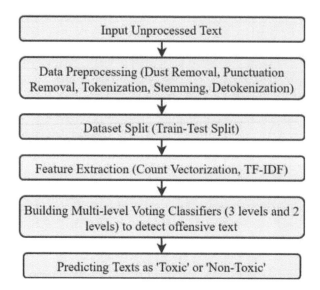

Figure 18.4: An overall workflow of the system.

18.4 EXPERIMENTAL RESULTS

To detect cyberbullying from our data, we have constructed multilevel-based voting models. From preprocessed data, we have applied 'BoW', TF-IDF and trained it to our prediction scheme. Different well-known classifiers (Linear SVC, LR, Multinomial NB, DT) and ensemble methods (GBoost, AdaBoost and Random Forest) have been used to build our model from a variety of machine learning algorithms. We have used a variety of performance indicators to estimate the performance of our system (Accuracy, F1-Score and AUC). Table 18.1 shows how our model differs from previous mining models in terms of performance.

Table 18.1: Performance evaluation of different classifier models.

Metric	Feature Generation		SVM	LR	DT	MNB	KNN	AdB	GB	RF	TLE	DLE
Accuracy	BOW		0.81	0.84	0.77	0.81	0.77	0.77	0.78	0.81	0.83	**0.83**
	TF-IDF	Word	0.85	0.84	0.77	0.81	0.67	0.78	0.78	0.82	0.85	**0.86**
		Char	0.87	0.84	0.75	0.80	0.84	0.83	0.85	0.86	**0.89**	0.87
		Unigram	0.85	0.84	0.77	0.81	0.67	0.78	0.78	0.81	0.85	0.84
		Bigram	0.74	0.70	0.68	0.70	0.56	0.59	0.60	0.69	0.65	0.67
F1-Score	BOW		0.79	0.81	0.75	0.75	0.63	0.77	0.78	0.80	0.80	0.81
	TF-IDF	Word	0.82	0.82	0.75	0.74	0.69	0.78	0.77	0.80	0.82	0.82
		Char	0.84	0.82	0.74	0.78	0.82	0.82	0.83	0.84	**0.86**	0.83
		Unigram	0.82	0.82	0.75	0.74	0.69	0.78	0.77	0.80	0.82	0.81
		Bigram	0.70	0.47	0.72	0.48	0.62	0.06	0.12	0.73	0.34	0.45
AUC	BOW		0.82	0.85	0.78	0.80	0.77	0.79	0.80	0.82	0.83	0.82
	TF-IDF	Word	0.85	0.85	0.79	0.79	0.65	0.79	0.80	0.82	0.84	0.84
		Char	0.88	0.85	0.78	0.75	0.83	0.85	0.86	0.86	0.87	0.86
		Unigram	0.85	0.85	0.80	0.79	0.65	0.79	0.80	0.83	0.84	0.85
		Bigram	0.74	0.64	0.72	0.64	0.59	0.51	0.53	0.73	0.63	0.62

Table 18.2: Cross-validation based performance evaluation of the proposed models.

Metrics	Cross-Validation Techniques	Feature Extraction		TLE	DLE
Accuracy	K-Fold	BOW		0.8581	0.8659
		TF-IDF	word	0.8845	0.8864
			char	0.8923	**0.8962**
			unigram	**0.8888**	0.8796
			bigram	0.6878	0.7123
	Shuffle Split	BOW		0.8405	0.8509
		TF-IDF	word	0.8630	0.8630
			char	0.8793	**0.8835**
			unigram	0.8724	0.8594
			bigram	0.6761	0.6943
F1-Score	K-Fold	BOW		0.8216	0.8347
		TF-IDF	word	0.8354	0.8390
			char	0.8556	0.8578
			unigram	0.8339	0.8401
			bigram	0.3887	0.4982
	Shuffle Split	BOW		0.8019	0.8234
		TF-IDF	word	0.8308	0.8290
			char	0.8467	0.8474
			unigram	0.8447	0.8278
			bigram	0.6663	0.4531
AUC	K-Fold	BOW		0.8447	0.8582
		TF-IDF	word	0.8587	0.8619
			char	0.8750	0.8770
			unigram	0.8576	0.8628
			bigram	0.5762	0.6549
	Shuffle Split	BOW		0.8338	0.847
		TF-IDF	word	0.8541	0.8524
			char	0.8666	0.8698
			unigram	0.8447	0.8474
			bigram	0.5962	0.6355

When extracting elements with TF-IDF ('Char'), we were able to achieve 89% accuracy for TLE, outperforming other models. When using TF-IDF ('Bigram') to extract features from the data, 65% accuracy has been achieved. The accuracy of prediction in [11], [12], [13] varied from 71% to 82%, which is resolved in our model. Since the plurality voting scheme is used, voting classifiers assist in justifying the class mark. As an example, if six of the eight algorithms agree on a name, the overall classifier would only use the outcome with the most votes. This is a one-of-a-kind strategy for achieving better results in this work. The DLE model was used to compare the findings to TLE. DLE can also outperform TLE in two or three context-based word analysis tests. As a result, both frameworks are beneficial in detecting bullying.

For detecting hate speech, voting classifiers based on different-level ensemble models have been proven to be superior. Our data were only partly balanced. To ensure that our model is unbiased, we used various cross-validation methods (Shuffle Split, K-Fold) to test it. In this study, 10-fold cross-validation was used. Table 18.2 shows the cross-validation outcome of our proposed model. While using the K-Fold cross-validation method, we were able to achieve 84% to 89% accuracy in DLE and TLE for all features except 'Bigram'. Other functions have also yielded

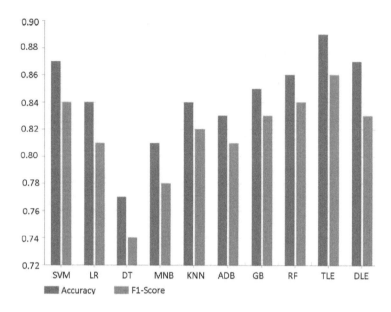

Figure 18.5: Performance visualization of different classifiers.

positive performance measurement metrics. Our literature review did not provide this cross-validation methodology distinction.

We have grouped similar category algorithms together in the DLE model, which has helped us to maintain objectivity. The outcomes we've achieved are truly remarkable. Ensemble based voting models are unique in this study and have achieved the maximum accuracy of 89% after cross-validation, with almost identical results for F1-Score. We measured precision and recall for comparison with other models. Since F1-Score can be calculated from recall and precision measures, we did not include them in the tables. In Figure 18.5, a bar chart depicts the performance of the above models based on the criteria (F1-Score and Accuracy). In this figure, F1-Score value and the average accuracy have been calculated using all the features. In the proposed voting framework, we observed balanced efficiency metric values. Our suggested DLE and TLE models have been reliable to optimize the classification method in this case. Cross-validation methods have also performed well in classifying social bullying.

18.5 CONCLUSION AND FUTURE WORKS

Cyberbullying, or hateful comments on social platforms, continues to affect people, especially teens and often results in several harmful effects, including psychological distress among victims. While a significant amount of work has been done for cyber-harassment identification on the English language, relatively few research has been conducted on Bangla text. We implemented various generic machine learning algorithms in this work, including LSVC, MNB, DT, etc., and also developed two voting classifiers, based on ensemble, to predict whether the Bangla text is hateful or not. We have found out that the best accuracy and other performance metrics were achieved by applying DLE and TLE classifiers on our dataset. The maximum accuracy we have achieved was 89% for the ensemble-based voting classifiers. In the future, we plan to include more diverse data to our dataset to ensure better performance. So far, we have only classified data into two categories. To overcome the limitation of our current work, we have future plans to apply our proposed models in multi-class classification and other text categorization problems.

Bibliography

[1] Li, Qing. 2006. "Cyberbullying in Schools: A Research of Gender Differences." School Psychology International. 27(2): 157–70. doi:10.1177/0143034306064547

[2] Dehue, F., C. Bolman and T. Vollink. 2008. "Cyberbullying: Youngsters' Experiences and Parental Perception." Cyberpsychology & behavior : the impact of the Internet, multimedia and virtual reality on behavior and society 112: 217-23.

[3] Dredge, Rebecca, J. Gleeson and X. Garcia. 2014. "Presentation on Facebook and risk of cyberbullying victimisation." Comput. Hum. Behav. 40:16-22.

[4] Schmidt, Anna and Michael Wiegand. 2017. "A Survey on Hate Speech Detection using Natural Language Processing." SocialNLP@EACL.

[5] Niu, Geng-Feng, J. He, Shanyan Lin, Xiao-Jun Sun and C. Longobardi. 2020. "Cyberbullying Victimization and Adolescent Depression: The Mediating Role of Psychological Security and the Moderating Role of Growth Mindset." International Journal of Environmental Research and Public Health 17.

[6] Wagner, A. 2019. "E-victimization and e-predation theory as the dominant aggressive communication: the case of cyber bullying." Social Semiotics 29:303-318.

[7] Alam, Kazi Saeed, Shovan Bhowmik and Priyo Ranjan Kundu Prosun. 2021. "Cyberbullying Detection: An Ensemble Based Machine Learning Approach." 2021 Third International Conference on Intelligent Communication Technologies and Virtual Mobile Networks (ICICV):710-715.

[8] Yadav, J., Devesh Kumar and Dheeraj Chauhan. 2020. "Cyberbullying Detection using Pre-Trained BERT Model." 2020 International Conference on Electronics and Sustainable Communication Systems (ICESC): 1096-1100.

[9] Muneer, Amgad and Suliman Mohamed Fati. 2020. "A Comparative Analysis of Machine Learning Techniques for Cyberbullying Detection on Twitter." Future Internet 12:187.

[10] Baruah, Arup, K Amar Das, F. Barbhuiya and K. Dey. 2020. "Aggression Identification in English, Hindi and Bangla Text using BERT, RoBERTa and SVM." TRAC@LREC.

[11] Hussain, Md Gulzar, T. Mahmud and Waheda Akthar. 2018. "An Approach to Detect Abusive Bangla Text." 2018 International Conference on Innovation in Engineering and Technology (ICIET): 1-5.

[12] Emon, Estiak Ahmed, Shihab Rahman, Joti Banarjee, Amit Kumar Das and Tanni Mittra. 2019. "A Deep Learning Approach to Detect Abusive Bengali Text." 2019 7th International Conference on Smart Computing & Communications (ICSCC): 1-5.

[13] Ahammed, Shovon, Mostafizur Rahman, M. Niloy and S. Chowdhury. 2019. "Implementation of Machine Learning to Detect Hate Speech in Bangla Language." 2019 8th International Conference System Modeling and Advancement in Research Trends (SMART): 317-320.

[14] Romim, Nauros, Mosahed Ahmed, Hriteshwar Talukder and Md. Saiful Islam. 2020. "Hate Speech detection in the Bengali language: A dataset and its baseline evaluation." ArXiv abs/2012.09686.

[15] Ghosh, Souvick, Satanu Ghosh and Dipankar Das. 2017. "Sentiment Identification in Code-Mixed Social Media Text." ArXiv abs/1707.01184.

[16] Ahmed, Md Tofael, Maqsudur Rahman, Shafayet Nur, Azm Islam and Dipankar Das. 2021. "Deployment of Machine Learning and Deep Learning Algorithms in Detecting Cyberbullying in Bangla and Romanized Bangla text: A Comparative Study." 2021 International Conference on Advances in Electrical, Computing, Communication and Sustainable Technologies (ICAECT): 1-10.

[17] Bangla Abusive Comment Dataset "https://github.com/aimansnigdha/Bangla-Abusive-Comment-Dataset/blob/master/train_data.xlsx.

CHAPTER 19

A Cognitive Approach for Load Adaptive MAC Protocol in Wireless Body Area Networks

Md. Mortuza Hossain, Md. Monirul Islam,
and Md. Obaidur Rahman

Department of Computer Science and Engineering
Institute of Information & Communication Technology
Dhaka University of Engineering & Technology (DUET), Gazipur
Gazipur, Bangladesh

CONTENTS

19.1   Introduction 224
19.2   Related Work 225
19.3   Proposed Model 226
    19.3.1   System Model 226
    19.3.2   Channel Rendezvous Phase 226
    19.3.3   Data Transmission Phase 227
    19.3.4   Channel Re-Rendezvous Phase 228
    19.3.5   Network Load Adjustment 229
19.4   Result 230
    19.4.1   Delay and Energy Equations 230
    19.4.2   Simulation Results 231
        19.4.2.1   Packet delay of protocols 231
        19.4.2.2   Energy cost of protocols 232
        19.4.2.3   Throughput of protocols 232
19.5   Conclusion 233

Wireless Body Area Network (WBAN) is an implementation of WPAN and is getting popular for monitoring health conditions of patients assuring movement flexibility and remote controlling. WBAN needs a reliable and energy-efficient MAC protocol to handle sensitive types of data in life-threatening situations. WBAN usually uses free ISM bands for communication purposes. However, various traffic demands of WSN applications make these limited ISM bands overcrowded. Cognitive Radio (CR) is one of the potential solutions to this problem for reliable data communication. To design an efficient MAC protocol metrics like energy efficiency, packet transmission delay, throughput, and traffic load should be considered to ensure better performance, reliable guaranteed data transfer, and longer lifetime. In this chapter, we have proposed the CALA MAC protocol which is very reliable and energy-efficient compared to few recent MAC protocols in WBANS.

19.1   INTRODUCTION

The Wireless Body Area Networks (WBANs) [1] are playing very important roles in different medical applications and our daily life. Especially during this COVID-19 pandemic, we have realized that remote health monitoring [2] is one of the most essential parts to stop the spreading of the corona virus. WBAN has many applications in healthcare, fitness and entertainment [3]. In medical applications various bio sensors (such as EEG, EMG and ECG, etc.) are placed inside, near and around the human body to monitor and collect data about body condition. WBAN is a special-purpose use of Wireless Sensor Network (WSN) [3]. WBAN gives an advantage of monitoring the health condition of any patient far way from a hospital or doctor clinic. This gives so much flexibility to doctors, also it confirms the safe distance from patients, especially for patients suffering from contagious disease such as COVID-19, Ebola, flu, etc. Also continuous monitoring is possible by WBAN for those patients suffering from chronic diseases such as diabetes, asthma, heart conditions [4], etc. by using bio sensors. These bio sensors can measure various physiological parameters like heart rate, body temperature, blood pressure, SpO2, ECG, EEG and EMGs [5], all of which are mainly battery-operated. In life-threatening situations a patient's sensor nodes send current health condition data, which are processed, and an emergency signal is sent to operators about the situation. That is why WBANs need a Media Access Control (MAC) protocol which is efficient in terms of energy, and has low delay in packet delivery and reliability in data transmission. WBAN uses the IEEE 802.15.6 standard for the purpose of MAC. The main challenge in WBAN is to utilize the energy of sensor nodes in an efficient way, so that a sensor node's lifetimes can be increased. Packets must be delivered with minimum delay in critical situations. The reliability of the protocol guarantees transmitting critical data to the receivers. So while designing a MAC protocol, these terms should be considered. Recently, a MAC protocol was designed for WBAN, named C-RICER [3]. It is based on cognitive task and receiver-initiated operation. In order to achieve good performance, C-RICER nodes use unused licensed bands instead of ISM (Industry Science Medical) bands. In C-RICER, nodes make an available channel list from the unused channels of licensed bands. During data transmission, only one channel is used, whose Signal-to-Inference Noise Ratio (SINR) value is less. In C-RICER, multiple channels are used only when the channel switching decision is made. Although C-RICER is good in performance, the protocol experiences few limitations: (i) C-RICER always uses one channel for data transmission, and (ii) traffic load issue is not considered in

C-RICER. To overcome those limitations, we have proposed a Cognitive Approach for Load Adaptive Media Access Control (CALA MAC). The proposed protocol shows good performance compared to the C-RICER in terms of packet delay and energy efficiency.

This chapter is organized as follows. Section 19.2 introduces the related MAC protocols. The proposed protocol operations are presented in Section 19.3. Simulation and results are discussed in Section 19.4. Finally, a conclusion is drawn in Section 19.5.

19.2 RELATED WORK

A survey on security issues and wearable sensors in WBAN for healthcare system [1] provides possible solutions of privacy and security challenges in WBAN. It evaluates the possible solutions of proper security maintainability in medical applications for few recent protocols in WBAN. It also clarifies the security enhancement issues in WBANs and offers prospective opportunity.

Optimum Placement of Relay Nodes in WBANs [2] is a system to improve the Quality of Service (QoS) of Indoor Remote Patient Monitoring (RPM) systems. It analyzes the effect of change in sight-of-communication due to human body orientation, estimates the path loss model for the angle rotation between coordinator and sensor nodes and different body weights of males and females, and provides the best position to place a relay node on the human body to improve the QoS. Authors design an adaptive cross-layer communication protocol for WBANs.

C-RICER [3] (Cognitive-Receiver Initiated Cycled Receiver) is an energy-efficient MAC protocol. It is specifically designed for WBANs to work cognitively in high interference environment. C-RICER protocol adapts both transmission power and channel frequency to reduce the interferences. C-RICER is able to outperform the traditional RICER (Receiver Initiated Cycle Receiver) protocol in terms of energy consumption, packet delay, and network throughput.

Multi-Dimensional Traffic Adaptive (MDTA) MAC [4] protocol is an energy efficient MAC protocol. It is used for WBANs. The majority of WBANs MAC protocols consider either application traffic class or traffic load. MDTA-MAC protocol considers both traffic class and load to increase the network performances.

B-MAC [6] is an asynchronous MAC protocol. It is based on carrier sense media access protocol for wireless sensor network. B-MAC provides a flexible interface to obtain ultra low power operation, effective collision avoidance and high channel utilization.

Cognitive Radio-based Medium Access Control (CR-MAC) [7] protocol utilizes cognitive radio transmission. In this protocol, the sensor nodes are classified into two groups, critical and non-critical health information collecting nodes groups. In CR-MAC, a priority is assigned for the higher priority packets and lower priority packets.

Traffic-adaptive MAC protocol (TaMAC) [8] dynamically adjusts the duty cycle of the sensor nodes according to their traffic patterns, thus solving the idle listening and overhearing problems.

RI-MAC [9] is an asynchronous duty cycle MAC protocol. It is the first Receiver Initiated MAC protocol. In RI-MAC, data transmission initiates based on the receiver beacon generation which is received by a potential sender node. RI-MAC significantly improves throughput, packet delivery ratio and latency.

X-MAC [10] is a low power MAC protocol for Wireless Sensor Networks (WSNs). X-MAC is also an Asynchronous MAC protocol and more efficient than B-MAC. X-MAC replaces the long preamble by using small preamble, called strobe preamble. This strobe preamble contains receiver address, which reduces overhearing and idle listening of other nodes in the network.

A Cognitive Radio Body Area Network (CRBAN) [11] is a Cognitive Radio enabled Wireless Body Area Network (WBAN). In this protocol, the Medium Access Control (MAC) layer plays a key role in cognitive radio functions, such as channel sensing, resource allocation, spectrum mobility and spectrum sharing. The authors compared the performances, collision ratio, channel access parameter, energy consumption and limitation of CR-MAC, DCAA-MAC, C-RICER, MBAN-MAC, and HCVP-MAC protocols.

19.3 PROPOSED MODEL

We have proposed a Cognitive Approach for Load Adaptive (CALA)-MAC protocol in WBANs. The purposes of the protocol are: reduce the packet delay, increase the energy efficiency and the traffic load in the network. Our proposed protocol uses multiple channels according to network traffic loads to adapt the traffic. Hence network packet losses rate is decreased and throughput becomes increased. The proposed CALA-MAC works in different phases to complete the tasks.

19.3.1 System Model

In our proposed CALA-MAC, the network has a coordinator node, and some sensor nodes called slave nodes. We consider a WBAN having "n" sensor nodes, denoted by Ni; where i = 1, 2, 3 . . . . . , n. Nodes are connected in a single hop star topology where a coordinator node collects data from all other sensor nodes in the network, which has no power limitation, is rechargeable and has two transceivers. On the other side, sensor nodes are placed around and deployed in the human body to collect different physical phenomena of the human body. All sensor nodes are battery-operated, hard to replace and have only one transceiver. The proposed CALA-MAC works in different phases to complete the tasks.

19.3.2 Channel Rendezvous Phase

Channel rendezvous phase defines how coordinator and sensor/slave nodes are rendezvoused into a channel. At the coordinator side, the coordinator senses all channels and makes a list of available channels which are not used by the primary users (PU). The available channels are detected by comparing SINR (Signal-to-Inference Noise Ratio) value of the channel with respect to the $SINR_T$ (SINR Threshold) value. If $SINR < SINR_T$ then the channel is added into the available list. If there are 5 channels

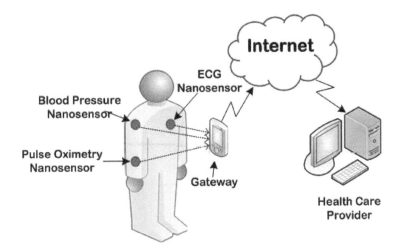

Figure 19.1: System model of CALA-MAC

and 2 are used by PU, then the other 3 channels are added into the list. Now for the simplicity of understanding, we set a rule where the coordinator chooses any of the channels randomly from the available channels list for sending/generating a beacon to initialize communication with the other sensor (slave) nodes in the network. This generated beacon contains the available channels list and schedule of the coordinator for data transfer. In the channel rendezvous phase, we consider slave nodes also as they sense the channels. According to Figure 19.2, let's consider the coordinator available channels as ch-1, ch-3, ch-5, and choose ch-5 randomly for generating a beacon. The coordinator node selects a channel randomly among the available channels list and generates a beacon in the channel to find the other sensor nodes in the network. The beacon is continuously generated by the coordinator after a fixed time interval T_B. At the slave node side, the node wakes up and senses all channels sequentially from ch-1 to ch-5. After sensing, if SINR value is found greater than $SINR_T$, the node stops listening to the channel and scans the next channel in a similar way. However, if it gets $SINR < SINR_T$, it starts listening to the channel at least for T_L until it finds the coordinator beacon, where T_L = Listening time for sensor nodes, and T_L is greater than or equal to the T_B ($T_L >= T_B$). Therefore, during the listening T_L times, if the coordinator beacon is received by the slave node, it sends an acknowledgement (ACK) to the coordinator for confirming the presence of the node in the network. The resulting coordinator receives an ACK from the slave and fills a check-list for the corresponding slave node to confirm slave presence in the network.

19.3.3 Data Transmission Phase

At the channel rendezvous phase, the beacon generated by the coordinator contains the available channels list information and schedule of coordinator for the next cycles. The beacon informs slave nodes when the coordinator will be available for the data transmission. In Figure 19.3 we assume for 3 available channels the coordinator schedule is: 1st T_{cycle} (consider, 1 T_{cycle} = 1000 ms) in channel-1, next T_{cycle}

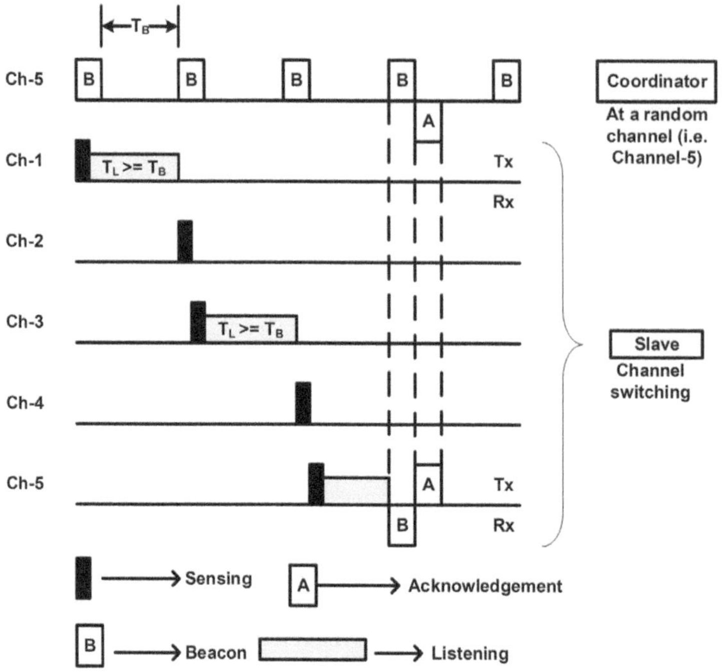

Figure 19.2: Channel rendezvous phase

in channel-3, next T_{cycle} in channel-5, and after that again in channel-1, and so on. Hence, all slave nodes know the schedule of the coordinator. If any slave node has data to send, it listens to the corresponding channel according to the schedule. Therefore, the slave node listens to the channel-1 at 1st T_{cycle} when it has data to send. During listening, if it receives the beacon from the coordinator, it takes a random back-off value to contend with other nodes. In this situation, the node that takes the smallest back-off value will send data after the back-off countdown and the other nodes will refrain from data sending. So after receiving data, the coordinator sends a beacon as an acknowledgment of data receptions and also invites other nodes for data exchange. After the end of the 1st T_{cycle}, the coordinator stops generating beacons in channel-1, and it starts generating beacons in the next channel according to the schedule and so on. It is worth mentioning that the newly generated beacon contains the latest schedule of the coordinator and newly available channels list of the network. Hence, shifting channels periodically is a cognitive task. Nodes use multiple channels to utilize all available channels.

19.3.4 Channel Re-Rendezvous Phase

Channel re-rendezvous phase is needed when, a slave node of the network loses its coordinator according to its current schedule. A slave may lose its coordinator if primary users (PUs) start using any available channel. If any PU occupies the channel, the coordinator immediately shifts to the next channel of its schedule and starts generating beacon in that channel and so on. If all previous free available channels are

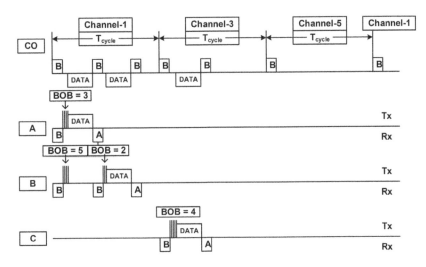

Figure 19.3: Data transmission phase

used by PUs, the coordinator makes an available channels list by following rendezvous phase strategy. A slave node always follows the schedule of its coordinator. So at time T_{cycle} it doesn't find its coordinator in the corresponding channel where the coordinator supposed to be. The salve node understands that the channel is currently used by some PU. As a result it immediately shifts to the next channel to find its coordinator. The slave listens to the next channel and if coordinator beacon is found, it continues the communication and data exchange. If slave node does not find its coordinator in the next channel, it goes to the next scheduled channel to find the coordinator. However, if it fails again to find the coordinator, it follows the rendezvous phase strategy. Therefore, when a slave completely loses its coordinator, it follows the rendezvous phase strategy to find the coordinator.

19.3.5 Network Load Adjustment

We consider three network traffic load strategies: low, moderate and high. Depending on the traffic load, the proposed protocol has utilized the available channels. In low load and moderate load strategies, the protocol considers delay for reducing channel switching cost for regular data.

In a low load strategy, the whole network has very low load. Say, one or two nodes generate data periodically. These are regular monitoring data, such as heart rate, temperature, blood pressure, etc. So these kinds of data are not necessary to send every cycle without a critical situation. Hence, in these types of situations, we can consider delay to saving the valuable energy of slave node by reducing the switching cost among the channels.

In a moderate load scenario, multiple channels are used for data transmission. In this scenario it is not necessary to utilize all the channels. After a specific time interval, i.e., $3 \times T_{cycle}$, nodes having data wake up when coordinator node is at a specific channel do not use all channels for data transmission. Hence channel switching energy is saved. We consider little delay for this situation.

In a high load scenario of the network, all available channels are used simultaneously to adapt with network traffic loads. High load situation is created when sensors sense life-critical data. Let's consider a sensor node has sensed an abnormal pulse rate, which will affect the other sensor nodes. Hence, those nodes will also sense different abnormal data simultaneously from the human body and try to send immediately. As a result, traffic load becomes high or overloaded. Now if a single channel is used in an emergency situation, nodes can't forward data to the coordinator on time. The proposed protocol fulfils the purposes of WBANs reliably and with less delay data transfer by using multiple channels data transmission simultaneously. Hence, all nodes can send data simultaneously at the same cycle in different channels, resulting in higher throughput as well as lower delay and contention. Furthermore, emergency data can be reached to the coordinator reliably.

19.4 RESULT

We develop a C/C++ based analytical model to simulate our protocol and compare it with C-RICER [3] protocol. We have simulated both protocols delay-packet/sec, energy-consumption to transmit packets/sec and finally compared both protocol throughputs. To calculate the value of parameters of both protocols, we use four mathematical equations.

19.4.1 Delay and Energy Equations

C-RICER:

$$Delay = \frac{T_{cycle}}{2} \tag{19.1}$$

Proposed CALA-MAC:

$$Initial\,Delay(I_{delay}) = n_{ch} \times T_{cycle} \tag{19.2}$$

$$Delay = I_{delay} + \delta \tag{19.3}$$

Where, $\delta \approx 0$. For Back-off time.
C-RICER:

$$Energy = 2 \times Tx_{Beacon} + Rx_{Beacon} + T_C \times IdleListen + Tx_{ACK} + \\ Rx_{ACK} + Tx_{Data} + Rx_{Data} + Tx_{ACK} + Rx_{ACK} \tag{19.4}$$

Proposed CALA-MAC:

$$Initial\,energy(I_{Energy}) = (n_{ch} + 1) \times Tx_{Beacon} + Rx_{Beacon} + Tx_{ACK} + \\ Rx_{ACK} + n_{ch} \times T_C \times IdleListen \tag{19.5}$$

$$Energy = I_{Energy} + Tx_{Beacon} + Rx_{Beacon} + Tx_{Data} + Rx_{Data} + Tx_{ACK} + Rx_{ACK} \tag{19.6}$$

These equations are used for calculating delay and energy of protocols. Equations (19.1) and (19.4) are used for calculating C-RICER [3] delay and energy consumption. Equations (19.3) and (19.6) are used for our proposed CALA. Equations (19.2) and (19.5) are used only for the rendezvous time of each sensor node. It means that these amounts of extra energy are consumed only for the 1st packet delivery in the rendezvous phase of each node. After that, the remainder parts of Equations (19.3) and (19.6) consider calculating the amount of energy needed by each node to send a packet.

19.4.2   Simulation Results

In this section, we compare the simulation result between proposed CALA and C-RICER [3] MAC protocols. We compare both protocols in terms of per packet delay, per packet energy cost, and throughput of network. Those three scenarios are given below.

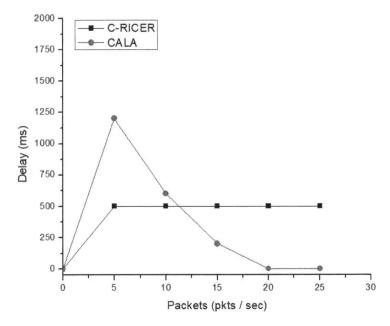

Figure 19.4: Compare packets/second vs delay of the protocols

19.4.2.1   Packet delay of protocols

In Figure 19.4 we compare proposed CALA protocol with C-RICER with respect to delay of packets/second. C-RICER doesn't have any contention window for the contention during data transmission; hence, the delay is considered $T_{cycle}/2$ on average for any cycle. As a result, the delay curve remains constant with respect to the load of the network. In Figure 19.4, the network average load of traffic is 5 packets/sec, C-RICER shows good performance than proposed protocols. At this point, our proposed protocol has an initialization delay for 1st packet delivery, but after that delay

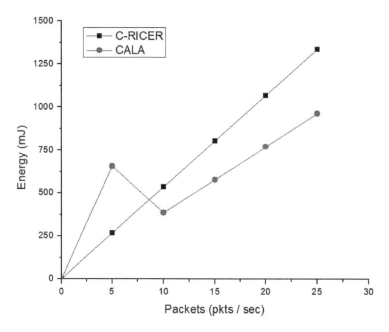

Figure 19.5: Compare packets/second vs energy of protocols

is approximate to zero. At 5 packets/sec and 10 packets/sec the situations are low load; at these points our proposed protocol needs a little more delay than C-RICER. Now, at 15, 20 and 25 packets/sec scenarios are moderated and high load situations, where probably every node of network generated packet. At these points, nodes these were transferred data earlier, need only δ (approximate to zero) amount of delay for each following packet transmission. Hence, delay at these points is much lower than the C-RICER.

19.4.2.2 *Energy cost of protocols*

In this scenario, we compared both protocols' energy consumption with respect to the packets/sec in networks. From Figure 19.5, we see that when the network generated 5 packets/sec data, our proposed protocol needed more energy compared to the C-RICER. This extra amount of energy is needed for the rendezvous phase of our protocol. From energy Equations 19.3 and 19.4, we see an extra amount of energy is needed only for the 1st packet generation of each node due to finding the coordinator schedule. After that, all nodes needed only a constant amount of energy to transmit each following packet. But in C-RICER protocol, every node needs a constant amount of energy for each packet generation.

19.4.2.3 *Throughput of protocols*

According to the analysis, we compare both protocols throughput with respect to the efficiency of protocols. The throughput of the network increases linearly with respect to the load increased in the network. In Figure 19.6, throughput is considered with

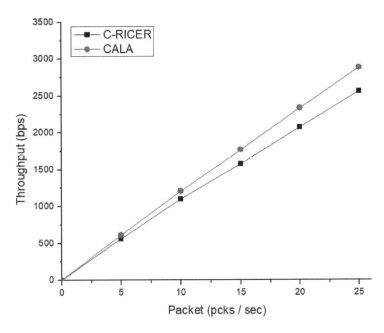

Figure 19.6: Compare throughput of protocols

respect to the generation of number of bits in network per second versus number of bits successfully transmitted to the receiver, where we consider our proposed protocol performance efficiency of 90 to 95% according to the analysis and C-RICER has performance efficiency of 80 to 88%. In low load situations, both protocols show good performance, C-RICER shows 88% efficiency, CALA shows 95% efficiency due to less collision and less packet losses. But in high load situations, both protocols' performance is reduced due to probability of packet loss and re-transmission of packets. In this situation, the C-RICER shows 80% efficiency but proposed CALA shows 90% efficiency.

19.5 CONCLUSION

In our proposed protocol we show better performances compared to an existing protocol C-RICER-MAC. In our proposed CALA-MAC protocol, we claim better energy efficiency for overall network of sensor nodes, reduce packets transmission delay of nodes, and achieve better throughput compared to C-RICER. We also derive a new process of initialization to rendezvous between coordinator and sensor nodes. For this rendezvous phase, sensor nodes need some extra energy and delay only for the 1st packet transmission. But after rendezvous, amounts of delay and energy consumption reduce very effectively. We also take network traffic loads into account and handle it very efficient way. In low load, we use few channels for data transmission, and in high load situations, we use all available free channels to increase network throughput. So that network packet loss is reduced, life-critical and important data reliably reach the destination. The proposed CALA-MAC protocol is very dynamic. Because if any of the free available channel is occupied by the primary user (PU), the coordinator immediately switches to the next free channel according to the schedule. Coordinator makes a new schedule of the available channels and delivers beacon to the network. Hence, packet delay reduces, and throughput also becomes high in the network. For this reason, inferences created by PUs do not affect our proposed protocol and protocol throughput. In our protocol, we do not consider the situation when all available channels are occupied by the PUs. In emergency situations when all channels are occupied by the PUs, the sensor nodes and coordinator may use the ISM band. We will find an alternative solution of this issue for our future implementation. At the end of the discussion, we can argue that our proposed protocol outperforms compared to the existing protocol in terms of energy, delay and throughput.

Bibliography

[1] Sawaneh, A. I., Sankoh, I., & Koroma, K. D. (2017). A survey on security issues and wearable sensors in wireless body area network for healthcare system. *14th International Computer Conference on Wavelet Active Media Technology and Information Processing (ICCWAMTIP)*, pp. 304-308.

[2] Vyas, A., & Pal, S. (2021). Optimum Placement of Relay Nodes in WBANs for Improving the QoS of Indoor RPM System. *Sensors Journal*, vol. 21, no. 13, pp. 14434-14442.

[3] Nhan, N., Gautier, M. & Berder, O. (2014). Asynchronous MAC protocol for spectrum agility in Wireless Body Area Sensor Networks. *2014 9th International Conference on Cognitive Radio Oriented Wireless Networks and Communications (CROWNCOM)*, pp. 203-208.

[4] Hossain, M., Dilruba., Kalyan, M., Rana, M. & Rahman, O. (2014). Multi-dimensional traffic adaptive energy-efficient MAC protocol for Wireless Body Area Networks. *2014 9th International Forum on Strategic Technology (IFOST)*, pp. 161-165.

[5] Ullah, S., Mohaisen, M., & Alnuem, M. A. (2013). A Review of IEEE 802.15.6 MAC, PHY, and Security Specifications. *International Journal of Distributed Sensor Networks*, https://doi.org/10.1155/2013/950704.

[6] Polastre, J., Hill, J., & Culler, D (2004) Versatile Low Power Media Access for Wireless Sensor Networks. *SenSys '04: Proceedings of the 2nd international conference on Embedded networked sensor systems*, Pages 95–107.

[7] Ali, A. K., Sarker, H. J., & Mouftah, T. H. (2010). A MAC protocol for cognitive wireless sensor body area networking. *Published online in Wiley Online Library, Wireless Communications and Mobile Computing*, Vol. 10: 1656–1671.

[8] Ullah, S., & Kwak, K. S. (2010). An Ultra Low-power and Traffic-adaptive Medium Access Control Protocol for Wireless Body Area Network. *Springer Science+Business Media, LLC*, Journal of medical systems. 36. 1021-30. https://doi.org/10.1007/s10916-010-9564-2.

[9] Sun, Y., Gurewitz, O., & Johnson, B. D. (2011). RI-MAC: A receiver-initiated asynchronous duty cycle MAC protocol for dynamic traffic loads in wireless sensor networks. *SenSys'08 - Proceedings of the 6th ACM Conference on Embedded Networked Sensor Systems*, Pages 1–14.

[10] Buettner, M., Yee, V. G., Anderson, E., & Han, R. (2006). R. X-MAC: A Short Preamble MAC Protocol for Duty-Cycled Wireless Sensor Networks. *SenSys '06: Proceedings of the 4th international conference on Embedded networked sensor systems*, Pages 307–320.

[11] Bhandari, S., & Moh, S. (2006). R. A Survey of MAC Protocols for Cognitive Radio Body Area Networks. *Sensors (Basel, Switzerland)*, Vol. 15: 9189 – 9209.

CHAPTER 20

Discrete Tone-Driven Directional Rate Controlled Communication System for Wireless Networks

Sweety Mondal, Md. Tareq Mahmud, and Md. Obaidur Rahman

Department of Computer Science and Engineering
Dhaka University of Engineering & Technology (DUET), Gazipur
Gazipur, Bangladesh

CONTENTS

20.1	Introduction	237
20.2	Background Study	238
20.3	Problem Statement	239
20.4	Objectives and Motivation	241
	20.4.1 Objectives	241
	20.4.2 Motivation	242
20.5	Research Methodology	242
	20.5.1 Assumptions	242
	20.5.2 Antenna Model	242
	20.5.3 P-Persistent Method	243
	20.5.4 Busy-Tone Packet	243
20.6	P-Persistent Tone Driven Rate Controlled MAC Operation	244
	20.6.1 Rate Controlling Methodology	245
20.7	Performance Evaluation	246
	20.7.1 Control Packet Overhead	246
	20.7.2 Throughput	247
	20.7.3 End-to-End Delay	248
	20.7.4 Per Packet Energy Consumption	248
20.8	Conclusion	249

D IRECTIONAL antennas not only can improve the spatial reuse of network bandwidth and capacity but also have a wider coverage area. Over the years, numerous directional medium access control (MAC) protocols have evolved and employed a single data channel, multiple radios or clock synchronization to mitigate directional hidden terminal and deafness problems which degrade network overall performances. However, single data channel and omni-directional control channel negotiation cannot thoroughly eliminate these problems. To resolve the mentioned limitations, we proposed a Discrete Tone Driven Directional Rate Controlled (DTD^{2}RC) Communication System for Wireless Networks utilizing multiple radios with directional antennas, multiple data channels and a discontinuous Busy-Tone Packet for medium access. The multi-channel concept is used to increase throughput avoiding unnecessary blocking of the exposed nodes. Busy-Tone Packet is sent in the common control channel using the p-persistent method stated in CSMA to solve the directional hidden terminal and deafness problems based on a calculated probability threshold. Moreover, the transmission rates of directional control packets and data packets are also adjusted using the *Shannon-Hartley* theorem which results in less energy consumption, increased throughput and eliminates the directional hidden terminal and deafness problems.

20.1 INTRODUCTION

Nowadays, the use of directional antennas is increasing for directional data transmission in lieu of omni-directional antenna, as it has great benefits like higher antenna gain with the higher data rate and larger transmission range over omni-directional antennas. Numerous medium access control (MAC) protocols designed with directional antennas increase spatial reuse and the capacity of the wireless networks.

However, designing a MAC protocol with directional antennas leads the researchers to go through some challenges such as hidden terminal and deafness problems. Hidden terminals in directional data transmission can be the cause of collision if these hidden terminals are not successfully handled. On the contrary, the deaf nodes which are engaged in transmitting or receiving can be the cause of energy loss or collision as they are unable to respond to other sources who want to communicate with the deaf nodes without knowing the existing directional data transmission. Hence, diverse intelligent mechanisms to mitigate these problems can pave a path to design new MAC protocols.

To work with directional antennas is tough due to its directional coverage range. In the case of directional data communications, a large number of nodes can be unaware of ongoing transmissions which lead to hidden terminal and deafness problems. Although the number of blocked/exposed nodes can be minimized with directional antennas to solve the hidden terminal problem, deafness problem is challenging without extra equipment. To do synchronization in large networks is also very difficult.

Enormous directional MAC protocols have already been designed using busy-tone (non-interfering sine wave to let other nodes know about business) with a single data channel and multiple radios [1], [2], [3]. All three protocols have used a busy-tone to solve the directional hidden terminal and deafness problems. However, the use of a single data channel may degrade the proper utilization of channel bandwidth.

Since synchronization is strenuous to achieve in large wireless networks, asynchronous MAC protocols are designed to achieve increased throughput and less energy consumption [4], [5]. Nowadays, protocol with the combination of cooperative information sharing, cooperative data relaying, multiple data channel and directional antennas is introduced to solve the directional hidden terminal and deafness problems with increased throughput [5].

In this paper, we propose an asynchronous multichannel MAC protocol employing both directional data transmission and omni-directional Busy-Tone Packet (BTP) using two half-duplex radios. Here, multiple data channel along with directional antenna not only are used to avoid unnecessarily blocking of the sectors which are used for concurrent data transmission, but also for increasing spatial reuse and wider coverage area which results in higher throughput. The proposed protocol also uses omni-directional BTP with *p-persistent* method instead of directional BTP in control channel to notify all the neighbor nodes about the ongoing data transmission to avoid the directional hidden terminal and deafness problems. Consequently, the joint participation of multiple data channels and multiple radios increases overall network throughput by minimizing directional hidden terminal and deafness problems.

Here, the main contribution of our proposed MAC protocol is the *p-persistent* method based discontinuous omni-directional BTP transmission in control channel which mitigates the following problems:

- Directional hidden terminal problem due to unheard directional control frames.

- Deafness problem due to using directional antennas.

Another significant contribution of our proposed protocol is that we have used the *Shannon-Hartley* theorem to calculate the directional transmission rate of control and data packets to eliminate the hidden terminal problems arising due to asymmetry in gain. Moreover, the rate of controlling mechanisms also reduces the energy consumption.

The residuum of the chapter is put in the following order: Section 20.2 confers about the existing directional MAC protocols. Section 20.3 contains the problems of recent busy-tone based directional MAC protocols. The objectives and motivations of proposed MAC protocol are listed in Section 20.4. We narrate the research methodologies in Section 20.5, and our proposed DTD^{2}RC MAC protocol operation is explained in Section 20.6. Finally, Section 20.7 shows the simulation results, and Section 20.8 concludes the chapter.

20.2 BACKGROUND STUDY

State-of-the-art research articles CAR MAC [6] and 2D-CMD MAC [5] proposed multichannel directional MAC Protocol for wireless networks. Both protocols use a control channel for cooperative information sharing and data channels for cooperative data relaying which eliminates the additional time for unwanted iterative negotiation in the control channel for data channel access. Moreover, the joint concept of cooperation solves the multichannel directional hidden terminal and deafness problems.

A recent research [2], has proposed Power Control Scheme for Directional MAC protocols for MANET. The protocol not only solves the hidden terminal and deafness problems but also mitigates the effect of side-lobe interference. For data transmission, a power control scheme is employed by calculating interference around the sender node and used to estimate the transmission power for the RTS (Request-to-Send)/CTS (Clear-to-Send) control packet as well as DATA/ACK (Acknowledgement) packet. An Energy Efficient MAC Protocol with Power and Rate Control in Multi-Rate Ad Hoc Networks is proposed in [7]. The protocol transmits data with adjusted rate, which results in decreased energy consumption.

The CDR-MAC [8] transmits RTS circularly in all directions through directional antenna sectors and encounters a delay. But, the protocol ensures increased spatial reuse and decreases hidden terminal and deafness problems by maintaining neighbor location information. To minimize the deafness problem, a Sectorized Directional MAC protocol is proposed in [9]. The protocol spends equal time periods in all the sectors having identical width circularly based on the Round-Robin algorithm to send or receive. To solve the deafness problem, the protocol assigns equal sector time which may increase the delay in data transmission, but it can save energy by minimizing the deaf nodes.

There are several Busy-Tone based directional MAC protocol [1], [2] to solve hidden terminal, exposed terminal and deafness problems. These protocols use the single busy-tone to solve these problems. However, the main drawback of these protocols are the uses of a single data channel which leads some nodes to sit idle for a certain period for some ongoing data transmission. DBSMA [3] is another busy-tone based MAC protocol proposed for multi-hop directional ad-hoc networks. Here, busy-tone is used to solve the directional hidden terminal problems. However, the protocol does not address the deafness problem.

20.3 PROBLEM STATEMENT

To solve the directional hidden terminal and deafness problem as well as the asymmetry in gain problem, different directional MAC protocols are designed utilizing the busy-tone signal. However, protocols with a single data channel lead to unnecessary blocking of some other neighbor nodes. In addition, the appropriate use of busy-tone signal is rarely found in those MAC protocols results in protocol overhead and energy consumption of wireless nodes.

In Dual Sensing Directional MAC (DSDMAC) [1], authors employed a busy-tone channel and a data channel. When a sender (S) sends a directional RTS (DRTS) to the destination (D) in data channel, the S also sends continuous busy-tone in the busy-tone channel towards all other directions to solve the hidden terminal problem. On the destination side, the D also sends a discontinuous busy-tone in the busy-tone channel towards all other directions except the directional CTS direction. Both the S and D send a discontinuous busy-tone at the time of data transmission. The DSDMAC is neither a single channel protocol nor a multichannel protocol. It is a Dual channel protocol with inefficient channel utilization. According to the MAC operation of DSDMAC, DRTS does not guarantee that the transmission must take

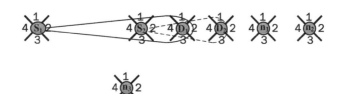

(a) Network scenario of DSDMAC.

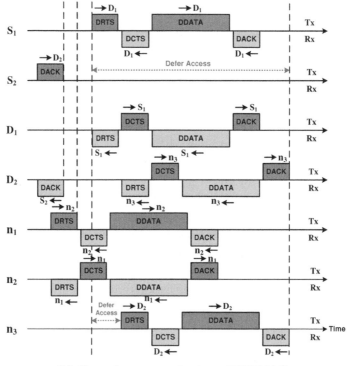

(b) Channel access mechanism of DSDMAC.

Figure 20.1: Protocol operation of DSDMAC [1] with network scenario.

place. So the DNAV setting before the DCTS reception is illogical and may result in unnecessarily blocking other neighbor nodes. Moreover, a continuous busy-tone will consume a great amount of energy of wireless node and restrict the parallel transmission in a different spatial direction.

Figure 20.1 illustrates the problem of DSDMAC [1]. Here, node S_1 transmits data directionally to node D_1 after successful negotiation by exchanging DRTS and DCTS, respectively. According to Fig. 20.1, node S_2 sets its DNAV by blocking the sectors upon overhearing the DRTS and DCTS form S_1 and D_1, and node S_2 can transmit data to D_2 only after the completion of S_1's data transmission to D_1 due to the single data channel. However, D_2 and n_3, as well as n_1 and n_2, can transmit as they did not block their directions. However, S_2 could directionally communicate with D_2 if there were multiple data channels.

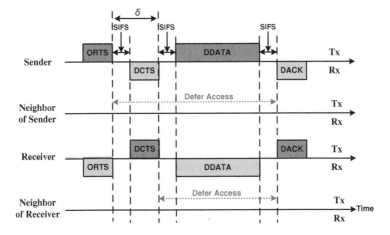

Figure 20.2: Medium access operation of PCDMAC [2].

The PCDMAC [2] also uses busy-tone to solve the hidden terminal and deafness problem but suffers from single data channel problem. As shown in Fig. 20.2, neighbors of both sender and receiver must be deferred until the sender and receiver finish the directional communication due to the single data channel. To solve hidden terminal and deafness problems the protocol uses busy-tone which forces the neighbors to go in silent mode. However, this MAC operation creates an exposed terminal problem for $\delta = $ (SIFS+DCTS) time because all directional antennas of the sender's neighbor are blocked for the δ time listening to omni-directional RTS (ORTS), and DNAV is set for the exact direction of receiver node after the δ time, which decreases the network capacity.

20.4 OBJECTIVES AND MOTIVATION

The objectives and motivation behind the protocol design are described in the following subsections.

20.4.1 Objectives

DSDMAC [1] and PCDMAC [2] use busy-tone to solve directional hidden terminal and deafness problems. However, considering the above-mentioned problems of DSDMAC and PCDMAC protocols, we have been motivated to develop a discrete tone driven directional rate controlled MAC protocol which intends to attain the subsequent objectives:

- Ensuring concurrent data transmission by employing multiple data channels to eliminate the hidden terminal problems of a single data channel.

- Utilizing the *p-persistent* method in discrete omni-directional busy-tone transmission to mitigate directional hidden terminal and deafness problems consuming minimum energy.

- Employing *Shannon-Hartley* theorem to calculate the directional transmission rate of control, and data packets to eliminate the hidden terminal problems that arise due to asymmetry in gain.

20.4.2 Motivation

In consonance with the preceding objectives as far as we know, no MAC protocol have designed employing the *p-persistent* based busy-tone along with utilizing multiple data channels. First and foremost, we have employed *p-persistent* method based omni-directional busy-tone transmission and directional data transmission in multiple data channels in our proposed MAC protocol to attain the outcomes that follow:

- By taking the advantage of directional antennas increase the spatial reuse and wider coverage area which results in higher throughput.

- The use of multiple data channels and multiple directional radios increases overall network throughput by ensuring concurrent data transmission and minimizing directional hidden terminal and deafness problems.

- *Shannon-Hartley* theorem based rate controlling mechanisms not only eliminates the asymmetry antenna gain problems but also reduces the energy consumption of wireless nodes.

20.5   RESEARCH METHODOLOGY

The research methodology consists of assumptions, adopted antenna model, P-Persistent method and Busy-Tone packet.

20.5.1   Assumptions

The proposed communication system has a dedicated control channel and multiple data. Each node is equipped with two half-duplex radios. One radio is dedicated to exchange directional control packets and omni-directional BTP in the control channel. Another radio performs directional data transmission in one of the available data channels. All the nodes maintain an asynchronous time slot in the control channel, where a sender node transmits only the DRTS and BTP at the beginning of the time slots. On the contrary, a receiver node transmits BTP at the beginning of its time slots.

20.5.2   Antenna Model

A switched beam antenna model [10] (as shown in Fig. 20.3a) is assumed to be used in our proposed communication system because switched beam antennas are inexpensive. The beamforming lobe (main lobe) with high gain and nulls (sidelobe) with a low gain is also demonstrated in Fig. 20.3a. It is also assumed that the proposed protocol can use all the sectors simultaneously to cover all the directions or it can

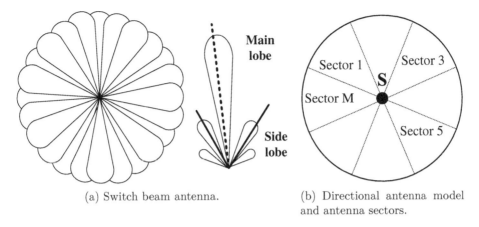

(a) Switch beam antenna.

(b) Directional antenna model and antenna sectors.

Figure 20.3: Antenna model of proposed DTD^{2}RC MAC protocol.

use switching methodology for a specific direction [1] shown in Fig. 20.3b. Here, M directional antennas/sectors with an angle of "$2\pi/M$" radians jointly form the transceiver [5] based on the 360° surroundings.

20.5.3 P-Persistent Method

In p-persistent method [11], a channel has time-slots and each time-slot span is equal to or larger than the highest propagation delay time in that channel. When a node has frames to transmit, it senses the channel to determine whether the channel is idle or busy. If the node detects that the channel is busy, it waits until the next time-slot. If the channel is discovered to be idle, it instantly transmits a frame with a probability p; whereas the node defers its transmission until the next slot with probability q=1-p. If the next time-slot is also found idle, it either transmits or defers again, with probabilities p and q. This process is repeated until either the frame has been transmitted or another station has begun transmitting.

20.5.4 Busy-Tone Packet

Discontinuous Busy-Tone Packet (BTP) is assumed to be sent in all the directions to avoid hidden terminal and deafness problems. The BTP will contain information such as node id, left communication time, communication direction and channel number to let the neighbor inform about ongoing communication so that the neighbor can avoid directional hidden terminal and directional deafness problems. As demonstrated in Fig. 20.4, during the directional data (DDATA) transmission and directional acknowledgement (DACK) transmission time in a data channel (DC), a sender and its receiver node transmit the BTP in control channel (CC) if the calculated probability is higher than or equal to a threshold value (β) according to the *p-persistent* method. In this proposed protocol, we have assumed the threshold value is half of the maximum probability value, i.e., $\beta \geq 0.5$.

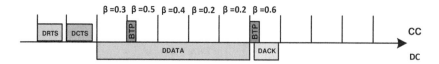

Figure 20.4: Busy-Tone Packet (BTP) with asynchronous time-slots.

20.6 P-PERSISTENT TONE DRIVEN RATE CONTROLLED MAC OPERATION

When a node has data to transmit, it senses the control channel (CC) using the dedicated radio to access and assess the CC occupancy. If it senses the CC is busy, then it will wait for the next time slot and senses the CC again. If the node doesn't sense any DRTS/DCTS or BTP in the CC, then it starts negotiation with its intended receiver for selecting one of the data channels (DC) for directional data (DDATA) and acknowledgment (DACK) transmission.

Sender node transmits DRTS at the beginning of an asynchronously maintained time-slot. If the receiver node successfully receives the DRTS, it will reply with a DCTS (waiting a SIFS time). Receiving DRTS, a neighbor waits for setting DNAV [2] until a DCTS packet is received. Receiver's neighbor nodes receive DRTS and DCTS where the receiving sectors will be blocked until DACK is received only for a specific data channel. Again, DCTS received sender's neighbor nodes; receiving sector will also be blocked until DACK is received only for a specific data channel. Thereupon, performing a successful negotiation sender and receiver switch to the designated DC and the sender starts directional data transmission towards the receiver.

During communication in DC, nodes will maintain asynchronous periodic slots in CC and in each slot with *p-persistent* methods sender or receiver will transmit discrete omni-directional BTP if the calculated probability is higher than or equal to the threshold value (i.e., $\beta \geq 0.5$). Here, the collision between DRTS/DCTS and BTP can be avoided by maintaining asynchronous time slots by all nodes. Also, the probability of the collision among BTPs is less due to the *p-persistent* method-based probability value in case of BTP transmission. However, if consecutive n numbers of slots are missed due to low probability value than the threshold value, then in $(n+1)^{th}$ slot a BTP will be sent forcefully. When the neighbors of a sender and receiver overhear BTP, they will stop their intended communication based on the information contained by a BTP. By this way, BTP is also exploited to eliminate hidden, exposed terminal and deafness.

As shown in Fig. 20.5, node S_1 transmits DRTS to node D_1 just after sensing the common CC is free. Upon receiving the DRTS, node D_1 sends DCTS to S_1 with the calculated rate according to the *Shannon-Hartley* theorem stated in Eq. 20.1. After DRTS, DCTS negotiation S_1 and D_1 select data channel-1 (DC$_1$) and starts directional data transmission with a controlled rate calculated using Eq. 20.2. Receiving data node D_1 sends a DACK with a controlled rate estimated by Eq. 20.3 to S_1 in the data channel. Here, based on the *p-persistent* probability value both S_1 and D_1 send BTP at the beginning of the asynchronously maintained time-slots (TS$_i$) in CC during DDATA and DACK transmission in data channel. In Fig. 20.5, node

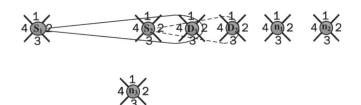

(a) Network scenario of DTD^{2}RC MAC.

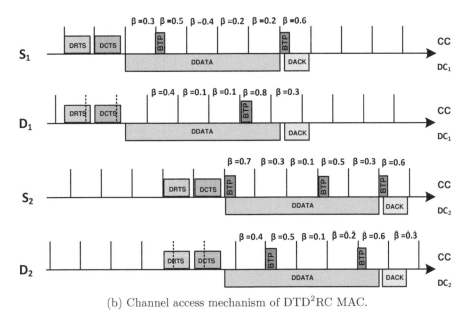

(b) Channel access mechanism of DTD^{2}RC MAC.

Figure 20.5: Protocol operation of DTD^{2}RC MAC with network scenario.

S_1 sends BTP in TS$_4$ and TS$_8$ of its own asynchronous time slots and node D_1 sends BTP of its TS$_7$.

20.6.1 Rate Controlling Methodology

The transmission rate of DCTS/DDATA/DACK is calculated using the *Shannon-Hartley* theorem. The DCTS transmission rate is calculated using Eq. 20.1, where C_{DCTS} is the transmission rate of DCTS and B is the bandwidth of the channel. The S_{DRTS} is the average received DRTS signal power over the bandwidth. N and I are the average power of the noise and interference, respectively.

$$C_{DCTS} = B\log_2 \left(1 + \frac{S_{DRTS}}{(N + I)}\right) \tag{20.1}$$

After the successful reception of DCTS from the receiver, the sender transmits DDATA with a controlled transmission rate using the following formula:

$$C_{DDATA} = B\log_2 \left(1 + \frac{S_{DCTS}}{(N + I)}\right) \tag{20.2}$$

Table 20.1: Simulation Parameters.

Parameter	Value
Simulation Area	$1000 \times 1000 \ m^2$
Node Deployment Type	Uniform
Number of Nodes deployed	$5 \sim 50$ nodes
Control Channel (CC) used	1 (Dedicated)
Data Channels (DC) used	6
Transmission rates for data packet	1, 2, 5.5, 11 Mbps
Transmission rates for control packet	1 Mbps
Data Packet Size	1024 Bytes
Packet Generation Rate	$5 \sim 50$ Pkt/s
Antenna Beamwidth	$15° \sim 90°$
Number of sectors (M)	$2 \sim 8$ per node
Frequency Band	$2.40 \sim 2.48$ GHz
Number of Simulation Runs	10
Total Simulation Time	100 Seconds

Similarly, the transmission rate of DACK is calculated using Eq. 20.3 by the receiver to send DACK the sender.

$$C_{DACK} = B\log_2 \left(1 + \frac{S_{DDATA}}{(N + I)}\right) \qquad (20.3)$$

20.7 PERFORMANCE EVALUATION

The performance of the proposed DTD^{2}RC MAC protocol is evaluated through an analytical simulation model. We have compared different aspects such as *Control Packet Overhead, Throughput* and *End-to-End Delay* of the proposed work with DS-DMAC [1], PCDMAC [2] and IEEE 802.11 [12] protocol. Based on this performance metrics, the proposed protocol significantly outperforms the compared protocols. The simulation parameters are listed in Table 20.1.

20.7.1 Control Packet Overhead

The comparison among IEEE 802.11, DSDMAC, PCDMAC and proposed DTD^{2}RC MAC protocol of control packet overhead for effective data communication between sender and receiver with respect to the data payload size of the network is shown in Fig. 20.6. Here a significant improvement of the proposed protocol is found in terms of control packet overhead because both the DSDMAC and PCDMAC require continuous busy-tone transmission for successful data transmission. However, the proposed MAC protocol transmits discontinuous busy-tone packets using the *p-persistent* method and results in less control packet overhead. Besides, IEEE 802.11 protocol suffers from hidden terminal and deafness problems for its straightforward nature in protocol operation. Therefore, it requires iterative handshaking and results in nearly

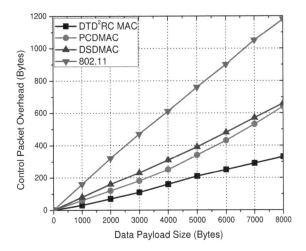

Figure 20.6: Comparison of control packet overhead with distinct data payload sizes.

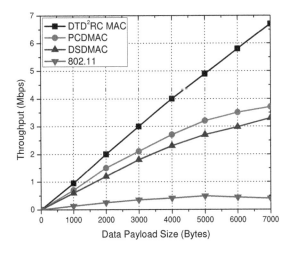

Figure 20.7: Throughput with different data payload sizes.

two times control packet overhead than the DSDMAC and PCDMAC. Moreover, IEEE 802.11 protocol requires nearly three times control packet overhead than the proposed DTD^{2}RC MAC protocol.

20.7.2 Throughput

Figure 20.7 demonstrates the comparison of overall network throughput among IEEE 802.11, DSDMAC, PCDMAC and proposed DTD^{2}RC MAC protocol with respect to different data payload sizes. Here, the overall throughput of proposed DTD^{2}RC MAC protocol is increased linearly and better than any of the three compared protocols due to joint employment of multiple data channels with multiple radios as well as rate control mechanism for directional communication using *Shannon-Hartley* theorem.

20.7.3   End-to-End Delay

End-to-End Delay of IEEE 802.11, DSDMAC, PCDMAC and proposed DTD^2RC MAC protocol with different number of nodes is shown in Fig. 20.8. We have assumed the maximum number of node is 50. Here, IEEE 802.11 protocol suffers from maximum average transmission delay for one hop communication due to excessive hidden terminal and deafness problems. However, DSDMAC and PCDMAC also suffer from single hop communication delay due to continuous busy-tone signal that blocks the handshaking process of other nodes in the same network. The proposed DTD^2RC MAC protocol suffers from minimum average transmission delay for one hop communication due to joint employment of multiple data channels with multiple radios and omni-directional discontinuous Busy-Tone Packet (BTP) with *p-persistent* method in control channel to solve the directional hidden terminal and deafness problems.

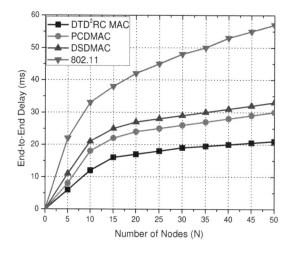

Figure 20.8: End-to-end delay with varying number of nodes.

20.7.4   Per Packet Energy Consumption

Based on the distinct node densities we have also compared the energy consumption rate of the proposed DTD^2RC MAC protocol with respect to IEEE 802.11, DSDMAC and PCDMAC protocol. Figure 20.9 demonstrates that the proposed DTD^2RC MAC protocol is more energy-efficient than the compared protocols because the proposed protocol consumes energy to a smaller extent than the IEEE 802.11, DSDMAC and PCDMAC protocol. Here, the IEEE 802.11 has the highest energy consumption rate. When the number of nodes increases in the network, the rate of collision also increases in IEEE 802.11. Hence, the huge number of packet retransmission in IEEE 802.11 results in a linear increment of energy consumption rate. DSDMAC has the second highest energy consumption rate because it minimizes the packet collision rate by utilizing busy-tones. However, huge energy is consumed for a successful packet transmission due to transmitting a continuous busy tone. PCDMAC is more energy-efficient than IEEE 802.11 and DSDMAC, but not more than the proposed protocol. PCDMAC gains more energy efficiency than IEEE 802.11 and DSDMAC due to

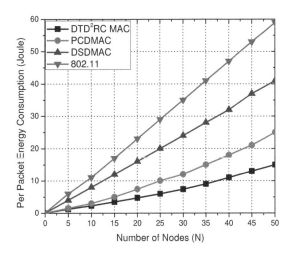

Figure 20.9: Per packet energy consumption with varying number of nodes.

using a rate-controlling mechanism. Finally, the proposed DTD^{2}RC MAC protocol achieves higher energy efficiency than IEEE 802.11, DSDMAC and PCDMAC protocols because of the joint employment of multichannel, multiple radios and *p-persistent* methods for discrete busy tone transmission. This joint notion limits the packet collision rate and saves a lot of energy that requires packet retransmissions by compared protocols. Moreover, the transmission rate controlling mechanism for control and data packet transmission minimizes the extra energy consumption for gaining unnecessary higher data rates for transmissions.

20.8 CONCLUSION

The DTD^{2}RC MAC protocol is proposed to solve and mitigate the hidden terminal problem and deafness problem in directional data transmission with rate controlling mechanism and multichannel concept. The proposed protocol is more energy efficient due to employing joint direction antenna, multiple data channels, multiple radios and Busy-Tone Packets as well as rate controlled mechanisms and fewer control packets. Overall throughput is increased with the use of multiple data channels. Overall delay decreases due to employing fewer control packets. In the future, we will perform a comprehensive mathematical analysis of the proposed protocol in order to validate the findings of simulation.

Bibliography

[1] Abdullah, A., Cai, L. & Gebali, F. (2012). DSDMAC: Dual Sensing Directional MAC Protocol for Ad Hoc Networks with Directional Antennas. *IEEE Transactions On Vehicular Technology.* vol. 61, 1266-1275.

[2] Yadav, S. & Lobiyal, D. (2017). Power Control Directional MAC Protocol for Mobile Ad Hoc Networks. *Wireless Personal Communications.* vol. 96, 4131-4144.

[3] Kulkarni, S. & Rosenberg, C. (2005). DBSMA: a MAC protocol for multi-hop ad-hoc networks with directional antennas. *2005 IEEE 16th International Symposium On Personal, Indoor And Mobile Radio Communications*. vol. 2, pp. 1371-1377.

[4] Ahmed, K., Uddin, M. & Rahman, M. (2018). Rate adaptive cooperative multi-channel directional MAC protocol for ad hoc networks. *2018 IEEE International Conference On Innovative Research And Development (ICIRD)*. pp. 1-6.

[5] Mahmud, M., Rahman, M. & Hassan, M. (2018). Two-Dimensional Cooperation-based Asynchronous Multichannel Directional MAC Protocol for Wireless Networks. *TENCON 2018 - 2018 IEEE Region 10 Conference*. pp. 1033-1038.

[6] Mahmud, M., Rahman, M., Alqahtani, S. & Hassan, M. (2021). Cooperation-Based Adaptive and Reliable MAC Design for Multichannel Directional Wireless IoT Networks. *IEEE Access*. vol. 9, pp. 97518-97538.

[7] Bandai, M., Maeda, S. & Watanabe, T. (2008). Energy Efficient MAC Protocol with Power and Rate Control in Multi-Rate Ad Hoc Networks. *VTC Spring 2008 - IEEE Vehicular Technology Conference*. pp. 66-70.

[8] Korakis, T., Jakllari, G. & Tassiulas, L. (2008). CDR-MAC: A Protocol for Full Exploitation of Directional Antennas in Ad Hoc Wireless Networks. *IEEE Transactions On Mobile Computing*. **7**, 145-155.

[9] Inzillo, V., De Rango, F. & Quintana, A. (2018). A sectorized directional MAC proposal for mitigating deafness and energy consumption in mobile ad hoc networks. *2018 15th IEEE Annual Consumer Communications Networking Conference (CCNC)*. pp. 1-2.

[10] Balanis, C. & Ioannides, P. (2007). Introduction to Smart Antennas. *Introduction To Smart Antennas*. vol. 2, 1-175.

[11] Cali, F., Conti, M. & Gregori, E. (2000). Dynamic IEEE 802.11: Design, Modeling and Performance Evaluation. *Networking 2000 Broadband Communications, High Performance Networking, And Performance Of Communication Networks*. pp. 786-798.

[12] IEEE Standard for Telecommunications and Information Exchange Between Systems - LAN/MAN Specific Requirements - Part 11: Wireless Medium Access Control (MAC) and physical layer (PHY) specifications: High Speed Physical Layer in the 5 GHz band. (1999). *IEEE Std 802.11a-1999*. pp. 1-102.

CHAPTER 21

Blockchain-Based Secure Medical Data Management with Enabling IoT

Naymul Ekram, Md. Nazmul Hasan, and Muhammad Sheikh Sadi

Khulna University of Engineering & Technology, Khulna, Bangladesh

Mohammad Shahriar Rahman

United International University, Dhaka, Bangladesh

CONTENTS

21.1	Introduction	252
21.2	Related Work	254
21.3	Preliminaries	254
	21.3.1 Internet of Things (IoT)	254
	21.3.2 Blockchain Technology and Security	255
	21.3.3 PoW Algorithm for Mining New Blocks	256
	21.3.4 Ethereum Blockchain	257
21.4	Proposed Methodology	257
	21.4.1 Steps in Our System	259
	21.4.2 System Model Representation	260
	21.4.2.1 Data Collected from IoT Nodes	260
	21.4.2.2 Creating a Blockchain for Each Patient in the Ethereum Network	260
	21.4.2.3 Encryption of Cloud Address with Doctor Public Key	261
	21.4.2.4 Store Patient Cloud Address to Blockchain	261
	21.4.2.5 Give Permission to the Doctor to Access the Block	262
	21.4.3 Smart Contract	262
21.5	Performance Evaluation	262
	21.5.1 Performance Comparison among Proposed Methods and Existing Methods	263
	21.5.2 Consumed Gas for Every Transaction	263
21.6	Conclusion	263

NOWADAYS, the Electronic Health Care System is rapidly expanding. The management of Electronic Health Records (EHRs) on cloud resources has undergone a paradigm change in recent years. The interconnection of devices for data collection and intelligent decision-making is known as the Internet of Things (IoT). However, IoT is vulnerable to privacy and security breaches due to a lack of inherent security controls. Data retrieved from IoT devices are mainly stored in a database. For a certain patient, this information is crucial. If the evidence is tampered with, the doctor will be unable to determine the true nature of the patient's condition and therefore will be unable to provide appropriate care, causing significant damage to the patient. As a result, it is important to ensure a higher level of security in the health sector. For this sake, different security systems have been introduced for the welfare of mankind. Such an emerging technology might be Blockchain. In this case, blockchain technologies would be extremely beneficial. We have created a framework that employs Blockchain technologies to eliminate anonymous data access in the cloud while also ensuring data security. Here, in this chapter, we have demonstrated a system prototype using IoT, blockchain, and a user-friendly website.

21.1   INTRODUCTION

The Internet of Things (IoT) refers to the expansion of Internet access to include physical computers and daily usable devices to make our daily life more comfortable [1]. These connected devices can be remotely controlled only with the help of IoT. But the data which are exchanged by the IoT nodes can be easily manipulated. Data security is one of the most important concerns for all in recent days [2]. Even if the data is less relevant, no one wants to share it with anyone. This data security is a burning question for critical patients.

If the data are accessed by an intruder, he can maltreat or blackmail the patient. If an attacker alters a patient's records, the doctor may be unable to provide adequate care. In that case, security is strongly needed. Assume that an intruder tries to change the information records. As soon as he edits the information from your ID, it will change the block's hash. To hide his tracks, the hacker will need to upgrade the next block in the chain, which would still contain the old hash [3]. In that way, he has to change the hash of that block, also the next, and one by one every block's hash. From another aspect, critical patients are not able to go to doctors daily, and on several occasions, these inabilities create problems for them. Hence, if the remote monitoring system of the patient is possible, then it will be supportive to them. Moreover, for elderly people, who are reluctant to travel to the hospital to demonstrate their condition, the remote surveillance device would be beneficial [4]. One of the issues found with the modern health system is that it is possible to evaluate a patient in multiple hospitals and not exchange the details between them [5]. As a result, it is a challenge that patients must retest if they change doctors. Thinking about the security concern of health systems, blockchain technology appears.

Blockchain technology has gained huge popularity in the health sector for its significance in solving the compatibility and security problems of Electronic Health Record

(EHR) systems in recent days [4]. Blockchain has shown tremendous promise in a wide range of e-health systems with its decentralized (there is no central authority) and trustworthy nature, including a fee exchange of electronic medical data records and shared data management among various healthcare systems [6]. Now, e-Health has become very popular among people. It is an emerging technology for medical science. Medical services and information about patients are delivered through the internet. This word doesn't apply to the technical aspect; it has also a wider context. There are many works in this field to solve this kind of security issue. Blockchain technology has made a secured decentralized database for this technology thereby decreasing patient suffering. They don't have to retest their physical conditions if they go to a new doctor because, using blockchain, they can share their secured data with the safest platform. Many researchers have worked with the cloud-based blockchain system. They have uploaded data in a blockchain-controlled cloud system to make them secure from intruders.

We are concerned about the security problems and physically visiting doctors that the patients face. So, we developed a blockchain-enabled IoT system that can be the solution to the above-mentioned problems. Patients upload their data and their symptoms in the cloud through the website; this data of patients should be secured. Blockchain technology describes the issue of safety and trust in many aspects [7]. The novelty of our chapter is that each patient's data is gathered from IoT nodes (such as various sensors which are connected with Raspberry Pi) and is stored in an encrypted form in the remote cloud linearly, and the cloud address will be kept in the blockchain which is impregnable. Storing every patient's huge data in the blockchain network is difficult and costly. In this regard, we have planned to store the patient's data in the cloud and the blockchain network will contain only the cloud address. Acquiring the help of this secured e-health system, critical patients can be monitored by proficient doctors. In this way, blockchain and IoT greatly serve the critical patient. We build a secure storage system using blockchain mainly using Ethereum blockchain. In that case, we have used blockchain algorithms proof of work, and other security algorithms. Here we can store an unimaginative number of blocks; there is no limitation and no central authority which is the most essential thing. In the database, the data are centrally maintained by a server, but in a blockchain, there is none of the central authority which is the reason why it is fully decentralized and secure from the attack of intruders. That makes the e-Health system fully safer than other systems. If an intruder attacks and changes any data of a block, the block's hash will be immediately changed, then the previous hash will also be changed one-by-one because it is a chain method. That creates a whole change in the blockchain. Patients should be concerned about the abuse of their data. From a medical data security viewpoint, our project prevents sharing any personal data with anyone.

The following is a description of the chapter's structure. In Section 21.2, we describe the related work. In Section 21.3, we explain preliminaries. In Section 21.4, we have discussed our system model that describes how the system will work. In Section 21.5, the performance evaluation of our proposed system is discussed. The final section concludes with a summary of our contributions and recommendations for future enhancements.

21.2 RELATED WORK

There are related research works that prove the feasibility of our work. In this section, we have discussed some of the recent works in this field.

In [8] the authors have used blockchain for empowering cloud e-Health. They have built the system for radiation oncology for mainly cancer patients. The prototype is built on Hyperledger Fabric which is an open-source permitted blockchain architecture [9]. Here data is uploaded in the cloud but in this prototype, there is no implementation of IoT so all the patient data has to be uploaded manually. Their infrastructure includes a web interface and a back end that includes a membership provider and credential authority, a network of nodes, a load balancer that can send a user to each of the network's trusted nodes, and different cloud-based storage for patient data as well as certificates. They could include real-time patient data uploading in the cloud through IoT.

In [6] the authors have used blockchain to introduce a secure Electronic Health Record (EHR) exchanging mechanism for mobile cloud-based e-Health systems. They are employing Ethereum Blockchain platform for building e-Health system; their prototype is mainly mobile-based patient monitoring which is different from us as we implemented our infrastructure in a web version that is quite apparent. Also, choosing AWS as their cloud server is a wise decision for them.

In [10] the authors have done quite similar work comparing the above two. They have built a prototype e-Health data access management using blockchain especially Ethereum blockchain. Ethereum is mainly a public blockchain that is used for data access management. For creating smart contracts, they have used solidity language to collect data from patients; they have used various sensors and Raspberry Pi. For file storage, IPFS is used as a database, but this is much too complex so they could choose cloud firestore for their purpose.

21.3 PRELIMINARIES

In this chapter, some formal statements and terminologies related to this section will be discussed. Some specifications will also be discussed which will be used to describe the proposed method. These statements and terminologies will be elaborated on using some examples and pictorial representation. Blockchain with IoT scheme will also be discussed. Some problems of the existing method will also be explained. Many of the existing methods have some problems. Some methods are used efficiently and some are not. In this chapter, some existing methods are described.

21.3.1 Internet of Things (IoT)

The Internet of Things (IoT) is a compact network of sensors and other devices to communicate with one another through the internet. Internet of Medical Things (IoMT) is a part of an IoT program that collects and analyzes data for testing and monitoring [11]. It has been deemed Smart Healthcare because it is the infrastructure that allows for the creation of a digitized healthcare system that connects accessible patient resources and healthcare services. Remote patient monitoring is now

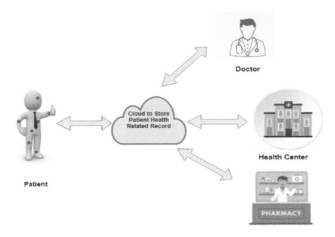

Figure 21.1: Internet of things (IoT).

thinkable only for the advancement of IoT. These health monitoring kits can be from wearable sensors to various sophisticated devices. A recent statistic shows that there exists around one-third of IoT devices in the health sector, and the analysts predict that it will be increased by 2025, which will be the digitalization of our health sector [12]. The tide of development in this sector not only makes our life comfortable, but also increases our average life expectancy. But with time, IoMT solutions are facing difficulties as security and privacy fragility. For security purposes, an emerging technology blockchain has been adopted which is quite new to people. Figure 21.1 depicts the data sharing procedure through the Internet of Things. Nowadays a patient's health data can be easily shared among doctors, pharmacy and other third parties with the cooperation of cloud computing.

21.3.2 Blockchain Technology and Security

Blockchain technology is a collection of blocks that are connected in an immutable and decentralized network. In IoT, blockchain works without the help of a centralized database. Blockchain is such a technology in which data are stored block-by-block, whenever new blocks are created, they are added at the end of the chain in a linear procedure. The blockchain network must verify the validity of a transaction after it has been certified. By giving proof of the transaction by a computer, the transaction is linked to the blockchain as a block. Each block on the blockchain network has a distinct hash. A hash is developed using an algorithm and is crucial for cryptocurrency blockchain management. In case of manipulating any information of a block, instantly it changes the block's hash value. However, this causes a change in the hash of the after block also. This is an ongoing process, so by changing or deleting any data, all other block hashes change automatically. To change a single block on the blockchain, an intruder will have to change every single block after that. It will take an immense amount of computational power to recalculate all of those hashes. So, no one can change a single thing in the blockchain network without notice.

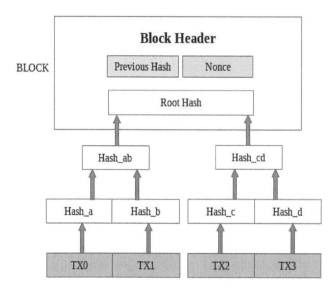

Figure 21.2: The block header (redrawn from [13])

In a blockchain system, there exist two variants of nodes: the first one wants to add new blocks in the network and the other receives these new blocks to create a chain of blocks. Blockchain consists of blocks, and blocks have block headers. And each block header has its unique hash, the previous block's hash, Merkle root, nonce, and timestamp [13]. Figure 21.2 shows a complete idea of the block header.

21.3.3 PoW Algorithm for Mining New Blocks

We use proof of work for mining transactions. It is not possible to alter any data in a block. But it can be somehow possible to generate all the block's hashes and regenerate the chain. If we use a transaction mining process, then it will require a very high-performance machine or even an impossible machine to do so. In our case, we use this method and test computation power before mining transactions. We also make the sender a miner. After making a transaction the sender mines the transaction also.

While creating a new block by a node, the receiving nodes will compute hash function of the block data and a nonce, which is called miners. A nonce is an arbitrary number in cryptography that we can use it only one time in a cryptographic communication [14]. It is often a randomized or quasi-random number that is provided in an identification protocol to ensure that previous contacts cannot be reused in replay attacks [15]. The predefined value must be greater than the computed hash value. If this criterion is not met, the nonce is increased and the hash function is recalculated using the modified nonce. After finishing its task by a miner, the newly created block has now its proof of work and it will be checked by other nodes in the network. But mining is not a simple process because for solving complex

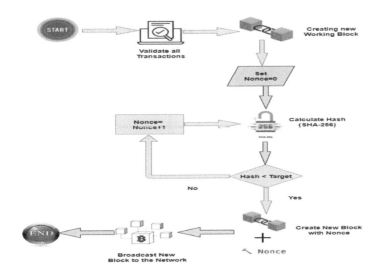

Figure 21.3: PoW algorithm.

mathematical terms, computers have to run high programs. Here, Figure 21.3 shows an algorithm of PoW.

21.3.4 Ethereum Blockchain

Ethereum is a decentralized and also public blockchain network that emphasizes operating a decentralized application programming code. It is a worldwide knowledge exchange network that cannot be manipulated or modified. Ether, also known as ETH, is a decentralized digital currency [16]. It is mainly used for paying transaction fees as well as computational services in the Ethereum network. As the Ethereum network expands, the process of business and transaction will change in the near future. Ethereum has a broad variety of possible uses, including voting, health records, the global supply chain, and the banking sector.

The big advantage of Ethereum is that it's an open system [17]; people from outside can join this, but it's a secure platform. Its transaction fees are lower than any other blockchain project. There is no need for third parties in ETH transactions. Any kind of complex agreement can be done on this platform. For many of those advantages, everyone prefers Ethereum blockchain over other blockchain technologies.

21.4 PROPOSED METHODOLOGY

In IoT technology, the conventional way is to store all data in the cloud. Nowadays, the security of this cloud data is a matter of concern. Users should be aware of who can access their data on the cloud. In our system, we also want to store a patient's

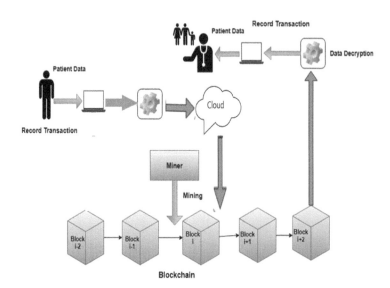

Figure 21.4: The overview of blockchain-based e-health system.

data in the cloud but following effective security procedures. Some data are very influential as well as confidential that should be secured in the cloud, and patients must have sufficient control over who can access this data from the cloud. So, security should be ensured on this data on the cloud. On this point of security, we use a very well-known blockchain technology. Many blockchain technologies are available, we use Ethereum blockchain for its high-security criteria. Some paramount reasons behind choosing this Ethereum technology are given below:

- Ethereum is a large existing network, and for many years this network is tested through many operations and lots of value. So, it is secure and safe.

- Ethereum has a lot of functions to use, is very good for using smart contracts, and also can store data very securely in a decentralized manner.

- Ethereum is so popular, and there are constant ways to improve this technology.

Thinking about all of these advantages, we build an Ethereum-based smart contract for communicating between patients and doctors. Doctors can easily monitor patients via this smart contract. The whole methodology can be divided into several parts. In this section, we describe all these parts one-by-one. Figure 21.4 shows the pictorial view of the key idea of our system that has two parts: IoT and blockchain. Patient data are collected from sensors and stored safely in cloud-first. Then, the cloud address is stored in the blockchain. That makes the entire system quite more secure than other IoT medical systems. Figure 21.5 also depicts the flow diagram of the proposed methodology.

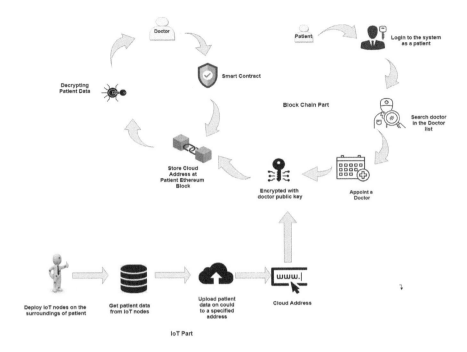

Figure 21.5: Flow diagram of the proposed methodology.

21.4.1 Steps in Our System

In this subsection, we want to establish our blockchain part step-by-step so that everyone has a clear point of view on how the system is working. The proposed steps are given below.

- **Step 1:** Create an Ethereum account for each patient/user;

- **Step 2:** Create own blockchain;

- **Step 3:** Deploy IoT nodes on surroundings;

- **Step 4:** Data Store on cloud database of Master Node;

- **Step 5:** Data preprocessing;

- **Step 6:** Encryption of cloud address;

- **Step 7:** Upload cloud address to a certain block;

- **Step 8:** Appoint a doctor;

- **Step 9:** Doctor decrypt the cloud address with his private key;

- **Step 10:** Doctor gives advice and suggestions on the patient block;

- **Step 11:** Ater a certain time access power is over.

21.4.2   System Model Representation

We have developed a system model that is suitable for remote patient monitoring as well as secure from data breaches. Critical patient data can be easily altered by anyone, and concerning this, we want to make a safe and trustable platform for the patient. The steps which are followed to develop the platform are described below:

21.4.2.1   *Data Collected from IoT Nodes*

The patient's sensible data are collected from IoT nodes. The IoT nodes consist of various sensors (temperature sensor (LM35), heartbeat measuring sensor) and medical equipment deployed in the surroundings of the patients. We continuously collect data from these nodes, and encrypt it, and save this encrypted value on the cloud. In the cloud, the data are saved chronologically. The individual patient can only access his data, not others. Then some preprocessing of data is done, and all the garbage and unnecessary data are filtered out from the data. Only crucial data are stored in the cloud. For our system, we use various kinds of sensors (temperature sensor(LM35), heartbeat measuring sensor) to collect data from the patient surroundings, and here Raspberry Pi works as a Master node. In Raspberry Pi, we write code in Python language to retrieve data from sensors and store those data in the cloud. The circuit setup is shown below in Figure 21.6.

21.4.2.2   *Creating a Blockchain for Each Patient in the Ethereum Network*

As we know, if anyone changes any block data in the blockchain network, that automatically changes every block previous to that block. So, if we create a single blockchain for all the patients in the same Ethereum network, and when any patient updates his data on his block, then it causes a vital change in every previous node

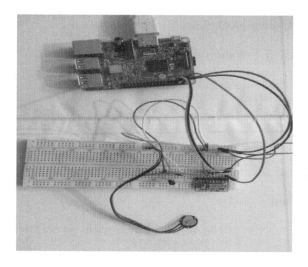

Figure 21.6: Circuit setup.

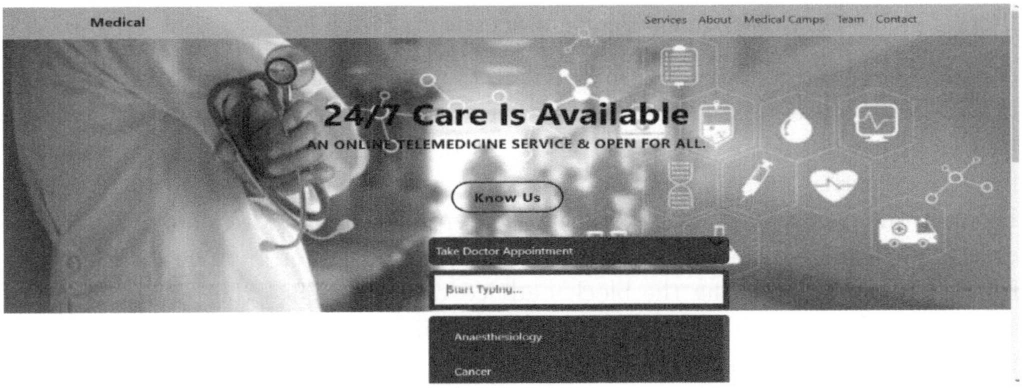

Figure 21.7: Home page of our website.

on this chain. This might be very costly, as the number of patients is gets increased day-by-day. For this purpose, we have created a new blockchain for each patient. Here we have shown this approach as a prototype by creating a new Ethereum account for each patient in the Ethereum network. The patient who created this node has only the rights of his block. Without his consent, none can access his data.

21.4.2.3 Encryption of Cloud Address with Doctor Public Key

After preprocessing, cloud data is ready for deployment to the patient block that was created by the patient earlier. All the data are encrypted with an asymmetric encryption technique with doctor public key for extra security. So only permitted doctors can decrypt the data with their private key and store them in the cloud, which is preferred to be secured from intruders. Instead of encrypting all data we just encrypt cloud address, as it is cost-effective to encrypt only an address and store in blockchain.

21.4.2.4 Store Patient Cloud Address to Blockchain

After logging into our website with valid information, the patient has to upload his encrypted cloud address to his block. Those blocks are stored one after another in a blockchain network linearly. Figure 21.7 depicts the home page of our website. We try to develop the website mainly to make a smooth connection between blockchain and IoT nodes as well as with the cloud. Then the whole system becomes a compact secured E-Health system. When a patient needs to upload data on the blockchain, he has to log into his account and upload the encrypted address. He also needs to fulfill necessary conditions for the read-write authority of his block. The smart contract is written in Solidity language on the Remix IDE online and deployed on the Ethereum blockchain network [18]. Mainly cloud addresses are stored for each patient in the individual Ethereum blockchain. Because of the high cost of ETH gas, we don't prefer to store all the data of patients, so we store only the cloud address of the IoT data. No one but the owner of this block can access it; otherwise, it will roll back the transaction on the Ethereum blockchain.

21.4.2.5 *Give Permission to the Doctor to Access the Block*

A patient can permit access of his block data to a trusted doctor by another function. If the doctor has a valid Ethereum account and valid permission from the patient, then he can read and write to the block. Also, a time-frame is set by the patient for extra security, and the doctor has to access this block within this time-frame. By using the doctor's private key, he can decrypt the cloud address and can directly observe patient condition for a certain time. Then the doctor gives necessary advice to the patient by updating the block's advice variables. Then the patient gets this advice from his block in the Ethereum blockchain network. After a certain period, the access is automatically turned off.

21.4.3 Smart Contract

Data security of IoT nodes is our first concern, so we use asymmetric data encryption techniques for ensuring security that makes the system quite secure from attacks. But we deployed our system in Ethereum blockchain to make it safer because cloud data can also be manipulated in any way. These data are stored in the cloud for remote access to the doctor and should be secure from intruder attacks, as this data is controversial for critical patients. In this case, patients can permit one doctor to access the cloud data through the smart contract. We make a smart contract that ensures a secure permission checking and gives only the desired doctors access to the cloud data of the particular patient. The pseudocode of smart contract is described in Figure 21.8.

21.5 PERFORMANCE EVALUATION

Our system has gained the faith of patients who were the victims of data extortion. Instead of following the conventional procedure, we use blockchain for the sake of data security and transparency. Any type of illegal attempt is contrabanded in this

```
BEGIN:
    # Patient
    Do:
        encrypt cloudAddress
        create new BlockChain
        create new Block
        set doctorUserID
        set patientUserID
        set timestamp
        set duration
        store Data
    # Doctor
    If doctorUserID == block.doctorUserID
            AND timeNow+duration > block.timestamp
        get cloudAddress;
    Else
        get error;
    EndIf

    Do:
        decrypt cloudAddress
        get patientData
END:
```

Figure 21.8: Pseudo code of smart contract.

architecture. So, the system is considered one of the safest platforms compared with the remaining e-health platforms.

21.5.1 Performance Comparison among Proposed Methods and Existing Methods

In this section, we make a comparison between our system architecture and other health systems. The comparison is based on the significant properties of different health systems. Here 'Y' sign means the corresponding system has a certain property

Table 21.1: Comparison Table.

Properties	Type			
	[6]	[8]	[10]	Proposed System
Remote Patient Monitoring	Y	N	Y	Y
High Level Data Security	Y	Y	N	Y
Use of Sensors	Y	N	Y	Y
User Authentication Advice	Y	N	N	Y
Store Data in Blockchain	Y	Y	Y	Y
Use of Cryptographic Function	Y	Y	N	Y
Use of IPFS File System	Y	N	Y	N

in it; on the other hand, the 'N' sign means that property is absent in it. Table 21.1 shows the comparison below.

21.5.2 Consumed Gas for Every Transaction

In the Ethereum blockchain, to perform every transaction a gas fee is charged. In another word, gas is a kind of currency to perform any transaction. As the gas fee is high in the Ethereum network, we don't store all kinds of patient data. So, we decide to store only the individual cloud address in the Ethereum, which costs a small gas fee. However, our system is more efficient than any other system. Figure 21.9 shows the graph between gas fee and input size in bytes.

21.6 CONCLUSION

In the health sector, IoT security is getting a lot of recognition these days. Due to high energy consumption and transmission overhead, existing security technologies are not necessarily suitable for IoT. Hence, to overcome this challenge, this chapter has proposed a blockchain technology that is highly recommended for privacy purposes. This initiative is primarily intended for patients' remote care, as well as the priority protection of sensitive patients' records. To maintain data security, we have implemented the Ethereum blockchain which is considered one of the most effective techniques which are used for data security. We have also used the asymmetric cryptography for hashing technique that makes the block transaction safer than other systems. The possible future enhancements of this chapter could be as follows: sensors, like accelerometer sensors, can be added to the system to measure the accurate

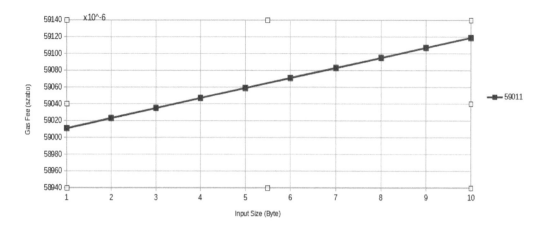

Figure 21.9: Gas vs input size used during the transaction Ethereum.

position of the patients; additional features could be added to the developed website to advance the functionalities of e-health systems.

Bibliography

[1] Ray, P.P., Dash, D., Salah, K., & Kumar, N. (2020). Blockchain for IoT-based healthcare: background, consensus, platforms, and use cases. *IEEE Systems Journal, 15*(1), 85–94.

[2] Fan, K., Wang, S., Ren, Y., Li, H., & Yang, Y. (2018). Medblock: Efficient and secure medical data sharing via blockchain. *Journal of medical systems, 42*(8). 1–11.

[3] Ge, C., Liu, Z., & Fang, L. (2020). A blockchain based decentralized data security mechanism for the Internet of Things. *Journal of Parallel and Distributed Computing, 141*. 1–9.

[4] SuselGóngora Alonso, Jon Arambarri, Miguel López-Coronado & Isabel de la Torre Díez(2019). Proposing New Blockchain Challenges in eHealth. *Journal of Medical Systems, 43*.

[5] Casado-Vara, R., & Corchado, J. (2019). Distributed e-health wide-world accounting ledger via blockchain. *Journal of Intelligent & Fuzzy Systems, 36*(3). 2381–2386.

[6] Nguyen, D. C., Pathirana, P. N., Ding, M., & Seneviratne, A. (2019). Blockchain for secure ehrs sharing of mobile cloud based e-health systems. *IEEE access, 7*. 66792–66806.

[7] Daneshgar, F., Sianaki, O. A., & Guruwacharya, P. (2019, March). Blockchain: a research framework for data security and privacy. *In Workshops of the In-*

ternational Conference on Advanced Information Networking and Applications , 960–974, Springer, Cham.

[8] Dubovitskaya, A., Xu, Z., Ryu, S., Schumacher, M., & Wang, F. (2017, September). How blockchain could empower ehealth: An application for radiation oncology. *In VLDB Workshop on Data Management and Analytics for Medicine and Healthcare*, 3–6, Springer, Cham.

[9] *Hyperledger Fabric, https://www.hyperledger.org/use/fabric, last accessed 2021/06/12.*

[10] Rifi, N., Rachkidi, E., Agoulmine, N., & Taher, N. C. (2017, October). Towards using blockchain technology for eHealth data access management. *In 2017 fourth international conference on advances in biomedical engineering (ICABME)*, 1–4, IEEE.

[11] *Internet of Things, https://en.wikipedia.org/wiki/Internet_of_things, last accessed 2021/06/29.*

[12] Qureshi, F., & Krishnan, S. (2018). Wearable hardware design for the internet of medical things (IoMT). *Sensors, 18*(11), 3812.

[13] Vujičić, D., Jagodić, D., & Ranđić, S. (2018, March). Blockchain technology, bitcoin, and Ethereum: A brief overview. *In 2018 17th international symposium infoteh–jahorina (infoteh)*, 1–6, IEEE.

[14] *Brief of nonce, https://en.wikipedia.org/wiki/Cryptographic_nonce, last accessed 2021/06/12.*

[15] Chen, L., Xu, L., Gao, Z., Lu, Y., & Shi, W. (2018, June). Protecting early stage proof-of-work based public blockchain. *In 2018 48th Annual IEEE/IFIP International Conference on Dependable Systems and Networks Workshops (DSN-W)*, 122–127, IEEE.

[16] *Ethereum Blockchain, https://ethereum.org/en/developers/docs/smart-contracts, last accessed 2021/06/13.*

[17] *Advantage of Ethereum, https://www.mittenmachen.com/advantages-and-disadvantages-of-ethereum, last accessed 2021/04/12.*

[18] Watanabe, H., Fujimura, S., Nakadaira, A., Miyazaki, Y., Akutsu, A., & Kishigami, J. (2016, January). Blockchain contract: Securing a blockchain applied to smart contracts. *In 2016 IEEE international conference on consumer electronics (ICCE)*, 467–468, IEEE.

CHAPTER 22

Bio-Inspired Meta-Heuristic Techniques for DC-DC Boost Converter with LQR Controller in a DC Microgrid

Md. Hassanul Karim Roni and M. S. Rana

Rajshahi University of Engineering & Technology, Rajshahi, Bangladesh

CONTENTS

22.1	Introduction	267
22.2	Literature Reviews	267
22.3	System Description: DC-DC Boost Converter	269
22.4	Controller Design: Proposed LQR Framework	270
22.5	Bio-inspired Optimization Algorithms	271
	22.5.1 Genetic Algorithm	271
	22.5.2 Particle Swarm Optimization	272
	22.5.3 Grey Wolf Optimization Algorithm	273
	22.5.4 Dragonfly Algorithm	274
	22.5.5 Whale Optimization	274
	22.5.6 Optimization Objective Function	275
22.6	Performance Evaluation and Discussion	275
	22.6.1 Optimization Performance	275
	22.6.2 Unit Step Response	276
	22.6.3 Discussion	276
22.7	Conclusion	276

S EVERAL bio-inspired meta-heuristic algorithms have been developed for solving real-world optimization problems, which mimic the social behavior of animals in nature. For control engineers, designing and tuning an optimal controller for a power converter has always been a challenge. This chapter presents a comparative analysis of the application of different bio-inspired meta-heuristic optimization techniques for designing a controller for a dc-dc boost converter circuit. This chapter has illustrated the development of a linear quadratic regulator (LQR) control framework with five different bio-inspired optimization algorithms, i.e., particle swarm optimization, genetic algorithm, grey wolf optimization (GWO), dragonfly algorithm, and whale optimization. GWO coupled with LQR has outperformed the other four optimization methods with 0% overshoot, 0.48% steady-state error, and the least execution time of 5.17 seconds. Hence, GWO has been proposed for power converter controller optimization due to its fast and efficient optimization performance. The controller design and optimization have been carried out in the MATLAB/Simulink environment.

22.1 INTRODUCTION

With the recent technological advances, power converters are getting more popular in residential and industrial applications. They have placed renewable power generation development on the next level with the integration of microgrid [1]. A DC MG consists of many DC-DC and dc-ac converters for voltage conversions and regulation as shown in Figure 22.1 (a). Due to the variable nature of renewable resources e.g., solar power generation, the generated voltage is not always stable with constant voltage and hence requires DC-DC boost converters to raise the voltage from input to output terminals. Basically, in DC MG DC-DC a boost converter helps maintain the voltage levels of the dc bus in photo-voltaic systems [2]. This chapter focuses on DC-DC boost converter modeling and control for DC MG application. The boost converter requires a closed-loop controller for the proper regulation of the converter output. Many control techniques are found in the literature for the closed-loop control operation of the DC-DC boost converter. This chapter represents a comparative analysis of the application of different bio-inspired optimization algorithms for optimizing a LQR controller for the DC-DC boost converter. A control framework with LQR has been presented for comparison with different optimization approaches.

Literature review is discussed in Section 22.2. System descriptions are discussed in Section 22.3. Section 22.4 illustrates the controller design approach, and Section 22.5 illustrates different optimization algorithms. Finally, the performance analysis and discussion are made in Section 22.6, with the conclusion drawn in Section 22.7.

22.2 LITERATURE REVIEWS

The proposed work here is based on an LQR control framework with different optimization algorithms that are inspired from nature. The plant used is a DC-DC boost converter model. The state-space model of the converter has been used for designing controller. This section illustrates the different literature related to the work presented in this chapter.

The proportional-integral-derivative (PID) control is a very popular control approach for power converters. In [3], a comparative analysis has been shown between proportional-integral (PI) and PID control techniques for a DC-DC converter with the application of an evolutionary optimization algorithm. In [4] an enhanced PID controller design for dc boost converter is presented. Many articles are referring to the application of the PID controller for DC-DC boost converter in the literature. But PID-based control lacks robustness and fails to handle system uncertainty

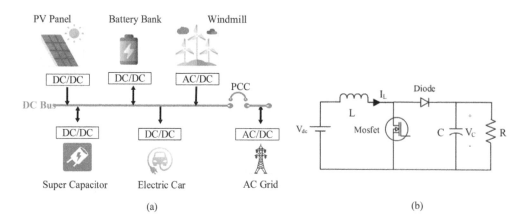

Figure 22.1: (a) Fundamental block diagram of a DC MG system [1], (b) fundamental circuit of a DC-DC boost converter

compared to optimal controllers, e.g., linear quadratic regulator (LQR), linear quadratic Gaussian (LQG). Again tuning a PID controller is another challenge for control engineers [5]. LQR, being a full state feedback optimal controller, can outperform PID controllers with proper design and tuning. Such a problem of tuning controllers can be solved with the help of optimization tools [6].

Many of the optimization methods have drawn inspiration from different natural phenomena [7], [8], and [9]. Animals in nature have many social norms. They search for food, communicate, interact in their society, and explore for prey in groups or herds. They can even execute a hunt with discipline and effective planning. Their social behavior has inspired the development of many optimization methods mimicking their activities. For instance, grey wolves hunt for prey in a pack. They follow the leadership hierarchy for approaching the prey. The hunting nature of grey wolves has inspired Grey Wolf Optimization (GWO) [9]. The Genetic algorithm (GA) was inspired by the evolution process of genes through generations based on Darwin's Theory [19]. Inspiration from the flock of birds or fish schooling Particle Swarm Optimization (PSO) was proposed [20]. The hunting nature of humpback whales in a bubble net strategy has inspired Whale Optimization (WO) [8]. How a dragonfly approaches food and gets away from the enemy for survival has inspired Dragonfly Algorithm (DA) optimization [10]. These bio inspired meta heuristic algorithms have been used in solving many real-world control problems [5], [6], [11]-[15].

Designing a controller with only simulation models or experiments is a time-consuming process and may not reach optimal solutions in many cases. A better approach is to go with optimization algorithms associated with simulation models and then reach for experimental validation. This approach is a more efficient, faster with guaranteed optimal solution and less prone to errors [12], [14]. A comparative summary of these three approaches is shown in Table 22.1.

Table 22.1: Pros and cons of different types of design approaches.

Design Approach	Pros and Cons
Design with experiments	Pros: 1. Simple approach and direct evaluation. Cons: 1. Tedious iterative process, 2. Costly, 3. Requires more time, 4. More human participation, 5. Less accuracy.
Design with simulated model	Pros: 1. Faster approach, 2. Less costly. Cons: 1. Slow Design process, 2. Medium human participation, 3. Susceptible to error.
Design with optimization algorithms	Pros: 1. Fast modeling, 2. Fast design process, 3. Automated (Minimum human participation), 4. Less error. Cons: 1. Complex optimization algorithm, 2. Difficulties of solving real-world problems

22.3 SYSTEM DESCRIPTION: DC-DC BOOST CONVERTER

DC-DC boost converter, a power converter circuit, boosts the input voltage at output. A control signal can be used to regulate voltage level using fast-switching devices (e.g., transistor, MOSFET, etc.) and changing charge-discharge cycles of the LC elements of the circuit [16]. There are many typologies available in the literature for boost converter [2]. This chapter demonstrates the very fundamental DC-DC boost converter circuit for optimal control application in a DC MG as shown in Figure 22.1 (b).

The state-space model of the DC-DC boost converter can be achieved by applying Khirchhoffs voltage law for circuit analysis for both on and off state of the switching devices and averaging the states matrices. The complete model of the DC-DC boost converter circuit can be represented in state-space form as shown in Eqs. (22.1) and (22.2). The DC-DC boost converter configuration is summarized in Table 22.2.

$$\begin{bmatrix} x_1' \\ x_2' \end{bmatrix} = \begin{bmatrix} 0 & -\frac{(1-d)}{L} \\ \frac{(1-d)}{C} & -\frac{1}{RC} \end{bmatrix} \begin{bmatrix} x_1 \\ x_2 \end{bmatrix} + \begin{bmatrix} \frac{1}{L} \\ 0 \end{bmatrix} u_1 \tag{22.1}$$

$$\begin{bmatrix} y_1 \\ y_2 \end{bmatrix} = \begin{bmatrix} 1 & 0 \\ 0 & 1 \end{bmatrix} \begin{bmatrix} i_L \\ V_c \end{bmatrix} + \begin{bmatrix} 0 \\ 0 \end{bmatrix} u_1 \tag{22.2}$$

Table 22.2: Configuration of the DC-DC boost converter circuit.

Description	Values
Inductor	2 mH
Capacitor	220 μF
Load Resistance	3 Ω
Input Voltage	12 V
Reference Output Voltage	24 V

22.4 CONTROLLER DESIGN: PROPOSED LQR FRAMEWORK

This section describes the controller design approach and the optimization framework. LQR is a full state feedback optimal regulatory control. A feedback gain K is designed in order to minimize the performance index function J [17]. Here, some trade-offs are made between how much controller effort is applied and how stable is the system performance. The system dynamics for a continuous LTI system can be described as follows.

$$dx/dt = Ax + Bu, \tag{22.3}$$

$$y = Cx + Du \tag{22.4}$$

The cost function for LQR is obtained by Eq. (22.5)

$$J = \int_0^\infty [x(t)^T Q x(t) + u(t)^T R u(t)] dt \tag{22.5}$$

Here, Q is the weight matrix and R is the weight matrix of controller effort. The cost function is minimized by the u.

$$u = -kx \tag{22.6}$$

Here, K and P is derived as follows.

$$K = R^{-1} B^T P \tag{22.7}$$

$$A^T P + PA + Q - PBR^{-1} B^T P = 0 \tag{22.8}$$

Choosing the right controller gains Q and R, which is a challenge in implementing the LQR controller. It is important to select appropriate weight matrices; otherwise the performance of the controller may not be satisfactory. Most of the research works present a manual trial-and-error based method for choosing the optimal values of Q and R.

This article proposes the application of an optimization-based approach for designing such controllers rather than depending on manual tuning methods. Different bio-inspired optimization methods have been used in this chapter for optimizing the LQR controller weight matrices, Q and R. The proposed controller structure with optimization framework is shown in Figure 22.2.

Here the error function $RMSE(r - y)$ has been minimized with the application of different bio-inspired optimization algorithms. The dotted lines in the figure indicate the optimization processes. The optimization algorithm updates the value of gains matrices Q and R to obtain the optimal performance by the controller.

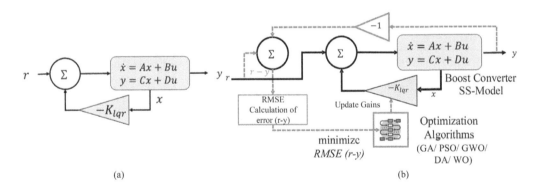

Figure 22.2: (a) Conventional LQR Control structure [18], (b) Proposed LQR Control design with optimization framework.

22.5 BIO-INSPIRED OPTIMIZATION ALGORITHMS

Nature has some inherent formulas of surviving for its animal realm. Many optimization methods have been developed inspired by the behavior of animals, insects, underwater lives, which are known as bio-inspired optimization algorithms. Some popular bio-inspired algorithms for optimization are: GA, PSO, WOA, DA, GWO, and many more. This section discusses the basic concept of these optimizations and how they work.

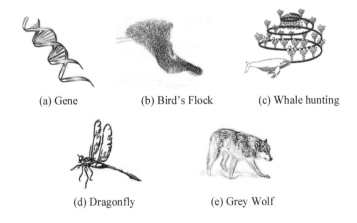

Figure 22.3: Inspiration for different optimization methods: (a) GA, (b) PSO, (c) WO [8], (d) DA, and (e) GWO.

22.5.1 Genetic Algorithm

Genetic Algorithm (GA) is a bio-inspired global and parallel search method for optimization problems. Motivated by Darwin's Theorem of Evolution, it was first introduced by Holland [19]. It is an optimization method based on population. It has four

Table 22.3: Set parameters for optimization with GA.

Parameters	Setup values
Types of Optimization	Single Objective Optimization
No. of variables	$3\ [r, q_{11}, q_{22}]$
Lower limit	$[0.001\ 0.001\ 0.001]$
Upper limit	$[1\ 1e9\ 1e9]$
Population Size	50
Fitness Scaling Method	Rank Based
Selection Method	Stochastically Uniform
Reproduction	Elite count: $0.05\times$ Population, Crossover frac.: 0.8
Mutation function	Adaptive and feasible
Crossover function	Intermediate
Migration	Direction: Forward, Fraction: 0.2, Intervals: 20
Stopping Criteria	Generation: 300, Fitness tolerance: 1e-6

basic phases in each iteration: (a) selection of genes, (b) crossover, (c) mutation, and (d) reproduction.

It imitates the biological development and the process of gene selection. For the improvements of gene species, genes are processed for crossover and mutation operations. The GA algorithm implies these operations mathematically and helps to resolve problems with optimization. In each generation, the genes will improve fitness following these steps, and will thus be able to survive in their surroundings. The best genes from n generations will offer solutions to the problem of optimization. The set parameters for optimization using GA used for this chapter are shown in Table 22.3.

22.5.2   Particle Swarm Optimization

The Particle Swarm Optimization (PSO) is a population-based search algorithm first introduced by James Kennedy and Russell C. Eberhart [20]. This method of optimization simulates the social behavior of birds within a flock or fish schooling while searching and exploring for foods or resources. Each of the particles in a swarm represents an agent with its own position, velocity, and acceleration representing coordinates in the search space of global solution. Each current position of the agents is evaluated with a fitness function and the particle with the best fitness value for the total exploration, i.e., iterations, is called the best global solution g_{best}. Each particle keeps track of its fitness function value over the whole explorations and the best fitness value is known as personal best, p_{best}. The swarm agents start their exploration at random positions but, as their explorations progress, all the particles approach the position of the best global and personal best according to Eqs. (22.9) and (22.10).

$$v_{n+1} = v_n + c_1 rand_1() \times (p_{best,n} - currentP_n)$$
$$+ c_2 rand_2() \times (g_{best,n} - currentP_n) \quad (22.9)$$

$$currentP_{n+1} = currentP_n + v_{n+1} \tag{22.10}$$

Here, v_{n+1}, v_n represent the velocity of particle at $(n+1)th$ and nth iteration accordingly. c_1, c_2 represents acceleration factor related to g_{best}, p_{best}.

Table 22.4: Set parameter for optimization with PSO.

Parameters	Setup values
Type of optimization	Single objective optimization
No. of variables	$3 \; [r, q_{11}, q_{22}]$
Lower bound	$[.0001 \; .0001 \; 0.0001]$
Upper bound	$[1 \; 1e9 \; 1e9]$
Max iteration	600
Swarm size	100

22.5.3   Grey Wolf Optimization Algorithm

The Grey Wolf Optimization (GWO), proposed by Seyedali Mirjalili [9], is a bio-inspired meta-heuristic optimization method inspired by the unique hunting nature of grey wolves. Grey wolves hunt in a pack and follow the leadership hierarchy among the alpha, beta, delta, and omega wolves. Their hunting process involves three main phases: (a) search for prey, (b) encircle the prey, and (c) attack the prey.

The encircling process of the prey by the wolves may be modeled as:

$$D = |C.X_p(t) - X(t)| \tag{22.11}$$
$$X(t+1) = X_p(t) - A.D \tag{22.12}$$
$$A = 2a.r_1 - a \tag{22.13}$$
$$C = 2.r_2 \tag{22.14}$$

where the A *and* C are co-efficient vectors, X_p, X position vector of prey and grey wolves, accordingly. The a components are reduced from 2 to 0 in linear fashion and r_1, r_2 are random vectors.

After spotting the position of prey and making the encirclement of the prey, the grey wolves prepare for hunting guided by the alpha. The participation of beta and delta in the hunt is optional and occasional. Their hunting behavior may be modeled as:

$$D_\alpha = |C_1.X_\alpha - X| \tag{22.15}$$
$$D_\beta = |C_2.X_\beta - X| \tag{22.16}$$
$$D_\gamma = |C_3.X_\gamma - X| \tag{22.17}$$
$$X_1 = X_\alpha - A_1.D_\alpha \tag{22.18}$$
$$X_2 = X_\beta - A_2.D_\beta \tag{22.19}$$
$$X_3 = X_\gamma - A_3.D_\gamma \tag{22.20}$$
$$X(t+1) = \frac{X_1 + X_2 + X_3}{3} \tag{22.21}$$

The final position is defined by the positions obtained by alpha, beta, and gamma wolves. Thus the hunts get terminated once the best solution is found with respect to the stopping criterion.

22.5.4 Dragonfly Algorithm

The Dragonfly Algorithm (DA) is another meta-heuristic optimization technique inspired by the dragonfly proposed by Sayedali Mirjalili [7]. This method mimics how a dragonfly behaves statically and dynamically swarming in nature. The necessary two phases for navigating, food searching, and protecting against the enemy are given by (a) exploration and (b) exploitation.

For getting attracted to food resources and getting away from enemies, they keep updating their positions based on five factors: (i) separation, (ii) alignment, (iii) cohesion, (iv) attraction to food, and (v) distraction away from harm. These steps may be modeled mathematically as follows.

$$Separation: S_i = -\sum_{j=1}^{N} X - X_j \tag{22.22}$$

$$Alignment: A_i = \frac{\sum_{j=1}^{N} V_j}{N} \tag{22.23}$$

$$Cohesion: C_i = \frac{\sum_{j+1}^{N} X_j}{N} - X \tag{22.24}$$

$$Attraction\ to\ food: F_i = X^+ - X \tag{22.25}$$

$$Distraction\ away\ from\ enemy: E_i = X^- + X \tag{22.26}$$

where X, X_j, X^+, X^-, N are current individual position, j_{th} individual position, position of food, position of the enemy, and the number of neighbors, respectively. With these steps, different exploration and exploitation are done. This DA method may be applied for single objective as well as multi-objective problems.

22.5.5 Whale Optimization

The Whale Optimization (WO), a bio-inspired meta-heuristic optimization algorithm, was first proposed by Seyedali Mirjalili [8]. This process of optimization is inspired by the social behavior of humpback whales while hunting for food with a bubble-net strategy. The WO process has three main phases: (a) search for prey, (b) encircle prey, and (c) attack the prey.

The encircling process may be modeled as follows.

$$D = |C.X(t) - X(t)| \tag{22.27}$$

$$X(t + 1) = X^*(t) - A.D \tag{22.28}$$

$$A = 2a.r - a \tag{22.29}$$

$$C = 2.r \tag{22.30}$$

Table 22.5: Set parameters for optimization with GWO, DA, and WO.

Parameters	Setup value
Types of Optimization	Single Objective Optimization
Max. Iteration	100
Search Agents	10
No. of Variables	3 $[r, q_{11}, q_{22}]$
Lower Bounds	$[.0001\ .0001\ 0.0001]$
Upper Bounds	$[1\ 1e9\ 1e9]$

Here A, C are co-efficient vectors, X, X^* are position vector and best position vector obtained so far, accordingly. a is linearly increased from 2 to 0, and r is a random vector between 0 to 1.

The search approach can be modeled as follows:

$$D = |C.X_{rand} - X| \tag{22.31}$$

$$X(t+1) = X_{rand} - A.D \tag{22.32}$$

where X_{rand} is a randomly chosen position vector.

The WO algorithm begins with random solutions with a set of search agents. At each iteration, each agent updates its search position either randomly or by the best-obtained solution so far. The whale may go for spiral or circular movement. Finally, with meeting the required stopping criteria, the algorithm is terminated.

22.5.6 Optimization Objective Function

In this chapter, the root mean squared error (RMSE) was used as the objective function to minimize the error $e(t)$, which is given by Eq. (22.33). The optimization parameters chosen for the controller optimization are shown in Tables 22.3 - 22.5.

$$RMSE = \sqrt{\frac{\sum_{t=0}^{T}(v_{out}(t) - v_{ref}(t))^2}{T}} \tag{22.33}$$

22.6 PERFORMANCE EVALUATION AND DISCUSSION

This section describes the performance of the optimization process of different methods and performance of the controller with the system.

22.6.1 Optimization Performance

Table 22.6 shows the optimized values for Q $[q_{11}, q_{22}]$ and R matrices. Three variables $[r, q_{11}, q_{22}]$ have been optimized to get the best optimal performance with the LQR control structure. Their fitting performance curves are illustrated in Figure 22.4 and fitting performances are summarized in Table 22.6.

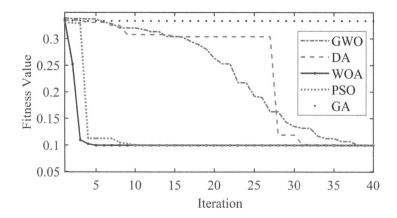

Figure 22.4: LQR fitting curves.

Table 22.6: Performance of different optimization methods.

Method	Optimized Values	Score	Min Iter.	time (sec)
GA	$[4.7e^{-3}, 4.56e^{7}, 9.4e^{8}]$	0.2865	4	16.39
PSO	$[7.8e^{-4}, 1e^{-4}, 9.9e^{8}]$	0.0995	17	22.07
GWO	$[7.8e^{-4}, 1.05e^{4}, 1e^{9}]$	0.0995	40	5.17
DA	$[1e^{-4}, 1e^{-4}, 1.27e^{8}]$	0.0995	36	23.90
WO	$[1.2e^{-4}, 1.3e^{-4}, 1.2e^{8}]$	0.0995	4	6.36

22.6.2 Unit Step Response

The unit step response of the DC-DC boost converter with LQR control architecture optimized by different bio-inspired algorithms is summarized in Table 22.7 and illustrated in Figure 22.5.

22.6.3 Discussion

From Tables 22.6 and 22.7, it is evident that among the different bio-inspired optimization methods, GWO obtained the fastest execution time, and the best score with 0% overshoot, 0.48% steady-state (SS) error with the least execution time of 5.17 seconds. WO scored the same with 6.36 seconds only, but it has an overshoot of 5.44%. PSO and DA also attained the best score but needed longer optimization time. But GA failed to attain the best score and also it has a 32% SS-error.

22.7   CONCLUSION

This chapter has demonstrated the application of different bio-inspired algorithms for optimizing LQR control for DC-DC boost converter circuit. With respect to optimization time and step performance, GWO outperformed the other four compared methods with 0% overshoot, 0.48% steady-state error, and only 5.17 seconds execution time for optimization. In real hardware implication, fast optimization is crucial

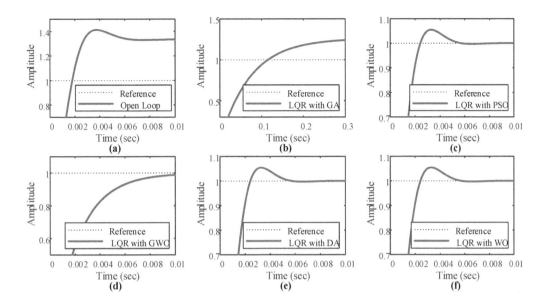

Figure 22.5: Step response for different optimization methods (a) open loop response, (b) LQR with GA, (c) LQR with PSO, (d) LQR with GWO, (e) LQR with DA, and (f) LQR with WO.

Table 22.7: Comparison of step responses with different optimization methods.

Description	Settling Time	Overshoot	SS-Error
Open Loop	0.0053	5.8661 %	32.99%
LQR with GA	0.2845	0 %	25.83%
LQR with PSO	0.0046	5.4499 %	0.15%
LQR with GWO	0.0047	0 %	0.48%
LQR with DA	0.0046	5.4499 %	0.15%
LQR with WO	0.0046	5.4499 %	0.15%

for maintaining system stability and ensuring better performance. Hence this chapter recommends GWO optimization approach for conducting optimization of controller for power converter circuits in DC MG application. This chapter has been limited to some of the most popular bio-inspired algorithms. There is also room for other methods. In this chapter, only LQR control architecture for DC-DC boost design was used. Other architectures of control can also be experimented with power converters.

Bibliography

[1] Tabatabaei, Naser Mahdavi and Kabalci, Ersan and Bizon, Nicu. Microgrid architectures, control and protection methods. *Microgrid Architectures, Control and Protection Methods*. 115–137, (2019). Springer.

[2] Babaa, Saleh E., El, M., Georges, Mohamed, F., Pamuri, S. et al. (2018). Overview of boost converters for photovoltaic systems. *Journal of Power and Energy Engineering*, 6–04: 16. Scientific Research Publishing.

[3] Namnabat, M., Poodeh, M. B., and Eshtehardiha, S. (2007). Comparison of the control methods in improvement the performance of the DC-DC converter. *2007 7th Internatonal Conf. on Power Electronics*, 246–251. IEEE.

[4] Adnan, M., Oninda F., Mohammad, A. M.,Nishat, Mirza, M., and Nafiul, I.(2017). Design and simulation of a DC-DC boost converter with pid controller for enhanced performance. *International Journal of Engineering Research and Technology (IJERT)*, 6:27–32.

[5] Roni, M.H.K. and Rana, M.S. (2021). Optimized PID Control Scheme for Three Phase Micro-grid System. *2021 2nd International Conf. on Robotics, Electrical and Signal Processing Techniques (ICREST)*, 77–80. IEEE.

[6] Roni, M.H.K. and Rana, M.S. (2021). Data-Driven Linear Quadratic Control Scheme for Three-Phase Microgrid System Optimized by Genetic Algorithm. *2021 International Conf. on Emerging Smart Computing and Informatics (ESCI)*, 549–554. IEEE.

[7] Mirjalili, S. (2016). Dragonfly algorithm: a new meta-heuristic optimization technique for solving single-objective, discrete, and multi-objective problems. *Neural Computing and Applications*. 27: 1053–1073. Springer.

[8] Mirjalili, S., and Lewis, A. (2016). The whale optimization algorithm. *Advances in engineering software*, 95:51–67. Elsevier.

[9] Mirjalili, S., Mirjalili, S.M., and Lewis, A. (2014). Grey wolf optimizer. *Advances in engineering software*, 69:46–61. Elsevier.

[10] Dragicevic, T., Lu, X., Vasquez, Juan C., Guerrero, Josep M. (2015). DC microgrids—Part II: A review of power architectures, applications, and standardization issues. *IEEE trans. on power electronics*, 31: 3528–3549. IEEE.

[11] Eltamaly, Ali M., Farh, Hassan, M. H. (2019). Dynamic global maximum power point tracking of the PV systems under variant partial shading using hybrid GWO-FLC. *Solar Energy*, 177: 306–316. Elsevier.

[12] Hasanien, Hany M. (2018). Performance improvement of photovoltaic power systems using an optimal control strategy based on whale optimization algorithm. *Electric Power Systems Research*, 157: 168–176. Elsevier.

[13] Veerachary, M. and Saxena, A. R. (2014). Optimized power stage design of low source current ripple fourth-order boost DC–DC converter: A PSO approach. *IEEE Trans. on Industrial Electronics*, 62:1491–1502. IEEE.

[14] De Leon-Alcado , S. E. et al. (2015). Metaheuristic optimization methods applied to power converters: A review. *IEEE Transactions on Power Electronics*, 30, 12:6791–6803. IEEE.

[15] Roni, M. H. K., Rana, M. S. and Pota, H. R. et al. (2022) Recent trends in bio-inspired meta-heuristic optimization techniques in control applications for electrical systems: A review. *International Journal of Dynamics and Control*, 1–13. Springer

[16] Tan, R.H.G., and Hoo, L.Y.H. (2015). DC-DC converter modeling and simulation using state space approach. *2015 IEEE Conf. on Energy Conversion (CENCON)*, 42–47. IEEE.

[17] Sarkar, S. K., Roni, M.H.K., Datta, D. and Das, S.K., and Pota, H.R. (2018). Improved design of high-performance controller for voltage control of islanded microgrid. *IEEE Systems Journal*, 1786–1795. IEEE.

[18] Wang, Haiquan and Liao, Lei and Wang, Dongyun and Wen, Shengjun and Deng, Mingcong (2014). Improved artificial bee colony algorithm and its application in LQR controller optimization. *Mathematical Problems in Engineering*. Hindawi.

[19] Holland, John H. (1984). Genetic algorithms and adaptation. *Adaptive Control of Ill-Defined Systems*, 317–333. Springer.

[20] Kennedy, J., and Eberhart, R. (1995). Particle swarm optimization. *Proceedings of ICNN'95-international conf. on neural networks*, 4: 1942–1948. IEEE.

CHAPTER 23

Mining Significant Pre-Diabetes Features of Diabetes Mellitus: A Case Study of Noakhali, Bangladesh

Md. Shahriare Satu

Department of Management Information Systems, Noakhali Science and Technology University, Noakhali, Bangladesh

Koushik Chandra Howlader and Avijit Barua

Department of Computer Science and Telecommunication Engineering, Noakhali Science and Technology University, Noakhali, Bangladesh

Mohammad Ali Moni

School of Health and Rehabilitation Sciences, Faculty of Health and Behavioural Sciences, The University of Queensland St Lucia, QLD 4072, Australia

CONTENTS

23.1 Introduction 281
23.2 Methods and Materials 282
    23.2.1 Data Description 282
    23.2.2 Machine Learning-Based Pre-Diabetes Feature Detection Model 283
    23.2.3 Data Balancing Techniques 284
    23.2.4 Baseline Classifiers 285
    23.2.5 Feature Selection Methods 285
    23.2.6 Evaluation Metrics 285
23.3 Experimental Result 286
    23.3.1 Derived Outcomes for Correlation Analysis 286
    23.3.2 Experimental Results for Classification Approaches 286
23.4 Discussion and Conclusion 289

D IABETES MELLITUS is a chronic condition which is due to the abnormally high level of sugar in the blood. It is an enduring disease that causes numerous harmful effects to human life. In Bangladesh, most of the computational works related to assessing the possibility of diabetes have occurred in urban regions. However, rural people do not properly consider for these analyses. Hence, the objective of this work is to predict the severity of pre-diabetes stages and find out significant features of rural people. As a consequence, we gathered pre-diabetes records of individuals from Noakhali, Bangladesh. This raw dataset have been cleaned, balanced and generated a number of datasets applying some oversampling techniques, respectively. Thus, many classification techniques have been employed into primary and derived datasets to analyze and predict the severity of pre-diabetes stages of controls. Then, this classification outcome has been used to explore significant features for identifying the possibility of diabetes. After assessing the performance of individual classifiers, random forest is found as the most accurate and stable classifier to predict and explore noteworthy factors along with other high-performing classifiers. Besides, MODLEM shows the highest 95.28% accuracy, 95.30% f-measure, and random forest provides 99.50% AUROC for random oversampling dataset. This work can be used as a complementary tool for diabetes treatment.

23.1 INTRODUCTION

Diabetes mellitus is a group of metabolic diseases where the pancreas cannot make sufficient insulin or the body is not absorbing insulin efficiently. A prolonged increase of insulin does not lessen blood sugar in the body. As a result, the human body cannot hold its metabolism properly. In three types of diabetes (i.e., Type I, Type II and gestational diabetes), Type II diabetes (i.e., diabetes mellitus) is the most dangerous and requires more care to avoid different complications. The prevalence of diabetes was considered 2.8% in 2000, but that will increase 4.4% by 2030 for all age groups worldwide [Wild et al.(2015)]. It causes one death per every 6 seconds throughout the world [Lukmanto et al.(2019)]. However, this number will possibly reach close to 700 million in 2045 [Nurjahan et al.(2021)]. The common symptoms of diabetes are weight loss, excessive thirst, hunger, fatigue, yeast infections, skin problems, slow healing wounds, abnormal cholesterol along with triglyceride levels, and tingling or numbness in the feet. Recent studies [Yu et al.(2015)] show that diabetes can be prevented by changing lifestyles and pharmacotherapy at the pre-diabetes stages. However, many people are not concerned about it.

The pre-diabetes stage of diabetes mellitus measures the possibility of it happening to the average person [Barber et al.(2016)]. However, its severity and risk requires careful detection and precautions for reducing its harmful impact. Various statistical and computational methods have been used to investigate and explore how we can prevent this disease in different ways. Recently, machine learning is efficiently used to analyze different types of complex malfunctioning diseases in the bio-medical sector [Ahammed et al.(2020), Akter et al.(2017), Akter et al.(2021), Rahman et al.(2021)]. Therefore, numerous state-of-the-art technology have been created for detecting diabetes mellitus using this technique [Nurjahan et al.(2021), Satu et al.(2020)]. For instance, [Nilashi et al.(2018)] proposed a hybrid intelligent model which implements clustering, noise removal, and classification methods to investigate incremental diabetes data. [Wang et al.(2020)] proposed an effective predictive method called Diabetes Mellitus classification on Imbalanced data with Missing values (DMP_MI) that uses Naïve Bayes (NB) to compute missing values of a Pima Indian Diabetes Dataset. Then, an adaptive synthetic sampling method (ADASYN) is implemented to balance and random forest (RF) is used to investigate this dataset. [Ramesh et al.(2015)] developed an end-to-end remote monitoring framework where the support vector machine (SVM) uses for diabetes risk prediction.

The motivation of this work is to identify essential factors of diabetes mellitus in the pre-diabetes stage using machine learning. In Bangladesh, there are few works about this issue, but most have been focused on urban people. Therefore, we gather numerous pre-diabetes records from rural people of Noakhali District, Bangladesh and propose a machine learning-based feature selection approach which can detect significant risk factors of diabetes at early stages. The contribution of this work is given as follows:

- Investigate pre-diabetes stages of controls using multiple machine learning models.

- Identify rural individuals rather than urban people to detect pre-diabetes.

- Employ different widely used data balancing and classification methods to select significant features of the pre-diabetes stage.

23.2   METHODS AND MATERIALS

The working steps of this system is described (see Figure 23.1) as follows:

23.2.1   Data Description

According to the following existing scales [Ouellet et al.(2011), Bamanikar et al.(2016), Woolley et al.(2015)] and the prescription of specialists of the Noakhali Diabetes Association (NDA), Maijdee, Noakhali, Bangladesh, several attributes are identified to detect pre-diabetes stages of people where the final classes are: healthy, possibility of disease and risky, respectively. Then, this scale was approved by the ethical committee of the Research Cell, Noakhali Science and Technology University (NSTU), Bangladesh. Then, we collected 210 pre-diabetes records (including both male and female) from different rural areas in Noakhali, Bangladesh. The age range of the patients are within 17-100 years old. This dataset is available at the following link: `https://github.com/shahriariit/Noakhali\_Diabetes/`. Therefore, the demographic description of numerical attributes in this dataset are given in Table 23.1.

Table 23.1: Demographic Review of Pre-Diabetes Dataset

Features	Abbrev.	Mean	Range	Median	STD
Age		49.492	17-100	48	13.62
Weight (kg)	W	62.106	36-93	62	11.411
Height (m)	H	1.566	1.4-1.76	1.57	0.078
Sistolic Blood Pressure (mm Hg)	SBP	120.497	60-180	120	18.39
Diastolic Blood Pressure (mm Hg)	DBP	79.387	50-155	80	12.056
Plasma Glucose (mmol/l)	PG	8.936	3.43-23.68	7.6	4.421
Plasma Glucose 2hr After Glucose (mmol/l)	PG2	13.662	5.16-29.38	12.53	5.879
Serum Cholesterol (mg/dl)	SChol	205.879	78-2210	191	146.435
High Density Lipoprotein Cholesterol (mg/dl)	HDLC	45.017	20-97	40	14.947
Low Density Lipoprotein Cholesterol (mg/dl)	LDLC	129.906	32-200	128	35.335
Triglyceride (mg/dl)	STr	198.781	66-589	175	102.325
Creatinine (mg/dl)	SCr	1.642	0.6-98	1.06	6.857

23.2.2 Machine Learning-Based Pre-Diabetes Feature Detection Model

- **Data Retrieval and Cleaning:** After gathering pre-diabetes records, several records have been removed from this dataset which contains multiple unclear, duplicate and more missing values. Some of them are filled manually with an approximation on each class. Finally, 199 records have been confirmed for further analysis which contains 52 healthy, 33 possible and 113 risky class labels of average people.

- **Data Balancing:** In pre-diabetes (primary) dataset, the classes of this dataset are not properly balanced. So, some oversampling-based data balancing techniques, such as random oversampling (ROS), Synthetic Minority Oversampling Technique (SMOTE) and SMOTE-NC, have been selected, which implements into its minority classes (see details in Section 23.2.3). After the balancing primary dataset, three oversampling datasets have been generated using these techniques.

- **Correlation Analysis:** Then we create correlation matrix for primary and newly generated oversampling balanced (derived) datasets and check the correlations of each feature. More highly correlated features (i.e., if the p-values of any two correlated features are greater than 0.90) have produced overfitted results that should be removed from these datasets.

- **Classification:** Many baseline classifiers such as Bayesian, functional, rule, tree based method (see the list of classifiers in Section 23.2.4) have been implemented into primary and derived datasets. After producing these outcomes, we

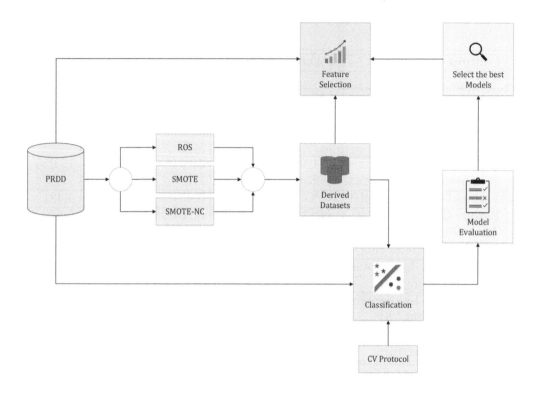

Figure 23.1: Machine Learning-Based Pre-Diabetes Feature Detection Model into PRe-Diabetes Dataset (PRDD).

compare and identify the highest performing classifier for each dataset. Then, the best stable classifier has been explored. To justify these results, various evaluation metrics such as accuracy, f-measure and AUROC are used in this work (see details in Section 23.2.6).

- **Feature Selection:** After identifying the best classifiers, we used them to select the most significant features for estimating pre-diabetes conditions. Therefore, two classifier based feature selection techniques, namely, classifier subset evaluator (CSE) and wrapper subset evaluator (WSE), have been used in this work. If the best classifiers cannot support these feature selection methods, another most suitable classifiers have been used to identify the most significant pre-diabetes features.

We outline different machine learning techniques of the proposed model briefly as follows:

23.2.3 Data Balancing Techniques

A brief review of implementing data balancing methods are given as follows:

- **Random OverSampling (ROS)** basically oversamples minority classes where it takes instances randomly with replacement.

- **Synthetic Minority Oversampling Technique (SMOTE)** is used to produce synthetic samples (i.e., based on nearest neighbor techniques) for the minority class. In this case, we use Weka to implement it.

- **Synthetic Minority Oversampling Technique for Nominal and Categorical Features (SMOTE-NC)** marginally changes the process of SMOTE by producing new samples for both categorical and numerical values.

23.2.4 Baseline Classifiers

The list of usage classifiers is given briefly as follows:

- **Bayes:** Bayes Net (BN), Naïve Bayes (NB)

- **Functions:** Logistic, Multilayer Perceptron (MLP), RBFNetwork (RBFN), Simple Logistic (SL)

- **Lazy:** Instance based K-nearest neighbour (IBk), IBkLG, KStar

- **Misc:** Composite Hypercubes on Iterated Random Projections (CHIRP)

- **Rules:** Decision Table/Naïve Bayes hybrid classifier (DTNB), Repeated incremental pruning to produce error reduction (JRip), MODLEM, PART, RIpple-DOwn Rule learner (Ridor)

- **Trees:** Best First decision tree (BFTree), Credal Decision Trees (CDT), Cost Sensitive Decision Forest (CSForest), Decision Forest by Penalizing Attributes (ForestPA), Functional Trees (FT), Hoeffding Tree (HT), J48, Logit boost Alternating Decision tree (LADTree), Logistic Model Trees (LMT), decision tree with Naïve Bayes classifiers (NBTree), Obtimized Forest (OF), Random Forest (RF), Random Tree (RT), Reduced Error Pruning Tree (REPTree), SimpleCart (SC), Systematically developed Forest (SysFor)

23.2.5 Feature Selection Methods

However, classifier subset evaluator (CSE) selects features by manipulating training/testing dataset and estimates credit of these attributes using a classifier. Also, wrapper subset evaluator (WSE) justifies feature sets by esteeming the accuracy of learning scheme using a classifier.

23.2.6 Evaluation Metrics

To assess the performance of individual classifiers, we generate confusion matrix which produces true positive (TP), false positive (FP), false negative (FN), and true negative (TN) values. Hence, the performance of classifiers are evaluated using the following metrics.

- **Accuracy** indicates the rate of perfect classifications that is represented as follows.

$$\text{Accuracy} = \frac{TP + TN}{(TP + TN + FP + FN)} \tag{23.1}$$

- **F-measure** is the harmonic mean of precision and recall which is shown as follows.

$$\text{F} - \text{measure} = \frac{2 \times \text{precision} \times \text{recall}}{(\text{precision} + \text{recall})} = \frac{2TP}{2TP + FP + FN} \tag{23.2}$$

- **Area Under Receiver Operating Characteristic (AUROC)** indicates how well positive classes are isolated from negative classes. It can be defined as follows.

$$\text{AUROC} = \frac{TPrate + TNrate}{2} \tag{23.3}$$

23.3 EXPERIMENTAL RESULT

In this experiment, Weka machine learning tool [Satu et al.(2020)] has been widely used for data cleaning, balancing (i.e., SMOTE) and implementing various classification methods. Besides, ROS and SMOTE-NC were implemented using imbalanced-learn library in Python. Therefore, the configuration of our working computer is 11th Gen Intel(R) Core(TM) i3-1115G4 processor with 3.00GHz clock speed and 8.00 GB RAM.

23.3.1 Derived Outcomes for Correlation Analysis

When we analyze feature correlation of primary and oversampling balanced datasets, PG and PG2 show high correlation (0.9) between them. If we remove one of them from the dataset, the correlation matrix of these datasets does not provide any higher correlation between two attributes. Hence, we removed PG2 from primary and over-sampling balanced datasets to avoid overfitted accuracies (above 90%) and get more feasible results.

23.3.2 Experimental Results for Classification Approaches

Then, ROS, SMOTE and SMOTE-NC are implemented to balance the class label of the primary dataset. Various classifiers (the list of classifiers in Section 23.2.4) have been used to analyze primary and oversampling balanced datasets. The results of individual classifiers for the primary pre-diabetes dataset are shown in Table 23.2. Most of the classifiers display good results as expected. Notably, CSForest determines the highest accuracy (82.92%) and F-Measure (82.90%). But, RF generates the maximum AUROC (95.50%) in this work. Moreover, the result of CSForest is slightly improved than OF and RF, respectively. Then, the classification results are rapidly increased for different derived oversampling balanced datasets, which is given in Table 23.3. For ROS dataset, MODLEM shows the best accuracy (95.28%) and f-measure (95.30%). Also, OF and RF engender the best AUROC (99.50%) respectively. In addition, RF produces the second highest findings among all of classifiers. Instead, OF and RF compute the best accuracy (91.32%), f-measure (91.40%) and AUROC (98.30%) for SMOTE dataset. Afterwards, RF generates the largest accuracy (91.15%) and AUROC (98.50%) for SMOTE-NC dataset. In this case, SC shows the top AUROC (93.10%) which is also nearest to the RF (91.20%).

Table 23.2: Experiment Results Individual Classifiers for Primary Diabetes Dataset

Classifier	Accuracy	F-Ms.	AUC	Classifier	Accuracy	F-Ms.	AUC
BN	78.89	78.70	93.70	CDT	78.89	78.50	88.40
NB	75.88	78.30	92.50	CSForest	**82.91**	**82.90**	94.10
Logistic	80.40	80.50	92.70	ForestPA	77.89	75.10	91.50
MLP	76.88	77.10	90.50	FT	78.89	79.10	88.50
RBFN	78.39	79.00	90.50	HT	76.38	78.60	94.30
SL	80.90	80.70	92.30	J48	75.88	76.20	84.50
IBK	72.86	73.60	78.80	LADTree	78.39	78.60	93.70
IBKLG	72.86	73.60	80.00	LMT	80.90	80.70	92.30
kStar	74.87	76.00	90.00	NBTree	80.41	80.10	90.00
CHIRP	77.89	75.70	79.70	OF	81.41	81.10	95.40
DTNB	77.89	77.80	77.80	RF	81.41	80.90	**95.50**
JRip	75.36	74.20	80.60	RT	77.39	77.30	81.50
MODLEM	80.40	78.00	80.90	REPTree	78.39	78.40	90.60
PART	76.87	76.70	86.20	SC	78.89	78.60	88.40
Ridor	77.89	77.70	82.90	SysFor	75.88	76.40	89.40
BF Tree	77.89	78.00	89.00				

When we notice the average results of individual classifiers (see Figure 23.2), RF shows the largest 89.57% accuracy (see Figure 23.2(a)), 89.50% f-measure (see Figure 23.2(b)), and 98% AUROC (see Figure 23.2(c)). Further, the average results of OF are close to RF and most tree-based classifiers show better outcomes than others. Therefore, it is proved that RF is the most stable classifier to investigate significant features and assess pre-diabetes risk more precisely.

Therefore, we explore individual pre-diabetes risk factors by investigating primary and oversampling balanced datasets respectively. In this experiment, different high performing classifiers have been found which are employed to scrutinize these datasets and provide the utmost findings. Hence, CSE and WSE methods have been used to identify significant features of pre-diabetes condition applying best performing classifiers. Also, most stable RF have been needed for different purposes in the feature selection approach. In the primary dataset, CSForest, and RF employ within feature selection methods to detect significant attributes. Many high performing classifiers (i.e, MODLEM and OF for ROS, SMOTE and SMOTE-NC dataset, respectively) are not properly supported within CSE and WSE methods. So, we use RF within

Table 23.3: Experiment Results Individual Classifiers for Various Oversampling Balanced Diabetes Dataset

Classifier	Acc.	F-Ms.	AUC	Acc.	F-Ms.	AUC	Acc.	F-Ms.	AUC
	ROS			SMOTE			SMOTE-NC		
BN	86.43	86.50	97.50	88.80	88.90	96.30	87.61	87.60	97.50
NB	77.58	78.30	91.60	83.75	83.80	94.30	81.12	81.60	93.50
Logistic	83.19	83.20	94.60	84.87	84.90	94.60	84.96	85.10	95.10
MLP	92.33	92.30	96.20	88.24	88.20	95.00	87.02	87.10	95.10
RBFN	80.24	80.60	92.80	84.59	84.70	91.60	83.19	83.60	93.30
SL	80.24	80.40	94.20	84.87	85.00	93.80	83.78	83.90	94.90
IBK	92.04	92.00	94.20	85.99	85.90	88.10	87.32	87.40	90.40
IBKLG	92.04	92.00	98.70	85.99	85.90	95.30	87.32	87.40	94.90
kStar	89.09	88.80	99.30	85.71	85.30	98.50	87.91	87.60	98.60
CHIRP	91.15	91.20	93.40	85.43	85.60	80.20	85.84	85.90	89.40
DTNB	90.56	90.50	97.70	89.64	89.70	99.90	85.84	85.90	97.00
JRip	91.15	91.20	95.50	85.43	85.50	92.40	85.25	85.30	92.00
MODLEM	**95.28**	**95.30**	**96.50**	86.55	86.60	89.60	84.96	84.60	88.70
PART	93.22	93.20	95.90	86.55	86.60	91.30	82.01	81.90	88.60
Ridor	88.20	88.20	91.20	83.19	83.20	86.70	86.73	86.80	90.00
BF Tree	89.97	98.60	94.90	88.80	88.80	92.70	85.25	85.30	92.90
CDT	87.02	87.00	96.00	88.53	86.60	93.20	81.71	81.90	92.60
CSForest	86.14	86.40	77.30	85.99	86.10	95.70	86.73	86.80	96.40
ForestPA	90.56	90.70	98.40	87.39	87.50	96.70	87.91	87.90	94.10
FT	88.79	89.00	93.70	86.27	86.30	93.50	85.55	85.70	92.50
HT	80.24	80.80	92.10	84.03	84.10	93.90	80.83	81.20	93.50
J48	91.15	91.10	98.40	88.52	88.50	92.70	84.96	84.90	90.80
LADTree	86.73	86.80	94.80	86.27	86.30	93.70	88.50	88.50	96.20
LMT	93.22	93.20	96.90	87.11	87.10	93.50	88.50	88.60	93.70
NBTree	93.22	93.20	98.60	82.91	82.90	92.60	85.84	85.80	94.90
OF	94.10	94.10	99.50	**91.32**	**91.40**	**98.30**	90.56	90.60	98.40
RF	94.40	94.40	99.50	**91.32**	**91.40**	**98.30**	91.15	91.20	98.50
RT	94.10	94.10	95.60	87.96	88.00	90.70	84.37	84.20	88.30
REPTree	86.73	86.70	95.00	84.87	84.90	91.80	81.71	81.90	93.10
SC	89.68	89.70	94.40	89.08	89.10	91.70	85.25	93.10	93.10
SysFor	86.73	86.90	94.00	85.15	85.20	92.40	85.55	85.60	93.30

these methods for detecting features for ROS, SMOTE, and SMOTE-NC datasets. All of the identifying significant features for each dataset are shown in Table 23.4. If different features are remarked, PG almost appears for all the feature selection methods. Therefore, it is detected as the most significant feature of pre-diabetes condition. Also, HDLC and SChol are selected many times by different procedure. Afterwards, SBP, SCr, STr, DBP, age, weight, and height are appeared several times in different evaluation. On the other hand, Body Mass Index (BMI) is a important factor to detect the pre-diabetes risk more efficiently. Therefore, this process is identified weight and height which is required to calculate BMI.

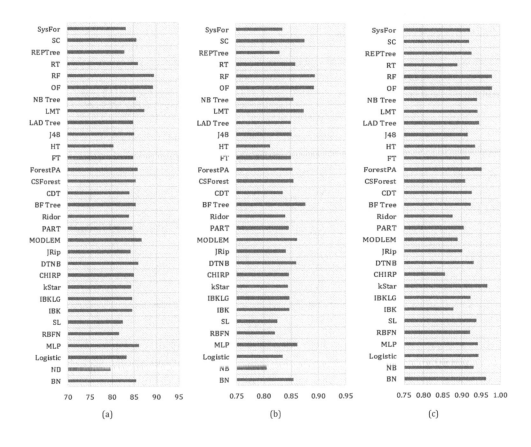

Figure 23.2: Average (a) Accuracy, (b) F-Measure, and (c) AUROC of Individual Classifiers for Primary and Oversampling Balanced Diabetes Datasets.

23.4 DISCUSSION AND CONCLUSION

In this aforementioned methodology, we explore several significant features that are useful to assess risk of pre-diabetes conditions. Our task is to identify most significant pre-diabetes conditions of suspected people in rural regions in Bangladesh using well-organized methodological structure (i.e., using different data balancing, classifier's variants and feature selection methods). Therefore, we gathered pre-diabetes records of various types of people in Noakhali District, Bangladesh who will get this disease. In this light, most state-of-art works did not properly consider rural people and did not apply multiple types machine learning models/tools to analyze remarkable factors of diabetes. However, there were numerous works about detecting early diabetes stages [Nurjahan et al.(2021), Lukmanto et al.(2019), Minh et al.(2020), Fahmiin et al.(2019)] and investigating this disease [Nurjahan et al.(2021), Islam et al.(2018), Pranto et al.(2020)]. But, most of them utilized the Pima Indian diabetes dataset to their machine learning applications [Lukmanto et al.(2019), Minh et al.(2020), Fahmiin et al.(2019)],

Table 23.4: Identifying Noteworthy Features using the Best Performing Classifiers and Feature Selection Methods

Dataset	Classifier	Feature Selction	Features
Primary	CSForest	CSE	Age, DBP, PG, SChol, HDLC, SCr
		WSE	AGe, SBP, PG, SChol, HDLC, STr SCr
	RF	CSE	PG, HDLC
		WSE	W, PG, HDLC
ROS	RF	CSE	PG, SChol
		WSE	SBP, PG, SChol, HDLC, LDLC
SMOTE	RF	CSE	PG, HDLC
		WSE	SBP, PG, SChol, HDLC, LDLC, STr SCr
SMOTE-NC	RF	CSE	PG, HDLC
		WSE	W, H, SBP, DBP, PG, SChol, HDLC, STr, SCr

and did not try those approaches with a new one. Again, proposed methodology is adaptable to another sector of machine learning applications. Besides, many related works in Bangladesh had not focused on pre-diabetes conditions at all [Islam et al.(2018), Pranto et al.(2020)]. However, some limitations occurred in this experiment, such as 220 records collected which are not large enough to predict early diabetes surroundings and discover major features. In the case study, we only gathered pre-diabetes associated instances from Noakhali, Bangladesh. This proposed model is designed in a way that it could be extended and improved for the automation of diabetes analysis. This study assists many researchers to optimize possible symptoms of diabetes which is helpful for treatment of this disease. In the future, we will gather more early stage data with significant attributes and improve this methodology to scrutinize heterogeneous types of methods/records (i.e., for diabetes/other related fields) more accurately.

Bibliography

[Ahammed et al.(2020)] Ahammed, K., Satu, M. S., Khan, M. I., & Whaiduzzaman, M. (2020). Predicting infectious state of hepatitis C virus affected patient's applying machine learning methods. In *2020 IEEE Region 10 Symposium (TEN-SYMP)* (pp. 1371–1374). Dhaka, Bangladesh: IEEE.

[Akter et al.(2017)] Akter, T., Ali, M. H., Khan, M., Satu, M., Uddin, M., Alyami, S. A., Ali, S., AKM, A., & Moni, M. A. (2021). Improved transfer-learning-based facial recognition framework to detect autistic children at an early stage. In *Brain Sciences, 11*(6), 734.

[Akter et al.(2021)] Akter, T., Khan, M. I., Ali, M. H., Satu, M. S., Uddin, M. J., & Moni, M. A. (2021). Improved machine learning based classification model for early autism detection. In *2021 2nd International Conference on Robotics, Electrical and Signal Processing Techniques (ICREST)* ((pp. 742–747). Dhaka, Bangladesh: IEEE.

[Bamanikar et al.(2016)] Bamanikar, S., Bamanikar, A., & Arora, A. (2016). Study of serum urea and creatinine in diabetic and non-diabetic patients in in a tertiary teaching hospital. In *The Journal of Medical Research, 2*(1),12-15.

[Barber et al.(2016)] Barber, S. R., Davies, M. J., Khunti, K., & Gray, L. J. (2014). Risk assessment tools for detecting those with pre-diabetes: a systematic review. In *Diabetes research and clinical practice, 105*(1),1-13.

[Fahmiin et al.(2019)] Fahmiin, M., & Lim, T. (2019). Evaluating the effectiveness of wrapper feature selection methods with artificial neural network classifier for diabetes prediction. In *International Conference on Testbeds and Research Infrastructures* (pp. 3-17).

[Islam et al.(2018)] Islam, M. M., Rahman, M. J., Roy, D. C., & Maniruzzaman, M. (2020). Automated detection and classification of diabetes disease based on Bangladesh demographic and health survey data, 2011 using machine learning approach. In *Diabetes & Metabolic Syndrome: Clinical Research & Reviews, 14*(3), 217-219.

[Minh et al.(2020)] Le Minh, T., Minh, T. V., Pham, T. N., & Dao, S. V. T. (2020). A novel wrapper-based feature selection for early diabetes prediction enhanced with a metaheuristic. In *IEEE Access,9,7869-7884.* doi: 10.1109/ACCESS.2020.3047942

[Lukmanto et al.(2019)] Lukmanto, R. B., Nugroho, A., Akbar, H., et al. (2019). Early detection of diabetes mellitus using feature selection and fuzzy support vector machine. In *Procedia Computer Science, 157,* 46-54.

[Nilashi et al.(2018)] Nilashi, M., Bin Ibrahim, O., Mardani, A., Ahani, A., & Jusoh, A. (2018). A soft computing approach for diabetes disease classification. In *Health Informatics Journal, 24*(4), 379-393.

[Nurjahan et al.(2021)] Nurjahan, Rony, M. A. T., Satu, M. S., & Whaiduzzaman, M. (2021). Mining Significant Features of Diabetes through Employing Various Classification Methods. In *2021 International Conference on Information and Communication Technology for Sustainable Development (ICICT4SD)* (pp. 240-244). Dhaka, Bangladesh: IEEE.

[Ouellet et al.(2011)] Ouellet, V., Routhier-Labadie, A., Bellemare, W., Lakhal-Chaieb, L., Turcotte, E., Carpentier, A. C., & Richard, D. (2011). Outdoor temperature, age, sex, body mass index, and diabetic status determine the prevalence, mass, and glucose-uptake activity of 18f-fdg-detected bat in humans. In *The Journal of Clinical Endocrinology & Metabolism, 96,* (1), 192-199.

[Pranto et al.(2020)] Pranto, B., Mehnaz, S., Mahid, E. B., Sadman, I. M., Rahman, A., Momen, S., et al. (2020). Evaluating Machine Learning Methods for Predicting Diabetes among Female Patients in Bangladesh. In *Information, 11*(8),374.

[Rahman et al.(2021)] Rahman, S., Khan, M. I., Satu, M. S., & Abedin, M. Z. (2021). Risk prediction with machine learning in cesarean section: Optimizing healthcare operational decisions. In *Signal Processing Techniques for Computational Health Informatics.* (pp. 293-314). Springer.

[Ramesh et al.(2015)] Ramesh, J., Aburukba, R., & Sagahyroon, A. (2021). A remote healthcare monitoring framework for diabetes prediction using machine learning. In *Healthcare Technology Letters, 8*(3),45.

[Satu et al.(2020)] Satu, M. S., Atik, S. T., & Moni, M. A. (2020). A novel hybrid machine learning model to predict diabetes mellitus. In *Proceedings of International Joint Conference on Computational Intelligence* (pp. 453-465). Dhaka, Bangladesh; Springer.

[Wang et al.(2020)] Wang, Q., Cao, W., Guo, J., Ren, J., Cheng, Y., & Davis, D. N. (2019). DMP_MI: an effective diabetes mellitus classification algorithm on imbalanced data with missing values. In *IEEE Access*,7,102232-102238.

[Wild et al.(2015)] Wild, S., Roglic, G., Green, A., Sicree, R., & King, H. (2004). Global prevalence of diabetes: estimates for the year 2000 and projections for 2030. In *Diabetes care, 27*(5),1047-1053.

[Woolley et al.(2015)] Woolley, E. (2020). 10 Causes of High Triglycerides in Diabetes.

[Yu et al.(2015)] Yu, W., Liu, T., Valdez, R., Gwinn, M., & Khoury, M. J. (2010). Application of support vector machine modeling for prediction of common diseases: the case of diabetes and pre-diabetes. In *BMC medical informatics and decision making, 10*(1),1-7.

CHAPTER 24

IoT-Based Smart Kitchen Security System

Al-Akhir Nayan

Chulalongkorn University, Bangkok, Thailand

Joyeta Saha

University of Surrey, Guildford, UK

Jannatul Ferdaous

European University of Bangladesh (EUB), Dhaka, Bangladesh

Muhammad Golam Kibria

IoT Lab, University of Liberal Arts Bangladesh (ULAB), Dhaka, Bangladesh

CONTENTS

24.1	Introduction	294
24.2	Related Work	295
24.3	Materials and Methods	296
	24.3.1 Proposed System Architecture	296
	24.3.2 List of Components	297
	24.3.3 Hardware Implementation	297
	24.3.4 Software Implementation	298
24.4	Result and Analysis	298
	24.4.1 Sensor Output	298
	24.4.2 Test Case Output	299
	24.4.3 Cost Analysis	299
	24.4.4 The Specialty of the System	300
24.5	Conclusion	300

THe increased rate of accidents in both domestic and commercial kitchens is a prime concern nowadays. Internet of Things enabled systems could be a solution to predict any possibility of an accident. Statistical analysis showed that among the victims, 30% were children injured using a knife and boiled oil or water. The application of the Internet of Things and the various aspects of smart kitchens is highlighted in this chapter. An Internet of Things-enabled prototype has been implemented to predict any vulnerability in the kitchen and perform immediate actions to ensure kitchen safety and security. Different sensors, including PIR, temperature, and gas, are used to detect human height and their movement, the presence of gas and flames, etc. The implemented prototype was tested in a kitchen that provided correct data regarding human movement and gas presence in the kitchen.

24.1 INTRODUCTION

Kitchen safety has become a significant concern because there are consistently fire incidents, resulting in an incredible loss of property and human lives. Records of disaster in the Asian nation reveal that around 300,000 people lost their lives in fire accidents between 2001 to 2014, while an average of 59 people died every day [1]. The annual damage caused by fires is estimated to be approximately $135 million. About 25,000 people die from fires and other related causes in Bangladesh and India each year, where 66% are women. According to the National Criminal Records Bureau (NCRB) statistics, deaths caused by fireplaces accounted for 5.9% (23,281) of the total deaths in 2012 [2]. According to the Bangladesh government report, compared with 19,642 accidents in 2018, national fire accidents have increased by 22.5% to 24,074, causing a loss of 330.41 million takas. Data compiled by the Bangladesh Fire Department and Civil Defense Department showed that the kitchen causes one-third of fire accidents [3], [4].

According to modern architecture, the kitchen is attached to the dining room directly. In Dhaka city, most of the kitchens do not have a door. The kitchen is kept open to visit at any time. This is suitable for adults, but unexpected incidents may occur when children or pets wander unsupervised into the kitchen. A child can be injured by a knife, boiling water, or a hot pan. If we look at newspapers, we will see many reports of accidents with children due to a lack of kitchen safety. A survey mentions that 5% of children are injured in the kitchen, and such accidents happen when parents are busy watching TV or working at the office [5].

Internet of Things (IoT) enabled smart kitchen makes life easier and enhances existing safety and security. To reduce the loss, meet fundamental objectives, and avoid an unspecified accident, we have proposed an IoT-based kitchen security system that detects a fire, identifies children and pets separately, collects and processes real-time data to take immediate action, and sends a notification to the user. A gas sensor detects gas leakage, prompts the microcontroller to turn off the gas supply, and powers a cooling fan to remove gas particles from the kitchen air. An electric motor associated with the system streams water to control the fire if detected. The system comprises a power backup unit that allows it to work during power cut-off. The data collected by the sensors are periodically transmitted to the system to update the status of the kitchen in real-time. An Android application also facilitates controlling the system through the internet.

Such type of system can ensure kitchen safety. Its rapid production may minimize unexpected incidents in the kitchen. In modern industries, chemical, gas, and fuel leakage lead to fires, resulting in economic loss. The features introduced with this project can be a helpful solution to protect industries from fire-related accidents.

24.2   RELATED WORK

In 2020, a study was conducted by Dauda et al. [6]. They considered fire outbreaks a significant problem in homes, offices, and industries and focused on the dangerous effects caused by fire. They suggested installing an automatic fire alarm detector at vulnerable locations to avoid danger. They proposed the Arduino-based fire alarm and control system. The system could detect heat and produce an alarm. The objectives of this project were achieved, and the system worked effectively. But the system did not perform any automatic operation to control fire. It alerted people about the fire, and the fire control was a manual process.

In 2019, another study focused on Arduino-based fire detection and security system. The study gave major priority to residential areas. To detect fire, they installed smoke detectors outside each separate sleeping area. There was a system to control fire by pouring water on it. Besides, they used an SMS notification system and buzzer sound to alert people about a fire. But the system was costly. They used many sensors that created system failure, and the system did not take any immediate action if a sensor failed to perform [7].

In January 2015, a study occurred on fire and smoke detecting systems. The authors claimed fire is the primary cause of accidents killing valuable lives and destroying property. They talked about the timely detection of the fireplace to avoid a severe accident. They developed a fire detection system to sense smoke and the rising temperature. In a critical situation, the systems activated a buzzer and sent commands on a virtual terminal of the Android phone through the Wi-Fi module. But the project failed to function when the electricity was cut off. On the other hand, fire control was a manual process [8].

In 2019, Mahzan et al. [9] described an Arduino-based fire alarm system for homes, adding a GSM module feature. The mission of the project was to avoid fire accidents in residential areas. An LM35 temperature sensor was used to detect the heat from the fire, and an alert message sending system was performed using a GSM module. When the system detected a temperature of 40 C or more, it immediately displayed an alert notification on an LCD and sent an SMS alert to the users simultaneously. The system worked successfully, but the fire controlling was done manually like other proposed systems described before.

Most articles describe similar techniques to detect fire and send alerts to its users. But the fire control is a manual process. The articles do not suggest preventing gas leakage and controlling fire automatically. Besides, the articles do not suggest a solution during the power cut-off. That paves the way to work on this project. In our project, we have tried to control gas and fire automatically. We have implemented a system that functions using battery power and ensures safety for everyone. Our implemented project provides solutions to the problems related to fire.

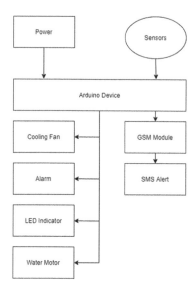

Figure 24.1: Proposed System Architecture

24.3 MATERIALS AND METHODS

24.3.1 Proposed System Architecture

We intend to implement an IoT-based intelligent kitchen that will ensure safety. Figure 24.1 exposes the recommended system architecture where a microcontroller serves as a brain by obtaining input from different sensors and interpreting the problems. An external battery provides the necessary power to the microcontroller. The device is programmed to recognize any issues transpiring in the kitchen by estimating the sensor data. The sensors can sense living bodies, gas particles, temperature, smoke, flame, and fire. The system observes the kitchen room quietly but responds immediately.

The system furnishes significant preference to children and pets. If the system detects movement in the kitchen, it produces noise through the buzzer and transfers a notification to the mobile phone using the GSM module. The temperature value is examined continuously, and if overheating is recognized, it produces a sound to alert someone. If any fire activities are identified, the Arduino device assigns a power signal to an electric relay that turns the electric motor on and scatters water in the kitchen to avoid fire expansion. The buzzer and SMS notification system are also activated.

The gas sensor measures the density of gas particles, and depending on the score, the gas supply is turned off, and the cooling fan starts to pull the gas particles out of the kitchen. The sensor's output can be monitored through an Android application. The application performs manual control while an internet connection is established with the system.

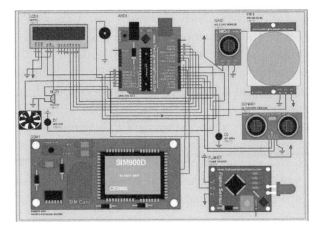

Figure 24.2: Smart Kitchen Security System Circuit Diagram

24.3.2 List of Components

To implement the project, we used the following components.

- Arduino Uno (ATmega328)
- PIR Sensor (HC-SR501)
- GSM Module (SIM800L)
- Ultrasonic Sensor
- LED Light
- Wires
- Buzzer
- Flame Sensor
- Smoke Sensor
- Electric Motor
- LED Display
- 5-Volt DC Relay
- Antenna
- Breadboard
- 9-Volt Battery

24.3.3 Hardware Implementation

Figure 24.2 represents the circuit diagram of the system where an Arduino Uno is related to other sensors and devices. The microcontroller is programmed by connecting with a computer via a USB cable. We have utilized a 9-volt battery with a register to ensure a 5-volt constant power supply to the Arduino device.

A SIM800L GSM [10], [11] module is integrated with the project, compatible with Arduino, and can be connected directly to a 5-volt power source to transmit VCC and TTL signal [12]. The module contains an antenna to transmit signals and is used to send message notifications.

HC-SR501 PIR sensor [13] identifies infrared radiation and detects animals and humans in the kitchen. On the other hand, an HC-SR04 ultrasonic sensor [14] detects the distance of the living body. These two sensors are responsible for detecting the existence and distance of the living body in the kitchen. A flame sensor that consumes 3.3- to 5.3-volt relates to the microcontroller device to detect the occurrence of fire or flame. In this project, we have used a DHT11 sensor [15], [16] to measure the temperature. But temperature sensors cannot identify fire incidents every time. So, the flame sensor is a backup of the temperature sensor. Values from both sensors are considered while deciding.

MQ2 gas sensor [17] is vital in detecting LPG, propane, methane, hydrogen, alcohol, smoke, and carbon monoxide. It measures the gas particles in the air and transmits a score to the microcontroller. The function of the cooling fan depends on the sensor. The working procedure of the system can be monitored via an LCD or LED lights, and a buzzer connected with the system is responsible for producing sound.

24.3.4 Software Implementation

We used Arduino Integrated Development Environment (IDE) [18], [19], [20] to write and upload programs to the microcontroller device. It is an open-source application developed by Arduino and hosted by GitHub that ensures Arduino software's active development. Installing the IDE on a PC, we performed further operations.

Internet connection problems may impede real-time monitoring, but the system is intended to function in critical situations integrating all functionalities with it and depreciating dependencies. At the time of internet connection loss, the system automatically stimulates the self-control mode. An android application is designed using JAVA and XML to monitor the sensor readings manually and control the gas supply, water motor, and cooling fan when the system is online.

24.4 RESULT AND ANALYSIS

After performing the software and hardware implementation, we located the prototype in the kitchen to examine the system's working performance. We distributed sensors with the gas pipe, door, and ceiling to observe the sensor outputs and check other functionalities. A laptop computer was utilized to monitor the sensor output, create graphs, and supply 5-volt DC power for the microcontroller. Figure 24.3 shows the prototype of the system.

24.4.1 Sensor Output

The sensors were experimented on creating dummy critical situations. In the test cases, the sensor distinguished the existence of a human or pet in the kitchen by generating high frequency, as shown in Figure 24.4. Arduino IDE monitored the sensor reading shown in Figure 24.5. The outputs confirm that the sensors are performing well and transferring readings accurately. The microcontroller manages these sensor outputs for additional processing and gaining the decision.

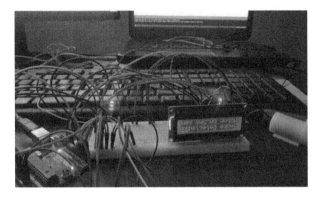

Figure 24.3: System Prototype

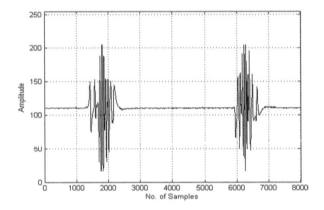

Figure 24.4: PIR Sensor Output

24.4.2 Test Case Output

According to the program, the microcontroller accepts an actual threshold value for an individual sensor. The microcontroller disregards sensor reading below the threshold and performs immediate action when the threshold is crossed. A total of 20 test cases were run to confirm the operational aptitude of the system. The system showed satisfactory performance and rendered correct responses against various critical situations. Therefore, few test cases among 20 are reported in Table 24.1.

Figure 24.6 (a) shows the GSM module output. The system successfully notified its user when a child entered the kitchen in the test case. Depending on the situation, the suggestion becomes different. For example, if a fire is detected, the system sends a notification saying, "Fire is detected in the kitchen." Manual control was also performed correctly, and a layout of the application is shown in Figure 24.6 (b).

24.4.3 Cost Analysis

The implementation cost has been estimated in Table 24.2. The ingredients used for the implementation are available everywhere, and we purchased them from a local Bangladeshi market, so the amount is estimated in Bangladeshi currency. In

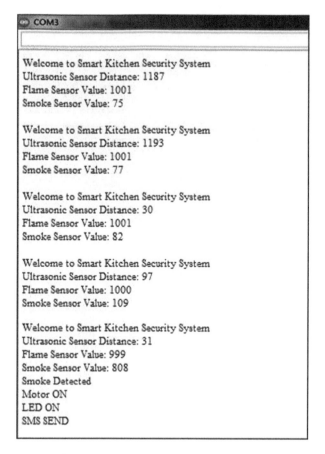

Figure 24.5: Output of the System

USD, the amount will be only $22, which is very cheap, and anyone can manage the implementation cost.

24.4.4 The Specialty of the System

The system comprises all features to defend against a fire like other associated works and provides some unique features. It gives special priority to children and pets and ensures protection. Two separate modes have been introduced that serve to control manually or automatically.

Most of the works related to this project are costly and appear with a complex installation process. On the other hand, anyone can purchase our system for $22, and the installation process is effortless. The code, an Android application, and an installation video will be uploaded to GitHub and YouTube accordingly and made public to complete the installation process effortlessly.

24.5 CONCLUSION

The increased accident rate in the domestic and commercial kitchens caused by fire and kitchen utensils is a significant concern. Besides, the number of urban areas

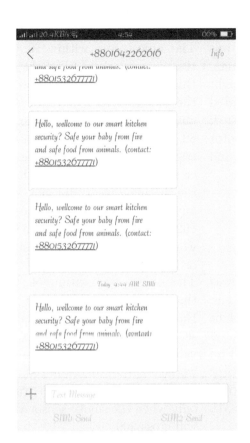 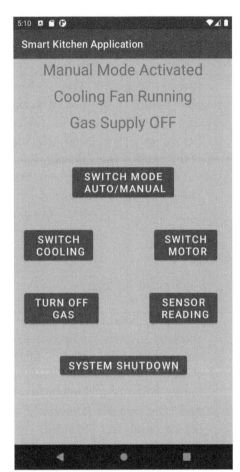

Figure 24.6: (a) GSM Output (b) Android Application Layout

and their increased demand for modern kitchen tools have inspired the manufacturer to transform into a smart kitchen. The IoT-based smart kitchen, its importance for safety and security, specifically for children and pets, and various roles of the smart kitchen have been highlighted in this article. An IoT-based prototype has been implemented using several sensors, microcontrollers, Arduino, etc. The implemented prototype has been tested, and it functioned well. The prototype monitored the kitchen environment automatically and notified the user regarding the status of the kitchen. The cost of implementing the system has been discussed considering the local market price.

The implementation of several identified functionalities has been going on to update the system and should be completed soon to contribute to society's well-being and sustainable development.

Table 24.1: Test Case Output

S. N.	Data	Result	Reason
1	Sensor received the value of 31 CM, Flame Sensor value was 802, and the smoke sensor value was 82.	The object was placed in the system. Red LED Light and the integrated Buzzer worked; however, the motor was not started, and SMS was not sent.	The object was within 50 CM; that is why the LED light and Buzzer were triggered. However, the smoke sensor did not send any signal because the value was 82. The system is programmed to trigger only when the value will cross 200. On the other hand, the Flame sensor did not send any signal because the value was 802. The system is programmed to work when the value is at least 800 or less.
2	Height Sensor received the value of 21 CM, Flame Sensor value was 748, and the smoke sensor value was 260.	The object was placed in the system. Red LED Light and the integrated Buzzer worked; Fire Detected, Motor Started to supply water, and an SMS was sent.	The object was within 50 CM; that is why the LED light and Buzzer were triggered. The fire sensor sent a signal because the value was 748. The smoke sensor worked as the value was 260. The system is programmed to trigger only when the smoke sensor value will cross 200.
3	Height Sensor received the value of 29. The flame sensor value was 996, and the Smoke Sensor value was 506.	The object was placed in the system. Red LED Light and the integrated Buzzer worked. Smoke Detected, Motor Started to supply water, and an SMS was sent.	The object was within 50 CM; that is why the LED light and Buzzer were triggered. The smoke sensor sent a signal because the value was 506. The flame sensor did not work as the value was 996.
4	The Height Sensor received the value of 30 CM, the Flame Sensor value was 1001, and the smoke sensor value was 82.	The object was placed in the system. Red LED Light and the integrated Buzzer worked; however, the motor was not started, and SMS was not sent.	The object was within 50 CM; that is why the LED light and Buzzer were triggered. However, the smoke sensor did not send any signal because the value was 82. On the other hand, the Flame sensor did not send any signal because the value was 1001.

Table 24.2: Cost Analysis

S. No.	Sensors and Accessories Name	Price (BDT)
1	Arduino Uno	450
2	9v Battery	39
3	PIR Sensor HC-SR501	130
4	Height Sensor HC-SR04	120
5	LED Light	2*2=4
6	Buzzer	15
7	Flame Sensor	120
8	Smoke Sensor MQ-2	100
9	5v DC Mini Water Pump	195
10	5v DC Relay	30
11	GSM Module SIM800L	450
12	Breadboard	100
13	Jumper Wire	1*50=50
14	16x2 LCD Display	159
15	1k resistor	1
	Total cost	1863

Bibliography

[1] Mahboob, M. M. (2012b). Characteristics of Fire Incidents in Asian Countries Particularly in Bangladesh. *Fire Science and Technology*, 31(3), 159–172.

[2] Chaturvedi, R. (2018). Fire loss is national loss-let us adopt fire safety measures. *Fire Engineer*, 43(1 and 2), 27.

[3] ILO'S Press Release on the tragic incident of fire in a garment factory at Ashulia. (2012, November 27).

[4] Fire accident. (2019). The Economic Times. https://economictimes.indiatimes.com/topic/fire-accident.

[5] Hirunpraditkoon, S., Dlugogorski, B., & Kennedy, E. (2008). Fire Properties of Refuse Derived Fuels: Measurements of Temperature Profiles and Mass Loss. *Fire Safety Science*, 9, 765–776.

[6] Shazali Dauda, M., & Toro, U. S. (2020). Arduino Based Fire Detection and Control System. *International Journal of Engineering Applied Sciences and Technology*, 04(11), 447–453.

[7] Goni, I., & Hassan, R. (2019). Intelligent Arduino Home Based Security System Using Global System for Mobile Communication (GSM) and Passive Infrared (PIR) Sensor. *Communications*, 7(2), 45.

[8] Jeevanandham, A. T. & Sivamurgan, P. (2015). IoT Based Automatic Fire Alarm System. *Bulletin of Scientific Research*, 29–34.

[9] Mahzan, N. N., Enzai, N. I. M., Zin, N. M., & Noh, K. S. S. K. M. (2018). Design of an Arduino-based home fire alarm system with GSM module. *Journal of Physics: Conference Series*, 1019, 012079.

[10] Rashid, M. M., Nayan, A. A., Simi, S. A., Saha, J., Rahman, M. O., & Kibria, M. G. (2021). IoT based Smart Water Quality Prediction for Biofloc Aquaculture. *International Journal of Advanced Computer Science and Applications*, 12(6).

[11] Mluyati, S., & Sadi, S. (2019). Internet Of Things (IoT) Pada Prototipe Pendeteksi Kebocoran Gas Berbasis MQ-2 dan SIM800L. *Jurnal Teknik*, 7(2).

[12] Integrated-circuit digital logic families. II: TTL devices. (1971). *Microelectronics Reliability*, 10(3), 147.

[13] Smallest PIR motion sensor in the world can now be adjusted for sensitivity. (2001). *Sensor Review*, 21(4).

[14] Turnip, P., Sitompul, E., Wibawa, B.M., Trisanto, A., Turnip, A. (2020). Motor speed control toward wall surface angle based on HC-SR04 ultrasonic sensor. *In: Proceedings of the International Conference on Culture Heritage, Education, Sustainable Tourism, and Innovation Technologies*. SCITEPRESS - Science and Technology Publications.

[15] Rahman, M. O., Kashem, M. A., Nayan, A. A., Akter, M. F., Rabbi, F., Ahmed, M., & Asaduzzaman, M. (2021). Internet of Things (IoT) Based ECG System for Rural Health Care. *International Journal of Advanced Computer Science and Applications*, 12(6).

[16] Saptadi, A. H. (2014). Perbandingan Akurasi Pengukuran Suhu dan Kelembaban Antara Sensor DHT11 dan DHT22. *Jurnal Infotel - Informatika Telekomunikasi Elektronika*, 6(2), 49.

[17] Pratama, R., Muid, A., & Sanubary, I. (2019). Perbandingan Kinerja Sensor TGS2610, MQ2, dan MQ6 pada Alat Pendeteksi Kebocoran Tabung Liquified Petroleum Gas (LPG) Menggunakan ATMega2560. *PRISMA FISIKA*, 7(1), 14.

[18] Prakash, A., & Singh, A. (2019). Development of an Arduino-Based Embedded System. *SSRN Electronic Journal.*

[19] Home Automation Using Arduino. (2018). *International Journal of Recent Trends in Engineering and Research*, 195–199.

[20] Dey, A., Haque, K. A., Nayan, A. A., & Kibria, M. G. (2020). IoT Based Smart Inhaler for Context-Aware Service Provisioning. *2nd International Conference on Advanced Information and Communication Technology (ICAICT)*, Dhaka, Bangladesh.

Index

Symbols

λ fading factor 64

Numbers

5Vs of Big Data 190

A

Acknowledgement packet 239
Adaboost 214
Adam optimizer (Adaptive moment estimation optimizer) 54
Adaptive decay and radius-based online clustering for stream data (ADROCS) 63
  application of 64
  overall performance 71–72
  performance evaluation 67–71
  testing of 67–71
Adaptive decay evolving clustering approach 61ff
Adaptive moment estimation (Adam) optimizer 54
Adaptive radius approach 62
Adaptive synthetic sampling method (ASASYN) 282
ADROCS *see* Adaptive decay and radius-based online clustering for stream data (ADROCS)
Affective computing 122–123
Aggression 212ff
Air quality goals and parking systems 5
Algorithms for clustering approaches 62–63
Allows 37
Alternative certainties 13
Amazon Web Resources Reviews in consumer research 13
Anaconda environment 92

Android interface development for seniors 180–181
Android smartphone application for smart parking system 7
ANN *see* Artificial neural network (ANN)
Antenna switched beam models 242–243
Antenna transmissions 237
Aquaculture for fish cultivation 83
Arduino 2
  in aquaculture 83ff
  in fire detection 295, 298
  mega 2560 controller 205–206
Arduino UNO 76–77, 89
Area under receiver operating characteristic (AUROC) 281–289
  accuracy 281
  use of Delay Tolerance Networking (DTN) 286
Artificial neural network (ANN)
  algorithm 85
  layers in 15
  performance 11–12, 16–17
AUROC *see* Area under receiver operating characteristic (AUROC)
Average latency 137–138, 144–146
Average remaining energy 139–144

B

BA *see* Behavioral attitude (BA)
Back-off value 228
Backpropagation algorithm 15
Bagging 214
Bag of Words (BoW) 102
  distributed vectors 126
  feature extraction 216

BanFakeNews dataset 49
Bangladesh parking systems 1ff
Bangla fake news detection 46ff
Bangla language
    detecting offensive language 213, 214
    low-resource 46
Bartlett's test 26
Baseline classifiers 285
Bayes classifiers 285
Beacon generated 227
Beamforming lobe 242–243
Behavioral attitude (BA)
    impact of 29
    toward online shopping 23
    utilization by retailers 29
BengaliGlove 51
Bengali language in user interface for
        seniors 183, 185
Bengali Named Entity Recognizer
        (Bengali NER) 99
    need for tool set 100
Bengali Natural Language Processing
        (BNLP) 50–51
Bengali NER see Bengali named entity
        recognizer (Bengali NER)
Bengali newspapers for crime data 97ff
Bengali Wikipedia dump dataset 51
BERT see Bidirectional encoder
        representations from
        transformers (BERT)
Best first decision tree (BFTree) 285
Bidirectional encoder representations
        from transformers (BERT) 59
    for emotion classification of
        COVID-19 pandemic tweets
        109ff
    performance 48
    processing with 113
    Sentence-BERT 123
Bidirectional long short-term memory
        (Bi-LSTM)
    hybrid deep learning model for fake
        new detection 47
    processing by 52
Big Data

5Vs 190
    properties 190
    visualization techniques 195–197
    visualization tools and techniques
        188ff
Bigram architectures 216
Bi-LSTM see Bidirectional long
        short-term memory (Bi-LSTM)
Bi-LSTM + CNN models 54
    performance for fake news detection
        55–58
Bio-inspired meta-heuristic techniques
        266ff
Bio-inspired optimization algorithms
        271–275
    performance comparison 276–277
Bio-sensors 224
BIRCH 63
Bitcoin
    development 36
    weakness in 40
Blockchain
    for each patient 260–261
    function of 35
Blockchain architecture
    Hyperledger Fabric 254
Blockchain attack manipulation 252
Blockchain-based healthcare system 38
Blockchain-based medical data
        management 251ff
Blockchain for secure communications
        252
Blockchain technology security 255–256
Blockchain transaction fee in gas units
        37
B-MAC 225
BMI (Body mass index) 288
BNLP see Bengali natural language
        processing (BNLP)
BOCEDS buffer-based algorithm 62, 64,
        69–70
Body mass index (BMI) 288
Boost converter 266ff
Border routers placement 3
BoW see Bag of Words (BoW)

Box and whisker plot visualization
    technique 195–196
BTP *see* busy-tone-packet (BTP)
Bullying on social media 212ff
Busy-tone based protocol 239
Busy-tone-packet (BTP) 237, 238, 243

C

CALA MAC protocol 224, 225
    efficiency 233
    see also Cognitive approach for load
        adaptive MAC (CALA-MAC)
        protocol
Camera detection for energy efficient
    lighting 75–76
Carp condition preference 93
CB *see* Circuit breaker (CB)
CC 243–244
CDMA *see* Code Division Multiple
    Access (CDMA) schedule
CDR-MAC transmission 239
CDT 285
CE *see* Consumer engagement (CE)
CEDAS Clustering approach 62, 69–70
CF (Clustering features) tree 63
CH 153
Channel rendezvous phase 226–227
Channel re-rendezvous phase 228–229
Channel shifting 228
Children in kitchens 294, 296
CHIRP 285
Circuit breaker (CB) 203–204
    status determination 203
    tripping 202
Circular helix 67
Classification algorithm accuracy 172
Classifier subset evaluator (CSE) 282
Classifier techniques 213
Class weights 54, 57–59
Clear-to-Send 239
Clickbait news 49
Cloud address encryption 261
Cloud-based smart parking systems 1ff
Cluster head (CH) 153
Clustering features (CF) tree 63

Clustering methods 62
Cluster purity 69–70
CNN *see* Convolutional neural network
    (CNN)
CNN + Bi-LSTM models
    performance for fake news detection
        26–28, 56–58
    processing with 54
CNN + LSTM models
    accuracy 47
    performance for fake news detection
        56–58
    processing with 52
CODAS clustering approach 63
Code Division Multiple Access (CDMA)
    schedule 154, 237
Cognitive approach for load adaptive
    MAC (CALA-MAC) protocol
    226
Cognitive radio (CR) 224
Cognitive radio-based medium access
    control (CR-MAC) protocol 225
Cognitive radio body area network
    (CRBAN) 226
Cognitive-receiver initiated cycled
    receiver (C-RICER) 225, 226
    delay 230–232
    efficiency 233
    MAC protocol 224
Communication techniques in IoT 75
Composite hypercubes on iterated
    random projections (CHIRP)
    classifier 285
Conditional Random Fields (CRFs) 99
Connectivity charts visualization
    technique 197
Consumer behaviors analysis 13
Consumer engagement (CE) 20
    definition 24
    impact of 29
    utilization by retailers 29
Control channel (CC) 243–244
Control packet overhead 246–247
Convolutional neural network (CNN) 99
    algorithm 85

for fake news detection 48
hybrid deep learning model for fake new detection 47
in hybrid system 48
for image processing 52
performance 48
Coordinator node 226
Correlation matrices visualization technique 196
Cost of processing in system 42, 43
Cost sensitive decision forest (CSForest) 285
Count Vectorizer 48, 51
Covariance matrix in PCA 14–15
COVID-19
E-learning satisfaction prediction 163ff
impact on purchasing habits 21
pandemic tweet emotion classification 109ff
shift to online classes 164–165
tweets dataset 111–112
CR 224
CRBAN 226
Credal decision trees (CDT) 285
CRFs 99
C-RICER see Cognitive-receiver initiated cycled receiver (C-RICER)
Crime collector 101
Crime data collection 100
Crime data visualization 97ff
Crime-finder system 97ff
Crime information use 99
CR MAC 225
Cronbach's alpha test 26, 169
Crustacean condition preference 93
Cryptocurrency cost to create prescriptions 38
Cryptocurrency cost to create sold medicine records 38
Cryptocurrency wallet authentication 34
Cryptocurrency wallet bridge 36–37
CSE 282
CSForest 285

CSMA 237
CTS 2
Cyber aggression detection 212ff
Cyberbullying consequences 213

D

D3.js visualization tool 194
DACK see Directional acknowledgement (DACK) transmission
Darwin's theory as inspiration for algorithms 271–272
DATA/ACK packet 239
Data balancing techniques 285
Data channel (DC) 243–244
Data migration in smart parking system 7
Data mining clustering techniques 62
Data quality in Big Data 192
Data sample evaluation tests 26
Datasets for clustering 63
Dataset splitting 216
Data stream 62
DBSCAN algorithm 63
DBSMA busy-tone protocol 239
DC 243–244
DCAA-MAC 226
DC-DC boost converter 266ff
DC microgrid 266ff
DCTS packets 244
DDATA 243
d-dimensional embedding 124
Deafness problem 237, 238
Deaf nodes 237
Decision Forest by penalizing attributes (ForestPA) 285
Decision support systems with heterogeneous WSNs 3
Decision table / Naive Bayes (DTNB) hybrid classifier 285
Decision tree algorithm 168
Decision tree visualization technique 196–197
Deep Learning implementation impact 85
Deep-sea communication use of Delay

Tolerance Networking (DTN) 137

Delay tolerance networking (DTN) 136ff

Delivery probability 139–142

Density-based clustering 62–63

Density threshold ($Th_{density}$) 64

Deploys 37

Diabetes dataset
  biomarker correlations 288–290
  classifier correlations 288–290

Diabetes mellitus
  classification on imbalanced data with missing values (DMP_MI) 282
  early detection 282
  feature detection 280ff
  symptoms 281
  types of 281

Digital signage 13

Dimensionality reduction 12–13

Dimming lighting for energy reduction 75–76

Directional acknowledgement (DACK) transmission 243, 244, 246, 248–249

Directional antennas 236–237

Directional data (DDATA) 243

Directional hidden terminal problem 237

Directional MAC power control 239

Directional RTS (DRTS) 239–240

Discontinuous busy-tone packet 237, 239

Discrete tone-driven communication 236ff

Discrete tone driven directional rate controlled (DTD^{2}RC) communication system 236ff

Dissolved oxygen impact 85

DistilBERT 59

Distress signal sending for seniors 179–180

Distributed Bag of Words vectors 126

Distributed memory paragraph vector (PV-DM) 126

DLE 212

DMP_MI 282

DNAV 240–241

Doc2Vec embedding technique 123, 126

DocDict see Document Dictionary (DocDict)

Doctor private key for record access 262

Doctor public key 261

Document Dictionary (DocDict)
  emotion detection embedding approach 122–123
  hybrid technique 128–130
  method performance 131–132
  using Doc2Vec 128

Dominant cluster 69

Double-level ensemble (DLE) models 212

Dragonfly algorithm (DA) 267
  inspiration for 274

Driver program 100

DSDMAC 239–241

DStream 69–70

DTD^{2}RC 238

DTN 136ff

DTNB 285

Dual channel protocol 239–240

Dual sensing directional MAC (DSDMAC) 239–241

E

EAMMH see Energy-Aware Multihop Multipath (EAMMH) routing

Earlystopping 54

Education see E-learning

Efficiency of density-based clustering algorithm 68

E-health systems 251ff

EHR 252

E-learning
  impact summary 172
  satisfaction prediction 163ff

Electronic health records (EHRs) 252

EmotiNet 110

Emotion
  shifts during pandemic 117–119
  types of 112

Emotional shifts during pandemic 117–119

Emotion classification of COVID-19 pandemic tweets 109ff
Emotion classification work flow 112
Emotion detection
    methods for 124, 126–127
    using embedding techniques 122ff
    workflow 124–126
Emotions, basic 123
Encryption of cloud address 261
End-to-end delay 248
Energy-aware DTN routing protocols 136ff
Energy-Aware Multihop Multipath (EAMMH) routing 152, 154
Energy awareness 142–148
Energy conservation and IoT application 75
Energy consumption per packet 248–249
Energy cost of protocols 232–233
Energy module 139–140
Entity-relationship diagram (ERD) 206
EOA 37
Epidemic DTN routing protocol 137, 138
    energy awareness 148–149
Eps (radius) 63
ERD 206
ETH 205, 257
Ether 38, 257
Ethereum blockchain 254, 257–258
Ethereum blockchain-based healthcare system
    consumed gas 263
    purpose 38
Ethereum blockchain-based system 34ff
Ethereum platform for sharing information 36
Ethereum Virtual Machine (EVM)
    covering large quantity of applications 36
    use of platform 34
ETH gas 261
EVM see Ethereum Virtual Machine (EVM)
Evolving clustering approach 61ff
Externally owned accounts (EOA) 37

F
Facebook e-commerce 11ff
Fading factor λ 64
Fake news
    definition 47
    detection levels in Bangla 47
    performance of models for fake news detection 57–59
Fake news dataset 49
fastText 123
    embedding 124
    hybrid embedding method 123
    method performance 131
F-Commerce (Facebook e-commerce)
    analysis 11–12
    consumer behaviors 12
Feature extraction 216
Feature vectors 123
Feedback gain 270–271
Fire danger from kitchens 294–295
Fish condition preference 93
Fish supply 84
Five Vs of Big Data 190
Fog nodes in IoT system 5
ForestPA 285
Fossil teeth data for dietary information 13
Friedman test 132–133
Functional trees (FT) 285
Function classifiers 285
Fuzzy neural network 85

G
GA see Genetic algorithm (GA)
Ganache platform 40
Gas units for transaction cost 37, 263
Gboost 214
Generated beacon 227
Genetic algorithm (GA) 267, 268
    inspiration for 268, 271–272
gensim 48, 126
Geocoder 103
Global optimal radius 62
GloVe Bengali Global Vector model (GloVe) 51

GloVe model 51
Google Charts visualization tool 193
Google Maps for parking application 2
Grey wolf optimization (GWO) 267, 268
    inspiration for 268, 273–274
GSM module communications 295–297
GWO *see* Grey wolf optimization
    (GWO)

H
Half-duplex radios 238, 242
Harassment 213
Hard threshold (HT) 154
Hate speech 213
HCI 110
HCVP-MAC 226
Healthcare system based on ethereum
    blockchain 34ff
Health interface for seniors 178
Health record management issues 35
Helical data dataset 63
Helical data series 67
Heterogeneity in Big Data 192
Heterogeneous routing technique
    comparison 155–159, 160–161
Hidden Markov model 110
Hidden terminals 237
Hierarchical routing methods 152
Histogram visualization technique 197
Hoeffding tree (HT) 285
HT 154, 285
Human-Computer Interaction (HCI) 110
Human perspective in Big Data 192
Hybrid deep learning models for fake
    news detection 46ff
Hybrid model for fake news detection 48
Hyper-elliptical clusters 62
Hyperledger Fabric 254

I
IBkLG 285
IBM SPSS application 26
i-CODAS algorithm 63
IE 97–98
IEEE 802.11 246–249
Image scale in Big Data 192

Incremental pruning to produce error
    reduction (JRip) classifier 285
Influencing factor on consumer behaviors
    12
Infogram visualization tool 193
Information extraction (IE) 97–98
Information loss in Big Data 192
Initialization delay 231–232
Injected Web3 platform 40
Interaktor application 176
Interface features for seniors 176–177
Internet of medical things (IoMT) 255
Internet of things (IoT)
    data collection from nodes 260
    definition 1–2
    geomagnetic tracker in 3
    for kitchen security 293ff
    power interruption monitoring 200ff
    for secure medical data management
        251ff
    solar street light and surveillance
        system 74ff
Inverse-regularization parameter (C) 105
IoMT 255
IoT *see* Internet of Things (IoT)
IPFS database 254
ISEAR dataset 110, 111, 113, 130
ITS and WSNs 3

J
J48 tree 285
JavaScript VM platform 40
Jestho 177
JRip 285
JSON
    for parking application 2
    in smart parking system 7
Jupyter notebook 92
Jupyter visualization tool 194

K
Kaiser-Meyer-Olkin (KMO) test 26
Kalerkantho 101, 104
KDDCUP'99 dataset 63
    in ADROCS evaluation 67

Keras callbacks functions 54
Keras python library 52
Kernel density estimation visualization
    technique 195
Key performance indicators (KPIs) 201
    for quality control 202–203
    require circuit breaker status 208
K-Fold 216
Kitchen accidents 294
Kitchen safety 293ff
Kitchen smart security system 293ff
KMO (Kaiser-Meyer-Olkin) test 26
K-Nearest neighbor (KNN) algorithm
    84, 168, 285
    implementation 87–88
KPIs *see* Key performance indicators
    (KPIs)
KStar 285

L
LADTree 285
Language tools availability 106
Latent semantic analysis algorithm 110
Lazy classifiers 285
LDR 74
LEACH *see* Low energy adaptive
    clustering hierarchy (LEACH)
    routing
LeafletMap 103
Leaf-size 88
Lexical-based analysis of crime data 100
Lexical networks 48
Light-dependent resistor (LDR) 74
Lighting for safety 75
Likert scale 25
LIME explanation approach 111,
    113–115
Linear quadratic Gaussian (LQG) 268
Linear quadratic regulator (LQR)
    control framework 266
    controller design 270–271
    and PID controllers 268
Linear support vector classifier 105
Linear support vector machine classifier
    102

Listening time 227–228
LMT 285
Load adaptive MAC protocol 223ff
Location mapper subsystem 103
Logic boost alternating decision tree
    (LADTree) 285
Logistic classifier 285
Logistic model trees (LMT) 285
Logistic regression 102
    algorithm 168
Long short term memory (LSTM) 99
    algorithm 85
    for fake news detection 48
    hybrid deep learning model for fake
        new detection 47
    model usage 52
    for tweet analysis 113
    see also under LSTM
Low energy adaptive clustering hierarchy
    (LEACH) routing 154
    energy awareness 152
LQR *see* Linear quadratic regulator
    (LQR) control framework
LSTM *see* Long short term memory
    (LSTM)
LSTM + CNN model
    processing with 52
LSTM + CNN model accuracy 47
LSTM RNN for consumer research 13

M
MAC *see* Media access control (MAC)
    protocol
Machine learning (ML)
    algorithms 216
    model for emotion classification
        109ff
    models for consumer research 13
    sci-kit-learn library 15
Mackey-Glass dataset 63
    in ADROCS evaluation 67–71
Macro-cluster formed 64
MANET 239
MATLAB/Simulink environment 267
Maximum Radius (R_{max}) 64

MaxProp DTN routing protocol 137, 139
    energy awareness 148–149
MBAN-MAC 226
MDTA *see* Multi-dimensional traffic
    adaptive (MDTA) protocol
Mean-time-to-failure (MTTF) 201
Mean-time-to-repair (MTTR) 201
Media access control (MAC) protocol
    223
    sectorized directional MAC protocol
    239
Media platform level of usage 47
Medical data exchange 252
Medication abuse detection 35
Medicine purchase illegality 35
Memory efficiency testing 69–70
Merkle root 256
Merkle tree
    for data integrity 40–41
    for transaction linking 36
Message delivery probability 137–138
Meta-heuristic techniques 266ff
Metamask browser extension 36–37
Metamask Wallet platform 40
MG 267
Micro-cluster energy 64
Micro-clusters 62
Micro-clusters formed 64
Microgrid (MG) 267
Microprocessor relays 204–205
Microsoft Power BI visualization tool
    193
Minimum Radius (R_{min}) 64
Minkowski distance 87–88
MinPts (minimum points) 63
ML *see* Machine learning (ML)
MLP 285
MNB classifier 48
Mobility models 138
MODLEM 285
    accuracy 281
MRStream 69–70
MTTF 201
MTTR 201

Multi-dimensional traffic adaptive
    (MDTA) protocol 225, 238
Multi-hop directional ad-hoc networks
    239
Multilayer perceptron classifier (MLP)
    285
Multinomial Naive Bayes 214

N
Naive Bayes (NB) classification
    algorithm 168, 285
    use of Delay Tolerance Networking
    (DTN) 214
Naive Bayes decision tree (NBTree) 285
Named entity recognizer (NER)
    application of 102
    deployment 98
    tool sets by language 100
Natural language processing (NLP) 13
NB *see* Naive Bayes (NB) classification
    algorithm
NBTree 285
NB-wireless vehicle owner authentication
    3
Neighbor location information 239
Neighbor node blocking 239
NER *see* Named entity recognizer (NER)
Network diagram visualization technique
    196
Network load adjustment 229–230
Network packet loss 226
Network performance parameters
    137–138
Network traffic load strategies 229–230
Neural networks for word vector models
    51
News crawler 101
N-gram analysis 110
NLP 13
Nltk library 50
Nonce 36, 256

O
OCC model 110–111
OF 285

ONE 136ff
One-vs-all strategy 130, 131
One-vs-rest strategy 130, 131
Online classes
    shift to 164–165
    see also E-learning
Online data 62
Online purchase intentions 25
    of social network users 20ff
OpenCage geocoder 103
OpenStreetMap 103
Opportunistic networking environment
    (ONE) simulator 139–140
Opportunistic networks routing protocol
    performance 136ff
Optimization algorithm performance
    276–277
Optimization objective function 275
Optimized Forest (OF) tree 285
Overdose deaths 35
Overhead ratio 137–138, 146–147
Ownership of Big Data 192

P
Packet delay of protocols 231–232
Pandas framework library 54
Paragraph vector (PV) 126
Parallel parking theory implementation 3
Parameter sensitivity study 70–71
Parking systems 1ff
Parody news 49
PART 285
Particle swarm optimization (PSO) 267,
    268
    inspiration for 268, 272–273
PCA *see* Principal component analysis
    (PCA)
PCDMAC 241
Perceptron model 214
Performance analysis of routing
    protocols 136ff
Performance indicators 218–220
Performance requirements in Big Data
    192
Permanent decay variable 62

Perspective in Big Data 192
Pets in kitchens 294, 296
Phone number for parking
    authentication 3
Photo-voltaic systems power control
    scheme for directional MAC 267
Physical impacts and E-learning
    satisfaction prediction 163ff
Physiologic parameters measurements
    224
PI *see* Purchase intention (PI)
PID *see* Proportional-integral-derivative
    (PID) control
PIMS 200ff
Plasma glucose correlations with
    diabetes 286
Positive influencer satisfaction 24
Post-padding 51
PoW 256–257
Power control scheme for directional
    MAC 239
Power interruption monitoring system
    (PIMS) 200ff
Power supply interruption determination
    209–210
p-persistent method 238, 241, 243
    tone driven rate controlled MAC
    operation 244–246
Prawn condition preference 93
Pre-diabetes data 281
Pre-diabetes feature detection 280ff
Preprocessing step required 49
Prescription management across
    pharmacies 35
Prescription mining 38–39
Prescription sharing 38
Primary users (PU) 226–227
Principal component analysis (PCA)
    for component reduction 12
    definition 11
    extraction of components 13
    methodology 13–15
Privacy in Big Data 192
Processing speed and dimension size
    71–72

Proof of work (PoW) for mining transactions 256–257

PRoPHET DTN routing protocol 137, 138–139

PRoPHET for energy awareness 148–149

Proportional-integral-derivative (PID) control 267–268

and LQR controllers 268

Protocol throughput 232–233

PSO *see* Particle swarm optimization (PSO)

Psychological impacts and E-learning satisfaction prediction 163ff

PU 226–227

Purchase information sharing 22

Purchase intention (PI) 22

online 25

of online social network users 20ff

prediction of 27, 29

utilization by retailers 29

varying definitions 22–23

Purchasing habits COVID-19 impact 21

PV 126

P-value 171

PyCharm 91–92

Python sklearn library 168

R

R *see* Reputation (R)

RA 34

Racism 213

Radius-based evolving clustering approach 61ff

Random Forest (RF)

algorithm 15, 85, 168

classifier application 104–105

performance 12, 16–17

tree classifiers 285

Random oversampling (ROS) for data balancing 285

Random oversampling dataset 281

Random tree (RT) 285

Raspberry Pi 2, 253, 254

data collection from nodes 260

for parking application 2

Rate controlling methodology 245–246

RBFNetwork (RBFN) 285

RCNN 48

Reactive routing methods 152

Receiver initiated cycle receiver (RICER) 225

Receiver initiated MAC (RI-MAC) protocol 226

Recurrent convolutional neural network (RCNN) 99

Recurrent neural network (RNN) 48

Reduced error pruning tree (REPTree) 285

Registration for parking system 3

Regularization method 87

Regulatory authority (RA) authentication 34

Relativity analysis 169

Relay output 204

ReLu activation function 53

Remaining energy 142–144

Remix IDE platform 40, 261

Remote patient monitoring 255–256

Rendezvous phase 232

Renewable power generation development 267

REPTree 285

Reputation (R) 23

business asset 23

impact of 29

utilization by retailers 29

Request-to-Send 239

RF *see* Random Forest (RF)

RFID tags

for parking application 2

RICER 225

Ridor 285

RI-MAC 226

Ripple-down rule learner (Ridor) 285

River water data-set 91

R_{max} 6

R_{min} 6

RNN 48

RoBERTa approach 111

Romanized Bangla 214
ROS 285
Round-Robin algorithm 239
Routing performance of heterogeneous
 techniques 155–159
Routing protocols energy awareness
 142–148
RT 285
RTS (Request-to-Send)/CTS
 (Clear-to-Send) control packet
 239
Rule-based technique 99
Rules classifiers 285

S
S *see* Satisfaction (S)
SAIFI 201
Salmonid condition preference 93
SARS-CoV-2 (Severe acute respiratory
 syndrome coronavirus 2) *see*
 COVID-19
SAS 202
Satire/parody news 49
Satisfaction (S)
 definition 24
 impact of 29
 utilization by retailers 29
Saudi newspaper crime data 100
SAW *see* Spray-and-wait (SAW) DTN
 routing protocol
SBERT *see* Sentence-BERT (SBERT)
SC 285
Scalability definition 68
Scale of Big Data 192
Scatterplot matrices visualization
 technique. 197
Schweitzer Engineering Laboratories
 204–205
Sci-kit-learn machine learning library 15,
 104
scikit-learn regression method 130
S-commerce 22
 impact in Bangladesh 30
Scrapy 101
Sectorized directional MAC protocol 239

Secured electronic health record
 management system 37
Secure electronic prescription system 37
Secure medical data management 251ff
Self-assistance interface for seniors
 179–180
Self-harm 213
SELogic control equations 204
SEL relay 204–205
Semantic networks 48
Senior citizen assistance application
 175ff
SeniorsAid application 175ff
Sensor nodes 226
Sentence-BERT (SBERT) 123, 126
 method performance 131
 pretrained 126
Sentence classifier 101, 102
 performance comparison 105–106
Sentiment analysis 124
Sexism 213
Shannon-Hartley theorem 237, 238, 242
Shopping environment 13
Shrimp condition preference 93
Shuffle Split 216
Side-lobe interference 239
Signal-to-inference noise ratio (SINR)
 224–225, 226–227
Signal-to-inference noise ratio threshold
 (SINR$_T$) 226–227
SimpleCart (SC) tree 285
Simple logic classifier (SL) 285
Single-busy-tone 239
Single hop star topology 226
SINR 226–227
 see also Signal-to-inference noise
 ratio (SINR)
SINR$_T$ 226–227
Skip-gram model 125
Sklearn library 168
SL 285
Slave coordinator 229
Slave nodes 227–228
Slot reservation 5–7
Small preamble 226

Smart contracts 262
    for decentralized electronic
        prescription system 37
    deployment 39–40
    for transaction integrity 36
Smart healthcare 255–256
Smart kitchen security system 293ff
Smart parking system
    functional diagram 5
    reservation flowchart 6–7
    use case scenarios 8–9
Smartphone application for seniors 176
Smoke detection systems 295
SMOTE see Synthetic minority
        oversampling (SMOTE)
SMOTE-NC see Synthetic minority
        oversampling technique for
        nominal and categorical features
        (SMOTE-NC)
SNF see Spray-and-focus (SNF) DTN
        routing protocol
SNoW learning architecture 110
SNS 22
Social commerce (s-commerce) impact in
        Bangladesh 30
Social goals of parking systems 5
Social interface for seniors 179
Social media
    impact of COVID-19 21
    impact on purchasing habits 21
Social networking services (SNS) 22
Social network users online purchase
        intentions 20ff
Social Network Visualizer (SocNetV) 194
Soft threshold (ST) 154
Solar street light and surveillance system
        74ff
Solar surveillance system 74ff
Sold medicine list 37
Solidity language 261
Solidity programming language 40
Spray-and-focus (SNF) DTN routing
        protocol 137, 139
    energy awareness 148–149

Spray-and-wait (SAW) DTN routing
        protocol 137, 138
    energy awareness 148–149
SPSS
    application of 26
SQLite3 use 103
ST 154
Stochastic Gradient Descent Classifier
        102
Stochastic gradient descent classifier 105
Stopword removal 50
Strobe preamble 226
Substation automation system (SAS)
        202
Suicidal thoughts 213
Support Vector Classification (SVC) 130
Support Vector Machine (SVM)
        algorithm 85
Support Vector Machine Classification
        algorithm 168
Surveillance system circuit 77–78
Surveys of students to evaluate
        satisfaction with E-learning
        165–167
SVC 130
SVM 48
    see also Support Vector Machine
        (SVM) algorithm
SVM classifier 48
Switched beam 154
Switched beam antenna model 242–243
Sybil attack for network disruption 40
Syntactic networks 48
Synthetic minority oversampling
        (SMOTE) 14, 285
    performance in fake news detection
        57–59
Synthetic minority oversampling
        technique for nominal and
        categorical features
        (SMOTE-NC) 285
SYSFor 285
Systematically developed Forest tree
        (SYSFor) 285

System average interruption frequency
index (SAIFI) 201

T
T 25
T5 model 59
Tableau visualization tool 193
TaMAC 225
TDMA 154
TEEN *see* Threshold sensitive energy
efficient sensor network (TEEN)
strategy
Teenagers and cyber aggression 212
Testnets 37
consensus-based 42
Test subset 54
TF-IDF 48, 99
for vectorization 51, 216
$Th_{density}$ 64
ThingSpeak for parking application 3
Threshold sensitive energy efficient
sensor network (TEEN)
strategy 152, 154, 159
Time Division Multiple Access (TDMA)
schedule 154
TLE 212
Tokenization of text datasets 50
Tokenizer for tweet data 113
Tone-driven directional rate controlled
communication 236ff
Traffic-adaptive MAC protocol
(TaMAC) 225
Traffic load strategies 229–230
Train and test scores 54, 88, 94
Train subset 54
Transaction-based state machine 36
Transaction cost in gas units 37
Transfer learning 111
Transformer-based models 59
Tree classifiers 285
Trip 4 All 176
Triple-level ensemble (TLE) models 212
Trust (T) 25
Trust-based shopper responses 12
impact on purchase intention 23

Tulip visualization tool 195–196
Turkish text analysis 99
Tweets dataset 111–112

U
Undergraduate students' purchase
intentions
American 23
Bangladeshi 20ff
Kurdistan 23
Unit step response 276
University students online purchasing
20ff
Unstable network paths 137
Unstructured data extraction 12
Usability of interface 178
User interface development for seniors
180–184

V
V2I (vehicle-to-infrastructure
communication) 2
VANETs communications technology 3
Variable decay response 69
Vehicle owners parking clients 5
Vehicle-to-infrastructure (V2I)
communication 2
Visualization of Big Data 189
Visualization tools for Big Data 193–194
Visual noise in Big Data 192
Voting classifiers 217
Voting system usage 99, 102, 105, 106

W
WASSA-2-17 dataset 130
Water data-set 91
Water in ecosystem 84
Water monitoring for aquaculture 84
WBAN 223ff
Web servers in smart parking system 7
Web-spider 101
Weka machine learning tool 286
Whale optimization 267
Whale optimization (WO) 268
inspiration for 268, 274–275

Wireless body area network (WBAN)
     223ff
Wireless personal area network (WPAN)
     223
Wireless sensor networks (WSN) 3
     multi-hop 3
     uses for 151–152
Wireless sensor networks (WSN) with
     VANETS 3
WO *see* Whale optimization (WO)
word2vec 123, 124–126
Word2Vec
     for fake news detection 48
     for vectorization 51
Word clouds visualization technique 196

Word embedding for vector
     representation of words 51
WORO 35
WPAN 223
Wrapper subset evaluator (WSE) 284
Write-once-read-only (WORO) 35
WSE 284
WSN *see* Wireless sensor networks
     (WSN)

X
X-MAC 226

Z
ZigBee for communication in parking
     application 2